Walls of Empowerment

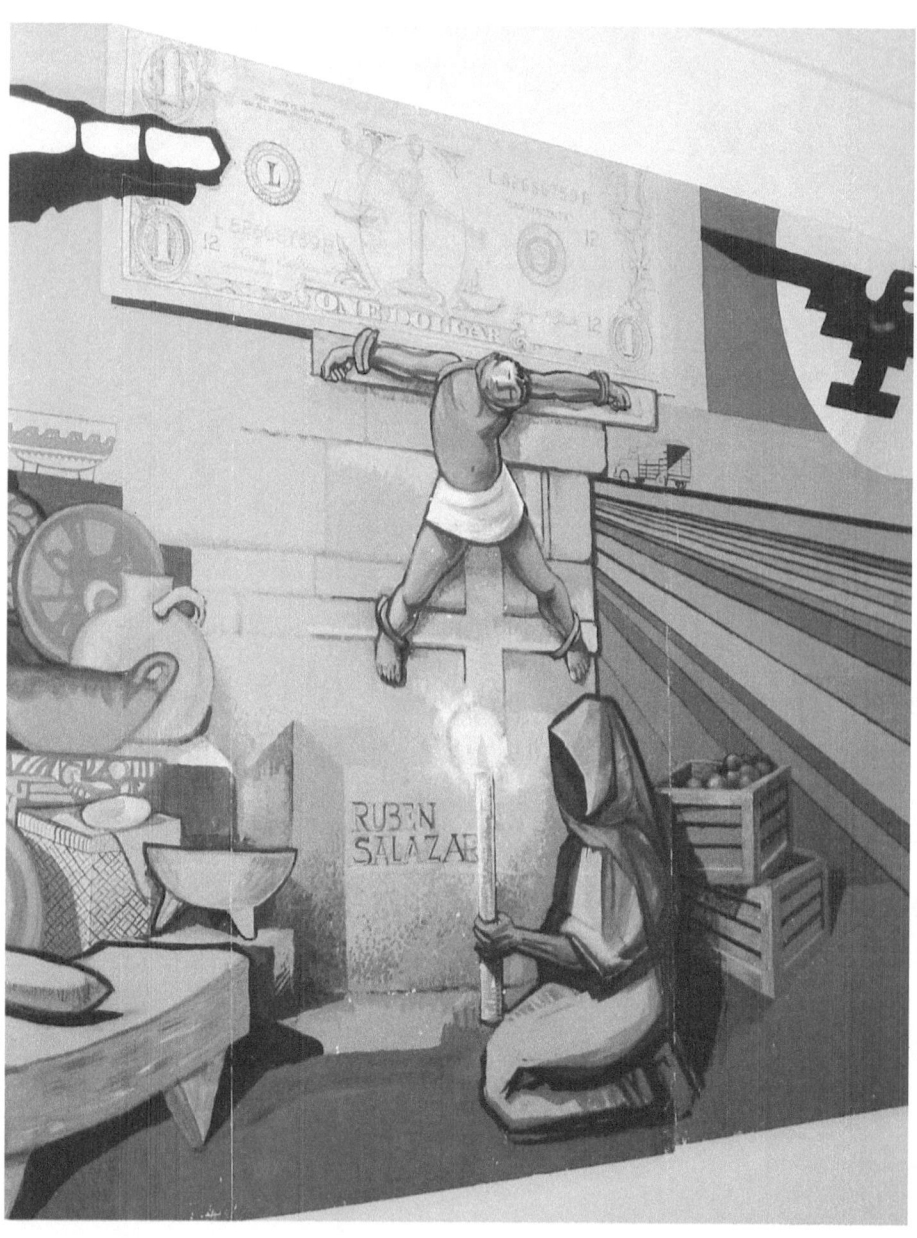

Sergio O'Cadiz, project director, assisted by Doris Baker, Emigdio Vasquez and Jennifer Winn, plus a team of 33 students of MECHA, © 1974, *The MECHA Mural* (detail), mural, Nealley Library, Santa Ana College, Santa Ana, CA. Courtesy of Nealley Library, Santa Ana College.

GUISELA LATORRE

Walls of Empowerment
Chicana/o Indigenist Murals of California

University of Texas Press, Austin

Requests for permission to reproduce material from
this work should be sent to:

    Permissions
    University of Texas Press
    P.O. Box 7819
    Austin, TX 78713-7819

    utpress.utexas.edu/index.php/rp-form

Library of Congress Cataloging-in-Publication Data

Latorre, Guisela, 1970–
  Walls of empowerment : Chicana(o) indigenist murals of California / Guisela
Latorre. — 1st ed.

     p.   cm.
  Includes bibliographical references and index.
  ISBN 978-0-292-71883-8 (cloth) — ISBN 978-0-292-71906-4 (pbk.)

  1. Mexican American mural painting and decoration—Political
aspects—California, Southern—20th century. 2. Street art—California,
Southern. 3. Indians in art. I. Title.
  ND2635.C22S685 2008
  751.7'308968720794—dc22
              2008011228

For my most precious little baby girl, *Judith*

Contents

Acknowledgments

While taking credit for the successful completion of a first book is something most scholars relish and anxiously await, none of us can truly say that we took this journey alone. So in the spirit of collectivism and mutual recognition of the Chicana/o mural movement, I would like to acknowledge those colleagues, mentors, organizations, friends, and *familia* who provided me with critical support—intellectual, institutional, emotional, spiritual, and otherwise—so that I could make *Walls of Empowerment* a reality.

The work that went into this book spanned nearly ten years and included my tenure in three wonderful institutions of higher learning, namely the University of Illinois at Urbana-Champaign; the University of California, Santa Barbara; and Ohio State University. At Illinois I counted with the tireless guidance and support of numerous mentors who patiently directed me through the early stages of this project. Jordana Mendelson (Art History), with a combination of kindness and professionalism, offered me vital insights into my work while always encouraging me to be rigorous in my scholarship. I am eternally grateful to Rolando Romero (Spanish and U.S. Latina/o Studies) for having introduced me to the discipline of U.S. Latina/o studies. His creative and visionary intellect irreversibly transformed the way I interpret cultural production. Historian Matt García—who at the time was a junior professor at Illinois and has since become a major scholar at Brown University—thoroughly trained me in Chicana/o history, thus allowing me to build a complex social context for Chicana/o mural production. In the process, both Matt and Jordana have become dear friends who continue to mentor and guide me to this day. Other brilliant and committed scholars at Illinois were instrumental to the intellectual development that eventually led me to write *Walls of Empowerment*: Alejandro Lugo (Anthropology), Angharad Valdivia (Communications), Oscar Vazquez (Art History), and Cynthia Radding (History).

After I completed my studies at the University of Illinois, an amazing dream came true: I was hired by the Department of Chicana and Chicano Studies at the University of California, Santa Barbara, to teach Chicana/o art. Working side by side with pioneers in the field of Chicana/o studies has been nothing short of astounding and exhilarating, not to mention humbling. Their support and encouragement have taken my scholarship to new heights of critical inquiry, something that is manifestly reflected in *Walls of Empowerment*. While every single faculty member of this renowned department directly or indirectly contributed to the intellectual impetus that drove my book project, I would specially like to thank María Herrera-Sobek, Chela Sandoval, Gerardo Aldana, Francisco Lomelí, and Horacio Roque Ramírez for their love and caring support, that is, for becoming my second *familia* away from home. I would never have been able to complete this project without the combination of intellectual and emotional reinforcement they provided during the past five years. While Chicana and Chicano Studies was my intellectual home at UC Santa Barbara, I cannot neglect to mention the help and direction of colleagues from other departments on this campus whose nurturing guidance always kept me grounded and focused, in particular, Claudine Michel (Black Studies) and Anna Everett (Film and Media Studies), who saw potential in me that I never realized I possessed. To my wonderful colleagues and *compañeras/os* at UC Santa Barbara: I will never forget you!

As I write these words of gratitude, acknowledgment, and recognition, I find myself at a critical crossroads in my career as I prepare to bid farewell to UC Santa Barbara and venture into a new scholarly terrain and personal journey with the Department of Women's Studies at Ohio State University, where I will become a new faculty member in the fall of 2007. I look forward to the intellectual coalitions and personal alliances I will forge with my new colleagues as I return to the Midwest. It was their recognition of my scholarly work, including *Walls of Empowerment*, as well as their deep commitment to women-of-color scholarship that persuaded me to join this illustrious group of feminist thinkers.

As I conducted research for *Walls of Empowerment*, several institutions and individuals assisted me along the way. During the early phases of my investigation, Christina Ochoa, from Self-Help Graphics & Art, happily made available to me the visual arts center's archives and allowed me to view the prints from its 1999 atelier. Francisco García-Ayvens patiently guided me through the collections of the UCLA Chicano Studies Library. Lillian Castillo-Speed, in the UC Berkeley Ethnic Studies Library, assisted me in finding the proper materials within their Chicano studies collection. Enrique Gonzales, Lab Technician at the Social and Public Art Resource

Center (SPARC), took a great deal of time from his busy work schedule to explain to me how the SPARC Digital Mural Lab functioned. I should also mention the contribution of Jean Bruce Poole, Historic Museum Director of El Pueblo de Los Angeles Historical Monument, who arranged for me to get a private showing of David Alfaro Siqueiros's *Tropical America* (*La América Tropical*). I would also like to specially acknowledge Dr. Shifra Goldman for having read and commented on early versions of my book proposal. In addition, Dr. Goldman kindly opened the doors of her home to me—as she has done with various other young scholars—where she housed one of the most impressive libraries and archives of Chicana/o and Latin American art in the nation. I would also like to mention the contribution of Alfred Arteaga, from UC Berkeley, who, during the summer of 2001, kindly agreed to meet with me and discuss my project. Isabel Castro-Melendez, from the UCLA Chicano Studies Research Center, also shared with me her valuable views on my work and research. In addition, Yolanda García, librarian at Santa Ana College's Nealley Library, took considerable time off from her numerous work duties to guide me through their invaluable collection. Moreover, I cannot overlook the kindness and generosity of Dr. Timothy Drescher, who has collected community mural imagery since the early 1970s and has thus preserved an important cultural patrimony of the United States. Dr. Drescher shared with me photographs of murals that are now partially or completely destroyed.

I am particularly grateful to two institutions and their staff for their dedication and support of my work, namely UC Santa Barbara's California Ethnic and Multicultural Archives (CEMA) and the Smithsonian Institution's Archives of American Art (AAA). Perhaps the most exhaustive and comprehensive collection of primary-source material on Chicana/o art in the world, CEMA provided me with an incredible wealth of material on my topic. With the help and guidance of Salvador Güereña, director of CEMA and archivist extraordinaire, I found numerous one-of-a-kind gems like artists' oral histories, diaries, letters, sketchbooks, newspaper clippings, and other ephemera. Unique slides, silkscreens, films, and sound recordings from CEMA also greatly enriched my scholarship in *Walls of Empowerment*. The AAA, in particular their West Coast Regional Office in San Marino, California, was instrumental in providing me with material on California mural imagery as well as information on specific artists through their Artist Oral History Program. While at the AAA, I counted with the valuable assistance of Paul Karlstrom and Marian Kolisch.

Of course, I cannot fail to acknowledge the hard work and dedication that the editorial staff of the University of Texas Press put into this book, in particular Theresa May, editor-in-chief, whose professionalism, commitment, and creativity were both refreshing and encouraging to me as a junior scholar who was still fairly new to the publishing world. I am also immensely grateful to editors Megan Giller and Nancy Warrington for their painstaking work of going through my manuscript literally inch by inch to prepare it for publication. Moreover, Nancy Lavender Bryan worked tirelessly to market and promote the book. It is my belief that editors and press staff in general do not receive the proper recognition in academia for their important contributions to scholarly work.

During the course of my work on *Walls of Empowerment*, I received numerous grants and fellowships that funded and supported the rigorous and meticulous research that this book demanded. While still at the University of Illinois, I was a recipient of fellowships from the Illinois Program for Research in the Humanities and the Center for Advanced Study. Small travel grants from the U.S. Latina/o Studies Program, the Graduate College, and the Fehl Research Fund (Art History) were vital sources of financial support. Participating in the Latino Museum Studies Program (LMSP) at the Smithsonian Latino Center during the summer of 2000 greatly enhanced the quality of my research for *Walls of Empowerment*. At UC Santa Barbara, I availed myself of various sources of funding geared toward promoting the research of faculty on campus: the Faculty Career Development Award, the University of California Committee on Latino Research (UCCLR) Grant, the Interdisciplinary Humanities Center (IHC) Faculty Fellowship, and the Academic Senate Faculty Research Grant.

Of course, none of what I wrote in *Walls of Empowerment* would have made any sense without the critical insights and accounts of Chicana/o artists themselves, who built the U.S. community arts movement literally with their bare hands. Juana Alicia, Santa Barraza, Yolanda López, Frances Salomé España, Diane Gamboa, Isabel Castro-Melendez, Alma López, Paul Botello, Emigdio Vasquez, Carlos "Higgy" Vasquez, Luis Garza, Salvador Barajas, John "Jota" Leaños, Posh One, Man One, Willie Herrón, Barbara Carrasco, Harry Gamboa Jr., Judy Baca, Judithe Hernández, Carlos Cortez, Esteban Villa, Eric Norberg, and Fred Alvarado all put down their paintbrushes and other artistic tools to sit down and talk to me. However, I am particularly thankful to Yreina D. Cervántez—whose spiritually empowering mural work graces the cover of this book—for having introduced me to the Los Angeles Chicana/o art scene, thus setting in motion one of the most profound intellectual and spiritual journeys of my life.

As most scholars realize, intellectual work cannot happen without the pillars of support provided by friends and *familia*. Faithful *compañeras* and friends Dana Katz, Chealon "Chili" Shears, Amanda Harris Nolacea, María Isabel Silva, Maricela DeMirjyn, Claudia Matus, and Lorraine Morales Cox all held my hand through the highs and lows of academia. But I cannot stress enough the importance of my dear parents, Guillermo Latorre and Teresa Huerta, scholars in their own right, who were my earliest mentors, sparking in me a passion for academic work since childhood. Moreover, it was their courage and determination to leave our native country of Chile during a time of political repression and immigrate to the United States that made everything I've accomplished possible. All that I am I owe to them. Nevertheless, my sister, Carolina, and brothers, Miguel and Guillermo "Yiyo" Latorre, also provided unconditional love and support throughout my career.

Finally, it was during the process of putting together *Walls of Empowerment* that I met my husband, Jorge Coelho, and gave birth to our beautiful daughter, Judith, in December of 2001. Having been blessed with a supportive and caring *familia* of my own while writing this book has truly made *Walls of Empowerment* a labor of love. Jorge, thank you for keeping it all together for me when things seemed to be falling apart, and, Judith, thank you *so much* for your patience when Mommy spent endless hours at the computer and for tagging along with me on my mural trips and tours. *¡Los quiero mucho!*

Walls of Empowerment

Indigenism and Chicana/o Muralism
The Radicalization of an Aesthetic

Chicana/o Murals and Indigenism

Two Aztec warriors, dressed in full regalia, clasp arms as they engage in a ritual dance with a mountainous landscape stretching behind them. Aside from inhabiting this idyllic environment, these heroes also physically reside within the barrio setting of East Los Angeles, where Ernesto de la Loza's *Danza de las Aguilas* (1978) mural is located. How did the meaning of these indigenous figures connect with the mostly Chicana/o and Mexican residents of East L.A. whose own experience was shaped by both urban life and native Mexican traditions? How was political, social, and cultural consciousness meant to be inscribed into this kind of iconography? As seen in the community murals that have transformed the urban landscapes of California since the late 1960s, the rehabilitation of indigenous history and culture became a crucial component in the growing politicization that saturated Chicana/o political thought with the onset of the Chicano Movement, or *el movimiento*. California became a significant site of mural activity because it possessed a mural tradition spanning most of the twentieth century, and, as art historian Shifra Goldman has written, the West Coast has led "the country in sheer [mural] quantity."[1] But most significantly, the state had endured a bitter and prolonged colonial, expansionist, and postindustrial history that directly and indirectly informed the Indigenist subject matter of these wall paintings. The Indian of the Americas emerged within these murals as a timeless ideal and a fluid allegory of cultural affirmation that reconstructed Chicanas/os' fragmented past while providing entire communities with a vocabulary that celebrated their contemporary cultural practices. Moreover, the recognition that the continent of America was essentially indigenous territory became one of the most fundamental steps toward decolonization and liberation of oppressed communities.

Chicana/o artists employed the monumentality of the public mural to disseminate an iconography radicalized in large part through its indigenizing qualities. These murals cited indigenous culture in a multiplicity of ways and for a variety of different reasons, yet composed part of an aesthetic that continuously sought to firmly establish Chicanas/os' sociopolitical place in U.S. territory. Indigenism, in the Chicana/o context, functioned as an elastic metaphor of political consciousness that allowed for innovative articulations of cultural and gendered identity. Though many artists outside the Chicana/o community also practiced community muralism, and despite the fact that indigenous imagery was part of a larger whole that defined Chicana/o decolonial consciousness, Indigenism contributed significantly to the politicizing process of Chicano *and* Chicana mural production. In the social and political context of late twentieth-century U.S. history, the idea of an autonomous and independent indigenous voice necessarily posed a threat to the foundations of postcolonial and capitalist orders.

In this introduction, I lay out the theoretical framework that informed Indigenism in California Chicana/o murals from the late 1960s to the turn of the twentieth century. In the process, I argue that through the public mural, Chicanas/os found a unique and effective tool with which to assert agency from the margins. In subsequent chapters of this project, this theoretical analysis provides a methodological foundation that allows me to engage the visual vocabulary of these murals as well as to discuss the activities and aspirations of the individual artists or collectives who created them. Focusing on three major centers of muralist activity—namely, the Los Angeles metropolitan area, the San Francisco Bay area, and San Diego—the question I ultimately want to raise is not whether the "subaltern" can speak, as Gayatri Spivak would posit, for we know that Third World and First Nation communities have achieved varying degrees of agency since the onset of colonialism, imperialism, and postindustrialization. Instead, the focus of this volume is to generate an understanding of the sorts of strategies deployed by the so-called subaltern in order to create a compelling and decolonized frame of self-representation. The Indigenist aesthetic that Chicana/o artists created provides a model for ways in which marginalized communities can empower themselves against the grain of dominant ideologies.

The images of indigenous America depicted in many California Chicana/o murals engaged a long history of Indigenist aesthetics and discourse in the Americas. The words "Indigenism" and "Indigenist" here will be distinguished and differentiated from the terms *indigeneity* and *indigenous*. Generally speaking, "Indigenism" refers to the act of consciously adopting an indigenous identity—which may otherwise not be fully self-evident—for a political or strategic purpose. The Indigenist posture often seeks to overturn historical processes in order to exact radical change. Indigenism as an ideology, however, can operate in favor but also against the needs of the native peoples themselves, and thus one must be cautious when resorting to it. Indeed, individuals or institutions outside of indigenous communities have utilized Indigenism in their quest to incorporate America's native cultures into articulations of national, cultural, or racial identity. Indigenism can constitute a political posture that seeks to construct race rather than define cultural practices. When such institutions or individuals generate Indigenist thinking, they are not necessarily identifying themselves as Indian but instead are acknowledging, in their own terms, the native presence in the country's cultural patrimony, with the ultimate goal of modifying or altering indigenous culture, often rendering it invisible or inconsequential. Mexican indigenous studies scholar Guillermo Bonfil Batalla argued that in most Latin American countries, modern Indigenist campaigns sought to assimilate and acculturate native peoples into national culture: "Indigenist policies in Latin American governments, in spite of their significant national differences, had one final objective in common: the assimilation of Indians."[2] Bonfil Batalla further argues that the assimilation and co-optation of indigenous people forms part of a larger project of preparing nascent nation-states for capitalist enterprising. In the Americas, especially Latin America, Indigenism also emerged as a solution to identity crises arising as a result of political and social turmoil (wars, radical changes in government, movements of civil or human rights, etc.). Paternalist forms of Indigenism make up an integral part of a Pan-Americanist spirit that seeks to rid itself of European control while still maintaining Western institutions.

By contrast, *indigeneity*, as understood in this book, will refer to the organic expressions that emerge from the indigenous communities themselves, which may or may not have anything to do with the official Indigenism often espoused by nation-states. While these expressions may be understood and even appropriated by non-natives, indigeneity primarily serves the spiritual and pragmatic needs of indigenous communities and nations without necessarily having to profess an overt political and anticolonialist agenda behind them.[3] Notwithstanding, Indigenist and indigenous expressions can overlap or even negate one another. Admittedly, we could argue that in colonial and postcolonial contexts, any expression of indigenous culture is inevitably Indigenist and thus political because, consciously or not, it counters dominant culture. We could also contend that there are cultural expressions within native nations and communities that fulfill both Indigenist and indigenous purposes. We will tread carefully in this volume as we navigate the nuanced and subtle distinctions between Indigenism and indigeneity and will proceed with caution through the problematic history of Indigenism.

The Chicana/o Indigenist aesthetic and discourse posed a unique phenomenon in the history of counterhegemonic struggles in the Americas, for it was positioned somewhere between Indigenism and indigeneity. As it emerged in various forms of creative and political expression during and after the Chicano Movement, Chicana/o Indigenism redeployed many of the strategies and tools of previous Indigenist initiatives but with critically different motives, goals, and outcomes. As with earlier Indigenist projects, Chicana/o artists sought to consciously and strategically embrace indigenous culture for political purposes. Some Chicana/o activists, intellectuals, and artists even looked to the Indigenist campaigns in Mexico after the Revolution of 1910 as a model for understanding how indigeneity can be incorporated in the construction of national formations. But within the cultural context of the United States, where indigenous culture is excluded on all levels of nationalist agendas, the act of proclaiming an indigenous identity as an identifying marker of the Chicana/o experience in this country was necessarily a subversive and transgressive move. Most importantly, however, Chicana/o Indigenism transcended the need to adopt politically strategic discourses and postures. While there were concerted efforts on the part of scholars, artists, activists, and intellectuals to adopt an Indigenist worldview that would challenge the stagnation of U.S. dominant culture, indigenous practices and beliefs have been important cornerstones of Chicana/o culture in North America predating U.S. expansionism and Spanish colonialism. The Indigenist aesthetic and discourse that would surface on the coattails of the Chicano Movement afforded the Mexican American community the unprecedented opportunity to be themselves, quite literally. Indigenous practices such as *curanderismo* (folk healing) and oral traditions, previously dismissed as backward, folkloric (i.e., quaint but not modern), and even superstitious by Western thought, were now celebrated and exalted during *el movimiento*, for these were the indigenous cultural markers that survived the ravages of colonization and connected the contemporary Chicana/o community to the great preconquest indigenous civilizations and cultures in the Americas. Moreover, in the process of reclaiming their indigeneity, Chicanas/os were seeking to rehabilitate the systems of collective support and communal protection that were prevalent among the native populations in the Americas prior to the arrival of Europeans who brought with them a more individualistic and capital-driven culture. Nevertheless, many of the Indigenist images and ideas Chicana/o artists and thinkers embraced did not come directly from their own personal indigenous experiences but from their process of politicization and self-education that prompted them to study Mexican history and culture, both ancient and modern. For example, the spiritual connection that Chicana artists and writers established with the Aztec earth goddess Coatlicue emerged out of their profound readings of Mesoamerican texts. Nevertheless, Coatlicue, whose abilities included the extraordinary power to give and take away life and whose anthropomorphic features were both beautiful and horrific, represented the embodiment of polar opposites and contradictions, a characteristic that mirrored and legitimized Chicanas' subject positions.[4] Because Chicanas/os were not indigenous in the same way that Native Americans were, their political consciousness reflected both Indigenist (politically motivated) and indigenous (organically manifested) proclivities. The hybridity, or *mestizaje*, within the Chicana/o community, while not negating the connection to other native populations, conditioned its activists to navigate between these two realms of political, social, and cultural being, namely, Indigenism and indigeneity.

If we think of ideology in its Marxist definition, that is, as a system of ideas that creates a "'false consciousness' [and] works in the interests of the powerful against the interests of the powerless,"[5] as John Storey explains, then we can perhaps think of Latin American Indigenism more as an ideology than as an aesthetic functioning independently of the needs of indigenous people. In Mexico, the construction of Indigenism implied no overt intention to work against the interests of native populations, but there was an attempt to diffuse the possibility of revolts or insurgences among the country's indigenous communities, whose consciousness had been dangerously awakened during the Revolution. As opposed to an ideology of oppression, Chicana/o Indigenism emerged as a methodology of decolonization that sought to create not a false consciousness but alternative models of oppositional thinking serving the needs of Third World communities.

Although representations of indigenous populations date as far back as the conquest, the use of such representations to construct the nation-state signals a fairly modern phenomenon. Prior to the nineteenth century,[6] European colonizers produced images of Indians in written and visual texts to further reiterate their own cultural identity and superiority in the face of growing miscegenation. Helmut Scheben, however, quickly pointed out that Indigenism, as an aesthetic and nationalist discourse, coincided chronologically with modernism,[7] and Debora Castillo asserted that the act of sidelining indigenous culture while romantically appropriating it lies at the crux of modernist and postmodernist debates in Latin America.[8]

Nations like Mexico, for instance, openly embraced indigenous iconography during the modern phases of their artistic development. This new aesthetic, though complicit with European coloniality, signaled a desire to proclaim a voice independent of foreign avant-garde trends. Indigenism, specifically in the Mexican context, did not provide platforms for self-representation for indigenous peoples, but rather created a state-sanctioned visual vocabulary that articulated a native identity according to the precepts of the new nation-state after the Mexican Revolution of 1910. As part of Mexico's educational reforms during the first few decades of the twentieth century, the education minister José Vasconcelos commissioned elaborate mural cycles to help the populace visually conceive the shape this new nation-state would take. The power of the public mural, as the Mexican muralists of the 1920s and 1930s knew, resided in its ability to not only prescribe ideology but also construct its own spectators.[9] When addressing Mexican indigenous history and culture, Diego Rivera was perhaps the one muralist who best understood the role that murals could play in the creation of a national collective identity. The unproblematized and often romantic Indigenism that emerged in the mural cycles he painted throughout Mexico became emblematic of the nationalist ideologies regarding the Mexican native communities.

Contesting Modernism and the Avant-Garde

The spirit of the Chicana/o arts movement presented a diametrically opposed school of thought to the prevailing discourses and practices surrounding the visual arts in the field of art history and criticism, in particular, modern and contemporary art history. The categories that defined established art history as well as time-honored museum practices proved to be utterly irrelevant to the practice of Chicana/o art. The categories pertinent to the standard periodization utilized in traditional art-historical methodologies—namely, prehistoric, ancient, medieval, Renaissance, modern, and contemporary art—proved to be inaccurate and even obstructive to the understanding of indigenous art, including Chicana/o creative expressions. The classification "non-Western" was also fraught with recurring colonialist visions and discourses that defined indigenous arts as exotic and primitive. Of particular interest to this study, however, is the way European and Euro-American academic thinking constructed the role of art and artists in the modern era. Art was the result of the most elevated form of creative endeavor coming from an intellectual elite. Art existed independently and quite above the mundane goings-on of everyday life and existence. The artist, as the human vessel for this creative force, held a special place in society, for he or she (though mostly he) held neither responsibility nor accountability toward a larger collective.[10] The artist often lived marginalized from society not because of any social injustice but because of his/her misunderstood genius and idiosyncratic lifestyle and personality. Modern and contemporary art history turned to the artist as the focus of attention, thus placing inordinate importance on an artwork's authorship.[11] This "cult-of-the-artist" approach deployed by many art historians and critics has led to the publication of hundreds, if not thousands, of lavish monographs on "modern masters" such as Claude Monet, Pablo Picasso, Henri Matisse, and Wassily Kandinsky, just to name a few, granting them all celebrity status.

The obstinacy of the structures of art history and criticism, coupled with the refusal on the part of many art historians and critics to recognize the legitimacy and value of Chicana/o art, conditioned numerous Chicana/o artists and intellectuals to create alternative historical and physical spaces for the free expression and deeper engagement of indigenous aesthetics. For Chicana/o artists who came of age during the Chicano Movement, the models offered by scholars of modern and contemporary art regarding the role of art and the artist were exceedingly inappropriate and even outmoded. Many Chicana/o artists had such strong ties to community concerns that they saw their roles as artists and activists as the same. So, as stipulated by Tomás Ybarra-Frausto, a critical "task was to re-think representation, the role of the artist, and the social function of art."[12] Conversely, indigenous aesthetics provided Chicana/o artists with more fitting and culturally sensitive models for creative expressions. The old adage "art for art's sake," which defined creative expression as a function of its own internal machinations, was supplanted in the minds of Chicana/o and indigenous scholars with the motto "art for life's sake." Mexican Indigenist scholar Guillermo Bonfil Batalla underscored quite eloquently the fact that many indigenous cultures regard commonplace experiences (*lo cotidiano*) as necessary mediating occurrences that happen between an individual and the rest of nature.[13] Without sacrificing individual creativity and artistic freedom, Native American scholar Daniel Heath Justice called for a form of creativity that is deeply ingrained in community concerns:

> [The idea of art for art's sake] frequently brings with it a hypernarcissism and self-centered conceit that contributes to the destabilization of the basic values and kinship ties of tribal communities. . . . I believe it's fair to say that most tribal artists . . . are creating art not only for themselves, but also for the survival and enduring presence of Native people . . . It becomes, as Cherokee/Appalachian poet Marilou Awiakta has noted, "art for Life's sake, as opposed to art for Art's sake."[14]

Like Native American artists, Chicanas/os were looking for ways to consolidate their creative needs with their commitment to community. Thus, by looking to various forms of indigenous aesthetics, both past and present, they found meaningful examples of art practices that existed in organic relationship to the community at large. The often collective nature of many indigenous arts also involved a process of transformation for both the artist and the community. While this transformation is primarily a spiritual one, it is also connected to other forms of transformations. For Chicana/o artists who invited local community members to collaborate in the creation of murals, this spiritual transformation also took the form of political revelation, whereby all those involved underwent a radical process of what Paulo Freire would call *conscientização,* or "conscientization," through which they became conscious of their own oppression but also of their own potential and power to bring about change at an individual and collective level.

Chicana/o artists could not afford to simply retreat into their studios to explore the contours of their own artistic imagination, for they were often compelled and driven to understand how their individual creativity related to the process of community building and preservation, a task they could not achieve by remaining in cultural, social, and political isolation. These desires of defining the self in relationship to community as well as to a spiritual universe were motivations that Chicana/o artists shared with other native peoples. But if artists had the responsibility of creating art that served objectives leading toward social justice, then art automatically became a form of decolonization. Through the process of developing an individual and collective creative expression, which can also be regarded as a form of empowerment and emancipation, artist and community alike begin to shed the mechanisms of a colonial system that has invaded their bodies, minds, and souls. By using art as a decolonizing agent, indigenous artists, including Chicanas/os, were subverting and overturning a very powerful yet pernicious tradition, namely, the practice on the part of colonizing powers of using art to further subdue and indoctrinate conquered and vanquished peoples. One must only look to the *casta* paintings of the sixteenth and seventeenth centuries in Latin America, to the nineteenth-century Anglo-American landscape paintings, or, even more recently, to the early twentieth-century political cartoons in major U.S. newspapers to understand how visual artists traditionally used the arts to literally and metaphorically reify colonial orders. The representations of indigenous peoples in these aforementioned visual traditions operated as circumscribing devices that contained and confined the social movement of the racial Other. If representation itself becomes hampered by a colonialist gaze, then self-representation necessarily implies a reversal of that process, as Steven Leuthold argues: "Indigenous self-representation primarily involves a shift in authority, implying that inherent in cross-cultural representations are the dynamics of power."[15]

Mexican and Chicana/o Indigenism in Murals

Though we can speak of several important Indigenist moments in the history of the Americas, Chicana/o creative expressions of the 1960s and beyond were most significantly influenced by the Indigenist revival that occurred during and shortly after the Mexican Revolution of 1910. Alfonso Caso, anthropologist and founder of Mexico's Instituto Nacional Indigenista, credited the Revolution itself with ushering in considerable changes in the way Mexico viewed its native populations: "One of the most permanent and constructive results of the Revolution was the consciousness and determination on the part of Mexico to resolve the indigenous problem."[16] Though Caso saw the presence of native communities as a potential liability to the country's progress and urged their assimilation as a way to solve the "indigenous problem," Chicanas/os' interest in the Revolution and its Indigenist proclamations was part of a more affirmative and potentially transgressive process of self-definition. While various Chicana/o thinkers regarded the Mexican Revolution as a metaphor for the contemporaneous struggles they waged, its historical importance also held a more tangible relevance to Mexican Americans. As historians have pointed out, many of the events prior to, during, and after the Revolution brought about one of the largest influxes of Mexican immigrants to the United States, with as many as 1.5 million people—approximately 10 percent of Mexico's entire population—crossing the border between 1900 and 1930.[17] Many of the Chicanas/os who came of age during the conflicts of the civil rights movement were either the children or grandchildren of these immigrants.[18] In the conscious imagination of many activists and artists, the Chicano Movement operated as an extension of the political and cultural debates instituted by the Revolution. After all, this event ennobled the cause of land reform to benefit Indians, and it also glorified leaders like Emiliano Zapata, whose indigenous blood symbolized the very essence of the Mexican nation.

Though Chicana/o muralism resides at the intersection of various currents and tendencies, the historical connection to the Mexican mural renaissance is quite self-evident. Nearly half a century prior to the flowering of Chicana/o muralism in California, the state had already become an important site for Mexican muralism.[19] José Clemente Orozco's *Prometheus* (1930) in Pomona College, Diego Rivera's California School of Fine Arts mural in San

Francisco (1930), and David Alfaro Siqueiros's *Portrait of Present-Day Mexico* (1932), originally located in Santa Monica,[20] all offered a politicized modernist vocabulary that was previously unfamiliar to the current artistic scene in California and the rest of the country. As far as the generation of Chicana/o artists of the sixties and seventies was concerned, however, the most pivotal Mexican mural was undoubtedly Siqueiros's *La América Tropical (Tropical America*; 1932), located on Los Angeles's Olvera Street. Laurance P. Hurlburt, author of *The Mexican Muralists in the United States* (1989), explained that the mural's bold critique of imperialism and capitalism centered around the figure of the crucified Indian, an image that must have struck a chord with the Mexican American residents of the area.[21] *La América Tropical* also demonstrated the powerful effects political statements coupled with Indigenist aesthetics could have when displayed in a public mural.[22]

Mexican Indigenist art also migrated to California via the work of Alfredo Ramos Martínez, who had led Mexico's Academia de San Carlos in the early twenties and eventually settled in Los Angeles in 1929. His open-air paintings and indigenous subjects had considerable influence on many Southern California artists of the period.[23] During the decades of the 1950s and early 1960s, several Mexican American artists contributed much to the area's artistic patrimony, even though their oeuvre often went largely unnoticed. Such was the case of Martín Ramírez, an artist active during the 1950s in the Los Angeles area, whose works on paper revealed, as Octavio Paz remarked, "forms, lines, volumes, and colors that express with a sort of exasperation the twin forces of separation and participation."[24] Referring to Ramírez's experience immigrating to the United States during the Mexican Revolution and his subsequent bouts with paranoid schizophrenia, Paz erroneously and dismissively described his work as that of a solitary and isolated genius who neither exerted influence on nor received influence from broader artistic currents.[25] Nevertheless, Chicago artist Jim Nutt "discovered" his drawings in 1968, and later, approximately one decade after Ramírez's death in 1960, the Mexican artist's work became the subject of various exhibitions around the country. Though he produced all his drawings while a mental patient at the DeWitt State Hospital (Auburn, California),[26] subsequent interest in his art reinforced the Mexican American artistic tradition in California. Chicano writer and activist Ricardo Bracho found Ramírez's drawings to be "exquisite, unsettling, dazzling in their intricate craft and deep with Mexican cultural referent," and in 2004 he began writing a play entitled "Mexican Psychotic," based on the artist's life.[27]

Painter and draftsman Carlos Licón, a Los Angeles artist whose style more closely resembled the Mexican School's social-realist tendencies than Ramírez's, established very early in his career a strong connection with his community when, in 1942, at the age of thirteen, he worked as a stage designer for the Mexican American venue Padua Hills Theater in Claremont, California. Four years later, Licón would actually meet the artist Alfredo Ramos Martínez and work as his assistant on a Scripps College mural. But, like Ramírez, recurring instabilities in his personal life often sidelined Licón's artistic production. A victim of drug and alcohol abuse, Licón spent a great portion of his adult life in prison on narcotics charges. But this period in the 1960s marked the most productive phase in his career.[28] Displaying the stylistic influence of the modern Mexican artists of the 1920s and 1930s, Licón's work nevertheless remained more personal and introspective. A tragic feeling of pathos and melancholy often saturated his iconlike portraits and figural compositions. The legacy of his artwork would greatly inspire the artists associated with the Chicano Movement.[29]

Though the work of Mexican American artists prior to the Chicano Movement remains largely unrecognized for its influence on subsequent generations of California artists, their contribution nonetheless provided an impetus and a sense of historical continuity to artists working during and after the civil rights movement.[30] But because Chicana/o artists during *el movimiento* sought to produce an art that would challenge social and political categories and classifications, they took greater interest in media like the graphic arts, such as posters, and, of course, muralism. As had the artists of the Mexican School during the earlier decades of the twentieth century, Chicanas/os, too, found in muralism a particularly fitting medium through which to profess and disseminate their new perspectives on Indigenism as it applied to their growing racial consciousness. On the one hand, wall paintings functioned as grand platforms of cultural expression for preconquest civilizations, and, on the other, they served as highly effective instruments for consciousness raising in modern Mexico.

The elements of Mexican Indigenism that influenced Chicana/o muralists are not unproblematic, however, and they present difficulties when addressing the similarities and differences between these two important moments of mural history. Indeed, scholars must problematize the relationship between modern Mexican and Chicana/o art history. On the one hand, Chicana/o community murals emphasized the narrative and discursive continuity between Mexican and Chicana/o history. Indigenous figures such as Quetzalcoatl, Cuauhtémoc, and Benito Juárez are as much a part of the Chicana/o pantheon of heroes as are individuals from the U.S. side of the border, like César Chávez and Reies López Tijerina. On the other hand, these community murals express the specificity, innovation, and originality that is unique to Chicana/o artistic production operating independently of the previous Mexican movements. Consequently, the Mexican influence on Chicana/o art poses a number of pressing questions regarding the nature of Chicana/o creative expressions. Can we think of Mexican Indigenist iconography as merely a form of artistic influence on these community murals? To what degree was Mexico a source of inspiration or a point of departure for Chicana/o artists? If Chicanas/os were seeking to carve out an autonomous space for themselves in the United States, why look at Mexican history and art? In addressing these questions, I found a genuine danger in applying essentialist frameworks to Chicana/o culture. Thinking of Mexico as a culture of origin inscribed in the Mexican American consciousness would obscure the complexity associated with the formation of bordered identities in the United States. If we maintain an essentialist model, the recurrence of Mexican Indigenism in these West Coast community murals would inevitably be described as part of a static model of unidirectional cultural flow simply migrating from Mexico to the United States, thereby denying a certain degree of creative agency to Chicana/o artists. By contrast, thinking of the relationship between Mexican and Chicana/o art as a *dialectic* provides a more fluid model of analysis. Anthropologist Charles W. Nuckolls described cultural systems as dialectical phenomena in that they are "made up of dynamic conflicts between the whole and its parts."[31] Drawing from Mikhail Bakhtin, communication studies scholars Leslie Baxter and Barbara Montgomery, in discussing the nature of interpersonal exchanges, commented on how forces of unity and difference (or *centripetal* and *centrifugal* forces) often collaborate in the formation of social relations.[32] The relationship between Chicana/o culture and Mexican culture can be described as a relational yet conflictive and oppositional dialogue. Chicana/o art then becomes conversant with Mexican currents, but often in a critical and contesting fashion. Though a visual dialogue takes place between the Mexican and Chicana/o muralists, this dialogue often involves a multivocal process whereby dissenting and consenting voices contribute to the creation of a unified cultural product. Chicana/o community muralism can be regarded as that product, given that it simultaneously embraced and digressed from the Mexican canon. This element of "contradiction" and "opposition," however, does not point to stagnation in the cultural process, but instead ushers in the creation of an emerging new cultural system.

As seen in community murals, the dialectic process played a particularly relevant role in the construction of Chicana/o Indigenism. Informed by Mexican Indigenist thinking and iconography, Chicanas/os revived their indigenous roots by reusing cultural paraphernalia already circulating in other spheres. Even though the social and political arenas were dramatically different, Chicanas/os frequently cited and alluded to Mexican Indigenism and muralism in their work during the civil rights movement. As in Mexico, the emergence of Indigenism and muralism in the United States happened after a period of critical social and political turmoil. In many ways, Chicana/o artists saw a model of socially engaged art in the Mexican mural renaissance. But while the Indigenist ideology, along with the muralist projects in Mexico, formed a symbiotic part of institutional initiatives to rebuild the nation-state after the Revolution, in the United States, both became phenomena occurring on the fringes of official discourses. As such, Indigenism among Chicanas/os initially emerged as a counterideology, that is, an alternative to hegemonic discourses about marginalized minorities not only in Mexico but also in the United States. Indigenist imagery for many Chicana/o muralists arose as a means to express forms of resistance and protest not sanctioned by state apparatuses.

Regardless of whether Chicana/o muralists constructed Indigenism through the borrowing of different styles, themes, or concepts, this process generally remained a highly critical and interventionist one. Behind this redeployment, Chicana/o artists subverted the traits of more canonic Indigenist discourses in Mexico that sought to keep indigenous communities from active participation in rebuilding the nation. Likewise, the use of wall painting itself functioned as an act of subversion and decentralization of other modern mural movements that were institutionally supported and state sanctioned, like the so-called Mexican School of painting.[33] The resurrection of Indigenist thought and aesthetics allowed Chicanas/os to build a nation without government sponsorship and on the fringes of the mainstream establishment. But, ultimately, the use of Mexican Indigenism signified for Chicanas/os the reclaiming of a culture and a history traditionally commodified by Western powers of colonization.

Aztlán and the Politics of Place and Space

When Chicana/o artists chose to use murals as vehicles for Indigenist aesthetics, it was not by coincidence or happenstance. One of the most significant connections between the concept of Indigenism and muralism involved the symbolic implications of space and place that both tendencies invoked. The concept of Aztlán composed an important element of Chicana/o Indigenism. According to Mexica history, the Aztecs migrated south to Tenochtitlán from a northern homeland called Aztlán. In the manifesto entitled "El Plan Espiritual de Aztlán" (1969), written primarily by the Chicano poet Alurista with assistance from Denver muralist Manuel Martínez,[34] Chicanas/os geographically identified this homeland as the U.S. Southwest. Regarding themselves as the descendants of the Aztecs who currently inhabited Aztlán, Chicana/o activists saw the Mexican American presence in this area as a fulfillment of this mythical return to the homeland. Not only did Aztlán, as a concept, contest the categorization of Chicanas/os as an invariably immigrant community, it also provided them with a physical and symbolic space that had previously been denied to them by official U.S. histories. To further legitimize the existence of Aztlán, many Chicana/o writers often cited a critical primary-source text, namely, the 1610 conquest chronicles of Gaspar Pérez de Villagrá entitled *Historia de la Nueva México*. In the first chapter, Pérez de Villagrá describes in great detail the lands of the U.S. Southwest while also identifying them as the former home of the Aztec Empire. But Aztlán was not only a geographical location for Chicana/o artists and activists; it was also a spiritual space where decolonizing frames of mind could be fully realized. Aztlán was a concept capable of converging into one discursive space many of the concerns affecting Chicanas/os, as Rafael Pérez-Torres elucidates: "The ideas embodied in Aztlán draw together geography, culture, history, genetics, migration, tradition, heritage, unity, authenticity."[35]

Like the notion of Aztlán, wall paintings, too, had the unique capacity to carve out physical and symbolic spaces for the articulation of identity.[36] In turn, Chicana/o Indigenism, of which the concept of Aztlán was a crucial component, sought to push the national and psychological border that had marginalized Mexican-descent communities in the United States. Thus, muralism celebrated the urban spaces prescribed to the Chicana/o nation and often transformed the barrio environment into an Indigenist realm. Moreover, Indigenism, as an aesthetic, and muralism, as an artistic medium, both seemed capable of conveying the specificities of place and time while simultaneously asserting broader statements of social and political consciousness. Ramón García, speaking in more general terms, stated that Chicanas/os "produce an art of place, where location is central to the representation of the self in many individual and collective guises."[37] Indigenism offered Chicanas/os a means by which to address the specificity of their indigenous roots without circumscribing their cultural identity. So when a Chicana/o muralist cited Aztec or Maya culture, for example, she/he generally did not seek to portray these images as, in the words of Ramón García, "static things to be imitated," but rather "as active things in the present."[38]

The notion that Chicana/o community muralism is essentially an "art of place" implies that this practice is essentially site specific. Nevertheless, although many community murals must be understood in the context of the barrio setting and in relation to the period in which they were made, they rarely, if ever, remain static signifiers of particular moments and places in history. However, the site specificity of the Chicana/o Indigenist murals in California aligned them with the movement of site-specific work that emerged simultaneously in the 1960s and 1970s within more mainstream artistic spheres in the United States and Europe. According to art historian Miwon Kwon, site-specific work "focused on establishing an inextricable, indivisible relationship between the work and its site and then demanded the physical presence of the viewer for the work's completion." Artists who engaged in this type of work, Kwon continued, resisted "the forces of the capitalist market economy, which circulates artworks as transportable and exchangeable commodity goods."[39] Site specificity functioned under the assumption that the space in which art resides is neither innocent nor devoid of meaning but rather laden with dynamics of signification and, as such, is necessarily complicit with its location. Chicana/o artists embraced site specificity for these reasons but also because of its connections to indigenous aesthetics, which, according to Steven Leuthold, are deeply rooted in space consciousness: "Indigenous representation rests upon social ties and a profound sense of place more than any particular medium, style, or subject matter."[40] Leuthold further argues that in indigenous art the sacred quality attributed to particular locations and sites is accompanied by a sense of responsibility toward that place, its community, and its environment. For the most part, Chicana/o muralists conscientiously sought to work with the qualities that are already intrinsic at any given site, thus avoiding interfering with many of the natural dynamics that are already in place there. Conversely, the practice of transforming and manipulating natural spaces is one closely aligned with colonialist and imperialist enterprises. For instance, the architects of the Roman imperial basilicas sought to re-create the vastness of exterior spaces inside these ambitious structures, and the colonial urban planners of El Zócalo in Mexico City dramatically altered the environment in and around Lake Texcoco to establish the seat of the Viceroyalty of New Spain. Chicana/o artists were conscious of how colonial and expansionist states often disturbed and ultimately destroyed natural environments, and they therefore developed strategies to interact rather than disrupt the natural dynamics of space and place.

Another significant dimension to the issue of space in relationship to

Chicanas/os' Indigenist consciousness centered around the signing of the Treaty of Guadalupe Hidalgo (1848) as a key episode in U.S./Mexican history. The annexation of Mexico's northern provinces during the mid-nineteenth century changed the citizenship rights and social status of some 100,000 Mexicans, many of whom were indigenous inhabitants of the area. Chicana/o activists argued that this particular event in U.S. history explained the current marginalization of Mexicans and Mexican Americans in this country. Richard Griswold del Castillo, in his 1990 monograph entitled *The Treaty of Guadalupe Hidalgo*, outlined the process of self-education Chicana/o activists underwent during the civil rights movement, when many learned about this treaty and its implications. During various public demonstrations, rallies, and meetings, activists like Rodolfo "Corky" Gonzales and Armando Rendón stipulated that the U.S. government had violated the terms of the treaty and that Mexico was indeed entitled to a number of the territories now under U.S. jurisdiction.[41] The historical dynamics triggered by the events surrounding 1848 were intimately connected to more recent histories of displacement such as the forced relocation of neighborhoods after the 1959–1962 construction of Dodger Stadium in the area of Los Angeles called Chávez Ravine. The significance and meaning of the Treaty of Guadalupe Hidalgo gave Chicanas/os not only the means by which to furnish their activist discourse with historical legitimacy but also an epistemological complement to the notion of Aztlán that further substantiated their mythical and innate right to inhabit North American soil. So while many Chicanas/os expressed the symbolic connection between land and indigenous consciousness in a performative manner through activist, oral, and written means, they most concretely achieved the reclaiming of this territory through the creation of murals that secured a place for Mexican Americans within the communities they resided in, as well as within the political and social landscape of the United States.

Chicana/o and Native American Indigenism

Knowledge of the Treaty of Guadalupe Hidalgo also provided a platform on which Chicanas/os forged alliances with Native American groups in the 1980s, given that the distinction between a Native American and a Mexican Indian was by and large determined by the redrawing of the U.S.-Mexico border in the mid-nineteenth century. Griswold del Castillo, for instance, cited an anonymous Chicano pamphlet entitled "Aztlán vs. the United States" that alluded to the common plight between Chicanos and Native Americans:

It [the pamphlet] argued that Chicanos in the United States were Indians by blood as well as heritage; they had suffered the same second class treatment as Indians. Aztlán ... was a spiritual and biological nation that included Indians as well as Chicanos. "This is the nation of RAZA INDIGENA, and the INDIAN NATIONS, or in other words nosotros los indios de Aztlán."[42]

Chicana/o Indigenist thinkers and artists recognized the importance of addressing the plight of indigenous people both south and north of the border. For example, Los Toltecas en Aztlán, an organization of artists and activists founded in San Diego's Centro Cultural de la Raza, would attend various meetings and events organized by Native American activists with the understanding that, like them, Chicana/o radicals were also pursuing the common goals of land rights and sovereignty.[43] In this respect, Cherríe Moraga commented that *movimiento* activists often joked that "Chicanos [were] usually the most Indian-looking people in a room full of 'skins,'" further maintaining that Chicanas/os carried not only indigenous blood from Mexico but also that of other "nations [in North America], including Apache, Yaqui, Papago, Navajo, and Tarahumara from the border regions."[44] The commonality of the Chicana/o and Native American Indigenist initiatives was also underscored by the shared experiences of having to contend with Anglo-Saxon expansionism and aggressive deterritorialization after having suffered the ravages of Spanish colonial campaigns. In many ways, the Anglo-American expansionist mentality posed different kinds of threats and challenges to indigenous peoples vis-à-vis the more parochial Spanish colonialism. Discourses about self-proclaimed racial superiority, accompanied by the support of scientific racism and the unrelenting quest for capital and prosperity, lent U.S. westward expansion an impetus and drive previously unheard of in other colonial enterprises.[45] Indigenous peoples in North America were now faced not only with virulent genocidal campaigns, the systemic usurpation of their ancestral lands, and other forms of devastation, but they were also confronted with the erection of institutions of power that would oppress indigenous nations for many generations to come. It is no surprise, then, that the forms of protest and civil disobedience enacted by Chicana/o and Native American activists later in the 1960s and 1970s would bear striking similarities with one another. For instance, in 1969, a group of more than three hundred Native American activists from fifty different indigenous nations took over San Francisco's Alcatraz Island, reclaiming the territory "in the name of all American Indians by right of discovery,"[46] as stipulated in a joint statement released by the group.[47] In a similar fashion, the Chicano radical group the Brown Berets arrived on California's Santa Catalina Island in September of 1972 and began what would end up being a twenty-four-day vigil in which a large group of Berets lined up along the island's Avalon Harbor holding flags. The Berets insisted that the island was not mentioned in the Treaty of Guadalupe Hidalgo and thus still belonged to Mexico. Chicano historian Richard Griswold del Castillo astutely pointed out that the aim of the whole operation was not to reclaim Catalina in the name of Mexico, but rather "to provide a forum for discussion of the problems confronting Mexican Americans arising from their colonized status."[48] Given its various strategies and modi operandi, as well as its worldview, the Chicano Movement, including its mural component, functioned in various aspects as an indigenous movement seeking to challenge the dominance of an overpowering nation-state. Nevertheless, the specificity of the Chicana/o and Native American experiences need not be collapsed when discussing the similarities in these two communities' colonial history. As a matter of fact, Native American studies scholars like Patricia Penn-Hilden have emerged as ardent critics of the way in which Chicana/o activists and intellectuals have, in her view, appropriated Native American narratives in an ahistorical manner, calling these appropriations "spiritual tourism and obfuscatory hybridization." Penn-Hilden has also argued that some Chicano historians have gone so far as to minimize the devastation of Spanish colonialism on Native American populations. The book *When Jesus Came, the Corn Mothers Went Away* (1991), by Chicano historian Ramón Gutiérrez, has been at the center of the controversy generated by Penn-Hilden and other Native American studies scholars and activists who argue that Gutiérrez relied too much on colonial sources for the book and, as a result, reproduced their exoticizing and eroticizing visions of the Pueblo peoples of the U.S. Southwest.[49]

Making space for previously silenced historical narratives of the Chicana/o experience also formed part of the mission behind the creation of Indigenist murals. Chicana/o artists were cognizant that modern Mexican and ancient Mesoamerican muralists alike had used this medium to "write" monumental epics of indigenous history. This project was of critical importance to Chicana/o activists, given that one of the most virulent aggressions directed at indigenous peoples in the Americas was precisely the obliteration of their history, for "without history, one cannot be, and with a false and foreign history, one cannot be oneself," as Guillermo Bonfil Batalla elucidates.[50] One of the major projects Chicana/o activists, artists, and scholars undertook during *el movimiento* was the recovery and recuperation of Chicana/o and Mexican history, a history that, of course, predated the encroachment of Spanish colonialism and Anglo-American expansionism.

This history reclaimed a crucial piece of cultural information that had been notoriously denied to most of these activists in the U.S. public school system. Historian and activist Ignacio García explained that art, in particular the public mural, played a pivotal role in the reconstruction of this history, which became a visual narrative that also underscored Chicanas/os' Indigenist consciousness:

> Art was another form of history, since most of it depicted the Chicano's Indian heritage and the community's legacy of struggle. Many Mexican-American children first learned about Pancho Villa, Emiliano Zapata, Benito Juárez, Cuauhtémoc, and other Mexican heroes from the murals in the barrio ... Much of the impetus for this "new" art came from the Mexican Revolutionary artists like Diego Rivera and David Alfaro Siqueiros.[51]

But with these Indigenist images, Chicana/o artists not only debunked dominant historical narratives to create autonomous spaces but also exposed the arbitrary and exclusionary character of these texts, thereby calling into question the whole business of writing history. In Western culture, written and visual history was the quintessential hallmark of legitimacy and truth. The myth of veracity associated with history was intimately linked with the preservation of hegemonic powers. Intellectuals in postcolonial and ethnic studies have long understood that most histories are merely elaborate discourses often created to maintain the social and political order. Postcolonial scholars Bill Ashcroft, Gareth Griffiths, and Helen Tiffin, for example, underscored how dominant historical constructs inform our very notion of reality, and that consequently we should regard the narrative component of these constructs as a product of imperialist thinking:

> The post-colonial task therefore is not simply to contest the message of history, which has so often relegated individual post-colonial societies to footnotes to the march of progress, but also to engage the medium of narrativity itself, to reinscribe the 'rhetoric', the heterogeneity of historical representation ... This, of course, is easier said than done for post-colonial societies which so often have failed to gain access to the very institution of 'History' itself with its powerful rules of inclusion and exclusion.[52]

Chicanas/os began to regard history as a subjective, positioned, and often arbitrary text that privileged the experiences and narratives of social elites and dominant culture. Nevertheless, if the act of writing history is equated with power, then Chicanas/os would undergo a radical process of empowerment through the writing and dissemination of their own history. Indigenism and muralism not only made Mexican American history more visible to a greater public, but also gave Chicanas/os access to the very institution of history itself. Moreover, the act of recuperating memory was a significant component within this historically enabling process. Indigenist imagery appeared in these murals not as a nostalgic longing for an indigenous existence, "but as a vision of a different time and space that enable[d] a critique of the present," as explained by cultural studies scholar José Esteban Muñoz when discussing the performative role of memory in Chicana/o art.[53] In this way, Chicana/o artists mirrored the strategies utilized by Native American scholars and activists who sought to explore past indigenous history to understand and address the issues affecting indigenous peoples in the present. Moreover, by depicting Mesoamerican images in their murals, Chicana/o artists were underscoring a historical continuity previously ignored or undermined by prevailing narratives. While scholars of indigenous history and culture recognized the scientific innovation, the social complexity, and the overall *greatness* of pre-Columbian civilizations, they systematically overlooked, consciously or not, the fact that contemporary indigenous people were the direct descendants of these civilizations and, as such, carried much of the sacred and intellectual knowledge of their ancestors. The images of preconquest civilizations rendered in Chicana/o community murals were then public reminders that this historical knowledge and continuity was also inherent in the contemporary urban Chicana/o community. As scholars and activists of indigenous resistance would argue, indigenous history did not end with the European conquest and colonization, thus establishing that, as Peruvian writer Guillermo Carnero Hoke contends, "the Indian nation lives in continuity with its past."[54]

The Chicano Movement ultimately questioned and contested the status quo of postcolonial systems in which the lives of oppressed and formerly colonized peoples are conditioned and compromised by the presence of a hegemonic and overpowering nation-state. Like many other indigenous movements, *el movimiento* sought to transform the relationship that the Chicana/o community had with the United States as a nation-state, a relationship necessarily defined by a center-versus-margin power dynamic. Given that all ethnic groups are "potential nations," as Guillermo Bonfil Batalla maintains, different writers and activists felt this relationship could be altered in many ways, some arguably more radical than others. These proposed changes ranged from the complete destruction or expulsion of the invading nation-state from native lands, to the return of territory belonging to indigenous nations while still allowing the foreign state to remain in the region, to merely devising strategies aimed at changing the *culture* of racism and marginalization that originally informed westward expansion and Manifest Destiny. Ward Churchill argued that the ultimate goal for Indigenist activists should be to find the means to subvert that status quo that regiments the dynamics between the colonizer and the colonized:

> [The Indigenist objective] is to arrive at a new set of relationships with peoples that effectively put an end to the era of international domination. The need is to gradually replace the existing world order with one that is predicated in collaboration and cooperation between nations. The only way to ever accomplish this is to physically disassemble the gigantic state structures—structures that are literally grounded in systemic intergroup domination; they cannot in any sense exist without it.[55]

Along similar lines, Bonfil Batalla argued that "ethnic groups are social entities with the proper conditions to justify their right to self-rule, be it as autonomous nations or as clearly differentiated segments of a broader social whole."[56] For the most part, Chicana/o writers, artists, and activists sought to redefine their relationship to the hegemonic centers of power by *indigenizing* rather than eradicating the nation-state. Advocating for a reconceptualization of the United States as a nation by acknowledging its indigenous foundations, Chicana/o thinkers imagined a relationship on equal footing between indigenous peoples and their former colonizers, but also nonoppressive ways in which communities can come together as nations without violating the rights, sovereignty, and autonomy of other nations.

In this quest to redefine the role of nations vis-à-vis historically oppressed peoples, public murals fulfilled a critical role. Chicana/o artists were acutely aware that murals had been historically complicit with nation-building campaigns by virtue of their highly visible and public status. Conscious of the fact that public art in general is intimately connected with the discursive construction of the nation-state, Chicana/o artists utilized this art form to formulate their notions of an indigenous nation as a contrasting model to the overpowering hegemonic state, namely, the United States. The images of indigenous America depicted in the Chicana/o murals not only posed counterexamples for the postcolonial state but also altered the prevailing definition of that very organism by connecting this Indigenist imagery to U.S. soil, thus indigenizing the state. The public murals became a call for the Chicana/o community and the U.S. nation-state to embrace their repressed and undermined indigeneity.

Radicalism, Identity, and Education

Constructing a radical discourse of resistance—though not always Indigenist in tone—was a critical move for Chicana/o activists during the civil rights era. Nevertheless, many of their proclamations expounding political and cultural difference borrowed much from the rhetorical vocabulary of past Indigenist moments in Latin America. For instance, Rivera's and Orozco's posture of reclaiming Mexico's pre-Columbian past also reemerged in the political discourse of Chicanas/os, and, in both cases, it functioned as a means by which to establish a position of difference and resistance in relation to dominant currents. But Chicanas/os knew all about the distinction between Indigenist identity politics enacted by state apparatuses in Mexico and those utilized by indigenous groups themselves to denounce and challenge their marginalization and continued colonization. Guillermo Bonfil Batalla identified some of the principal characteristics of indigenous protest and activism in Mexico, namely, resistance and innovation.[57] Such tactics, while not the sole property of indigenous protest, were also deployed by Chicana/o activists seeking to devise a radical political posture that would situate them in direct opposition to mainstream U.S. politics. Events like the school blow-outs in Los Angeles or the formation of highly oppositional activist groups like the Brown Berets pointed toward the greater radicalization in Chicana/o activist discourse, a discourse influenced by other civil rights activism of the time, such as the Black Power movement, as well as by indigenous movements of self-determination elsewhere in the Americas. Indeed, the Chicano Movement was a hybrid political struggle that combined various activist tactics that were both indigenous and nonindigenous; nevertheless, its public embrace of indigenous heritage, coupled with its open critique of coloniality and postcoloniality, distinguished it from other civil rights initiatives while simultaneously connecting it to hemispheric indigenous-rights campaigns.

The proclamation of Chicanas/os' indigenous roots also functioned as a distinct maker of difference, thus further reiterating their radical position concerning dominant culture. Within the Chicana/o radical perspective, the notion of difference functioned not as a marker of inequality or a justification for marginalization, but rather as a concept that contested homogeny and assimilation. Behind this conscious assertion of a separate and distinct cultural identity, Chicana/o radicals realized that identity itself was the result of constructed and positioned politics. Stuart Hall likens cultural identity to an act of "becoming" as well as "being." This meant that Chicanas/os themselves came to the conclusion not only that identity is dynamic and that, as Hall himself determined, its "meaning is never finished or completed,"[58] but also that it can often be subject to arbitrary manipulation. If society formulates identity more through "politics, memory, and desire" than through empirical criteria, then Chicanas/os could freely fashion their history and culture in a radically Indigenist vein.

For various Chicana/o artists and their constituent communities, the public mural fulfilled an educational role for a population culturally and politically excluded and isolated from the various schools and universities across the nation. Accordingly, community murals became part of a larger effort carried out by Chicana/o activists to reform the U.S. educational system on all levels. While accounts of the Chicano Movement speak at length of the important changes the student movement in high schools and universities brought to the U.S. educational system, Chicana/o studies scholars have said relatively little about the function that murals played as platforms for alternative educational experiences. Of course, the notion that public murals had the capability to educate entire communities was certainly not a new idea, as this was precisely what murals in early twentieth-century Mexico were meant to do. But Chicana/o artists and activists were all too conscious that both state-sponsored murals and government-funded educational initiatives had troublesome historical connections to public indoctrination, assimilation, and colonization. Like other indigenous peoples of the Americas, Chicanas/os had emerged from a public school system that sought to erase all forms of difference and cultural identity, thus creating a colonized subject who is capable of "seeing, hearing, but not speaking or critiquing," to borrow the words of Guatemalan indigenous activist Pedro Coj Ajbalam.[59] The push for reform and reorganization on the educational front to make schools and universities sites of decolonization rather than social control was part of the political agendas of various indigenous groups throughout the Americas. The demands placed on hegemonic educational systems by Chicana/o activists mirrored those initiated by other indigenous groups in the Americas: both advocated for bilingual and bicultural school curricula, state-funded outreach programs in deprived areas, increases in the hire of teachers and faculty of color, respect and support of family and community cultural traditions within educational institutions, the creation of specialized programs for the study of indigenous communities, and so on. Chicana/o artists, in particular, were also aware that public monuments like murals could carry much of the knowledge and history not taught in schools and universities.

Gender and Heterogeneity

Both Indigenism and muralism, as cultural phenomena in Mexico and the United States, failed to address how gendered subjectivities are deeply compromised by patriarchal systems. Hordes of Mexican and Chicana feminist scholars have written extensively about the peripheral or prescribed role women have had within nation-building processes in Mexico and the United States. In many ways, the history of modern mural movements in the Americas can be defined, in part, as a succession of emerging and contesting public discourses. To a certain degree, the male Chicano murals that would come out of the early 1970s directly or indirectly challenged everything from the style to the modes of production of the Mexican mural renaissance. But the fluid and dynamic nature of community muralism would soon allow for a more heterogeneous articulation of Chicana/o cultural identity. Just as Chicana feminist writers and activists found the need to challenge and problematize the orthodoxy of male Chicano identity politics, Chicana muralists, often by their mere presence up on scaffolding, offset the Chicano nationalist project. Artists such as Judy Baca, Juana Alicia, and Yreina Cervántez and the artists collective Mujeres Muralistas established a muralist tradition of their own, along with an alternative vision of Indigenist aesthetics. By conveying the critical contribution of Mujeres Muralistas, Alicia Gaspar de Alba further illustrated the highly gendered nature of muralism, both in its subject matter and its practices:

> They challenged the sexist and stereotypical notions within the Chicano Art Movement that women were physically not able and politically not "meant" to create murals, to build and climb scaffolding, to be on public display and withstand the comments of passersby.[60]

By default, then, women had little or nothing to say regarding how Chicano Indigenist nationalism would be constructed. This nationalist ideology would often revere male indigenous icons like Cuauhtémoc and Quetzalcoatl while rendering mestiza and indigenous women anonymously. As far as Chicanas were concerned, the Chicano Movement, along with its mural renaissance, had perpetuated patriarchal worldviews in the process of supposedly decolonizing the Chicana/o community.

Chicana muralists found themselves working in a medium that had historically excluded women for centuries. In the context of modern muralist activity in Mexico and the United States, there were at least two decisive episodes in the artistic traditions of these two countries that established muralism as an exclusively male artistic endeavor. The first episode involved the case of María Izquierdo, a Mexican easel painter and a contemporary to *los tres grandes* (the three great ones [Mexican muralists]: Rivera, Siqueiros, and Orozco). The Mexican government commissioned Izquierdo to design a mural for the government building in Mexico City in 1945. After she had made numerous preparations, purchased artistic materials, and created various sketches, Diego Rivera and David Alfaro Siqueiros launched accusations against her, claiming that she lacked the necessary experience to execute a mural,[61] accusations that resulted in the cancellation of her commission.[62] The scandal even reached certain sectors of the press, who continued belittling her qualifications as an artist: "María Izquierdo is not a muralist, she is an outsider in this branch of painting, she does not have the right to take over functions that do not pertain to her."[63]

Chicano muralism certainly inherited many of the gendered exclusions of the Mexican period. Marcos Sánchez-Tranquilino, in his account of the making of the Estrada Courts murals in East Los Angeles, recalled how the predominantly Chicano male organizers of this mural rejected Judy Baca's proposed design for the housing complex:

> According to Baca, her proposed mural was turned down because it was interpreted as being "negative." . . . [Her] finished drawing for the proposed Estrada Courts untitled mural focused on the pain and suffering of women as they have been historically impacted by different forms of male militarism.[64]

Though Sánchez-Tranquilino explains that Baca submitted her design at a time when the organizers and participants of the Estrada murals were trying to convey a more positive image of Chicano youth culture, and that other women did participate in other murals,[65] Baca's emphasis on women's experiences in times of crisis decentered the Chicano nationalist project taking place in Estrada Courts. In her own accounts, however, Judy Baca has stated that her original design was not rejected when she submitted it, but that she actually started doing work on it in Estrada Courts. Nevertheless, she was unable to complete it because, as she stated, "they [the organizers of the Estrada mural project] made it impossible for me to finish" by making the necessary artistic materials and equipment unavailable to her.[66] Both

Izquierdo's and Baca's failed mural projects demonstrated that muralism, as a transnational and transhistorical phenomenon, carried much of its *machista* baggage across time and space.

Chicana artists diversified the Indigenist aesthetic through their own muralist visions. Echoing the critiques of Chicano cultural identity proposed by Gloria Anzaldúa and other Chicana feminists since the 1970s, these artists provided an innovative alternative to the previous notions that Indigenism could only be articulated through the body, culture, and history of the male Indian. The work of Mujeres Muralistas, for example, often depicted indigenous landscapes and communities from Latin America in an attempt to distance themselves from what member Irene Pérez called the more "blood and guts" aesthetics of male Chicano murals.[67] Chicana muralists saw—as many other women of color did—that "their experience at the intersection of oppression . . . generated a multifaceted social critique."[68] In other words, their experiences of gender oppression afforded them insight into the varying degrees to which colonization functions for people outside and inside the Chicana/o community.

The work by Chicana artists inevitably introduced a greater heterogeneity to the mural practice, thus loosening the rigidity with which the medium had been defined. This heterogeneity, however, was also the result of a process that was already underway in Mexican and Chicana/o cultural practices. The process through which Chicana/o murals became increasingly heterogeneous can be linked to the interest in the concept of *mestizaje,* which, Rafael Pérez-Torres argues, was critical in Chicana/o identity formation: "The celebration of the racial and cultural mestizaje that, during the 1920s and beyond, found valorization in the construction of Mexican national identity resonates, during the 1960s and beyond, throughout the development of Chicano cultural identity."[69] In *La raza cósmica* (1925), one of the most important treatises on *mestizaje* read by many Chicana/o intellectuals in the early stages of *el movimiento*, Mexican philosopher and politician José Vasconcelos outlined the spiritual and social benefits that the synthesis of different racial and ethnic traits could bring to the global community. With regard to Mexico's own situation, Vasconcelos conceded that the indigenous presence in Mexico acted as "a good bridge [toward] racial mixing." While Vasconcelos thought of *mestizaje* as a means of assimilating Mexico's native populations, he also maintained that Mexican indigenous culture provided an appropriate starting point toward the achievement of greater heterogeneity.[70] In a curiously similar fashion, the Indigenist aesthetic served to incorporate Chicana/o cultural identity into the parallel and simultaneous articulations of differential consciousness of other marginalized groups in the United States. While the iconography of the early Chicano murals displayed a more monolithic Indigenist vocabulary, those created during the last couple of decades of the twentieth century began to reveal new forms and developments of Indigenist iconography and thought.[71] For example, during the 1970s, images of Aztec warriors and princesses embodied common muralist themes, but as the 1980s emerged, Chicana/o artists began to conceptualize the indigenous figure and landscape in relation to intersecting identities and currents. Indians began to share the muralist pictorial space with Black, Asian, Anglo, and other Latina/o figures. We also start to see collaborations among muralists from different communities whose only common goal is achieving greater social justice through creative avenues. Such a phenomenon, however, pointed not to a disintegration of these individual identities, but rather to the realization that all these distinct groups often shared the same physical and cultural spheres and suffered under the same systems of oppression. With Chicana cultural studies scholar Angie Chabram-Dernersesian calling for more in-depth academic analyses of "social relations that produce these heterogeneous social identities,"[72] it seemed fitting to think of muralist aesthetics and their Indigenist characteristics as phenomena significantly affected by intersecting social phenomena.

The very fleeting and ephemeral quality of many community murals created in California since the late 1960s, the majority of which are executed outdoors, exposing them to vandalism, to the wear and tear of the elements, or, in the specific case of Los Angeles, to local government graffiti-abatement programs,[73] further intensified this heterogeneity. Given that the majority of these projects lack the proper funding for maintenance and restoration, community murals often enjoy a relatively short life span. A large percentage of the artworks created during the 1970s, for instance, have disappeared or exist in a deplorable state of deterioration. This unfortunate reality, however, contributed to an inevitable and continuous renewal of the style and themes that inform muralist production, a phenomenon that greatly promoted much of this growing heterogeneity. As the century came to a close, Chicana/o Indigenism appeared to be a mere artifact of a bygone era of Chicano nationalism, but its elements were inadvertently reinscribed and fused into the increasingly hybrid aesthetics of the West Coast urban landscape.

On Indigenism, Nonessentialism, and Unstable Identities

In spite of its seemingly essentialist overtones, Indigenism as a theoretical tool for the articulation of a Chicana/o mural history offers dynamic rather than static definitions of cultural identity. Indeed, Indigenist aesthetics emerged from the Chicana/o political project as a way to find an origin, some sort of cultural essence that defined the Chicana/o being. But since identities are always "subject to the play of history and the play of differ-ence,"[74] as Stuart Hall has told us, the Chicana/o search for a quintessential indigenous essence always met with an unstable subject, impossible to pin down and open to numerous possibilities. As a posture that operates mainly on the level of consciousness, Indigenism can also transcend the specificities of race and class. Though it emerged from a specifically Chicana/o political project, Indigenism was not *exclusively* articulated, understood, and utilized by artists, intellectuals, and activists of Mexican or Chicana/o or Latina/o descent. A number of non-Chicana/o artists working within Chicana/o and Mexican community settings articulated Indigenist sensibilities in their public art by virtue of their often intimate contact with these populations or by their own political proclivities. It is because of the transcendental and unstable qualities of Chicana/o Indigenist aesthetics and identities that I include in this book the work of artists like Susan Kelk Cervantes, Posh One, Nicole Emmanuel, and others who are not Chicanas/os per se but whose work has done much to construct Chicana/o Indigenist identities. Community muralism has exemplified what Hall called the "de-centering of identity," in other words, "the fragmentation of social identity [, which] is very much part of the modern and . . . postmodern experience."[75] Moreover, the urban settings where these murals reside are often characterized by what George Lipsitz has called "dangerous crossroads" where cultural transac-tions and dynamic dialogues often take place among different communi-ties in ways that usually threaten monolithic notions of identity and so-cial expectations about race.[76] While these transactions do not erase power relations and communities' attachment to place, they are capable of tran-scending the strongholds of race, class, gender, sexuality, if only for a brief moment of contact.[77] Given the pervasiveness and visibility of Chicana/o Indigenist imagery in community muralism, it should come as no surprise that this aesthetic should traverse ethnic lines via these cultural transactions within the heterogeneous setting of the city.

The inclusion of non-Chicana/o artists in this volume on Chicana/o art is also prompted by their roles as community artists in the public and ur-ban settings of California. When these artists were working within a con-text of community involvement, their subjectivities were intertwined with that of the surrounding community, therefore their finished artwork inevi-tably reflects the two. Unlike artists working within a studio setting, com-munity artists are charged with the task of facilitating collective creativity rather than expressing individual artistic sensibilities. While I am not arguing that their individuality as artists is completely lost in the act of engagement, they are accountable to a larger constituency. These artists are engaged in what James Bau Graves calls participation in culture, a process through which community artists are conditioned to "[place] community interests at the center of the project's purpose and [rely] on community members' knowledge of their own heritage in the development of the most relevant programs."[78] Working within these contexts, an individual artist can legitimately articulate sensibilities, anxieties, concerns, feelings, and other expressions that fall outside her or his personal experience. In this way, works of art created within a Mexican American community context while organized or led by a non-Chicana/o can also further Chicana/o collective empowerment. Seana S. Lowe argues that when artists are engaged in the creation of a communal art project, individual and collective identities are dialectically defined through one another,[79] thus further problematizing fixed and unilateral notions of identity.

Vision, Methodology, and Configuration

This volume brings together two bodies of literature that until now have operated in complete oblivion of one another, namely, the existing scholarship on U.S. community muralism and the various writings and treatises on indigenous agency and resistance throughout the Americas. In this study, I argue that the complexity and multivalency of Chicana/o community muralism is best understood through the theoretical, discursive, and pragmatic lens of autonomous indigenous expressions. Rather than following a rigid chronological framework that does not properly represent the dynamic nature of Chicana/o mural history, this volume opts instead to privilege a thematic approach whereby the history of Chicana/o muralism unravels in an episodic fashion. Nonetheless, these different episodes or themes do follow a sequential order in that they discursively and theoretically build upon one another. We begin in Chapter 1 by directly addressing the connection between Mexican and Chicana/o muralism. In this chapter, the text focuses on the importance of the various murals created by David Alfaro Siqueiros and Diego Rivera in California to the generation of Chicana/o artists working nearly half a century later in the region. I then carry out close iconographic readings of Chicana/o murals that utilize Indigenist imagery "borrowed" from the work of Siqueiros, Rivera, and, to a lesser degree, José Clemente Orozco. I argue that this imagery emerges in the mural work by Chicana/o artists neither as an artistic "influence" nor a form of "appropriation," but rather as a dialectic element that allows Chicana/o artists to establish a critical dialogue with their Mexican predecessors.

Chapter 2, by contrast, focuses solely on the early phases of Chicana/o mural history, namely, the period from 1968 to 1978. This chapter identifies and interprets the most recurrent and persistent Indigenist motifs in Chicana/o muralism, images that were meant to aid in the formation of a Chicana/o nationalist identity. The frequent representations of the Aztec calendar stone, the mestizo tripartite face, and Mesoamerican pyramids pointed to the ways in which artists consciously sought to develop a visual vocabulary that further stimulated their growing political consciousness in the 1970s. But like any prominent civilization and culture, the Chicano Nation needed not only individual motifs but also *obras maestras* (masterpieces) that epitomized its spirit and essence, such as Guillermo Aranda's *Dualidad* and East Los Streetscapers' *Chicano Time Trip*, murals that are now considered emblems of Chicano nationalist zeal.

Chapter 3 moves into the ambiguous terrain of graffiti art and culture and the ways in which these modes of expression influenced the Chicana/o mural movement and its Indigenous aesthetic. Marcos Sánchez-Tranquilino astutely observed that cultural critics as well as community entities often thought of muralism and graffiti as opposite and contesting systems of visual signification, when in fact the relationship between the two was a dialectical and symbiotic one. The presence of graffiti calligraphy in community murals and the emergence of actual graffiti murals further complicated the mural vs. graffiti dichotomy. In this chapter, I further argue that graffiti calligraphy was particularly influential to Chicana/o muralists because of its similarities with Mesoamerican glyphs; the two generally operate as both image and text, in other words, as sign and signifier simultaneously. Moreover, in Chapter 3, I discuss artists whose work transcends or problematizes the distinction between muralism and graffiti, such as Charles "Chaz" Bojórquez, Esteban Villa, and Posh One, among others. While this volume identifies various individual murals that are important to the history of Chicana/o muralism, in Chapter 4, I discuss the phenomenon of the mural environment. These environments consist of initiatives to create series of murals in close proximity to one another and within a defined and limited space. With these murals, the public is expected to see them not as single works of art, but rather as components of a larger and collective artistic project. The position and iconography of the individual murals within the environment should be understood as functions of one another and in relation to the space in which they reside. I cite the murals in San Diego's Chicano Park, East Los Angeles' Estrada Courts, and San Francisco's Balmy

Alley (Mission District) as examples of mural environments, and I interpret their creation as responses to the history of displacement and marginalization traditionally suffered by Mexican and Chicana/o populations in the United States. As such, the mural environment operates for Chicana/o populations as a means to reclaim the spaces historically denied to them. I note that by reappropriating these spaces, Chicana/o muralists were seeking to physically restore the Aztec homeland of Aztlán on U.S. soil.

Though artists, art historians, and critics have traditionally construed muralism as an exclusively male art form, Chicana artists, with their substantial body of work, have radically subverted that belief. Chapter 5 provides a general overview of the contributions made by Chicanas to the history of community muralism in California. The first part of this chapter demonstrates how the mural movement often eroticized and exoticized the bodies of women, and the second part focuses on the actual work produced by women artists.

Finally, Chapter 6 examines the growing heterogeneity that has come to characterize the community mural movement in California. While muralism emerged as a seemingly unified artistic project that represented the spirit of the Chicano Movement, in actuality, mural history develops unevenly through the fragmented subject positions of the artists and the communities they served. There is no one mural Indigenist aesthetic, but rather a multiplicity of complementary and contesting aesthetics. I explore the nature of this heterogeneity by examining various examples of murals throughout California that for numerous reasons challenge traditional and time-honored notions about muralism. For instance, I discuss examples of new and innovative media utilized to create murals, such as recycled materials, performance, and digital technology. I ultimately underscore that, rather than creating a monolithic and static notion of Chicana/o identity through community murals, Indigenism allowed for a dynamic and heterogeneous notion of the indigenous.

CHAPTER ONE

The Dialectics of Continuity and Disruption

Chicana/o and Mexican Indigenist Murals

The art of our great señores,
Diego Rivera,
Siqueiros,
Orozco, is but another act of revolution for
the salvation of mankind.

RODOLFO "CORKY" GONZALES
from the epic poem *Yo soy Joaquín*

For the growing Chicano art movement, the aesthetics of Mexican
muralism coexist with the most avant-garde manifestations to express
the particular life experience of the urban Chicano.

SHIFRA GOLDMAN
"Siqueiros and Three Early Murals"

Mexican art and its various manifestations in California are not exotic.
We claim them as part of our cultural heritage as well.

PAUL KARLSTROM
"Rivera, Mexico and Modernism"

Mexican and Chicana/o Muralism: Continuity and Disruption

As stipulated in the introduction to this volume, Chicana/o Indigenism
was deeply influenced by the Indigenist discourses that emerged in Mexico after the Revolution of 1910. The various mural cycles commissioned by
the Mexican government throughout the first half of the twentieth century
were critical components of that discourse. In these images, Mexican indigenous history and culture were exalted as fundamental building blocks for
the postcolonial nation-state. Though artists had previously utilized indigenous images to legitimize a uniquely Mexican national identity,[1] the postrevolutionary period saw an interest in indigenous culture not as an artifact

of a bygone though idyllic era—as was the case with nineteenth-century representations—but as a living life force nurturing national culture in the present. Moreover, the Mexican muralists were among the first modern artists in the Americas to politicize indigenous imagery and figures to address issues of social justice and Marxist ideals about class struggle. Many Chicana/o artists admired the politicization of the indigenous enacted by modern Mexican artists and regarded the Mexican mural renaissance as the quintessential pairing of form and content. In other words, the public artworks by the likes of Diego Rivera and David Alfaro Siqueiros, among others, provided a powerful example of the political dimensions Indigenist discourse could take when articulated through the monumentality of the public mural.[2] Chicana/o artists, for their part, repeatedly sought out information and connections between themselves and the Mexican generation, as David Avalos explains:

> The link between Posada, the Mexican muralists and Chicano artists is vital. San Francisco artist and writer Rupert García has exchanged ideas on the Mexican and Chicano art movements with [Jean] Charlot.[3] San Diego's Salvador "Queso" Torres has witnessed and recorded for his colleagues the words of Siqueiros. The works of "The Three Greats" have been exhibited in Chicano neighborhoods like San Diego's "Varrio Logan Heights." Arsacio Vanegas Arroyo, the grandson of Posada's publisher, has maintained close contact with Chicanos and generously made his private collection available for touring at Chicano cultural centers.[4]

But the connection between these two generations of artists is not so much one of artistic influence as it is one of historical continuity. Both Siqueiros and Rivera had left their indelible mark on modern California history when they executed a series of murals in the 1930s that would critically inform the work of subsequent public artists like Works Progress Administration (WPA) artists and, of course, the Chicana/o group. Judy Baca, for her part, saw the Chicana/o mural movement not as a separate current but rather as a latter phase of the same creative phenomenon: "Chicano murals . . . [have] contributed to the shift in emphasis from Mexico to the United States as the center of mural production in the world."[5] Moreover, numerous Chicana/o artists sought to further their artistic training by going to Mexico and seeking out academies and workshops closely associated with *los tres grandes*, as Shifra Goldman explains: "Some [Chicana/o artists] sought training in Mexico as they developed into professional muralists (such as Ray Patlán, who worked with Arnold Belkin in the San Carlos Academy, and Judith Baca, who attended the Taller Siqueiros in Cuernavaca)."[6]

Nevertheless, the almost organic continuum between these two movements is neither seamless nor unproblematic. Eva Sperling Cockcroft and Holly Barnet-Sánchez were quick to point out the critical differences between these two mural moments:

> [The Chicana/o] mural movement differed in many important ways from the Mexican one. It was not sponsored by a successful revolutionary government, but came out of the struggle by the people themselves against the *status quo*. Instead of well-funded projects in government buildings, these new murals were located in the *barrios* and ghettos of the inner cities, where oppressed peoples lived.[7]

So, in spite of the historical connection between Mexican and Chicana/o muralism, it is not surprising that the contrasting sociopolitical contexts for both movements would lead to clearly divergent aesthetics and means of cultural production. What is not so self-evident, however, is the nature and character of this Mexican/Chicana/o mural connection. While Mexican muralism indeed functioned for Chicana/o artists as a source of artistic and political stimulus, it also operated as a distinct point of departure and difference. The dialectic relationship that Chicana/o muralism has had with Mexico points to the dynamic nature of the flow of cultural capital across the U.S.-Mexico border. Earlier in this monograph, I warned against the pitfalls associated with describing the Mexican influence on Chicana/o art as a unidirectional and static current of artistic movement. I argued that this approach trivialized the complexity and richness of Chicana/o art history and overlooked the critical importance of other factors that informed its development. I proposed, instead, the dialectic model formulated by critics like Mikhail Bakhtin and Charles Nuckolls as a more appropriate theoretical framework by which to articulate the Mexican-Chicano relationship. In this chapter, I highlight the markers of both unity and difference when discussing the continuity and disruption between the history of Mexican muralism and the development of Chicana/o public arts. I demonstrate how the thematic, iconographic, or stylistic elements of *los tres grandes* explicitly or implicitly emerged in the work of California Chicana/o artists, thereby forming part of a complex network of interrelated components that depend on one another but are also in conflict with one another.

As far as the Indigenist iconography in Chicana/o muralism is concerned, certainly the Indigenism upheld by the Mexican muralists had a profound effect on how Chicanas/os devised their own Indigenist imagery.

The fundamental difference, however, rested on the fact that Indigenism for Chicanas/os has not been an institution supported and endorsed by official ideologies, but a more introspective, self-affirming, and radical discourse occurring at the margins of the mainstream and one that sought to decenter hegemonic notions of nation and sovereignty. Nevertheless, the brand of Indigenist iconography that the Mexican muralists introduced to California, as indicated by Paul Karlstrom, "provided models for incorporating cultural past and ethnic identity into an alternative modernist vision, one that provided for a responsible fusion of the social and the aesthetic."[8] Moreover, while Mexican Indigenism formed part of an institutionalized canon, its meanings in the U.S. context did not form part of an official ideology. The work of artists like Rivera, Orozco, and Siqueiros provided a model for a politicized Indigenist aesthetic previously unseen in the history of modern art in Europe and the Americas.

Many Chicana/o artists, conscious of the historical and political specificity of the work by their Mexican predecessors, used their influence in strategic and measured ways. The reality they faced as members of a racialized U.S. minority contrasted greatly with that of Rivera, Siqueiros, and Orozco, who formed part of an elite group of artists in Mexico with training in the San Carlos Academy and even in Europe, as was the specific case of Rivera. Although these Mexican artists did expose the ills faced by the nation's marginalized communities, including indigenous populations, they did so from an outsider perspective, that is, from the position of someone trying to expose the suffering of the less fortunate. Chicana/o artists, on the other hand, dealt with social conditions in their work that they themselves had suffered, or were still suffering, in the flesh. For example, Ester Hernández, as well as various members of the Royal Chicano Air Force, came from farmworker families and had experienced first-hand the harsh working conditions in the fields and the ravages of pesticide poisoning in these communities. Amalia Mesa-Bains argued that this "need to blend a historical and personal identity as Chicano was a driving force in the activism of *el movimiento*."[9] These personal experiences lent a uniquely powerful and poignantly critical dimension to their work, thus forming a radical aesthetic previously unheard of in the history of modern and contemporary art in the Americas. Chicana/o artists, unlike many of their Mexican predecessors, were faced with the painful and difficult task of dealing with their own personal suffering when making collective statements about social injustice.

The profound differences between the Mexican and Chicana/o historical and sociopolitical contexts, coupled, nevertheless, with the undeniable connections between the two developments, produced a dialectic relationship between their corresponding mural movements. This relationship was defined in part by the tension between their similarities and differences. Certainly, both Mexican and Chicana/o artists viewed muralism as a more democratic form of art that could be more accessible to a larger population. Both were also conscious of the important role the medium could play in nation-building processes. But Chicana/o artists saw the Mexican mural movement as a model for what they were doing in California as much as they regarded it as a point of departure. Conscious of their comparatively peripheral position within U.S. mainstream artistic currents and institutions, Chicanas/os pushed the medium to challenge exactly the kinds of government institutions that endorsed the work of *los tres grandes*. Not having access to the walls of major public and federal buildings, as Cockcroft and Barnet-Sánchez pointed out, Chicana/o muralists turned to the urban landscapes of barrios and neighborhoods as sites for the radical visual discourse offered by their Indigenist images.

Even the parameters of community involvement were redefined in Chicana/o community muralism. While Mexico's mural renaissance sought to include its community through the public location of its frescoes and through the greater heterogeneity in its representation of the Mexican population, the Chicana/o mural movement further embraced its audience by recruiting them for the actual production of the murals, as indicated by Shifra Goldman and Tomás Ybarra-Frausto: "The notion of an artistic team collaborating on a public mural can be found in the early writings of Siqueiros; however, the inclusion of (often untrained) community participants as painters appears to be unique to the U.S. street mural movement of the 1970s."[10] This community involvement often made Chicana/o murals into collaborative works of art that articulated a collective Indigenist consciousness. In the same way that art historian Jonathan Fineberg saw Jackson Pollock's canvases covered with drips of paint as mere documents or artifacts of the actual work of art—that is, the moment of production—the work of art created by many Chicana/o muralists occurs during production when the community is actively engaged.[11] In what follows, I explore the dialectic strategies that Chicana/o muralists utilized to reinscribe meaning into Mexican mural discourse on the one hand, and to establish an independent voice reflecting their own unique historical memory and political agency on the other.

Visual Quotations

The correlation between the Mexican and Chicana/o mural movements can be appreciated on various levels (thematic, iconographic, stylistic, etc.), but perhaps one of the most common devices Chicana/o artists use to establish a conscious connection to their Mexican predecessors is that of the visual quotation. Just as writers may quote the exact words of other writers in their text, modern artists have reproduced iconographic motifs by older artists in their work for various purposes by using direct and clearly recognizable visual quotations. Sometimes called artistic appropriation—albeit somewhat inaccurately—visual quotations generally take the form of overt allusions to well-known works of art or hegemonic aesthetic traditions in images by modern and contemporary artists. Examples of visual quotations, for instance, include the references to Italian Renaissance painting in Cindy Sherman's photographic self-portraiture or re-creations of European "old masters" in the work by Japanese artist Yasuma Morimura.[12] These quotations usually betray a conflicted relationship between the "quoted" and the "quoting" image, whereby these contemporary artists may either be revering or subverting "the original" (or both), but are often interrogating the authority, originality, and power of established aesthetic traditions, as contemporary art curator Shirley J.-R. Madill explains: "In the 'quotation' . . . the original is oddly reified and given an extended life of its own, while the new object's autonomy similarly shines through."[13] In literary studies, critics such as Bakhtin himself and Claudette Sartiliot have argued that *textual* quotations are the natural outcome of the dialectic element in language itself,[14] with Bakhtin postulating that "the word is shaped in a dialogic interaction with an alien world that is already in the object."[15] A similar dynamic holds true for images that are inevitably derived from older visual traditions to varying degrees and that, as a consequence, enter into an active dialogue with the past.[16] It seems obvious, then, that the relationship between these two art-historical moments, the Mexican and the Chicana/o periods, is necessarily a dialectic one rather than an example of creative submission. Chicana/o artists, though conscious of their own dialogue with the Mexican School, make concerted efforts to clearly and overtly elucidate this influence to their public, who, in the case of the muralists, are primarily barrio residents and community members.

Artists of color in the United States and elsewhere have utilized visual quotations in their work as strategies for decolonization, often in reaction to cultural and historical erasure. In most of these cases, however, the "quoted" image is one deeply associated with colonial regimes. This strategic emulation of sorts, as Olu Oguibe, historian of modern African art, explains, is "not intended simply to prove the equal competence of the colonized as an end, but . . . to undermine the ideological foundations of the colonial project and overwrite, as it were, the colonial text."[17] While there are elements of legitimization and subversion behind the Chicana/o quotation of the Mexican School, the relationship between the two is not one of colonizer and colonized, but rather one of estranged historical cohorts; in other words, these two generations of artists represented different phases of the same historical continuum, a connection, nonetheless, that had been severely disrupted by dominant narratives. This relationship, of course, complicates the nature of Chicana/o artists' visual quotation of the Mexican imagery and thus heralds a completely new form of visual quotation. In the contemporary art scene, visual quotations traditionally take place between opposite perspectives, that is, new work citing old work, women citing male art, queer imagery citing heteronormative aesthetics, non-European artists citing the Western canon, and so on, and it has often been the case that the "citing" image dislodges the "cited" reference. Though marked by clearly distinct cultural and historical experiences, contemporary Chicana/o artists and the Mexican artists from the twenties and thirties do not represent polar opposites. When many Chicana/o artists came of age in the 1960s and 1970s, figures like Rivera, Siqueiros, and Orozco were already acknowledged "modern masters" in avant-garde discourse, yet they were completely divorced from any form of creative expression that emerged from Chicana/o and Mexican American communities, which was often dismissed as vernacular, folkloric, or merely propagandistic. With these visual quotations, Chicana/o artists reclaimed their connection to the Mexican School and thus legitimized their own artistic productions, but they did so on their own terms. For example, they would often take a single vignette, motif, or figure that was clearly and unambiguously from Rivera's or Siqueiros's visual repertoire and place it within a completely new and original composition. While Siqueiros was influential to Chicana/o artists throughout California, Rivera was more important to artists in San Francisco. Regardless, the choice of images for these quotations was a strategic one, for Chicana/o artists often used motifs that had the potential to transcend the historical moment for which they were created. The controlled and calculated way in which they cited these Mexican artists also, paradoxically, underscored the originality and autonomy of their own artistic production; the Mexican quotation provided a frame of comparison that underscored how similar but also how different Chicana/o art was from Mexican modernism.

Siqueiros, *La América Tropical*, and Chicana/o Artists

During the 1970s, the Mexican muralists provided an ideal model for a nationalist vocabulary that could be articulated in public spaces. Given these

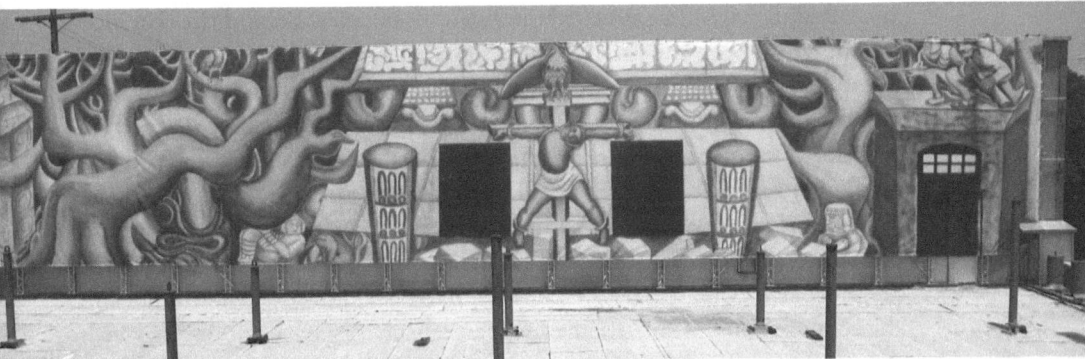

FIGURE I.I. David Alfaro Siqueiros, © 1932, *La América Tropical*, banner reproduction of original mural, Los Angeles, California. Courtesy of El Pueblo de los Angeles Historic Monument.

nationalist and Indigenist tendencies in Mexican art during the first half of the twentieth century, Chicana/o artists gravitated more toward these artists than to their direct contemporaries in Mexico during and after the 1960s. As noted in this book's introduction, some forty years prior to the Chicana/o mural movement David Alfaro Siqueiros had made a lasting impression in California art history with his mural *La América Tropical* (1932; Figure 1.1), painted in Los Angeles's Olvera Street,[18] a predominantly Mexican American area of the city at the time. Siqueiros had been commissioned by F. K. Ferenz, the director of the Plaza Art Center on Olvera Street, to do a mural with the theme "tropical America," as Siqueiros himself recalled: "The [director], like a good Yankee capitalist, had spent the whole night thinking up a theme. As one might imagine, for him, tropical America meant a continent of happy men surrounded by palm trees and squawking parrots where fruits fall voluntarily from trees into the mouths of happy mortals."[19] Siqueiros instead created a militantly politicized Indigenist mural that flew in the face of exoticizing conventions about indigenous cultures in the Americas. The artist placed a crucified Indian on a double cross at the center of the composition, where his twisted body dangles lifelessly from the cross. Perched above his head, we find an eagle, which functions here as a dual symbol. On the one hand, it is the American eagle, which, for the artist, represented U.S. capitalism and the harm it had wreaked upon indigenous communities in the Americas. On the other hand, the eagle in *La América Tropical* was an allusion to the eagle perched on a *nopal* cactus that appears in the Mexican flag, thus referring to the Mexican government itself and its own dismissive and often damaging treatment of indigenous peoples. Behind the crucified Indian we also see the architectural ruins of a pre-Columbian past while a serpentlike system of vines creeps toward the foreground. In a small architectural structure to the right of the composition, Siqueiros placed two additional indigenous figures who, at first sight, may appear to be mere afterthoughts to the central figure. Nevertheless, these two figures, a Mexican indigenous peasant and an Andean Indian, both armed, represent a kind of counterdiscourse to that of the crucified Indian. While the indigenous peoples of the Americas have fallen victim to the violence of colonialism and the economic disenfranchisement of capitalism, they have not done so without resistance. These two figures serve to remind the spectator that as long as indigenous communities are subjected to oppression and marginalization, the possibility of insurrection is always there. So for the many Chicana/o artists who were affected by this image, *La América Tropical* spoke not only of indigenous suffering but also of resistance, resilience, and agency.

While *La América Tropical* seemed radical and thus politically attractive to Chicana/o artists in the 1970s, it was simply too inflammatory for many audiences in the early 1930s. The mural would eventually be covered up with whitewash, and Siqueiros would be denied the renewal of his U.S. visa, which forced him to leave the country by August of 1932. Shortly after his departure, social pressure began to mount against the mural. F. K. Ferenz insisted that the sections of the mural that were visible from the street be whitewashed. Soon, however, local officials and residents managed to get the mural completely covered up. *La América Tropical* existed in virtual invisibility for three decades, until the late 1960s, when Chicana/o activists, artists, and residents of Los Angeles began to demand that the mural be restored. Shifra Goldman and Chicano filmmaker Jesús Salvador Treviño were among the first to raise awareness about the mural's deteriorating state and need for preservation. Goldman insisted that the mural be saved not only for its intrinsic artistic value but also because of its importance to the local Chicana/o community: "[The mural] establishes a link between the [Chicana/o] community in Los Angeles and that of Mexico in the work of this one great Mexican muralist."[20] Two professional restorers from Mexico, Jaime Mejía and Josefina Quezada, were brought in to assess the condition of the mural and to begin the salvage process. They found that the mural's imagery had faded considerably due to the peeling and cracking of the mural surface, which was caused by the whitewashing, years of neglect, the elements, and Siqueiros's own use of experimental techniques. Although restoration was not advisable, as Mejía and Quezada explained, the preservation and protection of what remained of the mural should become a priority. Many years later, in 1988, the Getty

Conservation Institute, in a partnership with El Pueblo de Los Angeles Historical Monument, took over the cleaning and preservation efforts for *La América Tropical.*

The relevance and importance of *La América Tropical* to Chicana/o artists operated on several levels. On one level, it was created during a particularly sensitive time in Mexican American history, when the U.S. government was staging mass deportations of Mexican nationals and Mexican Americans to supposedly alleviate the economic devastation of the Great Depression. On another level, Siqueiros utilized strategies in the creation of this mural that would later be used by Chicana/o artists who would also, like Siqueiros himself, try to survive in a country that ignored its own indigenous history. Siqueiros took elements imposed by the dominant culture, as was the case of the "tropical America" theme given to him, and reformulated them with transgressive and even subversive implications, a strategy Chicana/o artists would later use. In addition, many of these artists found that the systems of social control that sought to censor and curb Siqueiros's artistic production in the United States were the same systems that oppressed the Chicana/o community, as Chicano artist Gilbert Luján explained: "The whitewashing of the Siqueiros image is clear evidence of the inability of racist institutions to allow us to express our experiences as we see them."[21] Moreover, Siqueiros's experimentation with new artistic media in *La América Tropical,* such as industrial paint applied with an airbrush technique, led some contemporary observers to laud him as the first graffiti artist of Los Angeles. Even Siqueiros himself saw his work in the United States, which began in Los Angeles, as marking the beginning of his experimental journey with new media: "It was in [the United States], that country of great industrial development, that I began the true history of my self-proclaimed technical tricks."[22] But, most importantly, Siqueiros's ideas about the sociopolitical role of public art were most closely aligned with Chicana/o artists' own formulations about the importance of community muralism. In many of his public speeches, Siqueiros would argue that true public and monumental art possesses a quality he called *integración plástica,* or "aesthetic integration," which is the seamless and organic incorporation of elements from architecture, sculpture, painting, and sociopolitical discourse into the creative whole. He further contended that the most legitimate and authentic examples of *integración plástica* could be found in the monumental art by indigenous peoples of the Americas prior to the conquest. Moreover, Siqueiros felt that he himself did not achieve true *integración plástica* until he arrived in Los Angeles, where he worked for the first time in a truly collective and politically conscious way: "*Integración plástica* is the most advanced form of teamwork. My first experience with this mode of working happened in Los Angeles in 1932 when—with the close collaboration of painters, architects, photographers, draftsmen, and masons—we produced paintings on the exterior walls of the Chouinard School of Art and the Plaza Art Center."[23]

In spite of the critical precedent that La América Tropical and the figure of Siqueiros himself posed for Chicana/o artists who came of age during the civil rights movement, the question remains: Why did Siqueiros's impact take nearly four decades to materialize, that is, to mark its presence in the work of Mexican American artists? The existence of other Mexican American artists like Martín Ramírez and Carlos Licón in California prior to the 1960s established a general link between the Mexican and the Chicana/o generation, but the specific connection to Siqueiros seems more elusive. Luis Garza, Chicano artist and former project manager for the América Tropical conservation project, explained to me that Siqueiros had planted a seed for social consciousness and political affirmation in California that lay dormant until the civil rights movement, a period of greater freedom that allowed that seed to germinate and bear fruit.[24] Moreover, of the three Mexican muralists, Siqueiros was the most conscious of the plight suffered by Mexicans north of the U.S.-Mexico border and the one who lived long enough to learn about the emerging Chicano art movement in the United States serving as a kind of historical bridge between the Mexican School of painting and Chicano community muralism.[25]

Chicana/o artists in the Los Angeles area, the very site of La América Tropical, would be among the first to come under the influence of Siqueiros's powerful Indigenist vision. In 1974, members of the Chicana/o student activist group MEChA (Movimiento Estudiantil Chicano de Aztlán) in Santa Ana College mobilized the local community to create the now-legendary MEChA Mural on the campus's Nealley Library (Figure 1.2). This initiative was sparked when the students approached art historian Shifra Goldman, who at the time was teaching Mexican and Chicana/o art at the college, to organize a field trip to East Los Angeles for students to see the Chicana/o murals there. The trip created such a buzz among the students that they decided to make their own mural on campus. Mural making, they realized, need not be an activity requiring government sanction and lavish funding, as the budding Chicana/o mural movement happening in the barrios certainly proved. The late Sergio O'Cadiz, a local Santa Ana artist, was invited to be the artistic director of the project, along with three professional assistants, Doris Barker, Emigdio Vasquez, and Jennifer Winn. In addition to them, a total of thirty-three Santa Ana College students, many of them

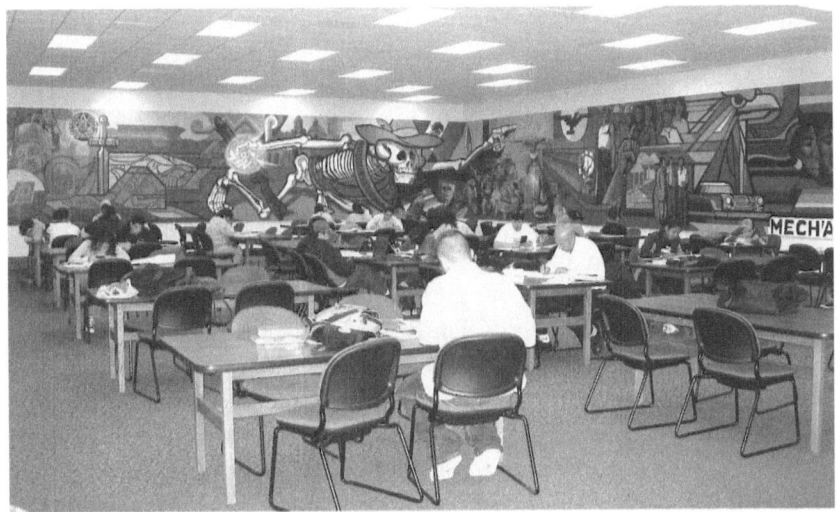

FIGURE 1.2. Sergio O'Cadiz, project director, assisted by Doris Baker, Emigdio Vasquez, and Jennifer Winn, plus a team of thirty-three students from MEChA, © 1974, *The MEChA Mural*, mural, Nealley Library, Santa Ana College, Santa Ana, California. Courtesy of Nealley Library, Santa Ana College.

members of MEChA, assisted the artists in the creation of the mural while also actively participating in every aspect of the decision-making process.

The working process behind the creation of the *MEChA Mural* began with a viewing of Jesús Salvador Treviño's documentary *América Tropical*, a film that recounts the making of Siqueiros's mural and the renovation efforts that took place afterward. Emigdio Vasquez, who was also a student at the time, recounted how O'Cadiz soon began soliciting ideas and sketches from the student body for the creation of the mural. He was invited to participate after he submitted a series of sketches. For his part, Vasquez had come under the influence of the Mexican muralists, whom he called "the great masters," through courses on Mexican art he had taken with Shifra Goldman at Santa Ana College.[26] So it was through direct student input that the iconographic program of the *MEChA Mural* was created. Originally conceptualized as a long, friezelike composition, the mural narrates, from left to right and in a loosely chronological order, key moments and images from Mexican and Chicana/o history and culture. The narrative begins with the preconquest indigenous cultures represented by the Aztec Calendar stone next to Quetzalcoatl and stylized representations of pre-Columbian pyramids. The development of the pre-Columbian period is then interrupted by a Spanish helmet and sword, which here symbolize the violent disruption of indigenous culture by the European conquest. Soon the pre-Columbian architectural motifs morph into colonial religious architecture, alluding to the critical role played by the Catholic Church in colonizing campaigns. Almost jumping out of the pictorial space, the figure of a gigantic skeleton with a huge skull, or *calavera*, suddenly emerges from within the composition, signaling a break in the general linearity and chronology of the mural. As pointed out by Shifra Goldman, the *calavera* operates here as an allegory of cultural duality and change.[27] A reference to the Mexican celebration of El Día de los Muertos (the Day of the Dead) as well as to the work of printmaker José Guadalupe Posada, the *calavera* wears a bandolier and holds a rifle, personifying the Mexican revolutionary soldier. Rather than sporting the traditional *sombrero* from the Mexican Revolution, however, the *calavera* instead wears a blue feathered hat associated with U.S. pachuco culture. The cultural duality of this figure points to the ways in which Mexican culture and history became transnational after 1848, thus heralding the rise of a new modern era. The artists depict the *calavera* lunging forward and pointing toward the second half of the mural, which depicts images more closely associated with Mexican culture in the United States. Reminiscent of Siqueiros's mural style in Chapultepec and at the Universidad Autónoma de México, the second half reveals the image of a migrant farmworker toiling in the fields; a group of white- and blue-collar Chicana/o workers looking toward the future; pachucos and cholos next to a lowrider car; and, to conclude the composition, a representation of the artists and students themselves working on the *MEChA Mural*. The inclusion of this last scene served the primary function of situating the creation of this mural within broader Mexican/Chicana/o history for the spectators as well as the mural participants themselves.

Couched between the *calavera* and the contemporary scenes of Chicana/o life, we find a visual quotation of Siqueiros's embattled crucified Indian from *La América Tropical*. O'Cadiz and the assisting artists of the *MEChA Mural* sought to recontextualize the crucified Indian within the specificity of the current Chicana/o struggle. Directly beneath this figure, a woman whose face is covered completely by a blue *rebozo* (shawl) kneels as she holds a large votive candle. The color of her *rebozo* and her position vis-à-vis the crucified Indian are reminiscent of crucifixion and lamentation scenes in Christian iconography where Mary mourns over the body of Christ. The artists, however, are quick to subvert this possible reading by also placing this woman next to a crate of produce, thus implying she is a farmworker mourning the loss of a loved one, possibly her son, to the hazardous and inhumane labor conditions in California's fields. The crucified Indian who emblemized the colonized and enslaved indigenous populations of the Americas in Siqueiros's original rendering here becomes an allegorical reference to the martyred farmworker. The multivalency of the scene and the theme of martyrdom is heightened by the inscription of Rubén Salazar's name beneath this figure. Salazar was the *Los Angeles Times* reporter who died when a tear gas canister thrown by police struck him during the Chicano Moratorium in 1970. By 1974 when the MEChA *Mural* was executed, Salazar had become a celebrated icon and martyr of *la causa chicana* (the Chicano cause). Shifra Goldman deemed the grouping of these three figures as a secular trinity of sorts: "The Indian, the slain Chicano reporter, and the field laborer picking crops form a symbolic triumvirate of Chicano life in the United States."[28] But the connection between the three is further complicated by the inclusion of a dollar bill above the Indian's head, which here operates as an even more overt symbol of U.S. capitalism than Siqueiros's eagle. The promise of financial reward after hard work, which seems to be the ultimate goal of the "American dream," does not apply equally to all those who labor in the United States, as indicated by the unequally balanced scales of justice that replace George Washington's face on the dollar bill. The way the crucified Indian is depicted in the MEChA *Mural* points to the openness of Siqueiros's visual vocabulary, but also to the creative resourcefulness of Chicana/o artists who were devising new iconographies that spoke directly to the Chicana/o experience.

   While Siqueiros's *América Tropical* was most influential to Chicana/o artists from Southern California, muralists in the San Francisco Bay Area were also deeply affected by this critical mural. *Homage to Siqueiros* (1974), a mural executed by Luis Cortázar, Mike Rios, and the late Jesús "Chuy" Campusano in the lobby of San Francisco's Bank of America, exemplified the dialectic relationship that Chicana/o artists had with Mexican mural nationalism, and particularly with Siqueiros. The cycle was one of the few corporate commissions given to Chicana/o community artists in the 1970s; the artists were given a $15,000 budget to paint a Liquitex mural on birchwood panels above the teller stations. The three muralists who worked on *Homage to Siqueiros* went to great lengths to create a continuum between what they were commissioned to do in the Bank of America and what the Mexican muralists had done in California some forty years earlier. While working on the mural, Cortázar, Rios, and Campusano called themselves *los tres muralistas,* echoing the *los tres grandes* designation given to Rivera, Orozco, and Siqueiros.[29] Moreover, various visual quotations of the Mexican muralists' U.S. work appear in the mural's iconographic program. Rivera was particularly important to this cycle's iconography as well as to its social-realist style. The muralists of this Bank of America mural counted on the guidance and advice of Emmy Lou Packard, who had been Rivera's assistant back in the 1930s and had become a good friend and mentor to Chuy Campusano in the early 1970s.[30] For example, the figure group of the nurse tending to a child in *Homage to Siqueiros* could also be seen in Rivera's vaccination panel in his *Detroit Industry* cycle. In both instances, these figures allegorize the positive effects of medical discovery on the community at large. In close proximity to this nurse-child motif in the Bank of America mural, we find a representation of a monumental male figure who holds a book in his hand while his body is being sculpted out of stone by a group of construction workers standing on scaffolding that surrounds this entire figure. Once again, a very similar figure was executed by Rivera in his San Francisco Art Institute fresco entitled *The Making of a Fresco Showing the Building of a City* (1931), where the Mexican muralist depicted a gigantic industry worker whose body is also being erected by figures standing on a scaffold in front of him (including the artist himself). Rivera was illustrating the construction of a proletarian worker, but Cortázar, Rios, and Campusano reformulate the older motif to make this figure into an architect who symbolizes the emergence of a new Chicano male who is now the "architect" of his own future. Moreover, though Rivera wanted to underscore the flatness of the mural by making a commentary on the production of a fresco, the Chicano muralists were attempting to convey a sense of three-dimensionality by having the figure of the architect sculpted out of stone and by having the scaffolding wrap *around* him.

In spite of the references to Rivera, perhaps the most important Mexican source for *Homage to Siqueiros*'s Indigenist aesthetic was, as the title plainly states, the work of Siqueiros himself and the imagery of *La América Tropical*. Siqueiros had passed away in the very year this mural was made, 1974, so Cortázar, Rios, and Campusano would also pay him tribute in their Bank of America mural by reproducing the Indigenist motif of the crucified Indian in the form of a visual quotation. In this particular panel, the artists placed this figure on his cross lying horizontally in the foreground, in contrast to Siqueiros's frontal and vertical placement. This modification of the Mexican artist's motif further underscores the indigenous figure's powerlessness before the forces of colonization and industrialization. Flanking this indigenous figure in *Homage to Siqueiros* are two figures, a child farmworker carrying a sack of cotton and, right next to him, a ghostly apparition of Emiliano Zapata walking by his side. In front of the crucified Indian, we see the figure of another farmworker holding out a book with the inscription "Our sweat and our blood have fallen in this land to make other men rich," a statement quoted from *El Plan de Delano*, written by the celebrated California farm-labor activist César Chávez. Cortázar, Rios, and Campusano modified Siqueiros's Indigenist iconography to fit the specific context of Chicano history in California. Not only does the crucified Indian become an allegory of the ills of colonization and capitalism, but he also becomes a personification of the abuses suffered by the Mexicans and Mexican Americans who toiled in the fields of California's prosperous agribusiness for over a century.

Siqueiros provided a radical vocabulary for Cortázar, Rios, and Campusano, but this language needed to speak more directly to the specificity of the Chicana/o experience while still underscoring the connection to Mexican muralism and Indigenism. For this reason, *Homage to Siqueiros* is also saturated with iconography that is unique to the predominantly Latina/o Mission District in San Francisco where this bank is located. For instance, the muralists included a train from the Bay Area Rapid Transit (BART) system zigzagging forward to document the construction of the subway's extension into the Mission District. Nearby, an ethnically diverse group of engineers look over the plans for this subway extension. The activities of these engineers are then likened to those of the artists who executed this mural, for we also see them standing next to the BART train, working on a sketch for this very mural. Cortázar, Rios, and Campusano were not only highlighting the specificity of the Mission District with these motifs but also redefining the role of the artist. Like the engineers who improved the lives of Mission District residents by bringing BART to their neighborhood, the artists here are also depicted as "workers" toiling for the betterment of the community rather than just to fulfill their individual creative needs. Cortázar, Rios, and Campusano saw themselves as putting into practice the notion that during the 1970s, Chicana/o artists, as stipulated by Tomás Ybarra-Frausto, "could be both workers and artists."[31]

Art historian Alan Barnett regarded both *La América Tropical* and *Homage to Siqueiros* as fine examples of radical visual statements articulated from within the "belly of the beast,"[32] in other words, U.S. corporate culture.[33] But unlike Siqueiros in his L.A. mural, Cortázar, Rios, and Campusano incorporated the specificity of place into more universalizing themes of social and political justice, whereas Siqueiros was seeking to create a Pan-American understanding of indigenous suffering and resistance. Nevertheless, the impact of both Siqueiros and Rivera in this mural functioned in a dialectic fashion in that these San Francisco muralists engaged in a discursive dialogue with the Mexican canon. Not only did they reinscribe new meaning into iconographic motifs like the crucified Indian through visual quotation devices, but they also subjected these motifs to a careful selection process whereby the muralists chose and discarded elements as they saw fit. In the process, they established the Mexican mural movement as a strong historical precedent for their work while also proclaiming a distinct voice independent of this tradition.

The importance of *La América Tropical* points to the ways in which Chicana/o artists were using visual quotations to specifically engage the Mexican Indigenist vocabulary but at the same time assert an independent indigenous aesthetic. Indigenous resistance in the Americas has included the use of cultural appropriation among its numerous strategies. Native peoples have a history of strategically appropriating elements from the colonizer's culture only to subvert or transform their meaning and thus challenge the colonial system.[34] Nevertheless, the quotations that Chicana/o artists produce in their work form part of a strategic essentialism of sorts. Given that many Chicana/o artists chose to do murals, the Mexican School was not only an influence for them but also an expectation coming from the outside looking in. Rather than rejecting this expectation, Chicana/o artists opted to embrace it in order to offer a certain degree of legitimacy to their subjectivities, as anthropologist Edward Fischer argues about indigenous peoples in general in the late twentieth century: "[Indigenous peoples] have begun to embrace a form of essentialism to justify their political legitimacy."[35] As part of the larger project to turn difference into empowerment, Chicana/o Indigenism often traversed the vertiginous space between stereotype and authentic selfhood. The strategic adoption of the Mexican canon by Chicana/o artists indicates that they were not only seeking to proclaim a decolonized identity but also to exert a certain degree of control over discourses articulated about Chicana/o culture by others. Indeed, Mexican visual quotations, in their measured and strategic positions within the Chicana/o visual repertoire, established a dialogue not only with the Mexican canon but also with U.S. hegemonic culture, which was cognizant of the work by *los tres grandes*. Visual quotations in the Chicana/o art context then function as cross-cultural engagements that modify all the discourses involved: the Mexican, the Chicana/o, and the U.S. dominant perspectives.

Viva la Raza

Chicana/o artists during the 1970s were not only aware of Mexican mural imagery in California but were also deeply knowledgeable about the work *los tres grandes* had done in Mexico itself. *Viva la Raza* (1977; Figure 1.3), a mural executed by Oakland-based Chicano artist Daniel Galvez, with assistance from Osha Neumann, O'Brien Thiele, and Stephanie Barrett in Berkeley, California, also contained visual quotations from the Mexican muralists

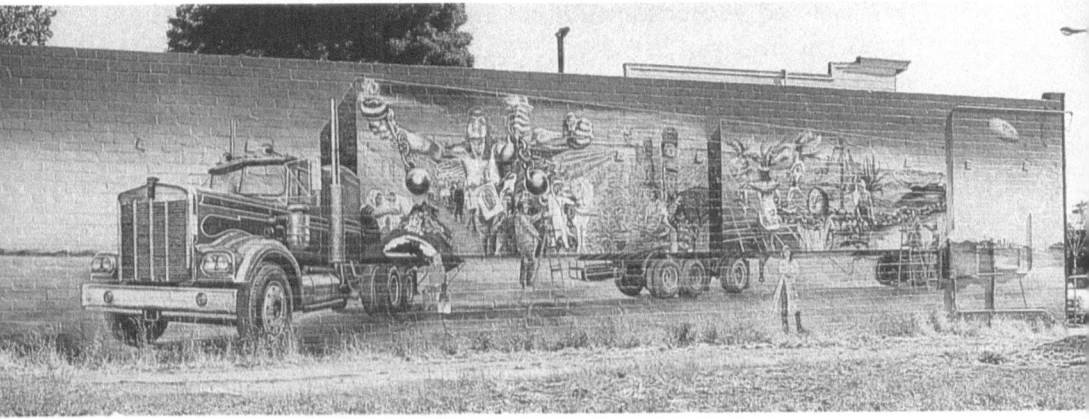

FIGURE 1.3. Daniel Galvez, assisted by Osha Neumann, O'Brien Thiele, and Stephanie Barrett, © 1977, *Viva la Raza*, mural, Berkeley, California. Courtesy of Timothy Drescher.

that addressed issues particularly relevant to the Chicana/o community in California. As mentioned earlier, the San Francisco Bay Area had become an important site for the work of Diego Rivera, who had also executed *Allegory of California* (1931) and *Pan American Unity* (1940) in San Francisco, in addition to *The Making of a Fresco*. During the 1970s, community muralists in this area, Chicanos and non-Chicanos alike, devised a variety of visual markers to underscore their artistic connection to the Mexican School. The area had also become an important site for the various WPA murals commissioned between the 1940s and 1950s. The WPA program was actually fashioned after the state-funded mural initiatives that had taken place in Mexico a decade earlier.[36] The social-realist style, coupled with themes about social justice, introduced by the likes of Rivera and Siqueiros in the 1930s, had become a trademark characteristic of the public art scene in Northern California during the mid-twentieth century. But in the sixties and seventies, San Francisco Bay Area Chicana/o artists breathed new life into the pairing of social realism and political subject matter by devising an Indigenist aesthetic that interrogated unilateral and hegemonic definitions of nation. Having done away with some of the romanticism and detachment of Mexican Indigenism, particularly in the work by Rivera, Chicana/o Indigenism sought to question the assumed European foundations of the U.S. nation-state by underscoring the importance of indigenous cultures in the country's history.

Viva la Raza was the first mural commission for Galvez, who at the time was employed through the Comprehensive Employment and Training Act (CETA) in the city of Berkeley.[37] In *Viva la Raza,* the artist limited the majority of the mural's iconography to pictorial representations of two trailers of a tractor-trailer parked near the Berkeley shore in the Bay Area, with the Golden Gate Bridge and the San Francisco skyline visible in the background. A blimp floats in the upper-right section of the composition, and it bears the inscription "Viva la Raza," a celebratory exclamation often used by Chicana/o activists to proclaim their identity, which loosely translates as "Long live the Mexican/Chicano race." Galvez here fused recognizable imagery belonging to two specific murals by Siqueiros and Rivera, respectively, with scenes of California cornfields and various figures of farmworkers. Although Galvez established a visual dialogue with Mexican mural images and iconography, the mural conveyed ideas and concerns that were specific to the Chicana/o reality of the 1970s. The motif of the truck in *Viva la Raza's* iconographic program functions as a clever visual device that divides the pictorial space into two realms, that of the truck itself and that of the images within the trailer panels.[38] The truck also acts as a reminder of the constructed nature of the mural pictorial space and creates a buffer zone between the illusionistic space of the mural itself and that of the spectator. Alan Barnett interpreted the truck in *Viva la Raza* as a signifier of the way in which Mexican culture was "transported" to the United States via migration and other phenomena of displacement.[39] Nevertheless, Chicana/o artists understood Mexican and U.S. history as two symbiotically interrelated narratives. Moreover, for many artists, Chicana/o indigenous identity was deeply rooted in both U.S. and Mexican soil, thus subscribing to the conviction that Chicanas/os had not crossed the border, but rather the border had crossed them, in particular after the redrawing of the national boundary between Mexico and the United States in the mid-nineteenth century. The motif of the truck, then, instead of signifying physical movement and migration from one geographic location to the other, functions as a metaphor for the less literal forms of mobility that define the Chicana/o experience, such as transnationalism and heterogeneity.

Perhaps the most prominent reference to Mexican mural imagery in *Viva la Raza* takes the form of a direct quotation from Siqueiros's allegory of *The New Democracy,* his 1944 mural in Mexico City's Palace of Fine Arts. Siqueiros in *The New Democracy* depicted a bare-breasted female figure that bursts out of a volcano while still bearing the chains of her oppression. Influenced by the aftermath of World War II, along with the fall of the Nazi regime in Germany, Siqueiros was seeking to create a figure that epitomized the liberation of the world from the forces of Fascism. In spite of the woman's state of triumphal empowerment, her facial expression still bears, as

Antonio Rodríguez explained, "the bitterness of war, full of suffering and pain."[40] Even though *The New Democracy* was inspired by actual historical events, Siqueiros fashioned his central figure, like the crucified Indian in *La América Tropical*, as a generalized symbol of the victims of oppression who have managed to break the bonds of their subjugation, regardless of historical context.[41]

In *Viva la Raza*, this figure of the "New Democracy" emerges from the California cornfields, rather than a volcano, while thrusting her body forward as if sheltering the procession of UFW (United Farm Workers) activists marching below. The close proximity between her and the farmworkers suggests that Galvez was attempting to establish a discursive relationship between the two. Siqueiros's universal allegory for emancipation and democracy here becomes a more specific symbol for the critical importance of labor organizing for groups like the United Farm Workers, who took on the powerful California agribusiness in their quest for a proper living wage, humane working conditions, and greater social justice in labor relations. The universality of Siqueiros's figure, coupled with the specificity of the UFW struggle, speaks of how localized social movements form part of larger global systems of oppression and how aggrieved communities throughout the world share many plights in common.

Near the procession of farmworkers in *Viva la Raza*, Galvez also provides the spectator with yet another recognizable image from *los tres grandes*, namely, that of Diego Rivera's figure of Emiliano Zapata alongside his horse, from his *Conversion of the Indian* cycle in Cuernavaca's Cortés Palace (1929–1930), which he would later transfer to a movable fresco in 1931. On one side of an arched doorway of the Cortés Palace, Rivera depicts this Zapata figure with a group of armed indigenous peasants behind him, and on the other side of the doorway, we see throngs of indigenous people enslaved and working on the construction of this palace. Zapata's role in agrarian reform and his tireless campaigns in favor of indigenous land rights seem like a fitting precedent for the struggles over labor abuses waged by the UFW. Galvez certainly makes the connection here between these two historical moments by placing Zapata among a procession of striking farmworkers, as if he was joining them right on the picket line.

In *Viva la Raza*, however, Galvez is not only addressing the historical importance of Zapata as an Indigenist figure; he is also alluding to the significance of Rivera's particular image. The artists of *Viva la Raza* depicted Rivera himself, standing on a ladder before the image of Emiliano Zapata, in the process of painting the figure of this celebrated revolutionary hero. The space in which Rivera resides, the buffer zone mentioned earlier, is also shared by representations of Galvez, Neumann, Thiele, and Barrett. Having the muralists represent themselves occupying the same space as Rivera suggests a dialectic relationship between them and the Mexican muralist; they are not only inhabiting the same temporal and spatial domain, but they're also shown collaborating on the same mural and are thus on a par with one another. The entire scene is then contained by two groups of figures that act as bookends to this panel's composition. On the lower left, we find a woman and a priest standing before a coffin covered with the UFW flag, a reminder of the fatal consequences of working in the fields around harmful pesticides and under harsh labor conditions. As a thematic contrast, on the lower-right half of the panel, we find a more idealized depiction of farmworking and agricultural labor. A woman grinds corn (*maíz*) on a metate while a man carries a box of produce next to her. Behind them is a row of Toltec deity sculptures that line the fields of *maíz,* implying a correlation or continuity between contemporary and ancient forms of farm labor.

Zoot Suit Riots

Some visual quotations of Mexican art by Chicana/o artists were overt and clearly recognizable, while others functioned as a mere afterthought to the central composition. Judy Baca, who since the early 1970s had become a highly influential figure in the Los Angeles mural scene, often used the visual conventions utilized by *los tres grandes* and redeployed them with a particularly feminist reading, thus dislodging the masculinist codes often present in their work. For instance, her movable mural entitled *Uprising of the Mujeres* (1979) borrowed from Siqueiros's powerful color palette and use of dynamic perspective to illustrate, paradoxically, a theme often absent in this Mexican artist's own work, namely, the vital contribution of women to social and labor movements. In Baca's mural, this theme was represented as women's contribution to the UFW struggle. However, in her seminal mural cycle *The Great Wall of Los Angeles* (1976–1983)—discussed in greater detail in Chapter 5 of this volume—Baca would exhibit the many ways in which the Mexican mural renaissance informed her stylistic and thematic development. The panel in the *Great Wall* entitled *Zoot Suit Riots* (1981; Figure 1.4) displayed what Paul Karlstrom termed "echoes of Rivera" in Baca's work.[42] Here Baca retells the events surrounding the 1943 aggressions suffered by Mexican American youth in Los Angeles. From June third to the seventh of that year, a mob of servicemen and civilians took to the streets of L.A. in search of zoot-suiters, who, in the popular imagination at the time, posed a threat to national unity and social cohesion. As a result, various young Mexican American men were physically assaulted and stripped of their zoot

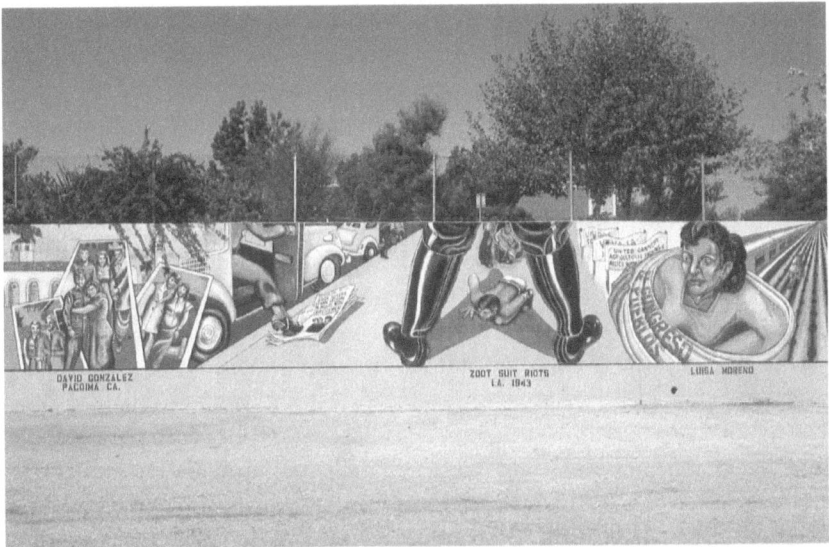

FIGURE 1.4. Judy Baca, © 1981, *Zoot Suit Riots* panel from *The Great Wall of Los Angeles*, mural, Tujunga Wash, San Fernando Valley, Los Angeles, California. © SPARC (www.sparcmurals.org)

suits. While the conservatism of the WWII period condemned pachucos' blatant disregard for authority and outrageous dress style, Chicana/o activists and thinkers regarded them as cultural heroes who boldly resisted accommodation into mainstream U.S. society. Marcos Sánchez-Tranquilino interpreted the removal of the pachucos' clothes as the symbolic elimination of their oppositional identities.[43]

Baca loosely based her mural panel *Zoot Suit Riots* on the press photographs that captured these actual events, but she also took some stylistic pointers from the Mexican School. Mirroring Rivera's use of volumetric and schematized form when depicting indigenous figures, Baca in this image utilized the Mexican muralist's visual conventions along with a visual quotation as a point of departure for her rendition of this event in Los Angeles history. The Chicana artist here cites a very small vignette from Rivera's 1935 easel painting *The Flower Carrier*, which depicts an indigenous man crouching on his hands and knees as a woman adjusts an enormous flower basket on his back. Baca transposes Rivera's rendering of this male figure's splayed hand to her own depiction of the defeated zoot-suiter in *The Great Wall of Los Angeles*. I would argue that this small vignette does not merely indicate Rivera's stylistic influence on Baca, but also acts as a conscious visual quotation on the part of Baca, who is here acknowledging the importance of the Mexican mural tradition. Simultaneously, the significantly different thematic content of the two images points to the ways in which Baca purposely departs from the Mexican canon to underscore her unique contribution to the history of mural painting. While this particular Rivera motif acts as a point of contact between the two artists' formal treatment of the human figure, Baca's very distinct reconfiguration of her zoot-suiter's pose and anatomy disrupts a linear and static reading of the Mexican influence on her work. This "Rivera" hand motif, then, acts as a marker of continuity and discontinuity between Mexican and Chicana/o mural history. Baca's scene of the Los Angeles Zoot Suit Riots embodies the often contestatory way in which Chicana/o artists engage Mexican Indigenist visual discourse. The relatively oppositional dialogue that Baca establishes with her Mexican precursors exemplifies the very nature of dialectic social and historical relations, where centripetal and centrifugal forces—that is, forces of unity and difference, as explained by critics Leslie Baxter and Barbara Montgomery—give rise to an original and unprecedented cultural product.

Nevertheless, Rivera's flower carrier and Baca's zoot-suiter also demonstrate the parallel yet critically distinct ways in which the Mexican and Chicana/o muralists approached Indigenist themes in their work. Rivera's oil and tempera panel painting is an example of a series of Indigenist-genre scenes the artist created with the purpose of glorifying and monumentalizing the everyday activities of native Mexican communities, thereby incorporating them into the national Mexican culture. Baca likewise sought to inscribe Chicana/o Indigenist consciousness into the collective U.S. cultural psyche. The figure of the zoot-suiter was considered an Indigenist symbol by Chicano nationalists in that he was regarded as a contemporary personification or reincarnation, if you will, of a fallen Aztec warrior. This idea was illustrated in Luis Valdez's 1978 play *Zoot Suit* where the battered zoot-suiter rises from the ground dressed as an indigenous figure near the end of the play. But the romanticized and highly idealized Indigenist vision seen in Rivera's rendition is absent in Baca's almost pessimistic representation of this event. As I argue in Chapter 5, Baca's version of the scene is a somewhat covert critique of the exaltation and monumentalization of the male Aztec and zoot-suit figures commonly seen in the work of male Chicano muralists. The zoot-suiter's powerlessness is further accentuated by his fetuslike pose, the framing device of the serviceman's legs enclosing him, and his extremely reduced size in relation to the figures and scenes around him. This scene of the Zoot Suit Riots is flanked within the broader iconographic program of *The Great Wall* by the depiction, on the right, of a figure stepping on a newspaper that features the actual headlines published in 1943 relating to this event and, on the left, of the comparatively gigantic representation of 1940s Guatemalan labor activist Luisa Moreno. With the zoot-suiter image, Baca critically addresses the male-centered Indigenist vocabularies of both her Mexican and her male Chicano counterparts, thus revealing, in the process, the gendered exclusions that their dogmatic nationalist postures upheld.

L.A. History: A Mexican Perspective

At about the same time that Baca had finished her panel on the Zoot Suit Riots in *The Great Wall of Los Angeles*, another Chicana artist began work on perhaps one of the most controversial murals in Los Angeles during the 1980s. Barbara Carrasco's *L.A. History: A Mexican Perspective* (1981; Figure 1.5), like Baca's *Great Wall of Los Angeles*, narrated a history of Los Angeles

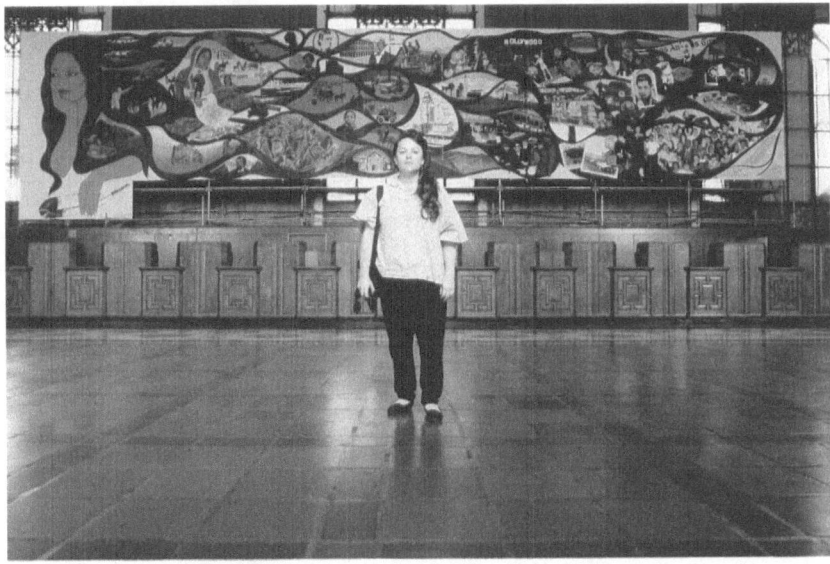

FIGURE 1.5. Barbara Carrasco, © 1981, *L.A. History: A Mexican Perspective*, portable mural (various locations). Courtesy of Barbara Carrasco. Photograph of Carrasco taken by Harry Gamboa Jr. during the mural's two-month-long display at Union Station in downtown Los Angeles as part of the city's 1991 festival. This was the only time the sixteen-by-eighty-foot mural was ever exhibited in its full form.

from the perspective of minority groups. Assisted by Los Angeles area youth in the creation of this sixteen-by-eighty-foot portable mural, Carrasco highlighted the abuse and injustices that these various groups suffered in the course of the city's history. Sponsored by the Community Redevelopment Agency (CRA) on the occasion of the Los Angeles bicentennial celebration, the mural proved to be, as Paul Von Blum described it, "critical rather than laudatory"[44] of the city's turbulent history. Soon Carrasco found that one of her most ambitious projects to date would be rejected by city officials due to the type of imagery with which the artist chose to tell this history.

The forty wood and Masonite panels that made up *L.A. History* came together to show the figure of an indigenous-looking Chicana holding a feather in her hand while the long tresses of her dark hair begin to reveal scenes from the city's past. Carrasco actually used preexisting documentary visual material, particularly photographs, to piece together an alternative history of the city. The images that are revealed through her hair unfold like the folios of an indigenous codex. According to Marcos Sánchez-Tranquilino, a codex generally consisted of "glued, accordion-folded panels of amate bark paper in which information was presented through painted pictures."[45] The value of the codex to modern-day scholars of Mesoamerican history and culture rested on its role in recovering the lost voices and experiences of indigenous peoples in the Americas, not unlike Carrasco's own attempt to reconstruct the contributions of Los Angeles's aggrieved communities.[46] Among the most prominent images in her mural we find that of a Japanese American girl sitting on a suitcase waiting to be taken to a U.S. internment camp during the 1940s, an image Carrasco had borrowed from a famous Dorothea Lange photograph. Directly above that figure we find yet another depiction of the Zoot Suit Riots from the same decade.

But even before the mural was completed, the CRA began to voice its objections by claiming that the images were too negative. As Carrasco recounts: "After the mural sketches were finished, the CRA put the mural on the wall and they outlined several images in purple and some images in red. The red images had to go and the purple images were kind of questionable to them but okay. . . . I was in the middle of being censored."[47] Carrasco defended herself by insisting that she had not included any images that were historically inaccurate; in fact, she had worked closely with three historians as consultants—Bill Mason, Jean Bruce Pool, and Rudy Acuña—just to make sure she was not misrepresenting the history of the city. In addition, she even carried out oral history interviews with city elders to get a more complex perspective of the city's history. But the CRA not only objected to the events being represented in Carrasco's mural, but also went so far as to question her artistic abilities by claiming that the mural was composed of a series of "cluttered" images.[48] "I had a real concern she was trying to put too many images in that thing," explained CRA architect Gary Williamson, "which was not doing justice to the mural as a whole."[49] Though the mural would be exhibited in other venues, it was never shown during the bicentennial celebrations. The CRA even attempted to destroy the mural, which forced the artist to seek legal counsel in order to retain co-ownership of her own mural and thus have a say in what ultimately happened to it.[50]

One of the other scenes the CRA objected to in *L.A. History* was a depiction of the whitewashing of Siqueiros's *América Tropical* mural, a representation situated next to the image of the Japanese American child and the zoot-suiters. She showed the Mexican muralist standing on scaffolding in the process of creating his now-infamous mural while buckets of white paint are being hurled at his imagery. Like many other scenes in Carrasco's mural, the one representing the incident with Siqueiros's work in Los Angeles formed part of a history that city officials who had commissioned Carrasco wanted to ignore or undermine. Carrasco soon saw the irony in her decision to include this particular incident in *L.A. History*, realizing that her own experience with her mural was not unlike that of Siqueiros's almost half a century before. These similarities created a continuity, albeit an unfortunate one, between Mexican and Chicana/o muralists working in California. The whole fiasco surrounding Carrasco's mural made her and her supporters realize that attitudes toward racialized minorities in Los Angeles had not significantly changed in fifty years. But what ultimately seemed to be at stake in the whole controversy surrounding this mural was the issue of who had access to the institution of history, especially when it came to illustrating this history in such a mainstream venue like the city's bicentennial. While Siqueiros's image of the crucified Indian would initially form part of a larger alternative historical narrative for Carrasco, the transhistorical significance of this Indigenist image would make itself all the more palpable when her own mural suffered a similar fate.

Resurrection of a Green Planet

As we near the decade of the 1990s, we begin to see a shift in the subject matter and a greater heterogeneity[51] in the themes that inform Chicana/o community murals in California. Moving away from the overtly nationalist vocabulary of the late sixties and early seventies, Chicana/o artists begin to take an interest in a variety of issues, including environmental concerns. Using Mexican iconographic motifs to enrich his compositions' aesthetic,

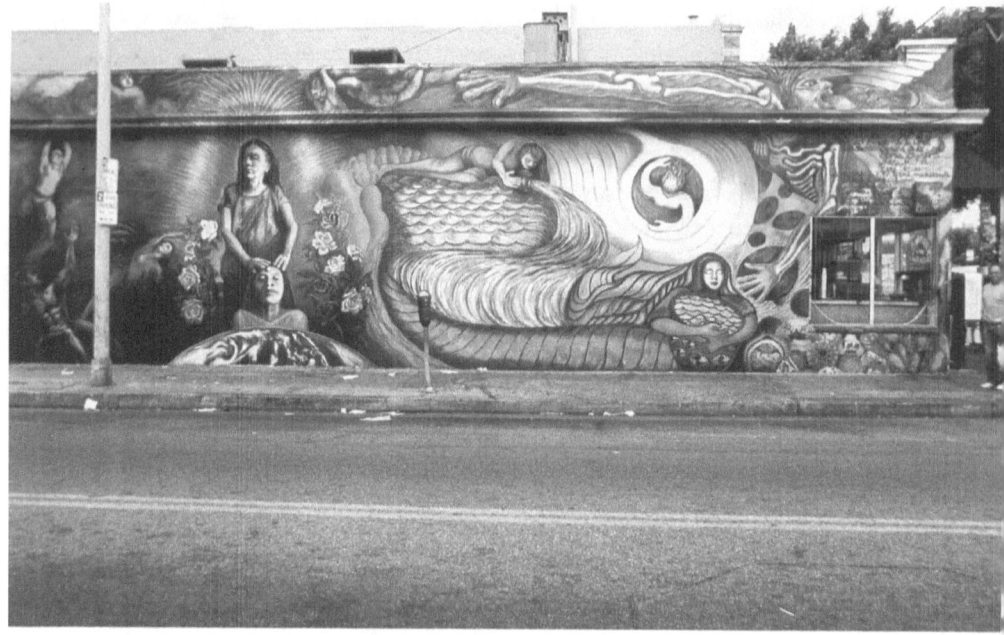

FIGURE 1.6. Ernesto de la Loza, © 1990–1991, *Resurrection of a Green Planet*, mural, East Los Angeles, California. © SPARC (www.sparcmurals.org)

Chicano artist Ernesto de la Loza has made a number of murals around East Los Angeles that deal with heterogeneous themes. He has spoken about the joys of living in the culturally diverse city of Los Angeles and has proudly exhorted the richness of his artistic influences: "I've been accused of being an Expressionist. Fifteen years ago they told me my style of super-realism wasn't art. But the truth is I don't hold on to any one style. In trips to Europe and Mexico, I've learned from them all."[52] Aside from displaying his multiplicity of influences, de la Loza's mural entitled *Resurrection of a Green Planet* (1990–1991; Figure 1.6) provided idyllic scenery of lush earthly and marine life interfused with symbolic and allegorical figures personifying fertility, rebirth, wind, fire, and other elements. De la Loza placed this visionary spectacle right on the corner of Breed Street and César Chávez Avenue, a particularly urbanized and commercially active intersection of East Los Angeles, with a doctor's office across the street, perhaps an unexpected yet effective place to make an environmentalist statement. The way in which the artist synthesizes concerns about global warming and pollution with those of a Mexican or Chicana/o cultural identity is perhaps one of the most striking elements of this mural. De la Loza reuses preexisting Mexican iconographic motifs to construct this utopian milieu. The figures of the Zapotec *curandera,* or traditional healer, and her young patient, located to the left-hand side of this mural's composition, are directly taken from an image by contemporary Mexican photographer Graciela Iturbide of women from Tehuantepec, Mexico. But unlike Iturbide's photograph, which focuses solely on the *curandera,* de la Loza's image depicts these indigenous Mexican healing practices as being directly connected to the intrinsic cycles of nature and as examples of environmentally safe medical procedures.

But of greater relevance to this study is the motif of the swirling wind goddess floating above the ocean in *Resurrection of a Green Planet,* a visual quotation from Diego Rivera's 1926 representation of *The Mechanization of the Countryside* in Mexico City's Ministry of Education. In many ways, both murals dealt with environmental issues that appeal to an Indigenist identity. Rivera presents us with a rural scene presided over by a seated Xilonen, the Nahuatl goddess of tender corn, whose schematic anatomy is reminiscent of Mesoamerican sculpture.[53] To her right, we see the same female deity portrayed in de la Loza's mural, who here represents lightning instead of wind. She is shown casting a triple-ended bolt onto a group of figures that Rivera considered to be the trinity of modern-day evil: the capitalist, the clergyman, and the military man. Stretching behind them, we find a Cubist-like landscape exhibiting Rivera's belief in the positive effects of technology in rural Mexico. While the swirling goddess acts as a punishing and aggressive deity in Rivera's representation, in de la Loza's image, she is a benevolent agent of Mother Earth whose movements revolve around the rhythms of nature. Though Rivera seems to suggest that a rural life, native Mexican belief systems, and industrial innovation could coexist harmoniously in a cosmic balance, de la Loza, as an artist of his generation, places no faith in technological advances and imagines an undisturbed natural realm free from the evils of industrialization. Nevertheless, Rivera provides de la Loza with a model for an Indigenist aesthetic that upholds a utopian vision of a natural habitat, a means by which to connect environmental concerns with issues of cultural and national identity.

El Quinto Sol

The decade of the 1990s also gave way to self-referential and introspective Chicana/o community murals that commented on the nature and history

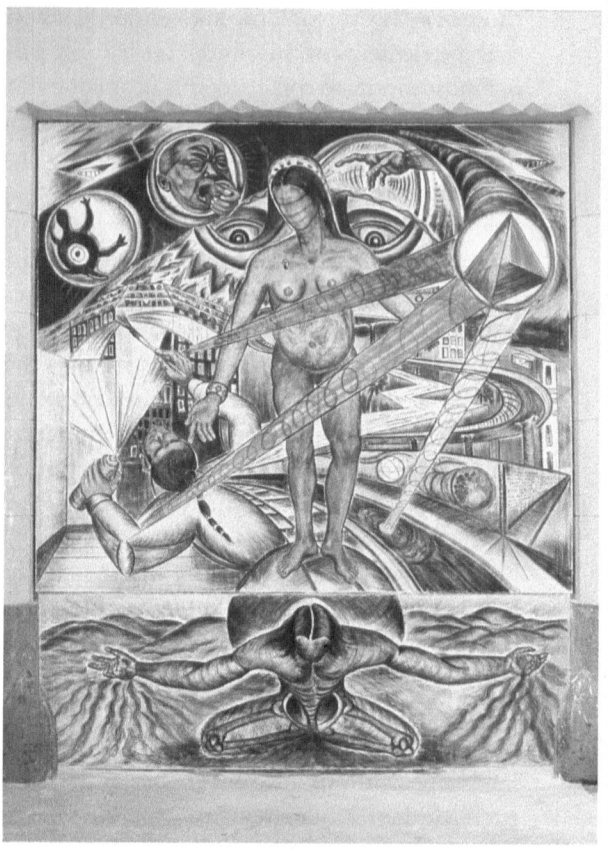

FIGURE 1.7. Frederico Vigil, assisted by Sergio Barrón and Robert Sánchez, © 1992, *El Quinto Sol*, mural fresco, SPARC building, Venice, California. © SPARC (www.sparcmurals.org)

of the medium itself, thereby operating as sorts of "metamurals." *El Quinto Sol* (1992; Figure 1.7), created by Frederico Vigil, who was assisted by Sergio Barrón and Robert Sánchez, is perhaps one of the most traditional Chicana/o murals in the Los Angeles area in terms of its style and medium. Located on Venice Boulevard, the mural sets itself apart in that it was executed using the fresco technique. By applying paint on wet lime plaster, the artist established a great contrast between this work and the majority of Chicana/o community murals that are usually rendered in acrylic paint. Rather than using the brightly colored and often linear form that the acrylic medium tends to offer, Vigil opted for a more subdued and earthy color palette, an effect more aptly achieved through the use of fresco. A native of Santa Fe, New Mexico, Vigil began his artistic career doing *retablos* (religious altar paintings, usually on board) as a way to explore the Southwest's Mexican history and culture. He would soon take up fresco painting and give rise to a renewed interest in the medium around the Albuquerque area, where he resides.[54] Though *El Quinto Sol* is his only mural in California, its subject matter, nevertheless, directly addresses the specific history and culture of Los Angeles. His presence in the area was also influential to a group of seven students who learned the fresco technique from Vigil and his assistants and later put it to practice in their own mural entitled *City of Los Angeles*, located just a few footsteps from *El Quinto Sol*.[55]

Vigil's choice of medium in *El Quinto Sol* was an aesthetic decision, but it also established a historical genealogy between this mural and other important wall-painting traditions. Contributing to this composition's overall Indigenist theme, the fresco technique itself has roots in ancient Mesoamerican and even Native American art, with important mural sites in Teotihuacán and Bonampak, Mexico, and with amazing fresco decorations found inside Anasazi kivas in Arizona and New Mexico.[56] But Vigil here also acknowledges the mural traditions from Renaissance Italy, and, most importantly, from modern Mexico. Aside from the use of fresco, Vigil makes reference to the work of Siqueiros through the utilization of a visual quotation placed above the central figure of the composition. This Chicano artist's choice of medium and his inclusion of such a quotation establishes *El Quinto Sol* as a direct descendant of the Mexican murals. Vigil had also received his training from Lucienne Bloch and Stephen Pope Dimitroff, assistants to Diego Rivera both in his *Detroit Industry* cycle and in his failed mural at the Rockefeller Center during the early 1930s,[57] an experience that undoubtedly reinforced Vigil's affinity with the Mexican School. Vigil's citation of Siqueiros's work can be found in a floating sphere the Chicano artist includes in the upper-left-hand corner of the composition. This sphere contains a composite image that makes reference to two different Siqueiros paintings, *Echo of a Scream* (1937) and *El Coronelazo* (1945), both examples of the Mexican artist's nonmural oeuvre. Vigil fuses the face of the screaming infant in *Echo of a Scream* with the projecting fist with which Siqueiros depicted himself in *El Coronelazo*. The heroic scale and monumentality that these motifs possess in the Siqueiros paintings are undermined in *El Quinto Sol* by their relatively peripheral position within this mural and by their reduced size.

This specific visual quotation of Siqueiros's work contributes to *El Quinto Sol*'s broader depiction of an Indigenized mural history in Los Angeles. The nude figure of a pregnant indigenous woman stands at the center of this rather small wall painting (nine by eleven feet), and her body and anatomical proportions greatly resemble those of the Malinche figure in José Clemente Orozco's National Preparatory School murals (1926). Vigil taps into

Orozco's archetypal and generalized depiction of indigenous female figures with stalky proportions and earth-tone skin color. Though her facial features, and by default her individual identity, have been obliterated, a radiating halo emerges from her head, a kind of abbreviated version of the body halo that usually surrounds the Virgin of Guadalupe in traditional representations. Nevertheless, this halo also acts in this case as a signifier of this figure's otherworldly and divine status. Furthermore, she stands on a sphere symbolizing the universe, which, at the same time, leads the viewer's eye to the lower register of this mural, where a male figure resides within an underworld-like domain resembling a geological soil stratum. Sitting cross-legged before the sphere, this figure extends his arms outward in a Christ-like crucifixion gesture as his skeletal structure is revealed through his skin. In spite of the Christian motif in this lower register, the artist also makes this section of the mural resemble descriptions of the underworld in Mesoamerican ancient texts. Called Mictlan Opochcalocan by the Aztecs and Xibalba by the Maya, this underworld, located in the lower strata of the earth, was a place of death and decay through which the souls of the recently departed had to travel before they could arrive at their final resting place. It was inhabited by the Lords of Death, whose bodies resembled, according to pre-Columbianists Linda Schele and Mary Ellen Miller, "skeletal creatures of the most distasteful countenance,"[58] not unlike the figure in the lower register of El Quinto Sol. In spite of the treacherous and fearsome nature of Mictlan Opochcalocan or Xibalba, as described in Mesoamerican texts, this underworld and its inhabitants formed a crucial part of indigenous conceptions of the universe and held an interdependent relationship with the middleworld, that is, the world of the living. Moreover, according to Aztec creation myths, Quetzalcoatl had to venture into Mictlan Opochcalocan to fetch the bones of the ancestors in order to create present-day human beings.[59] Vigil in El Quinto Sol creates a similar dynamic between his lower and upper registers, which could be interpreted, respectively, as parallels to the world of the dead and the realm of the living. In addition, the two figures presiding over the two registers of this mural are aligned along the same vertical axis, suggesting that these two entities allegorize a set of different dualities that have historically interacted with one another in the Americas, such as male/female, underworld/world of the living, and Christian/indigenous belief systems.

Vigil uses the mythic overtones of El Quinto Sol as a way to contextualize the history of mural painting in Los Angeles within a broader cosmic framework. Behind the female figure in El Quinto Sol, we see images of a more worldly nature. The artist provides depictions of recognizable architectural structures from the Los Angeles urban landscape, namely, representations of the city's complex freeway system and illustrations of buildings from the downtown area. In front of these buildings, we see the artist himself with a paintbrush in one hand and a spray can in the other, an allusion to the bordered position often held by Chicana/o muralists, who are usually caught between the world of established artistic institutions and the realm of urban youth culture. His two hands, however, are guided by beams of colored light that emanate from a prism gliding across the picture plane, suggesting that his creative impulses are channeled by a higher power. Vigil adds a dynamic quality to this predominantly symmetrical composition by saturating the entire scene in *El Quinto Sol* with crossing diagonals, projecting elements, and overlapping forms, echoing the influence of Futurism in the work by Siqueiros.

Finally, the actual title of *El Quinto Sol* lends an added dimension to the transcendental and mystical theme of this fresco while also making a commentary on the nature of mural history itself. The expression *quinto sol*, or "fifth sun," directly alludes to Aztec creation myths. According to the Mexica, the gods created the world on their fifth attempt. The first four were unsuccessful because of the constant disagreements and cosmic clashes between Tezcatlipoca and Quetzalcoatl, events that led to chaos and disorder in the universe. During the fifth creation, the gods met in the ancient city of Teotihuacán, discussed the problem, and ultimately succeeded in ushering in a new era of cosmic balance and stability in the universe and on earth: the Fifth Sun. Vigil cites the myth as a way to legitimize the artistic patina of the Chicana/o mural movement in Los Angeles. He also capitalizes on the idea of the various phases of creation and foregrounds it as a metaphor for the different stages of mural history. Though the Mexican tradition, as exemplified by the Siqueiros citation, holds a prominent position in this mural's iconographic program, it is nevertheless sidelined by the two central figures and by the images depicting the Los Angeles scene in *El Quinto Sol*. Like the Aztec myth, mural painting also went through five stages of creation, namely the pre-Columbian, the Native American, the modern Mexican, the WPA era,[60] and the Chicana/o periods. These five notwithstanding, the Chicana/o community mural movement, as illustrated by the central figures and images, represents a renewed and innovative phase of mural creativity, not unlike our present era of the "fifth sun." Like other Chicana/o muralists before him, Vigil recognizes the significance of the Mexican canon to the contemporary Chicano artist, yet he establishes a visual dialogue with this particular tradition that allows for an articulation of the specificity and centrality of Chicana/o experience. The importance given to the Los Angeles mural scene in *El Quinto Sol* is further underscored by this work's actual location. Gracing one of the exterior walls of the Social and Public Arts Resource Center (SPARC) building in Venice, California, this mural indirectly acknowledges the critical role that this organization has played in fostering the development of public arts in the Los Angeles area since 1976, when it was founded by Judy Baca. So through the medium, the subject matter, the style, the iconography, and the location, Vigil in *El Quinto Sol* creates a composite history of mural painting that places the Chicana/o contribution at the forefront.

Conclusion

Chicana/o muralists' reinterpretation or adaptation of the Mexican mural Indigenist canon through the recurring use of visual quotations, among other devices, points to the malleable, multivalent, and even timeless quality these artists found in this type of imagery. While remaining reasonably skeptical of the highly idealized and often dogmatic conceptions of the Mexican muralists, many Chicana/o artists recognized a prescriptive and visionary element in their work, qualities that were useful to them, as explained by Chicano painter and printmaker Rupert Garcia: "Even though we can be critical about the revolutionary murals in Mexico . . ., what's wonderful to me is that . . . [they] can represent something that should be rather than only that which is."[61] Furthermore, the Mexican Indigenist mural aesthetic had a pivotal role in the construction undertaken by these artists of a Chicana/o or Mexican American history, a history that until the late 1960s remained unwritten and undermined. By claiming the Mexican mural canon as a historical precedent, Chicana/o artists established connections to an already validated artistic tradition. While the Mexican mural movement remained a model for what Chicanas/os were doing in the urban landscapes of California, the reputations of artists like Rivera and Siqueiros as major figures in the history of modern art lent a certain degree of legitimization to their own work. As a result, Mexican muralism worked for Chicanas/os as a sign of cultural difference, but one that was even familiar to mainstream artistic institutions; it provided for them an autonomous space that functioned as a buffer between the Chicana/o community and U.S. dominant culture. The dialectic relationship that Chicana/o artists then established with their Mexican predecessors allowed them to keep a continuous critical eye toward an artistic tradition and history that was both relevant yet far removed from their own reality as a racialized minority in the United States.

Though many Chicana/o artists found a fascinating though fragmented continuity between their work and that of *los tres grandes*, it was also vital for them to establish a distinct visual vocabulary that specifically spoke of the Mexican experience in the United States. Like other movements during the civil rights period, the Chicano Movement was characterized by an often radical sense of nationalism. The Chicano indigenous nation, in the minds of many activists and thinkers, would be built within U.S. soil yet in strict defiance of dominant culture. The arts would then play the crucial role of providing a visual representation of this "nation."

The following chapter outlines and identifies the principal mural motifs and works of art that most effectively exemplified and even upheld the spirit of *el movimiento*. It also explains how Indigenism contributed to growing nationalist sentiments of the early to mid-1970s.

CHAPTER TWO

The Chicano Movement and Indigenist Murals
The Formation of a Nationalist Canon and Identity

Chicana/o Murals and Cultural Nationalism

By the early 1970s, once Chicana/o activists had established the civil rights movement and the Chicano Movement as viable platforms through which people of color could articulate their newly politicized identities, they also needed a visual repertoire to accompany or complement the nationalist discourses they formulated. Luis Valdez and his formation of the theater troupe Teatro Campesino in 1965 set a powerful precedent for the celebration of indigenous images and culture, an important model for the visual artists. For Chicanas/os, Indigenist imagery in murals became a crucial component of this repertoire and, as such, formed an important part of the budding Chicana/o cultural nationalism that began to take root in the 1960s and 1970s. This nationalism proclaimed cultural autonomy for Mexican-descent peoples in the United States and declared that Chicanas/os are a "*nation* autonomous and free—culturally, socially, and politically" (italics mine), as stipulated in "El Plan Espiritual de Aztlán," the prototypical Chicana/o nationalist manifesto drafted during the Denver Youth Conference of 1969.[1] According to this assessment, Chicanas/os were more than just a minority or ethnic group in the United States; they had formed a new *nation,* and this nation, identified as Aztlán, was undeniably indigenous in nature. This indigeneity, as Genaro M. Padilla argued, lent a mythical and spiritual component to the political struggles waged by Chicanas/os, thus giving *el movimiento* an added impetus.[2] *La causa chicana* was important not only because it fostered social justice and equality among peoples but also because it achieved a greater cosmic balance between indigenous and Western worldviews in a postcolonial era.

While the Chicano Movement shared many characteristics with other modern nationalist movements that eventually led to the formation of new nation-states in places like Africa and Eastern Europe, Chicanas/os were not necessarily seeking to break away from U.S. jurisdiction, nor were they trying to rejoin Mexico. Activists, artists, writers, and radical thinkers understood the uniqueness of the Chicana/o experience and maintained that Aztlán as a nation was situated somewhere in a political, geographic, and spiritual borderland between Mexico and the United States, even though we don't really know its exact location.[3] In this respect, the Chicano Movement resembled other indigenous movements in that it sought not separation from the state but rather legitimate participation within its inner workings. Michael Murphy, for instance, explains that "indigenous nationalism does not represent an absolute rejection of the state's authority . . . [but rather seeks] shared rule in state institutions."[4] As a matter of fact, most of the challenges that the Chicano Movement posed to the U.S. nation-state—such as critiques of the educational, labor, and legal systems and subsequent calls for the reform of these—were articulated within the purview of the law and in keeping with this country's democratic tradition of protest and free speech. So the Chicana/o nation was built, not through legalistic or geographic means, but through the celebration and protection of culture, which, in many cases, was defined as indigenous to the Americas. The cultural capital that Chicanas/os invested in, and continue to invest in today, signified a new strategy for survival and self-determination that actively challenged previous attempts at assimilation and Americanization. Through the celebration and maintenance of cultural nationalism, many Chicana/o nationalists believed, other pragmatic needs such as socioeconomic, racial, and even gender equality could more easily be accomplished.[5] Though one could argue that Chicana/o nationalist consciousness was more about group solidarity and collective community building than nation building, the nationalism that informed *el movimiento*'s political thinking insisted on the concept of a Chicana/o nation over "minority" or "group." Scholars on nation building argue that the boundaries between these various concepts are indeed blurry. While they agree that a "state" can be relatively easy to define along quantifiable, legalistic, and geographic terms, "nation is much more difficult because the essence of a nation is intangible," Walker Connor tells us.[6] He further argues that the bonds that bring a nation together are more "psychological," "emotional," and "primordial," and that nations are more often "self-defined" rather than "other-defined."[7] While all of this may hold true about Chicanas/os, there was an added political strategy behind the use of the word *nation* to define Chicanas/os. The term *nation* evoked a certain political power that the words *minority* and *group* simply did not have; in many contexts, the words *nation* and *state* were even used interchangeably.[8] The intangibility but also the political authority behind the term *nation* were particularly well suited to the radical and oppositional temperament of the Chicano Movement. Chicana/o thinkers were also well aware that other indigenous groups in the Americas, particularly in the United States and Canada, used the word *nation* to define themselves but also to challenge the primacy of the postcolonial state. The notion of a Chicana/o nation was further radicalized by its denomination as Aztlán, an indigenous nation. But indigeneity was not just a component of the Chicana/o nation; it was the very means by which Chicanas/os transformed themselves from "minority" to nation.

Without a doubt, visual imagery would play a critical role in the formation of a Chicana/o nationalist and Indigenist vocabulary. Visual representations in murals were perhaps the most powerful means by which to disseminate ideas about nation building because of their public nature. In the process, Indigenist imagery in murals would become inevitably and necessarily politicized and radicalized. These images not only served as reminders to the Chicana/o and Mexican community that they shared common cultural and historical roots with other indigenous groups in the Americas, but they also demonstrated that their indigenous consciousness could become a rallying cry for collective decolonization and denunciation of a discriminatory and inequitable social system. Furthermore, artists, like activists and community organizers, were at the forefront of the political struggle. Genaro Padilla even went as far as stating that the "role of the artist . . . proves to be a significant and often more continuous one than that of the political nationalist."[9] By establishing the visual as a conduit for the political, the distinction between activism and artistic activity during the early phases of *el movimiento* became nearly indistinguishable. Artists like Yolanda López, for example, found themselves acting as political activists before they became practicing artists. In a similar fashion, the members of the Chicano artists collective the Royal Chicano Air Force (RCAF), as the children of farmworkers, dedicated most of their creative energies to the cause of César Chávez and the United Farm Workers by creating posters for the various rallies and events organized by the UFW. Though these posters initially possessed the sole pragmatic purpose of getting the word out about these gatherings, the RCAF gradually began to see the production of these banners and billboards as creative endeavors in themselves and they eventually started putting greater care into the composition and iconography of the designs.[10] Artists, intellectuals, and activists alike came to the realization that political activism and artistic expression during *el movimiento* would have an almost symbiotic relationship and that the visual would become a critical component for the construction of the new Chicana/o nation emerging from the margins of U.S. dominant culture.

Indigenism and Murals

Indigenist imagery would become a critical element of the iconographic program associated with the Chicano Movement. The highly nationalistic and often militant nature of *el movimiento* required a visual language free from the trappings of colonized and co-opted aesthetics. At the same time, its language needed to possess a certain elasticity of meaning that could accommodate itself to the unique social, cultural, and political position of Chicanas/os as a marginalized and disenfranchised community in the United States, especially within the urban environments of California. Indigenist iconography—given its various sources as well as its transnational and transhistorical qualities—provided an ideal tool to promote and disseminate Chicana/o activist discourse, as this aesthetic celebrated cultural difference while still upholding social justice. In Latin America, Indigenism as an aesthetic and as an ideology was more closely associated with the representation of indigenous communities by government institutions and nonindigenous individuals, thus eliding any form of legitimate indigenous self-representation, but Chicana/o artists and activists effectively liberated it from its postcolonial predicaments. By using Indigenism as a means to establish an introspective and self-affirming identity, Chicanas/os personally identified with the plight of the indigenous peoples of the Americas instead of relegating them to the sphere of the Other: "*We are* a bronze people with a bronze culture. Before the world, before all of North America, before all our brothers in the bronze continent, *we are* a nation, we are a union of free pueblos, we are *Aztlán*" (italics mine).[11] This statement from "El Plan Espiritual de Aztlán" declared that Chicanas/os share a common culture and history with the rest of indigenous America and that, furthermore, this consciousness itself provided the building blocks for the existence of a Chicana/o nation within the U.S. nation-state. While Indigenism provided Chicanas/os with a sense of belonging to the American continent, including the United States, paradoxically it also endowed the Chicana/o identity with a heightened sense of cultural difference vis-à-vis Anglo and European-American culture. But even though indigenous consciousness among Chicanas/os can be traced back to the 1960s and *el movimiento*, it proved to be an aesthetic and political discourse capable of transcending even the limitations imposed by the often strict, militant, and even male-centered nationalist discourse formulated by many activists.[12] The new life that the Chicano Movement breathed into Indigenist aesthetics proved to be decisive for the construction of a cultural nationalism that challenged the hegemony and monolithic culture of the United States as a nation-state.

Chicana/o artists, particularly during the early stages of *el movimiento*, were seeking a medium that could appropriately convey the political fervor and excitement of the moment. Conventional artistic media tended to be too elitist and exclusive to circulate among public spheres in a nonrestrictive and uncompromising way. Many of these artists echoed the sentiments of the Mexican muralists, who, through the "Manifesto of the Union of Mexican Workers, Technicians, Painters, and Sculptors" (1923), denounced easel painting as bourgeois and apolitical. Even though most Chicana/o artists, like their Mexican predecessors, did paint on canvas and did not think of themselves as strictly muralists, they nevertheless attached a heightened political and indigenous consciousness to the practice of mural making. Furthermore, Chicanas/os, as well as many other artists of color, had long been excluded from the museum and gallery circuits and would need to find alternative spaces to show their work and express their independent aesthetics. Asco, a charismatic artists collective formed during the early 1970s in East Los Angeles, challenged this exclusion. Using performance art and public theatrics to convey their unique brand of Chicana/o stylistics, Asco made history when in 1972 they signed their names in spray paint near the entrance of the Los Angeles County Museum of Art (LACMA) as a way to protest the museum's unwillingness to exhibit Chicana/o art.[13] But the Chicana/o search for alternative artistic media and exhibition venues was also deeply connected to the burgeoning indigenous consciousness that characterized the Chicano Movement; the medium that would best represent Chicana/o political ideals not only needed to publicly disseminate indigenous consciousness, but it also had to reflect the *actual* artistic practices carried out by other indigenous peoples of the Americas.

As I established in the previous chapter, the Mexican artistic renaissance that occurred from the 1920s to the 1940s served as an important precedent for many Chicana/o artists active in the 1960s and 1970s and provided innovative approaches to media. The use of public murals and the graphic arts by the Mexican artists would be taken up again by Chicana/o artists in the form of community murals and posters.[14] While both media represented a more democratic means of artistic expression because of their availability to a larger public and their independence from the museum and gallery system, muralism, in particular, publicly monumentalized Chicana/o political discourses in an unprecedented fashion. Chicana/o artists, however, took the concept of community involvement in the mural arts quite a few steps further than their Mexican predecessors. Aside from placing the artwork in the public sphere, thereby making it available to a larger audience, these artists also recruited the community itself for the conception and creation of the public mural. Following a common practice among community artists across the nation, Chicana/o muralists also recruited local youth for the creation of these public works of art. As a result, all involved partake in the process of empowerment that is associated with mural making. Not only are the work and the responsibility shared, but so are the authorship and the credit for the artwork. The idea of community empowerment through public image making became a leitmotif in the history of Chicana/o muralism.

The coupling of Indigenist iconography with the community mural seemed like the perfect marriage between thematic content and artistic format. While both muralism and Indigenism created new symbolic and physical spaces for the articulation of a Chicana/o identity,[15] they also functioned as dialectic components belonging to a unified system of visual signifiers. Within this dialectic, the community mural lent a monumentalization to Indigenist imagery that could not be achieved through any other medium, while said iconography saturated these murals with an aura that harked back to the pre-Columbian era. Without a doubt, the use of the public mural signified a highly effective way to assert an Indigenist identity that needed to be absorbed in a collective way. Chicana/o artists inscribed these images in wall paintings—usually located in the barrios of cities like San Diego, San Francisco, and Los Angeles—within the everyday experiences of the residents. The presence of these murals amid the urban visual paraphernalia of the streets, like advertising billboards, storefronts, traffic signals, and so on, made Indigenist murals part of lived reality in the barrio setting, and, as such, they became familiar to almost every sector of Chicana/o and Mexican society in urban areas.

Indigenist Motifs

The repeated use of simplified yet highly coded Indigenist symbols and motifs characterized Chicana/o nationalist murals. These recurring motifs helped to construct the various components and levels of Chicana/o cultural nationalism, yet their general simplicity and directness had an immediate impact on the public reception of these symbols, thus situating themselves at the core of Chicana/o identity. Each of these individual symbols and motifs was strategically chosen by Chicana/o artists and community members and performed a very specific function in the construction of this new nationalist aesthetic. Given that most of these motifs had roots in ancient Mesoamerican iconography and belief systems, they all held the common purpose of legitimizing Chicana/o nationalism by providing a historical precedence that went back several centuries.

Among these ubiquitous pre-Columbian motifs, we find the recurrence of the Aztec Calendar Stone, an image that seemed to lend itself particularly well to the Chicana/o community mural aesthetic. Its flat yet highly complex and striking design elements turned out to be ideal for collective mural making. Its intricate and crowded composition, to which Chicanas/os added a colorful palette, offered a stark contrast to the often drab and utilitarian character of barrio architecture, much of which included federally subsidized housing projects. The image of the Aztec Calendar Stone was based on the famous low-relief stone sculpture, dating back to the mid-fifteenth to early sixteenth century, found near the Cathedral of Mexico City, and Chicana/o artists turned it into a colorful two-dimensional wall design. Once these various artists established the basic layout of the calendar, filling in the color of the different registers and motifs within the image proved to be an ideal activity for the children and young people who wished to participate in the making of a neighborhood mural. This simple yet effective exercise facilitated community interaction and empowerment in the process.

But, as might be expected, the Aztec Calendar Stone held an importance to Chicana/o artists and *el movimiento* as a whole that went beyond its purely stylistic and aesthetic qualities. The function as well as significance of this calendar in the pre-Columbian context became relevant to the emerging and increasingly politicized nature of Chicana/o identity during the civil rights period. The calendar's iconography became familiar early on to many Chicanas/os through the nationalist quarterly magazine *Con Safos* published in Los Angeles in the late sixties and early seventies. In 1970, *Con Safos* reproduced a diagram illustration of the Aztec Calendar Stone with detailed explanations of its iconography and meaning.[16] As an Indigenist image with roots in preconquest America, the Aztec Calendar Stone legitimized Chicanas/os' claim to Mexica spirituality and cosmology while simultaneously constructing an alternative and independent history from canonical U.S. narratives. Of particular importance to the calendar's complex iconographic program is the central glyph, identified by various Mesoamerican scholars like Mary Ellen Miller and Cecilia Klein as a personification of the sun (also thought to be Tonatiuh, the day sun). This particular personification also refers to the Fifth Sun, the final stage of creation in Mexica cosmology and the one representing our present era. The concept of cosmic time, as stipulated by the Aztecs and represented by the Aztec Calendar Stone, appealed to Chicanas/os because it offered more dynamic and spiritual ways to conceptualize history. The notion of cosmic time, as opposed to linear time, allowed Chicanas/os to situate their emerging identity in the past, present, and future. The Aztec Calendar Stone permitted Chicanas/os to write themselves into a narrative of both historical and cosmic dimensions.

In terms of its function, pre-Columbian scholars believe the Aztec Calendar Stone also served as a type of platform where sacrifices were performed. Emily Umberger explained that calendar stones such as the one found in Mexico City were usually created in commemoration of Tlaxcaxipehualiztli, the Flaying of Men ceremony. The event commemorated and glorified warfare and military victories while also legitimizing the power of Aztec rulers. The sacrifice of war prisoners constituted the culminating portion of the ceremony, and according to Umberger, the act was "performed on the sun itself."[17] Chicanas/os took quite an interest in the concept of sacrifice, not for its violent connotations but for its capability to perpetuate the cycles of life, as believed by the Aztecs. Among the creative expressions of U.S. Latina/o communities, we often find a concern about survival, be that cultural or natural survival. On the one hand, Chicana/o activists exposed the social ills that threatened the lives of their community, such as the disproportionate number of Chicanos who lost their lives in gang warfare and during the Vietnam War, as well as the sterilizations imposed on Chicana and Mexican women. This preoccupation with survival was also closely associated with the fear of assimilation into the U.S. mainstream, a phenomenon that could lead to the death of Mexican culture in this country. Sacrifice, as it surfaced in a metaphorical way within artistic production, reinforced the concept of survival on several levels.

But the calendrical function emerged perhaps as the most important element of the Aztec Calendar Stone that appealed to Chicanas/os. The calendar included glyphs corresponding to various dates in historical and cosmic time important for the Aztecs. Directly above the face of the Fifth Sun, the date 1 Flint is inscribed in hieroglyphic form. This date functioned as a symbol of the Aztec nation because it referred to the year in which the Aztecs, led by Huitzilopochtli, left their homeland of Aztlán to migrate south and establish their empire in Tenochtitlán. This particular event in Mexica cosmology, as I explained in the introduction to this volume, had a special importance to Chicana/o nationalist discourse in that it identified Aztlán as the U.S. Southwest or, as clarified by Luis Leal, as "the Mexican territory ceded to the United States in 1848."[18] Finding out about the existence of Aztlán through the chronicles of Gaspar Pérez de Villagrá was, for many Chicana/o artists, a definitive revelation: "To be given that information when you're looking for your roots is liberating; it empowers you," explained artist José Montoya; "it lets you know that you have a very legitimate claim to what you're talking about. . . . We have taken our *indigenismo* and we have taken everything that makes us mestizos, everything that makes us Chicanos."[19] Michael Pina further emphasized the importance of Aztlán to Chicana/o nationalism, stressing that "a nation without its 'homeland' is almost unthinkable."[20] But the 1 Flint inscription on the Aztec Calendar Stone also commemorates the migration from Aztlán to Tenochtitlán as a particularly spiritual event. This sculpture, then, legitimizes the Mexican presence on U.S. soil by providing an ancient account of Aztlán, thereby giving Chicana/o history in this country a mythical connotation.

The ubiquity of the Aztec Calendar Stone was only rivaled by the recurrent use among Chicana/o muralists of the mestizo or tripartite face. This motif was an important symbol with Indigenist overtones that saturated Chicana/o community mural imagery, and it generally depicted a three-sided face in which the flanking figures represent the Spaniard and the Indian. The central face then illustrated the merging of the two, the mestizo or the contemporary Chicana/o. This figure was originally formulated by Denver artist/muralist Manuel Martínez, inspired by a tripartite face featured prominently in the building of the School of Medicine (Facultad de Medicina) in Mexico City's Universidad Nacional Autónoma de México (UNAM). The UNAM mural (1953–1954) was created by Mexican artist Francisco Eppens, who depicted a tripartite face as the composition's central motif, surrounding it with other indigenous symbols and figures such as references to Tlaloc and Coatlicue, among other Mesoamerican allusions.[21]

The tripartite face, in spite of its Mexican mural origins, came to define, in its most basic and direct form, the essence of Chicana/o cultural and ethnic identity. Drawing from the ideas on *mestizaje* formulated by intellectuals like José Vasconcelos during early twentieth-century Mexico, Chicana/o *mestizaje* included the added dimension of the U.S. experience. Chicanas/os found Vasconcelos's notion of *mestizaje* particularly important, given that it had a cultural as well as a spiritual component. He believed that the four "races" that exist in the world—that is, the Caucasian, the Indian, the Asian, and the African ethnicities—would converge into one superior and cosmic fifth race that would be free of the vices and weaknesses of the previous four: "What will come out of this [convergence] is the definitive race, a synthetic or integral race, made with the genius and with the blood of all people and, for that reason, it will be more capable of true fraternity and universal vision."[22] Chicano nationalists like Nicandro F. Juárez regarded this philosopher/politician's own childhood growing up near the U.S.-Mexico border in Eagle Pass, Texas, as a crucial experience that shaped his ideas about ethnicity and culture.[23] Though many Chicana/o intellectuals knew that Vasconcelos regarded *mestizaje* as a way to assimilate the Mexican Indian into the national culture, they nevertheless saw his critical postures as creative alternatives to then-current postulates about racial and cultural identity. For instance, Vasconcelos harshly criticized the British and Anglo-Americans as colonizers because of their refusal to intermix and reproduce with the groups they were subjugating. According to him, Spanish colonization at least had the merit of initiating *mestizaje* in Latin America, whereas "the British man continued procreating only with whites and exterminated the Indian."[24] These ideas gave Chicanas/os a critical basis for the internal colonialism they suffered under the Anglo-American system in the United States. But while Vasconcelos saw the Indian as a mere bridge toward a greater *mestizaje*, Chicanas/os saw their indigenous blood as a crucial and necessary component of their being. The tripartite face in community murals thus acted as a public call for Chicanas/os to embrace the complexity of their identity, which many thinkers saw as the result of the union between European and Indian communities, a union further complicated by Mexican culture's contact with U.S. Anglo-American society.

While the Aztec Calendar Stone and the mestizo face underscored both the cultural and spiritual elements that informed Chicana/o identity, the repeated mural representations of Mesoamerican pyramids, be they Aztec or Maya, transformed the community's physical environment. Chicana/o artists would usually include these pyramids, often rendered in rather intuitive ways, to provide a visual backdrop to the pre-Columbian scenes so prevalent in Chicana/o community murals. But more than a historical and geographic backdrop, these pyramids functioned as trompe l'oeil complements to barrio architecture, that is, as visual stand-ins for the real structures. The representation of these pyramids seemed to imply that, even though many Chicanas/os and Mexicans have been conditioned to live in places like low-income housing projects and government-subsidized buildings, they once built and inhabited grander Mesoamerican structures. Moreover, these portrayals attempted to transform the urban environment into an almost mythical Indigenist realm, thereby transcending the pictorial space of the mural surface. For example, in his mural *Inspire to Aspire* (1987), located in San Francisco's Mission District, Chicano artist Michael Rios juxtaposed a

Teotihuacán-like pyramid with San Francisco's Transamerica Pyramid. This pairing disrupted the assumed cultural homogeneity of San Francisco's skyline and allowed such a transformation of these public spaces to take place. Furthermore, when studying ancient cultures, scholars such as archaeologists and art historians have often regarded large-scale public architecture as a reliable indication of the existence of a complex and sophisticated civilization. Pyramids, then, as classic representatives of this type of architecture, alluded to the Aztec civilization as a direct historical antecedent to contemporary Chicana/o culture, thus likening it to the alleged greatness of ancient Greece or Rome. In their quest to uncover and reconstruct a history that had been denied to them in their public school and even college education, Chicana/o artists and activists utilized the pyramid as perhaps the most monumental example of Mexican Americans' legitimate role among the world's leading and most advanced civilizations.

The *Obras Maestras*

While recurring Indigenist motifs in community murals played a pivotal role in the construction of Chicana/o cultural nationalism, their inclusion within more specific and recognizable murals created by well-respected artists had an even bigger impact on the way Indigenist iconography inscribed itself in the collective psyche. Individual motifs like the Aztec Calendar Stone or the tripartite or mestizo face had the advantage of acting like polyvalent symbols that could adjust themselves according to the theme of any given mural. However, by themselves, they lacked the site specificity and narrativity that characterized Chicana/o community murals. So, like any prominent civilization and culture, the Chicana/o nation needed a group of master artworks, or *obras maestras,* that epitomized its spirit and essence in the same way that Michelangelo's and Leonardo's work encapsulated the humanism of the Italian Renaissance. Unlike European or Eurocentric traditions, however, the Chicana/o artistic tradition would not be centered around an individual genius or be the privilege of an exclusive cultural elite. Chicana/o art, rather, needed to expound a more collective aesthetic that could embrace the sentiments of the community in a democratic way. The role that murals would play, then, would be that of *obras maestras* that represented the ideals of the community-oriented concerns defining Chicana/o cultural nationalism.

A great deal of mural production during the early stages of the Chicano Movement took place in conjunction with the establishment of cultural centers and institutions founded in the mid- to late 1970s to show the work of

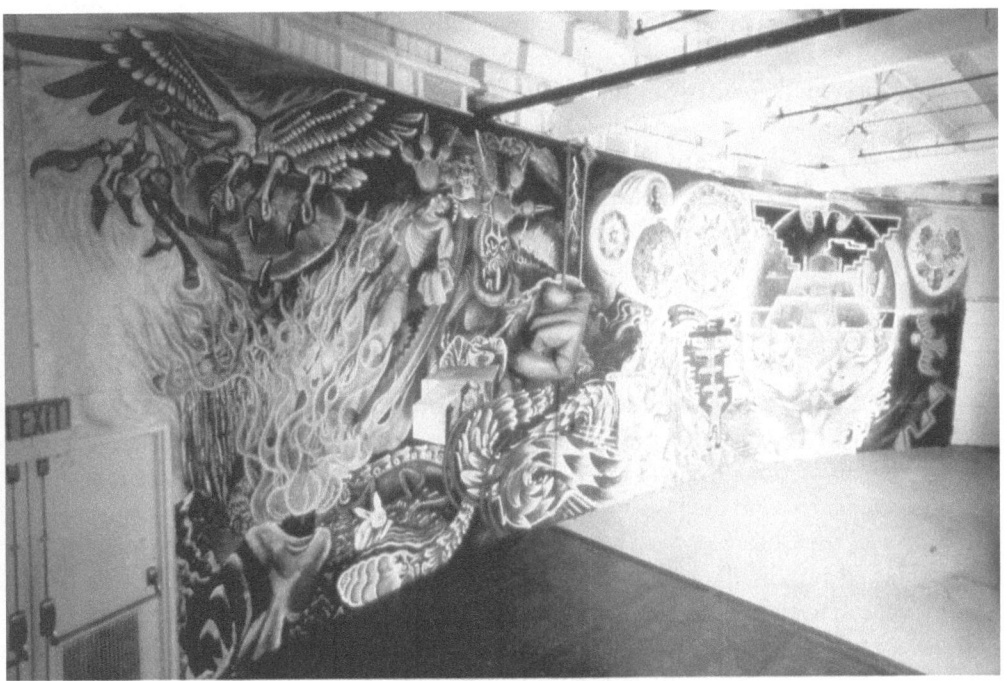

FIGURE 2.1. Guillermo Aranda and others, © 1970–1984, *La Dualidad*, mural, Centro Cultural de la Raza, San Diego, California. Courtesy of Guillermo Aranda and Centro Cultural de la Raza.

Chicana/o artists and to cater to the needs of its corresponding communities. Such was the case of the billboard murals attached to the Galería de la Raza in San Francisco and the various mural projects associated with the founding of the Social and Public Art Resource Center (SPARC) in Venice. But Guillermo Aranda directed perhaps one of the most ambitious early mural projects, inside San Diego's Centro Cultural de la Raza in Balboa Park. *La Dualidad* (Figure 2.1), begun in 1970 and finished more than a decade later in 1984, graced the curved interior wall of the Centro's main gallery space. Although Aranda engineered the mural's general design and layout, other artists such as the Toltecas en Aztlán and Tupac Enrique also participated in its creation throughout the years.[25] The mural was, in many ways, the result of the various intellectual dialogues about Indigenism that took place at the Centro in the late sixties and early seventies. Alurista himself had come to the Centro and was an early contributor to the indigenous sensibilities taking place there, which in turn affected the work of artists like Aranda and the Toltecas en Aztlán. The artists used a variety of Indigenist themes within *La Dualidad* that not only celebrated Chicano/Mexican culture, but that also served as platforms to critique Anglo-American and European imperialism and industrialization in the United States and abroad. The title, "Duality," also functioned on many levels, but most directly alluded to the general distribution of iconography across the mural's composition. The left half of *La Dualidad*, dominated by turbulent tones of red and orange, focused on the negative effects that colonization and war have had on American indigenous cultures. The right half, composed primarily of bright yellows, illustrates what the artists regarded as the utopian nature of native cultures once they're liberated from the grasp of these destructive forces. The concept of duality, however, does not necessarily imply a complete opposition between these contrasting notions, but rather an interdependence and correspondence between the two, implying that, paradoxically, one cannot survive or exist without the other. Chicano writers like Mario Garza recognized that the Mexican American experience contained a persistent duality: "This duality started since the origin of the Chicano when the Spanish element and the native Indian element united and fused together to form the *mestizo*—the Chicano. It still continues today as the Chicano is continually exposed to the Mexican and American forces around him."[26] Adding to that, the duality inherent in growing up bilingual further inscribed the notion in the Chicana/o psyche.[27] Alurista also argued that the Maya saw the different elements of the universe, including human beings themselves, as interdependent parts of a unified whole. The expression *in lak'ech*, "you are my other self," epitomizes the relationship that every human being has with one another.[28] For individuals to understand themselves, they must first understand their relationship with others. This idea was particularly appealing to Chicanas/os because it opposed the notion of the "Other" postulated by European colonialist thinking.

In *La Dualidad*, Aranda alludes to this Maya concept in order to address the complex and interconnected relationship between the colonized and the colonizer, but also to illustrate that the two spheres depicted in the mural act as opposites that, nevertheless, form part of a cosmic balance. In the right-hand side of the composition, Aranda and his colleagues rendered the body of an indigenous male figure crucified on a silver dollar, a symbol of U.S. capitalism. The fire underneath his feet identifies him as Cuauhtémoc, the last of the Aztec warriors and emperors who offered radical resistance to the Spanish colonizers in the sixteenth century, a fitting role model for the contemporary Chicana/o radical. He is surrounded by various figures and creatures who act as allegories for indigenous oppression in the Americas. Soaring above Cuauhtémoc and grasping his heart within its claws is a bird identified by art historian Alan Barnett as a cross between a vulture and an eagle.[29] Behind him, a neatly lined-up troop of soldiers wearing gas masks charge forward toward an unseen enemy, an image reminiscent of the troops depicted in Siqueiros's mural *Portrait of the Bourgeoisie* (1939–1940), located in Mexico City's Electrician's Syndicate. With regard to these particular figures, Aranda commented the following: "I think my purpose was to educate people about the status of society in the sense of being a mechanized world, half-human, half-machine."[30] The fire that burns Cuauhtémoc's feet comes from a torch held by a disembodied hand, perhaps an allusion to the torch held by the Statue of Liberty. Rather than placing Cuauhtémoc within a specifically Mexican context, the artists of *La Dualidad* contextualized his oppression and eventual torture within a more generalized setting that also includes direct and indirect references to U.S. imperialism. Cuauhtémoc thus stands not only as the fallen Aztec hero but also as a personification of the contemporary Chicano, whose own subjugation began with the European colonization of the Americas in the fifteenth and sixteenth centuries and continued with the U.S. domination of Mexican territory in the nineteenth and twentieth centuries.

But the choice of including Cuauhtémoc as an allegory of the Chicano struggle bears greater significance. During the siege of Tenochtitlán, Cuauhtémoc offered the last and most courageous posture of resistance toward the Spanish invaders who had decimated this impressive Aztec city. After his capture, the Spaniards demanded that Cuauhtémoc reveal his alleged plot against Hernán Cortés as well as the whereabouts of Emperor Moctezuma's gold. When he refused to volunteer any information, his Spanish captors tortured this Aztec warrior by setting his feet on fire. Chicanas/os saw this act of unparalleled bravery and conviction as a model for the types of resistance they needed to offer to the systems of authority that oppressed them in the United States. While torture did not necessarily form part of the Chicana/o experience, the figure of Cuauhtémoc as the last Aztec ruler before the beginning of colonization stood as an enticing model for the militant male Chicano who joined the ranks of *el movimiento*.

The right-hand side of *La Dualidad* offers a great contrast to the images of destruction and devastation in the Cuauhtémoc section. The iconography here centers around the image of an Aztec pyramid surrounded by various symbols associated with indigenous culture from both sides of the U.S.-Mexico border. Behind the pyramid we see the UFW eagle majestically spreading its wings while acting as a thematic opposite to the eagle/vulture creature on the Cuauhtémoc side. A pair of hands that emerge from a lake underneath, in turn, support this structure. These hands are conjured up by the earth goddess below them, whose own wings echo those of the UFW eagle above. Representations of the sun and the moon in the form of an Aztec stone relief sculpture hover nearby while the figures of a U.S. Native American man and woman are engaged in ritual hunting-and-gathering activities beneath them. The artists closely associate indigenous culture on this side of the mural with the earth's natural habitat, whereas the forces of colonialism and imperialism on the other side are connected to industrialized and artificial environments. *La Dualidad* espoused an Indigenist vocabulary that constructed an ideal Chicana/o cultural nation while also directly challenging the U.S. postindustrial nation-state. In other words, Indigenism in *La Dualidad* became a tool for both cultural celebration and social critique almost simultaneously.

The combination or conflation of Mexican and U.S. Native cultures in *La Dualidad* points to the alliances that Chicana/o and Native American activist groups formed during the civil rights movement. For instance, in San Diego's Centro Cultural de la Raza itself, the Toltecas de Aztlán attended various meetings with Native American groups. They even visited Indian reservations in San Diego's La Jolla and in Arizona.[31] They, like other Chicana/o activists, realized that Native Americans and Mexican Americans shared a history of dispossession, displacement, and discrimination. Moreover, the distinction made between Mexican and Native American Indian cultures depended on where European colonialism and U.S. expansionism chose to trace their national boundaries. Many Chicana/o artists, like the ones who worked on *La Dualidad*, sought to erase or undermine this distinction, thereby creating a sort of Pan-Indigenist aesthetic in their work. Furthermore, the Indigenist symbols and motifs on the right side of the mural also functioned as the allegorical solutions to the predicaments and problems posed on the Cuauhtémoc side.

As evident in many community murals throughout California, the use of ancient Mesoamerican and pre-Columbian imagery became a common strategy to construct Indigenist imagery. In their visual, written, and oral discourses, Chicana/o artists and activists established a direct lineage between precolonial cultures and contemporary Chicana/o communities. This strategy became part of their campaign to construct a history that had been ignored or undermined by the dominant narratives upheld in most educational institutions. Reclaiming the pre-Columbian past also lent a sense of legitimacy to the cultural nationalism that Chicana/o activist ideology espoused. In muralism itself, pre-Columbian imagery not only reminded or taught the community about their history and culture but also re-created a piece of that history in the barrio setting. The utilization of

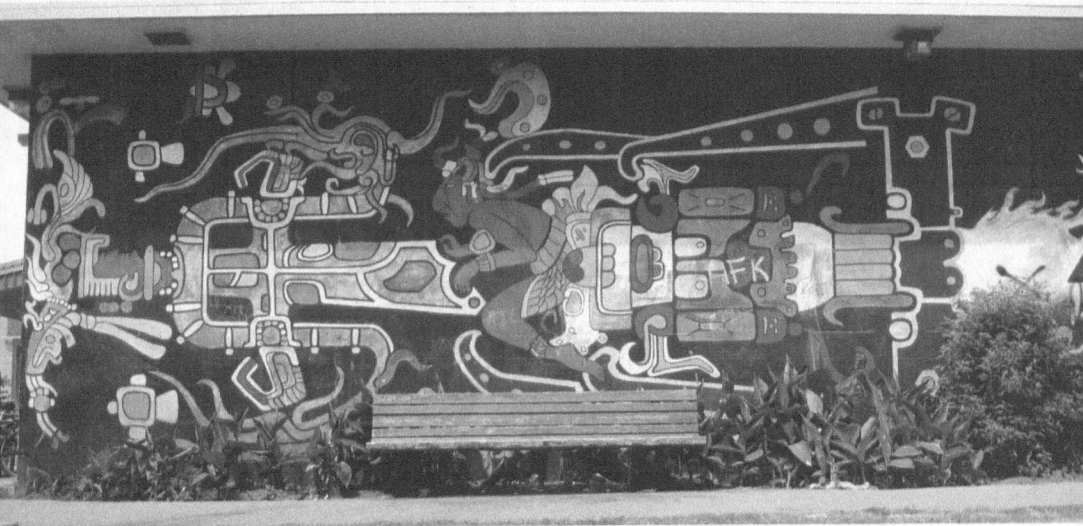

FIGURE 2.2. Domingo Rivera, © 1975, *Psycho-Cybernetics*, mural, San Francisco, California. Photograph by Guisela Latorre.

pre-Columbian visual language took many forms, including direct transcriptions or appropriations of images and symbols found in actual Mesoamerican monuments or objects. Such was the case of Domingo Rivera's *Psycho-Cybernetics* (Figure 2.2) mural from 1975 in San Francisco's Mission District.[32] Here the artist rendered a somewhat humorous image of a Maya figure piloting an elaborately decorated rocket ship made of machine parts and indigenous glyphs. The Mayas' profound knowledge of science, cosmology, and astronomy led to some rather creative and imaginative Indigenist representations of this Mesoamerican culture among Chicana/o artists. In spite of the rather tongue-in-cheek tone of the image, Rivera here makes reference to the scientific inventiveness of the Maya for an audience not accustomed to associating indigenous civilizations with technological progress. The image, in part, functioned as a response to the pseudo-archaeological claims made by Euro-American and European writers like Erich von Däniken, who in his popular book *Chariots of the Gods? Unsolved Mysteries of the Past* (1968) argued that visitors from outer space were responsible for the scientific and architectural feats of the Maya, among other civilizations, thus indirectly denying indigenous peoples' intellectual autonomy and agency. In spite of the mural's "science fiction" theme, Rivera

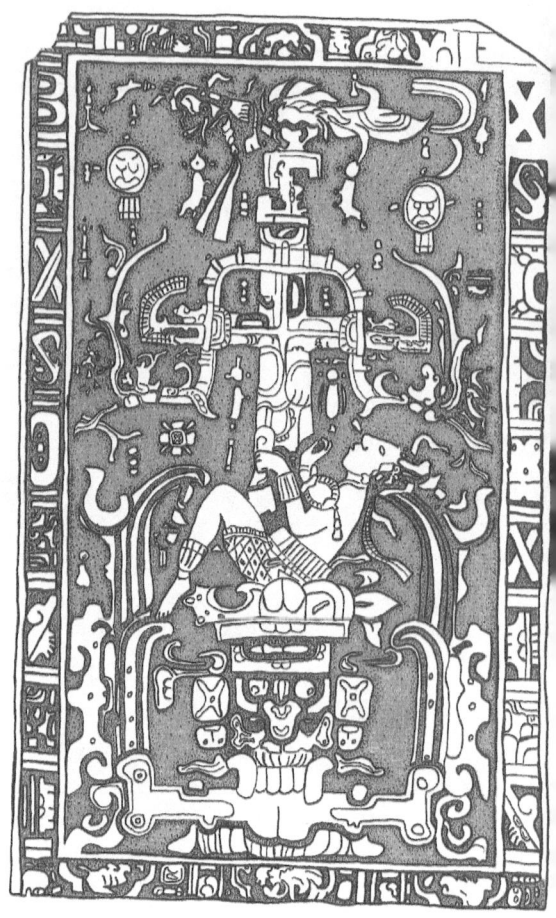

FIGURE 2.3. King Janaab' Pakal, stone relief (seventh century), Palenque, Veracruz, Mexico. Pen-and-ink drawing by Guisela Latorre.

places emphasis on the Maya figure piloting the craft, an unambiguously *earthly* indigenous figure. Furthermore, the artist has taken the image of the pilot and his spaceship from a well-known Maya stone relief sculpture dating back to AD 683 (Figure 2.3). This sarcophagus lid found within the Temple of the Inscriptions in Palenque, Guatemala, presents an image of Maya ruler Janaab' Pakal as he enters the world of the dead. He seems to be reclining on a small canoe or water vessel that emerges from the open jaws of an earth monster. Mary Ellen Miller points to how the Tree of Life springs from his body as if suggesting that his death can generate life itself.[33] This relief combines the themes of death, afterlife, and rulership into a unified and seamless visual construction.

In *Psycho-Cybernetics*, on the other hand, Rivera chooses instead to construct a kind of science-fiction fantasy by turning the entire scene on its head, quite literally. He rotates the original composition ninety degrees, creating a horizontal rather than a vertical orientation. After omitting many of the complex iconographic motifs from the sarcophagus, all Rivera needs to do to make Pakal's surroundings into a rocket ship is add a fiery combustion at the end. In spite of the stoic spirituality and solemnity of this Maya relief's subject matter, Rivera's version of this Palenque relief seems to fluctuate somewhere between respectful rendition and irreverent parody. Indeed, an essential component of the Chicano nationalist aesthetic is precisely the use of humor and irony. Rather than using it as a means to relax the seriousness of the messages being conveyed, Chicana/o artists and writers used humor as a lure to articulate more vehement critiques of existing social and political paradigms. Ricardo Favela, a member of the artists collective the Royal Chicano Air Force, explained that humor was often used "as a means of resistance, as a means of defiance, as a means of doing something to your oppressor where he doesn't understand or know that you're doing it to him [*sic*]."[34] Everything becomes subject to parody, even elements belonging to the Mesoamerican cultural patrimony that Chicanas/os so admired. But parody does not necessarily imply a complete subversion or disrespect toward that which is being imitated. The use of parody and humor in Chicana/o creative expressions becomes a means by which to decode and then reformulate the different components of preexisting cultural and social norms, thus adjusting them to the specificity of the Chicana/o experience. Similar to *rasquachismo*, the aesthetic of the underdog and downtrodden identified by Tomás Ybarra-Frausto, Rivera's reading of the Palenque relief reflects what this writer called the "resourcefulness and adaptability" inherent in Chicana/o survival tactics and creativity.[35] Rivera transforms Janaab' Pakal into a rocketship pilot, thereby modifying Mesoamerican culture with elements of pop culture easily identifiable by the community at large. The artist then uses the lure or hook of the humorous "science fiction" theme in this mural to direct his audience toward the importance of Mesoamerican culture as a viable and legitimate historical predecessor to contemporary Chicana/o society.

Pre-Columbian history and culture certainly became legitimate sources for the nationalist Indigenism found in Chicana/o muralism, but modern Mexican history was also utilized to explain the current state of affairs affecting the Mexican community in the United States. The Mexican Revolution of 1910 became a particularly important event for Chicanas/os on various levels. As explained in the first chapter of this volume, the event triggered one of the largest influxes of Mexican immigrants to the United States to date. Many Chicana/o artists and activists claimed direct connection to the Mexican Revolution because they were either the children or grandchildren of those immigrants who came to the United States during the first few decades of the twentieth century. But, of course, Chicana/o nationalists also regarded the Mexican Revolution as a historical precedent to their struggles during the civil rights movement in the 1960s and 1970s. Figures such as Emiliano Zapata and Francisco Villa became recurring icons in community mural walls and stood as the forebears of Chicano activists like Reies López Tijerina, César Chávez, and even slain journalist Ruben Salazar. As a matter of fact, the repetitiveness of their use deeply ingrained these revolutionary figures in the public psyche of Mexican neighborhoods in California. The images of these heroes became timeless ideals that transcended the Mexican Revolution itself and made themselves current to the contemporary activism of Chicanas/os on U.S. soil. The Mexican Revolution, along with its protagonists, provided a model for what many nationalists thought was a radical political uprising led by the country's underdog that deeply affected all echelons of Mexican society and culture. Chicana/o artists also presented the Mexican Revolution as an event that gave a voice to the nation's indigenous population, thereby making it an important event in Indigenist history. Not only were many Chicana/o radicals initially convinced that this revolution liberated many Mexican Indians from oppression and poverty, but they also focused on figures who were known to possess indigenous blood, like the *soldaderas* (female soldiers) and Zapata himself.

Wayne Alaniz Healy and David Rivas Botello are perhaps two of the most prolific Chicano muralists in Los Angeles, starting in the 1970s and working well into the 2000s. Their murals constituted the public works that most faithfully epitomized the nationalist ideals of the Chicano Movement. They came together in 1975 to form the legendary muralist group the East Los Streetscapers, which later also included Chicano painter George Yepes. Healy and Botello completed their first collaboration in 1977 with the mural *Chicano Time Trip* (Figure 2.4), which graces the exterior walls of what was then Crocker Bank (now EastWest Bank) in Lincoln Heights at the intersection of North Broadway and Daly Street. Funding for this work came from the bank itself and from the Citywide Mural Project, an early initiative led by Judy Baca in which the city of Los Angeles agreed to fund community-based mural works.[36] This five-panel mural depicts various figures that represent the numerous components of Chicana/o identity. Meant to be read from right to left, the last and largest panel, *La Familia*, presents the spectator with a representation of the archetypal Chicana/o

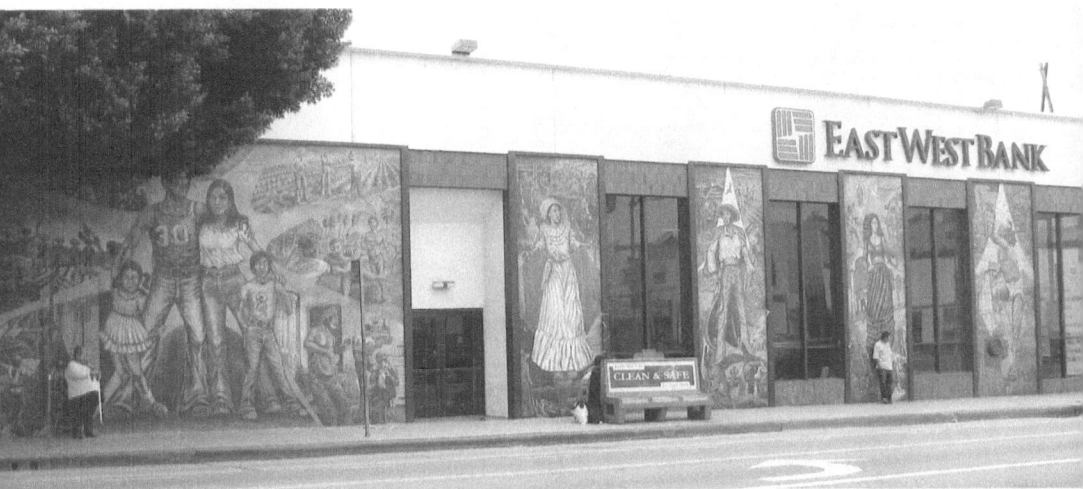

FIGURE 2.4. East Los Streetscapers, © 1977, *Chicano Time Trip*, mural, Lincoln Heights, Los Angeles, California. Courtesy of David Botello and Wayne Alaniz Healy.

family consisting of two young parents and their devoted children. Healy and Botello seem to suggest that this family has come together thanks to the political struggles and everyday cultural expressions of the Chicana/o community, as indicated by the scenes surrounding the family group. The artists rehashed the old trope of equating the family with the nation. So, in keeping with the goals of *el movimiento*, this mural sought to construct the Chicano nation through the social unit of the family and with the help of public imagery. The four single-figure panels adjacent to the family scene would act as additional building blocks to this nationalist construct. These panels would also represent four moments in Mexican history that deeply affected the present-day Chicana/o, displayed from most recent to oldest, moving from left to right: the Mexican Revolution, the Wars for Independence, the Colonial Era, and the pre-Columbian world, allegorized respectively by *La Soldadera* (Figure 2.5), *El Hacendado, La Española,* and *El Indígeno* (Figure 2.6), a Maya priest. With the Maya and *soldadera* figures in particular, the artists underscored the importance of Indigenist history to Chicana/o culture. Shown amid many indigenous cultures, the figure in the *El Indígeno* panel is a male priest grasping a flint knife in one hand and holding up a human heart in the other while resting his right leg over a sculpted head of Quetzalcoatl. Behind him, various scenes from the Mesoamerican world emerge: a group of Olmec artists working on one of the colossal heads found

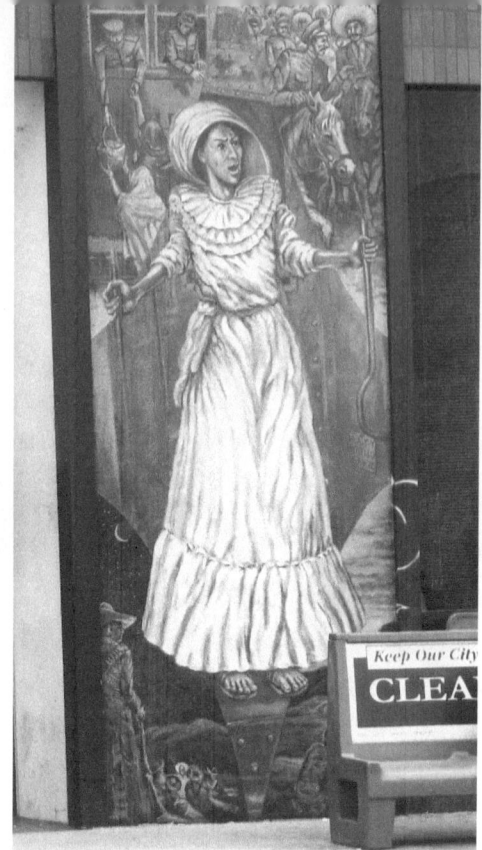

FIGURE 2.5. East Los Streetscapers, © 1977, *La Soldadera* panel from *Chicano Time Trip*, mural, Lincoln Heights, Los Angeles, California. Courtesy of David Botello and Wayne Alaniz Healy.

FIGURE 2.6. East Los Streetscapers, © 1977, *El Indígeno* panel from *Chicano Time Trip*, mural, Lincoln Heights, Los Angeles, California. Courtesy of David Botello and Wayne Alaniz Healy.

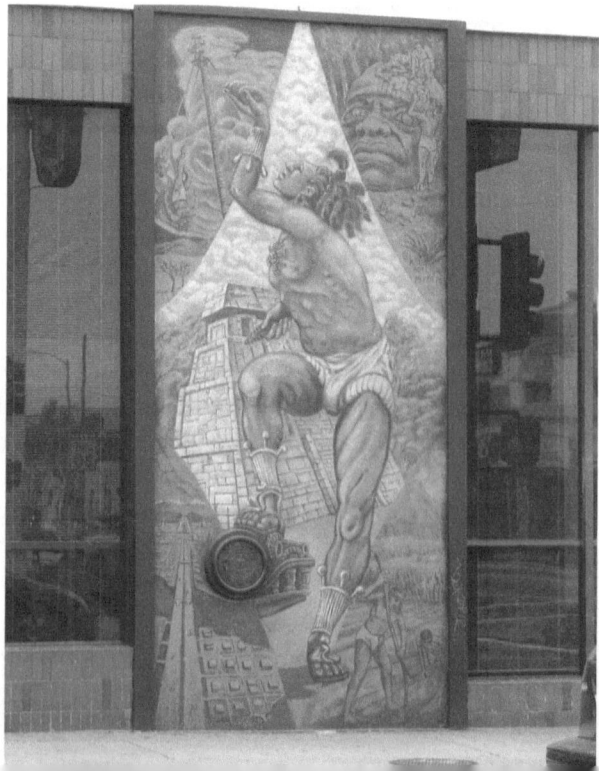

at the sites of La Venta, San Lorenzo, and Los Tres Zapotes in Veracruz; an aerial view of the ancient city of Tenochtitlán, revealing the complexity of Mexica city planning; a farmer planting maize; and others. The emphasis on and monumentalization of this Maya priest speaks to the general tendency among certain thinkers of *el movimiento* to hail these larger-than-life figures as the direct ancestors of the contemporary Chicana/o community. If places like East Los Angeles were reclaimed as significant parts of the new Aztlán, every working-class Chicano who labored endlessly to provide for his family was the reincarnation of a Mesoamerican warrior or king.

Another important Indigenist figure in *Chicano Time Trip* was that of the *soldadera*. *Soldaderas*, or Adelitas, as they were later mythicized, were the mostly indigenous and mestiza female companions to Mexican soldiers during the Revolution of 1910.[37] These women provided the men with everything from cooked meals to assistance in combat. Healy and Botello even highlighted her role as a cook with a scene in the upper-left corner of this panel that shows a *soldadera* handing a food basket to a soldier on a train. To Chicano nationalists, the *soldaderas'* contributions to the Mexican Revolution epitomized the ideal role a woman could take in nationalist struggles: a loyal follower who supposedly felt content with her secondary role to that of the men.[38] She was a loyalist who stood by her man for the greater cause of the Revolution. Chicano nationalists imagined Chicanas who joined *el movimiento* as fulfilling a similar role; some of the female members of the Brown Berets even dressed like *soldaderas* during public rallies and demonstrations. The *soldadera's* contribution would not be unlike that of the woman within the family depicted in this mural's main panel, thereby establishing a direct historical connection between the two.

Healy and Botello looked to the work of Mexican revolutionary photographer Agustín Víctor Casasola for their *soldadera* rendition in *Chicano Time Trip*. Casasola photographed various important historical events during the early twentieth century in Mexico. In the early 1920s, the photographer established the Casasola Archive, a collection that amassed thousands of photographs from the period, which included his work and that of other photographers. Drawing inspiration directly from a photograph in the Casasola Archive dating to around 1915 that depicted *soldaderas* (Figure 2.7), these artists were attracted to the immediacy and sense of urgency of the image. The scene shows a group of *soldaderas* descending from a train car, many of whom carry food items for the male soldiers. These Chicano artists chose to focus on the figure of the *soldadera* standing to the left-hand side of this photograph's composition. As she leaves the train, she looks to her left with an expression of desperation as the wind billows her *rebozo*.

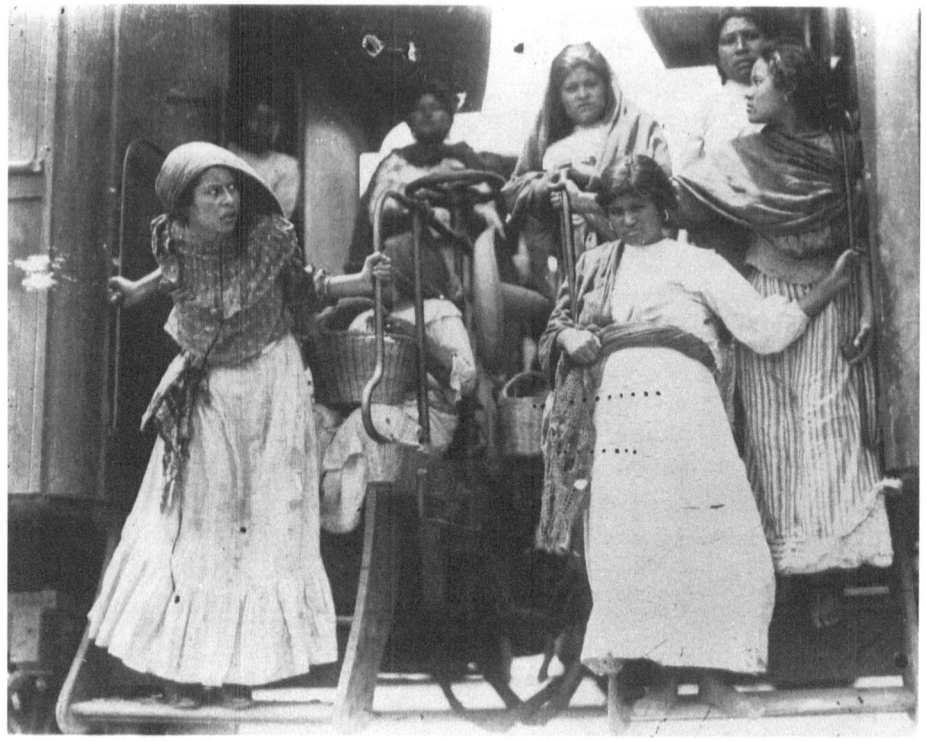

FIGURE 2.7. Agustín Víctor Casasola, © ca. 1915, *Soldaderas en Buenavista*, photograph. Used with permission by SINAFO-Fototeca Nacional.

When Healy saw this image, he commented that it seemed that the Revolution was taking place in her very eyes.[39] Healy and Botello took this figure, gave her a pair of Indian *chanclas* (sandals), and placed her within the backdrop of other scenes from the Mexican Revolution, many of which were also based on Casasola photographs.

For Chicana/o artists, Casasola's photography was perhaps the most faithful historical record of the Mexican Revolution. Having been excluded from historical canons within the United States, Chicana/o activists during *el movimiento* became conscious of history's subjectivity and function as a positioned text. Writing Mexican Americans back into U.S. history constituted one of the most important goals of the Chicano Movement. While Casasola's work, in most respects, represented modern *Mexican* history, Chicanas/os found the Mexican Revolution to be extremely relevant to their history in the United States. As a result, this photographer's images became one of the many threads Chicanas/os used to weave their own historical tapestry. Moreover, Casasola's photography depicted a political, social, and cultural revolution that included the participation of the native communities in Mexico and therefore contributed to the growing Indigenist consciousness that characterized the Chicano Movement. In addition, many Chicana/o artists believed that his work provided irrefutable proof of the Revolution's importance because of the veracity of the photographic image. While photographic historian Flora Lara Klahr asserted that "the objectivity of the photographic image" [40] thoroughly convinced postrevolutionary audiences in Mexico of the historical truth depicted in these images, many Chicana/o artists felt attracted to the seeming veracity of Casasola's photographic record. Texas-based Chicana artist Santa Barraza, who started using Casasola imagery in the mid-1970s and whose own family members had participated in the Mexican Revolution, found in his work a social, political, and cultural validation:

> I was attracted to the images of Casasola because they not only gave me a sense of history, but they also made me "real." They "validated" me ... Those Casasola photos brought into focus, for me, a reality that I had heard my grandparents talk about. It gave me a history, a belonging, a validity, a continuum.... I suppose that I was reclaiming a past that I had lost through colonization.... Those photos helped me to de-colonize myself. [41]

Chicanas/os' interest in Casasola was not limited to California and the Southwest but was a national phenomenon. During the fall of 1976, the Chicago-based Mexican American journal *Abrazo* featured the work of Casasola at the same time that an exhibition of his photographs was taking place at the University of Illinois in Chicago.

Transposing Casasola's photography to the mural medium also required a discursive shift of the significance attached to his imagery. The presence of his images in murals seems almost paradoxical, given that photographs are generally intended for smaller showcases. In the photographic medium, the figures and images functioned primarily as historical data, but when they were transferred to a public mural, they became monumental icons capable of defining the formation of Chicana/o national identity. The alleged historicity of Casasola's images operated as the motivation behind the creation of *La Revolución Mexicana* (*The Mexican Revolution*) mural on the pylon

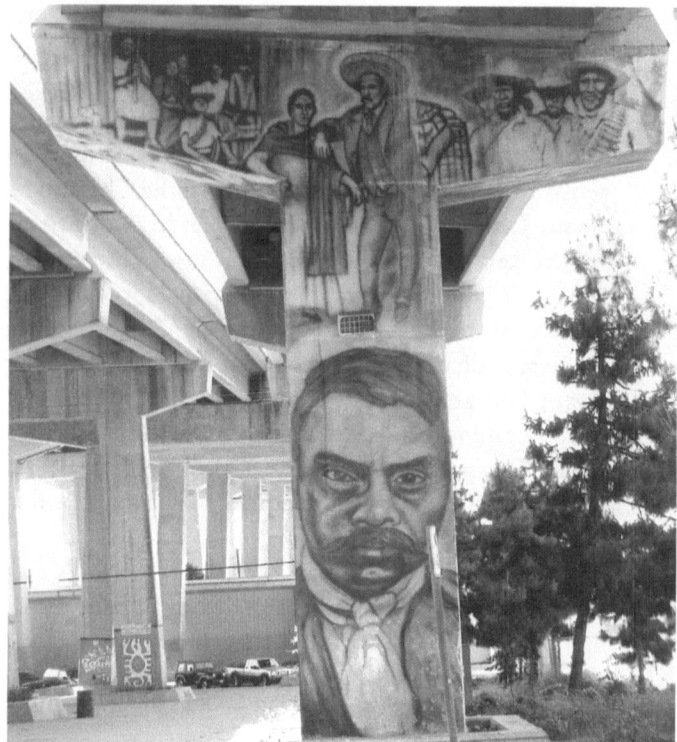

FIGURE 2.8. Víctor Ochoa, © 1978, *La Revolución Mexicana*, mural, Chicano Park, San Diego, California. Courtesy of Victor Ochoa.

in San Diego's Chicano Park, painted by Víctor Ochoa in 1978 (Figure 2.8). Ochoa had been inspired by a recent exhibition of Casasola's work at the Centro Cultural de la Raza and by the celebrations of the Mexican Revolution in San Diego. As a result, he constructed a composite of the Casasola images in his Chicano Park murals. Ochoa, who had been the director of the Centro from 1971 to 1974, invested much in the ideals of *el movimiento* and saw his work as a way to promote the goals of the Chicano Movement. In *La Revolución Mexicana*, the artist utilized a color palette that emulated the photographic medium. By using a sepia tone in his mural, Ochoa's figures remained, in his own words, "as authentic to the photograph as possible, so the image [was] as representative as possible of that part of the history of Mexico."[42] Like Barraza, Ochoa, too, was conscious of the historical accuracy and veracity often associated with the photographic medium.

On the east side of Ochoa's *Revolución Mexicana* pylon, he utilized four different Casasola photographs to put together the mural's composition. Taking advantage of the pylon's T shape, the muralist distributed the images in a way that reconfigured the meaning of the "original" pictures. In between the "arms" of the pylon, we see the famed revolutionary hero Francisco Villa standing next to his wife, Luz Corral. Flanking the couple, on the left, we find a group of *soldaderas,* most of whom are sitting inside a train wagon, and on the right, next to Villa himself, is a lineup of male indigenous peasants ready for combat. Ochoa carefully divided the upper register of this pylon to clearly delineate gendered spaces; the left half is clearly female, and the right half is distinctly male. By creating this gendering of the mural space, Ochoa embraced a view of the Mexican Revolution that assumed the roles of men and women in this struggle were unequivocally prescribed. Furthermore, Ochoa constructs the Revolution as a predominantly male political event by placing the larger-than-life figure of Emiliano Zapata at the base of the pylon. As with the other images, the artist used as a direct source Casasola's 1912 portrait of the revolutionary hero (Figure 2.9). Zapata was particularly

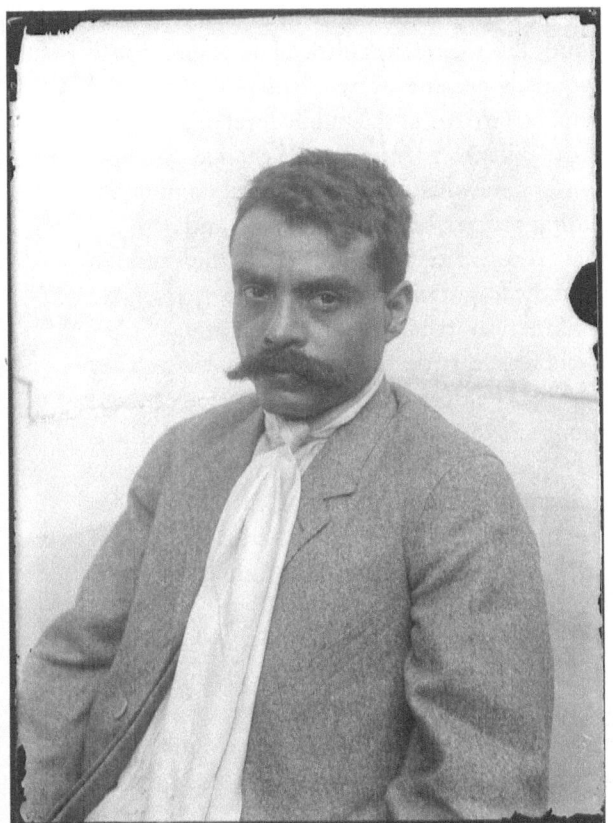

FIGURE 2.9. Agustín Víctor Casasola, © 1912, *Emiliano Zapata*, photograph. Used with permission by SINAFO-Fototeca Nacional.

important to Chicana/o nationalists because of his mestizo background and his strong bond with Mexico's indigenous peoples, whose lands had been plundered by colonization and industrialization. Like Mexico's native populations, Chicanas/os, too, were driven away from lands that were once part of Mexico, and leaders like Reies López Tijerina and César Chávez, who were concerned with issues of land and farmworkers' rights, could be considered contemporary reincarnations of Zapata himself.

Ultimately, for Chicana/o artists, Casasola functioned as a signifier of resistance and difference vis-à-vis the U.S. mainstream. In the Mexican context, this photographer's work formed part of an institutionalized ideology and official culture, but in the United States, his images characterized a marginalized though emerging cultural identity. His photographs contributed to the formation of an Indigenist canon that Chicana/o nationals were attempting to create in the 1960s and 1970s. As a whole, the visual component of this canon was particularly important because it circulated the ideals of *el movimiento* in ways that textual and oral means could not; the visual provided an immediate and direct message that could be more readily understood across cultural, social, political, and even linguistic divides. Chicana/o activists and artists alike very quickly became aware of the power of visual imagery saturated with Indigenist aesthetics at the public level of a community mural and capitalized on its ability to promote social change.

Given that the construction of a new history was a critical component of the Chicana/o nation-building process, artists, historians, and activists developed numerous strategies to re-create these previously undermined narratives. Historians uncovered the forgotten and ignored experiences and contributions of the Mexican American community in the United States by resorting to oral traditions such as legends, folktales, and *corridos*. They also carried out countless oral history interviews among the Mexican and Chicana/o communities throughout the Southwest and elsewhere. These activities gave rise to completely new and unique accounts of the Chicana/o experience that legitimized and empowered an assumed Chicana/o readership. These new narratives were sometimes woven into preexisting histories that formed part of canonical Mexican and U.S. history. A number of Chicana/o muralists, wishing to create visual histories with their work, resorted to the narrative threads provided by Chicana/o, Mexican, and U.S. historians. They pulled these threads together in often creative and unexpected ways to craft completely unique historical tapestries. Such was the case of Orange County Chicano artist Emigdio Vasquez, who became well known and respected, starting in the late 1970s, for his historical murals as well as his photorealistic style. A self-proclaimed Chicano social realist,[43] Vasquez often assembled the visual histories in his murals with the aid of photography (including Casasola's work): "I rely a great deal on photography. . . . I have gone through many magazines and newspapers and have cut out many photos of reference material that I feel can be useful for future paintings."[44] His approach to mural making was not unlike that of Chicana/o historians who had to restore the Chicana/o experience through the collection and recovery of historical fragments and loose narrative threads.

During the late seventies and early eighties, however, Vasquez, who had become politicized by the ideals of the Chicano Movement and the beliefs of socialism and Marxism, found himself in the problematic position of working for the city of Anaheim, carrying out a number of mural commissions:

> I started doing murals in 1977 and the reason I started doing them was that the city of Anaheim hired me to lead a program called the Youth Murals Program. . . . They were hiring low-income kids to work in different endeavors throughout the city and so I had a crew of ten to twenty kids to work with me. I worked with the city of Anaheim for about eight years and we did about eight murals throughout the city. That's how I actually got my start as a muralist.[45]

Though the commissions were fortuitous for the young artist, Vasquez usually found himself having to tone down the political message of his murals when working for the city: "In Orange County, I was kind of subjected to [a] certain amount of restraints, especially when you need to get approval for a mural from the city. They want to make art that is 'safe.'"[46] The forms of subtle and not-so-subtle censorship that the artist faced posed serious challenges to his belief in murals as collective histories and to his understanding of the role that history has in the nation-building process for the Mexican and Chicana/o communities in Orange County. Vasquez found himself caught between two captive audiences: the city officials who controlled the means of production and who closely monitored the content of the mural, and the largely Mexican and Chicana/o populations who lived with these murals on a daily basis and who sought a certain degree of empowerment from those images. As a result, Vasquez developed both visual and thematic strategies to negotiate his position within the politics of public art: "All I could do was be subtle," he commented, adding that much of the political content of his murals tended "to go over [the city's] heads" anyhow.[47] The artist stressed the experiences of struggle and racism suffered by the Mexican/Chicana/o

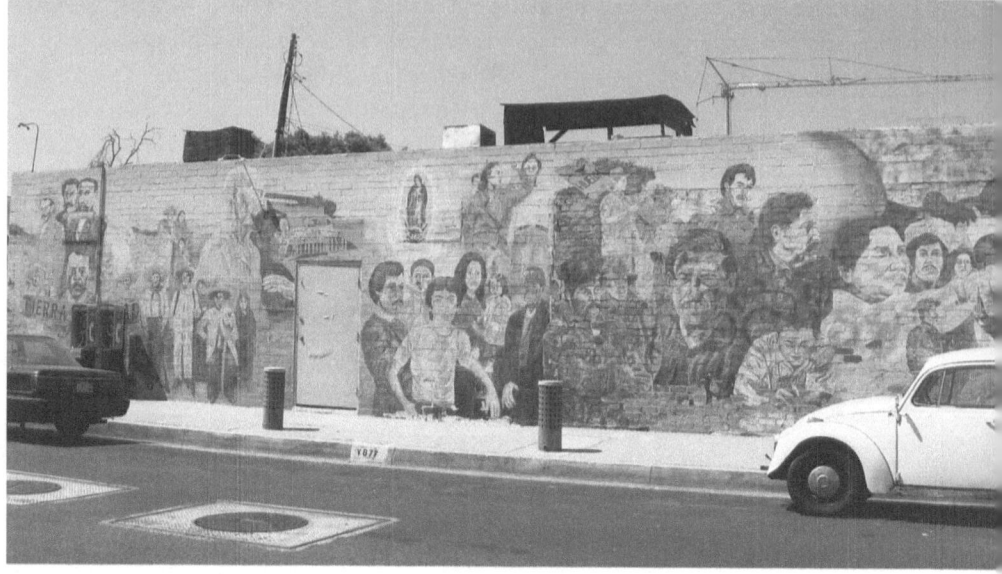

FIGURE 2.10. Emigdio Vasquez, © 1978, *Memories of the Past, Images of the Present*, mural, Ibero-American Market, Anaheim, California. Courtesy of Emigdio Vasquez.

community in Orange County, thereby indirectly critiquing the U.S. social system responsible for these inequities, a message that was often lost on the city officials who commissioned him.[48]

One of the first murals that Vasquez created under the auspices of the city of Anaheim and with the help of local youth was *Memories of the Past, Images of the Present* (1978; Figure 2.10). Like many of his other public works, this mural provides a historical backdrop or explanation for what he regarded as "the political and economic forces that shaped the [current] Chicano experience."[49] Here Vasquez traces the beginning of Chicana/o history to the Mexican Revolution of 1910, putting particular emphasis on Zapata and the indigenous/peasant participation in this armed struggle. The artist credited the Revolution with engendering a renewed admiration and respect for Mexico's native peoples and cultures: "[When the Revolution came along,] there was an appreciation of Mexico's Indian heritage."[50] As was true for many of his fellow artists, Vasquez's family also migrated to the United States as a result of the social unrest caused by the Revolution, and thus he regarded Chicana/o history as being profoundly connected to this particular moment in time. In *Memories of the Past*, the Revolution is represented by a series of figures of leaders like Zapata and Villa as well as the brothers Ricardo and Enrique Magón, who formed part of the intellectual arm of the revolutionary cause. Next to them are the anonymous indigenous peasants who bravely fought during this struggle, though many of them were eventually forced to migrate north to the U.S. Southwest in search of work. Vasquez uses their figures as transitional visual devices moving from the Mexican to the Chicana/o experience, placing particular emphasis on an elderly couple who are depicted gazing toward the future, namely, their new lives in the United States. "I [wanted] to convey the impact that this transition had on several generations of Chicanos," Vasquez explained, "and acknowledge the contributions that this process made on American society."[51] The Chicana/o experience is then rendered through episodes of both struggle and triumph. Vasquez illustrates how Chicanas/os were inducted into the low-paying and menial labor force in the United States, on the one hand, but also how they empowered themselves by becoming leading labor organizers, as was the case with César Chávez and Emma Tenayuca, both of whom are prominently featured in this mural. The working-class and Chicana/o experiences are intimately intertwined in much of Vasquez's work and reflect the collective but also personal subjectivity of the artist himself: "[I use] my life in my barrio as a microcosm of [the Chicano] experience."[52]

While Vasquez and his assistants utilized a left-to-right chronological narrative in *Memories of the Past*, the schema is suddenly disrupted in the last panel of the mural. Here the artist depicted two large figures, a Spanish soldier and an Aztec eagle warrior, both of whom function as allegorical rather than overtly historical figures. Vasquez explained that these figures were meant to "represent the fusion of the Indian and the Iberian cultures that resulted in the Mestizo. These are the ancestral forebears of the present-day Chicano."[53] Though Vasquez seems to be more interested in the working-class roots of Chicana/o culture,[54] the indigenous experience depicted in *Memories of the Past* further heightens the marginalized position of the Chicana/o population. Indigeneity here also underscores the mestiza/o consciousness of the community, a consciousness defined not only by its members' European-indigenous ancestry but also by their contact with Anglo-American society. The Spanish soldier and Aztec warrior are seen in this panel looking at a kind of hybrid landscape with lush vegetation, a Mesoamerican pyramid, and other indigenous figures sitting next to ancient stone sculptures. This rural scenery suddenly morphs into a city landscape with the identifiable Anaheim skyline in the background, thereby alluding to the transition from agrarian to urban lifestyles experienced by many Mexicans and Chicanas/os. The inhabitants of this landscape are now the disenfranchised workers of a postindustrial society. Among them, however, we find a traditional flute player, a native of the Andean highlands in Peru or Bolivia. Thus, the Chicana/o indigenous experience, Vasquez seems to imply, is not only connected to the struggles of the U.S. laboring classes, but is also mirrored in the history of colonization suffered by other native groups in the Americas.

Two years after the completion of *Memories of the Past*, Vasquez was commissioned to carry out another mural for the city, this time in Anaheim's Salvation Army Church. The result was another epic mural documenting twentieth-century Chicana/o history, appropriately entitled *Nuestra Experiencia en el Siglo Veinte* (*Our Experience in the Twentieth Century*; 1980). His experience with *Memories of the Past*, among other mural projects, had undoubtedly aided him in the perfection of multifigure arrangements and in the seamless incorporation of different visual sources into a unified composition. Nevertheless, his method of storytelling would remain virtually unchanged: Chicana/o history is told from left to right, starting from the Mexican Revolution and ending with the present era. As the story unfolds in rich colors and in stark realism, we witness the 1929 Stock Market Crash, the Zoot Suit Riots, the Vietnam War protests (including the untimely death of Ruben Salazar), the UFW demonstrations, and the inauguration of the Bracero Program, among other events. Of greatest importance to this mural, however, is the way Vasquez approaches Indigenist themes within the Chicana/o historical tapestry he constructed here. In the Mexican Revolution panel (Figure 2.11), the figures of Zapata and the brothers Flores Magón return; Ricardo stands close to the foreground and Enrique excitedly addresses a mass of indigenous peasants rallying under the banner of land reform. Disenchanted and disenfranchised by the unfulfilled promises of the Revolution, this group then migrates north in search of a better life. What awaits them there, however, are the harsh realities of the United States' overdeveloped industrialism, signified here by the smokestack-filled map of the United States, and the back-breaking labor in the Southwest's agricultural business. The indigeneity of this mass of figures is accentuated by their connection to land; in Mexico they participated in the Revolution's land redistribution campaigns, and in the United States they were drafted into farmwork. Within the political imagination of *el movimiento*, the organic connection to land was a critical function of Chicanas/os' indigeneity. According to "El Plan Espiritual de Aztlán," the territory of Aztlán "belongs to those who plant the seeds, water the fields, and gather the crops and not to the foreign Europeans." Though the relationship to land defined the indigenous consciousness during the Chicano Movement, it also contributed to Chicanas/os' oppression; they were forced to work the land, yet were not entitled to its benefits.

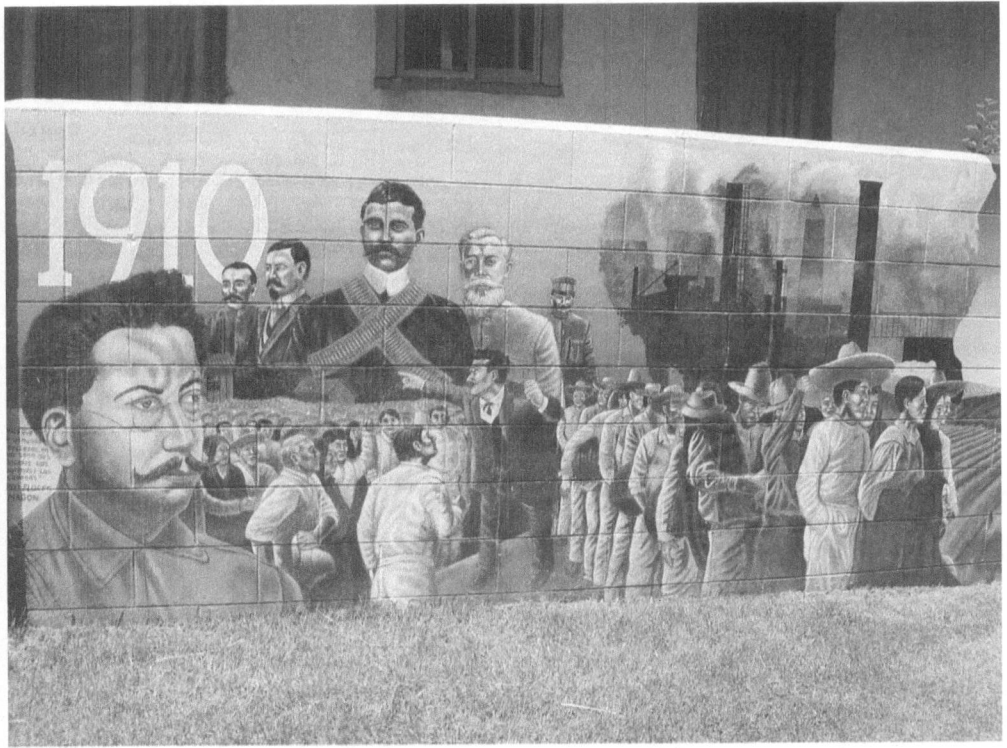

FIGURE 2.11. Emigdio Vasquez, © 1980, *Nuestra Experiencia en el Siglo Veinte*, detail, Salvation Army, Anaheim, California. Repainted in 1996. Courtesy of Emigdio Vasquez.

The monumentality with which Vasquez depicts these figures signifies the artist's refusal to represent indigenous and mestiza/o farmworkers as simply abject victims of oppression, as Shifra Goldman points out:

> Considering the attitude toward working-class themes in the United States and the prevalence of racism that made the Mexican peoples either stereotyped or invisible in U.S. history, [Emigdio Vasquez's figures] correspondingly attain a solid presence with great dignity and singularity. For the artist, no further social comment is required.[55]

The other Indigenist motif that Vasquez elaborated in *Nuestra Experiencia* emerges in the panel on the 1930s. Here Vasquez returns to a familiar theme, namely, the visual citation of David Alfaro Siqueiros's crucified Indian from the Los Angeles mural *La América Tropical*. Six years earlier, Vasquez had

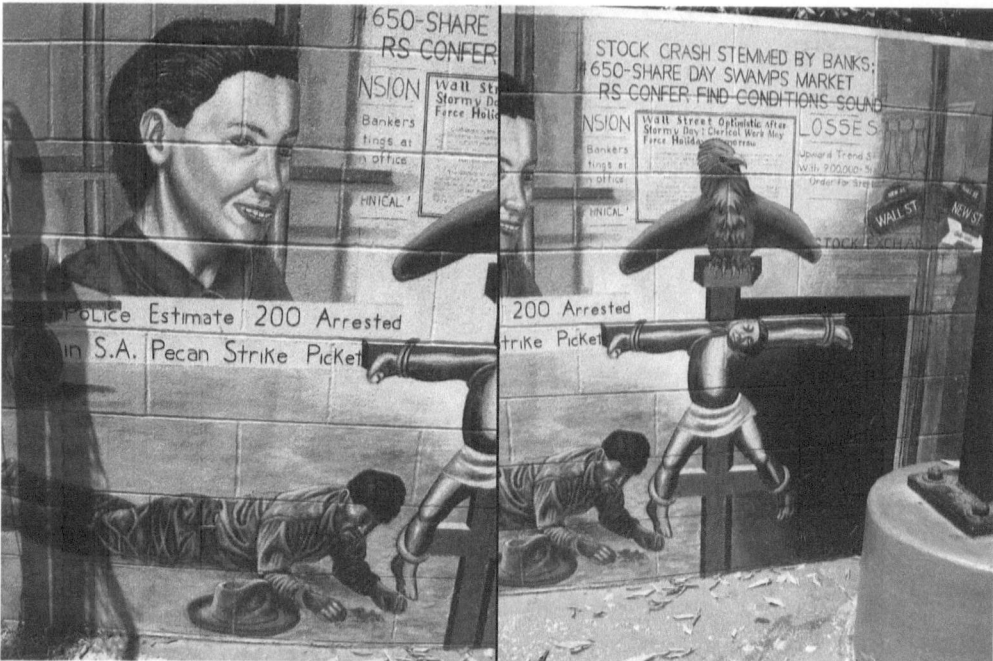

FIGURE 2.12. Emigdio Vasquez, © 1980, *Nuestra Experiencia en el Siglo Veinte*, detail, Salvation Army, Anaheim, California. Repainted in 1996. Courtesy of Emigdio Vasquez.

assisted Chicano artist Sergio O'Cadiz in the creation of the MEChA *Mural* along with other students from Santa Ana College, where the mural is located.[56] During that time, Vasquez realized the multivalent quality of Siqueiros's figure and found it particularly relevant to the Chicana/o experience. In *Nuestra Experiencia*, the artist places this now-legendary figure before a series of headlines announcing the Stock Market Crash of 1929. While the newspapers seem to focus on the effects of this event on the national economy, the artist puts greater emphasis on the consequences for the country's most vulnerable population, the working-class laborers. Adjacent to the crucified Indian we find the image of Emma Tenayuca, the celebrated labor activist from San Antonio, Texas, who organized pecan shellers in the 1930s (Figure 2.12). Tenayuca hailed from mixed Mexican and Native American background and thus established a powerful bond with many of the workers she organized who shared a similar indigenous ancestry. Here, she is depicted inside a prison cell during one of her many arrests as a result of her activism. Directly below her, the newspaper headlines read "Police Estimate

200 Arrested in S.A. Pecan Strike Picket." As a contrast to the cold and mat-ter-of-fact tone of these headlines, we see a striking Mexican worker with clearly discernible indigenous features who has been thrown to the ground bleeding, surely as a result of a violent confrontation with police during the pecan shellers' strikes. These three figures—the crucified Indian, Tenayuca, and the striking worker—are connected through their common experience of hardship but also through their inherent indigeneity. By grouping these together, Vasquez is also establishing historical connections between events that are not generally regarded as being related, namely the colonization of indigenous peoples and the abuse of the Mexican/Chicano proletarian worker. Here, the striking worker and the labor activist are presented as the modern reincarnation of the colonized and decimated Indian.

Conclusion

The Chicana/o art movement's role in nation building and Indigenist image making often provided muralists with a clear-cut directive for their creative activities. The spirit of collectivity that fueled the Chicano Movement's po-litical agenda gave many artists a meaningful purpose to their pursuits as cul-tural producers; they were not just doing art for art's sake, but they were re-sponding to a call to serve their community. This impetus behind their work at times endowed their murals with a certain degree of uniformity. The recur-rence of certain motifs or subject matter often made it seem as if Chicana/o muralism in California was unified in its ideological and iconographic goals. But the urban setting of these artworks made mural making susceptible to various other influences that circulated within these spheres, thus disrupt-ing any possibility for true uniformity and homogeneity. Graffiti was per-haps the most important influence that affected the production of murals in California, sometimes with negative consequences, but more often with positive and enriching outcomes. In Chapter 3, I document the often tense and confrontational, but also intimate and dialectic, relationship between graffiti and murals. In spite of the many differences that separate these two urban visual expressions, this chapter reveals how both forms often adopted Indigenist iconography in their respective visual repertoires.

CHAPTER THREE

Graffiti and Murals

Urban Culture and Indigenist Glyphs

The *plaqueasos* are beginning to be designated by some Chicano activists and artists as indigenous expressions of *Chicanismo.* Outdoor
murals in barrios, originally an attempt to cover and discourage graffiti, are now appropriating the street writer's techniques, symbols and
verbal content to design walls mimicking the vigor of street writing.

SALLY R. ROMOTSKY AND JERRY ROMOTSKY
"Plaqueaso on the Wall," 1975

The "Problem" of Murals and Graffiti

It should come as no surprise that Chicana/o muralism emerged in the
same spaces where graffiti, tagging, throw-ups, and *plaqueasos/placas*
were and continue to be prominent in the urban landscapes of California.
Though community muralism, Chicana/o Indigenism, and graffiti are creative expressions that have operated more or less independently of one another, this chapter explores the contested site where all three intersect in
the urban spaces of California. Given that these three currents were sharing
the same spaces and were being produced by similar communities, it stands
to reason that they would encounter one another at various junctions. This
chapter is also dedicated to examining the complex relationship between
Chicana/o graffiti and muralism, as well as the Indigenist aesthetics that
influenced, to varying degrees, many mural and graffiti practitioners in California. While I do not argue for a direct historical connection between
graffiti calligraphy and indigenous glyphs, I do maintain that both forms
explore the uncertain territory between image and text and offer alternative aesthetics to the Western canon that many Chicana/o artists sought.
While Euro-American culture established clear demarcations between text
and image, graffiti represented one of the first artistic movements in the
Americas since the indigenous preconquest periods that took text back into

the realm of the aesthetic. This interstitial territory that both graffiti writers and muralists traversed necessarily posed a challenge to the status quo. Ivor L. Miller, author of *Aerosol Kingdom* (2002), argued that graffiti represented "the idea of constructing an identity in opposition to the state and the consumer culture; and the idea that resistance through cultural production is reinforced with a consciousness of ancestral spiritual traditions."[1] Hence, the values at the core of graffiti's existence were not unlike those of community muralism.

Graffiti is a complex urban creative expression characterized by different criteria and fueled by varying degrees of motivation. Since its earliest forms, from the 1960s to the 1970s, graffiti has often been associated with youth gang culture because different groups or cliques would tag words, letters, numbers, or signs in public spaces, usually with spray paint or felt-tip markers, to stake their claim over a particular territory or neighborhood. In this way, they would make their presence known to local residents while also aggressively challenging prior claims by rival gangs. Gangs would also tag walls with "roll calls," that is, listings of the various members of any given gang or clique. Claims for social and physical space as well as group identity are important elements of gang-related graffiti, not unlike Chicana/o indigenous murals themselves, even though they functioned in significantly different ways. The complex system of symbols produced by gangs was not unlike the heraldic tradition in Europe of creating coats of arms, Marcos Sánchez-Tranquilino argues: "[This tradition] served *barrio* calligraphers as a discursive model for displaying what was common to both heraldry and *placas*, namely, the public display of kinship ties, corporate liaisons, territorial ownership (or dominance), and collective strength."[2] Jerry Romotsky and Sally Romotsky further argued that another related European tradition taggers adopted was the use of old English script: "Perhaps the alphabet most generally admired . . . is old English lettering. The style conveys dignity and respect."[3] Through their adoption of this type of visual vocabulary, gangs were seeking to legitimize their group identity and informal youth memberships within the public sphere.

Many graffiti scholars like Miller and Joe Austin, author of *Taking the Train* (2001), also locate the origins of graffiti in the civil rights movement during the 1960s, especially on the East Coast: "Radicalized youth of color had an especially strong presence in the city, particularly the Black Panthers and the Young Lords [Puerto Rican nationalist organization], who were active in many of the neighborhoods the writers called home."[4] Nevertheless, starting in the late 1960s on the East Coast and the mid-1980s on the West

Coast, graffiti began to increasingly operate independently of gang culture. Though gang graffiti continued to exist and develop, this new era of street writing saw the emergence of what came to be known as hip-hop or crew graffiti, in part influenced by the growing visibility and importance of rap music and dancing. Urban youth would now come together in crews where collective identity and social affiliations were defined solely by "getting up," in other words, by the practice of graffiti as an urban art form. Austin argued that the social organization of graffiti crews was an essentially hybrid one, "combining the informal organization of a peer group, the shared-goal orientation of a sports team, and the collective identity and protective functions of a gang."[5] Chicana/o muralism, which has existed simultaneously with both gang and crew graffiti, has been directly and indirectly affected by these two forms of public art and expression, although the relationship between the two has not always been harmonious.

The criminalization of graffiti and connection with gang culture has generally prevented some Chicana/o muralists from fully identifying with the practice. Even though many muralists recruited gang members and taggers for the creation of murals, they often distanced themselves from the lifestyles associated with graffiti. Graffiti artists like L.A.'s Man One, however, cite the media as the most significant agent responsible for the criminalization of graffiti:

It was in the early nineties, FOX Channel 11 did an undercover investigation and they came up with this term called "tag banging" that didn't exist. But what they started promoting on the TV was that there were kids doing graffiti and they had guns. Before that nobody had ever heard of "tag banging," not even us. It was a completely made-up term, but the kids believed the hype. They saw kids with guns and spray cans on TV. After that, I remember, people started getting shot in the streets, within weeks of that airing. Kids started thinking they had to carry guns; gangs started thinking graffiti writers are encroaching and they have guns.[6]

Media reports such as these not only further tainted the image of graffiti in the eyes of the general public, but also fostered an atmosphere of hostility between taggers, gang members, and muralists. This criminalization possessed a deeper history beyond damaging media reports. Joe Austin argues that the idea of graffiti as a "social problem" was the result of a long and sustained history of criminalization around the presence of working-class youth of color within urban settings: "Amid the rapid economic, demographic, social, and cultural transitions taking place in New York City and the nation during the early 1960s, fears of urban youths intensified as the spectacular visibility of youths within public spaces became strongly associated with the 'urban crisis.'"[7]

Nevertheless, the way many muralists commanded the urban space was clearly similar to that of graffiti writers staking claims over street territory. For those Chicana/o artists who did recognize graffiti as an influence and as a viable form of public creative expression, this art form best communicated the visceral and harsh nature of the Chicana/o urban experience. Issues that were connected with the practice of graffiti making or tagging were also at the core of Chicana/o subjectivity as a whole; concerns about criminality, legality, and ownership affected the community on a day-to-day basis. Muralism and graffiti alike became art forms that functioned as reactions and rebellions against the urban surroundings.[8] The stances of resistance, defiance, and radicalism that defined the early Chicana/o arts movement were indeed partly borrowed from the same postures inherent in graffiti practices, as Chicano artist David Avalos explained:

There's some social defiance as in the street graffiti tradition, but mainly the mural is a device to circumvent the gatekeepers of culture, the galleries and museums, and go directly to the people for acceptance; to serve, to inspire, to inculcate Chicano pride.[9]

In many ways, the knowledge about and sensitivity toward the urban environment that graffiti writers possessed facilitated muralists' own engagement in barrio and neighborhood life. Graffiti writers and muralists both understood that, as folklorist Sojin Kim explained, "neighborhoods are not simply geographic units, [but] they are also social, emotional, and stylistic environments."[10] Yet taggers and graffiti writers like Posh One often criticized the practice of muralism for not recognizing its roots in graffiti and for disavowing these.

Marcos Sánchez-Tranquilino has been quick to point out that starting in the early 1970s, graffiti and muralism were defined as two distinct and opposing systems of visual signification; the former represented the negative and even violent elements within Chicana/o youth culture, whereas the latter embodied the legitimization of Mexican culture in the United States as well as the community's feelings of collective civic pride. Sánchez-Tranquilino has openly denounced the dichotomous language that emerged in discussions about graffiti and muralism, a language that has often forced Chicana/o artists into two ideological camps. One camp argued that muralism was the natural outgrowth of graffiti, thus implying that the public mural was the more evolved and developed art form of the two.[11] Art historian Alan Barnett also subscribed to this Darwinian argument, insisting that the distinction between the two was characterized by a development from a symbol-based visual language (graffiti) to a narrative-based aesthetic (muralism):

> The distance in figuration from graffiti to murals is a gradual transition from bare initials through increasingly elaborated lettering to symbols—like hearts, stars, and peace signs—to representational parts of the human body—fists, heads, genitals—or other objects of interest like cars, and finally to detailed scenes, which themselves range from symbolic to narrative.... What begins as graffiti frequently concludes as a mural.[12]

Such an argument is difficult to maintain when we see that graffiti continued to exist and develop as an art form after the emergence of community murals.[13] While they still functioned as distinct artistic currents, the individual histories of murals and graffiti continually intersected and mutually influenced one another. The other and perhaps less conservative camp regarded murals and graffiti as symbiotic and interdependent parts of public urban aesthetics, thus refusing to privilege one over the other.[14] The anxiety stemming from the role that graffiti played in the development of Chicana/o muralism had a lot to do with the ideologies of the agencies and institutions that sponsored early mural projects. City governments, schools, and local barrio businesses would often commission Chicana/o muralists to beautify the environment and to prevent or discourage graffiti on public and private property, thereby establishing muralism as the *remedy* to the graffiti "problem."[15] By the 1980s, law-enforcement agencies like the Los Angeles Police Department (LAPD) had internalized the difference between graffiti and muralism to the point of stating that the only form of wall painting they didn't consider illegal were the "city-organized and approved murals."[16] This atmosphere often created tense relationships between graffiti artists and muralists, who often worked in close proximity to one another. L.A. graffiti writer Man One felt many muralists upheld these distinctions:

> To me, when I started doing [graffiti] professionally, I considered myself a muralist the whole time. I just thought, "I'm on the street, I'm painting, so I'm a muralist." Not only that, "I'm a Chicano and I'm painting in the streets, and I'm doing murals, so I'm a Chicano artist." That's what I thought and then I started meeting Chicano muralists,

and they didn't think the same thing. They would give us attitudes. They didn't consider what we were doing art and they didn't consider what we were doing murals. They considered it graffiti. They were the muralists, they were the professionals, and we were just kids doing whatever on the streets. There was no respect for us as artists, as muralists, not even as Latino/Chicano artists. They would see us just as graffiti kids. I got that for a long time, and it was weird because I looked up to a lot of these guys.[17]

Though artists who felt the need to legitimize their work and city authorities who continually sought to regulate the practice of public art both drew distinctions between muralism and graffiti, in everyday practice the genres constantly morphed into one another. The emergence of the Chicano Movement and its accompanying visual arts component in the 1970s further undermined the difference between graffiti and muralism, with the former becoming more politicized and the latter becoming increasingly daring and audacious. Additionally, artists such as Man One would later concede that, as the twentieth century came to a close, muralists began to recognize the importance of graffiti, crediting artists like Judy Baca and Ernesto de la Loza with reaching out to graffiti writers and building bridges between the two communities of artists.[18] Muralists also found themselves being victimized by the same mechanisms of social control that sought to eradicate and censor graffiti, as Esteban Villa recounts: "I've lost about one hundred murals that have been destroyed by the government, by the city. They even use Chicanos to clean up the neighborhoods of graffiti."[19] Villa has even been charged with violation of Executive Order 113 (Vandalism Against State Property) for repainting murals the city has covered up. Nevertheless, Susan Phillips, in her groundbreaking monograph *Wallbangin'* (1999), saw muralism as ultimately working against the interests of graffiti by "[pitting] neighborhood elements against each other."[20] Joe Austin concurred, arguing that while "writing [graffiti] was being cast as dangerous and demoralizing vandalism in local papers, the federal government was dispensing millions of dollars through the National Endowment for the Humanities for community murals in the same neighborhoods from which graffiti sprang."[21] Though muralism did often construct itself in opposition to graffiti, Phillips's and Austin's critiques of the supposedly divisive effects of muralism seem to overlook the organic relationship between these two art forms. Moreover, the fact that the city government and local business owners often commissioned Chicana/o murals to discourage graffiti did not necessarily mean that Chicana/o muralists saw themselves as complicit either with graffiti-abatement programs or with hegemonic systems of power. Furthermore, many muralists were subject to the same systems of social control and censorship that graffiti artists experienced, as Villa's testimony attests.

Image and Text: Indigenous Glyph and Graffiti Calligraphy

Graffiti scholar Ivor L. Miller argued that street writers took "the letter beyond its literary functions and into the realm of feelings and images," thus ritualizing "the alphabet, making it futuristic and primal, forging the letter into a verb."[22] Mayanist Adam Herring—speaking of a very different kind of visual imagery, namely, Maya glyphs and other images—posited that the beauty and intricacy of these visual signs was "a function of [the Mayas'] efforts to mediate the complicated world of experience with their own material and formal structure of things."[23] In both cases, we have two visual systems that not only produce a middle ground between image and text but also seek representations in art that speak to the subjectivity of feeling and experience. How to translate into images the angst, marginalization, isolation, but also exhilaration of the urban experience? Many Chicana/o artists resorted to graffiti or indigenous imagery as an alternative language to articulate the specificity of the Chicana/o urban experience. Both graffiti and indigenous imagery spoke of an urban subjectivity that fell outside dominant narratives or that connected urbanization to Eurocentric notions of progress and development. While many of the indigenous glyphs and images that influenced Chicana/o artists are connected with the rise of urban centers in preconquest Mesoamerican cultures, graffiti signaled an urbanism experienced primarily by youth of color. Consequently, both visual systems represented an alternative urban experience that told a different story from the discourses of progress that excluded Chicanas/os and other disenfranchised communities. These discourses of progress would eventually allow cityscapes to be taken over by corporate entities that would saturate the urban environment with monumental billboards and signs advertising consumer products, all within the realm of legality. Graffiti, then, functioned as an oppositional discourse that challenged and competed with the growing corporate aesthetics in the city. Street writers often argue that the reason why corporate billboards are legal forms of public display rests solely on the fact that companies *pay* for these spaces, thus making them socially acceptable, whether or not they meet with public or community approval.

While the graffiti influence on Chicana/o art emerged primarily from the artists' firsthand experience of growing up in barrios and neighborhoods where tagging and street writing was prevalent, these artists' interest in indigenous aesthetics emerged from the process of politicization connected to the

Chicano Movement. I would argue, however, that their familiarity with graffiti—whether these artists recognized its artistic merits or not—predisposed them to a greater sensitivity toward the visual dynamics of indigenous glyphs and symbols, particularly the ways in which these traversed the conflicted territories between text and image.

Moreover, the claims over territory that many graffiti taggings declare in many ways mirror Chicana/o artists' desire to reclaim Aztlán through the use of the public mural, as is discussed in Chapter 4. The insider codes deeply embedded in graffiti calligraphy—in other words, the limited legibility of these texts to a select few within the barrio or urban scene—were not unlike many Mesoamerican glyphs and texts that were created for an exclusive audience.[24] Jerry Romotsky and Sally Romotsky claimed that reading barrio calligraphy required a kind of street literacy in order to be understood: "Decoding graffiti requires one to interpret the symbols, the abbreviations, and the designs as well as the names and the terms in the plaqueasos."[25] Marcos Sánchez-Tranquilino further maintained that graffiti was indeed "visible to everyone but 'readable' only to a few," thus requiring a kind of "street intelligentsia" to decipher it.[26] When discussing Maya texts and glyphs, Michael Coe and Mark Van Stone explained that while inscriptions on public monuments were coded for widespread legibility among the Maya citizenry, ceramic texts reveal a "subtlety and complexity" probably reserved for a political or intellectual elite. Though most Maya glyph writing—whether it was on ceramic vessels or monuments—was state sanctioned and sponsored, unlike present-day graffiti, the subsequent conquest and colonization thrust indigenous art forms like these into the marginalizing sphere of the "Other" or the "exotic."

But graffiti's parallels to indigenous writing had to do with the way in which both possessed the qualities of text and image. As a matter of fact, graffiti practitioners are usually referred to as "writers" and "artists" interchangeably. Likewise, Mesoamerican scholar Dorie Reents-Budet has observed that "in all Mayan languages there is no linguistic or semantic differentiation among the words for painting, drawing and writing; all are referred to by the verb stem ts'ib."[27] Adam Herring, in his analysis of Maya aesthetics between AD 600 and AD 800, argued that "'painting,' 'representation,' and 'writing'—visual work, visual representation, and visuality put to work for linguistic ends—constituted discrete if overlapping domains of signification."[28] The use of glyphs, which are visual symbols that impart information nonverbally while also taking on the properties of both text and image, was characteristic of Mesoamerican writing systems, as George Cowgill states: "Many Aztec glyphs are pictographic or ideographic, using literal renderings of objects linked to particular concepts, but others employ the rebus principle" (i.e., the representation of a picture of one thing to stand for a word or syllable that has a similar sound).[29] Glyphs contributed to the ideographic nature of writing among the Aztec and Maya, for example. While glyph scholars like William Gates argue that all forms of text probably "go back to an original pictograph of some kind," they also contend that in many contemporary societies, that relationship "no longer [has] any effect or value in the current usage."[30]

With graffiti text, where readability is often secondary to visual impact and design, we witness a writing system that seeks to either return to an imagelike state or just undermine the distinction between the two. Ivor Miller contends that graffiti writers' manipulation of words represented "the resistance by colonized people to redefine themselves by manipulating the rules and logic of the colonizer's language."[31] Joe Austin maintains that "the twisted, fractured or crumbled letters" of graffiti make the Western alphabet come alive and disintegrate at the same time, thus allowing letters to be "released from their duties as conventional carriers of meaning." Graffiti artists understood these "modifications" as a "sweeping cultural critique of the Western Great Tradition."[32] Crispin Sartwell, for his part, argues that graffiti writers are reacting against the historical connection between written text and the rise of systems of power. Hence, Sartwell continues, the extreme stylization of graffiti text points to a process of disintegration and fragmentation of the text, which represents the symbolic destruction of those power structures.[33] Ultimately, graffiti sought to reverse the dynamics of power embedded in language and thus emerged in some quarters as a language of protest and defiance. Esteban Villa, for instance, used graffiti in his silkscreen print entitled *Ruben's Graffiti* (1988) to commemorate the slain *Los Angeles Times* reporter Ruben Salazar because, as Villa later explained, "he was a writer, and graffiti is a form of writing."[34] In doing so, the artist compared Salazar's politically engaged and Chicana/o-conscious brand of journalistic writing with graffiti's challenge to mainstream authority.

Susan Phillips, while not likening graffiti to Mesoamerican glyphs, also understood the conflicted space between text and image that graffiti occupied:

> As a medium of communication, graffiti lies somewhere between art and language. Words become signifiers, solutions, and slogans; that is, they cease to be individual words but become symbols and images, which communicate at a variety of levels.[35]

Man One, while not acknowledging Mesoamerican and non-European writing as an influence on his work, did find himself captivated by the way graffiti aestheticized the practice of writing: "To me [the appeal of graffiti] was giant letters on the side of a train. That was incredible to me. I had never seen anyone doing letter forms on that scale. Now the subject matter was letter forms.... To me the most unique thing about graffiti was that the letter forms were now the artwork."[36] Other artists, however, did directly or indirectly acknowledge the connection between graffiti and indigenous glyphs beyond the mere image/text dynamic. For example, Charles "Chaz" Bojórquez, who came to prominence in the contemporary art scene for his use of graffiti, also made recurrent allusions in his work to indigenous and non-European writing systems, which he had studied through various personal travels throughout the world.[37] Esteban Villa, a preeminent member of the artistic collective the Royal Chicano Air Force (RCAF), for his part, found that ancient hieroglyphic writing was very much like graffiti.[38] L.A. graffiti artist Posh One likewise became attracted to Mesoamerican texts and images because of what he saw as the similarity between the two: "The biggest similarity [between graffiti and indigenous glyphs and figures] is the simplicity of the characters yet the complexity of the language. It's amazing how much information is there, and if you looked at it without knowing what it is, it would say nothing to you, much like a [graffiti] piece does.... It's a language that needs to be learned."[39]

As many scholars in Chicana/o studies can attest, the study of native cultures of the Americas, in particular preconquest Mesoamerican civilizations, profoundly affected Chicana/o cultural production starting with the 1960s. Indigenous texts about the creation of the earth and the cosmos, as well as texts on pre-Columbian history, were particularly profound for Chicana/o artists and activists who were understanding their own contemporary history through an indigenous lens. But indigeneity also meant looking inward at the cultural capital inside Chicana/o spaces and social spheres, in other words, searching for what was *indigenous* to the Mexican community within a U.S. geographical context, which included urban areas. Graffiti was and continues to be a critical component of that urban indigeneity that Chicana/o artists were also celebrating.

Graffiti and Gender

Graffiti did much to loosen the definitions of public art, but the gendered dynamics and inequities that characterized the mural movement remained intact in this medium, too. Though issues of gender and the participation of women in the Chicana/o mural scene is discussed in Chapter 5, it is pertinent to mention here that the practice of graffiti has long been regarded as "a male-dominated sport," to borrow an expression used by Posh One during an interview with me. Other artists I spoke to agreed with this assessment: "[Graffiti] is very macho and jockish," Fred Alvarado lamented when discussing the scene with me. He further argued that fierce competition between crews and individual artists is a characteristic cultural trait of street writing, which tends to attract boys more than girls. Although women have managed to make their mark on the history of California community muralism despite all the odds stacked against them, the contribution of women to the West Coast *graffiti* scene continues to go largely unrecognized and is virtually invisible. The publication in 2006 of *Graffiti Women* by Nicholas Ganz has made an effort to correct this oversight by featuring the work of Chicana/Latina street writers Jerk and Luna, both active in Los Angeles.[40] Nevertheless, most of the available scholarship on graffiti puts greater emphasis on the male street writers, often relegating the work by women to a few paragraphs or sentences—if they are mentioned at all. My own attempts to identify women in the scene proved utterly fruitless. When I asked Man One whether there are many women in Los Angeles practicing graffiti, his response came in the form of a justification:

> There are women doing it, [but] not that many. I always tell people the reason is because L.A. is such a violent city, such a rough city to do anything in it, let alone go out there in the middle of the night. You got to deal with gangs, you got to deal with cops, you got to deal with other graffiti artists. ... There's cameras, there's gangs, there's cops, there's helicopters, there's everything. Women don't necessarily make it in this city. To go out there in the middle of the night, it's rough for a girl unless she's with some guys.[41]

The danger in the streets is a justification that many other male graffiti artists have used to explain the absence of women in the scene. In the 1980s, sociologist Richard Lachmann interviewed twenty-five graffiti artists in New York City. When asked about women, one of his informants replied the following: "You got to get into the yards [where the trains are parked at night] by going under and over those barbed wire fences. They have dogs loose. Women get scared and can't keep up."[42] Lachmann further observed that many graffiti artists refuse to train women in the craft of street writing, which cuts them off from a critical component of graffiti culture and learning, namely, the apprenticeship system. Unfortunately, the discourses that equate public space with maleness are deeply ingrained in California in both its graffiti and mural cultures, but street writing has emerged as a cultural practice that is particularly hostile to women. Without dismissing the legitimate danger that women do face in the streets, in particular with regard to police harassment and surveillance, it is undoubtedly the male-centered culture of graffiti and its accompanying scholarship that has marginalized women practitioners. At this juncture, however, I will limit myself to issuing a public call for more research and intellectual work on the participation of women, Chicanas or otherwise, in the graffiti scene, particularly in California.

Graffiti Influence on Early Chicana/o Murals: Los Angeles

It is no coincidence that Los Angeles would become a major mural site, given that for over half a century, it has also been a critical location for graffiti production. Susan Phillips noted that the city has been labeled "the graffiti capital of the world."[43] One of the earliest murals in the city to incorporate graffiti aesthetics into its visual program was Willie Herrón's *Quetzalcoatl* (1971; Figure 3.1), located on the back of Hidalgo Market in City Terrace, East Los Angeles. At the time he created this piece, Herrón was a young, multifaceted, yet largely untrained artist whose creativity was fueled primarily by his experiences as an urban Chicano. For him, the murals he created in the early 1970s were meant to communicate ideas to the resident communities, which included local gangs.[44] He saw his mural work from this time as a great departure from that of his Chicana/o contemporaries, many of whom were hired or commissioned to do murals with the purpose of discouraging or replacing graffiti:

> At that time there was throughout the community this anti-graffiti [attitude], which is still common today. . . . I was being criticized by the art world. I was criticized by other artists for the most part for incorporating graffiti rather than approaching muralism as a replacement [for] graffiti. Artists were getting hired in the early seventies to do murals so they could get rid of graffiti. I did the total opposite. I embraced graffiti, and graffiti became part of my work because I respected the voice of the community. And I added to their voice. I didn't get rid of their voice and say, "My voice is superior."[45]

Herrón's mural work from the early seventies embodied, according to Marcos Sánchez-Tranquilino, "a critical rethinking of graffiti as solely signifying vandalism, which in turn has led to a deeper understanding of the relationship between so-called Chicano graffiti and Chicano murals."[46] As

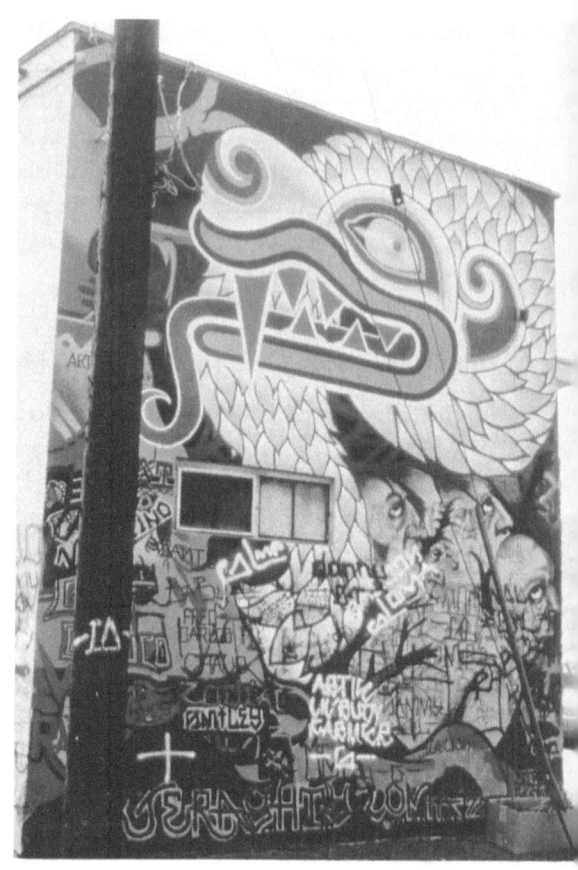

FIGURE 3.1. Willie Herrón,
© 1971, *Quetzalcoatl*, mural, City
Terrace, Los Angeles, California.
Courtesy of Willie Herrón.

Jerry and Sally Romotsky recount, Herrón visualized Quetzalcoatl's sinuous form emerging from the crowded and baroque graffiti *placas* tagged on the back of his grandparents' bakery in City Terrace.[47] Herrón rendered this Mesoamerican deity with a limited palette of greens and browns because, as he later explained, he had few colors at his disposal at that time. Nevertheless, the two-color scheme of the mural echoed the muted hues that characterized much of the graffiti texts of Southern California in the early 1970s. His emphasis on flatness, two-dimensionality, and boldness in design further complemented the surrounding environment. Below Quetzalcoatl's coiling body, we find the anguished faces of barrio residents who look up at the deity with expressions of fear but also awe. The relationship between this god and the anonymous figures below him is unclear. Is he protecting them? Are they running away from him? Perhaps both, given that the distinction between an aggressor and a protector is often blurred in the barrio. Unlike many of his fellow muralists who were using Indigenist motifs, Herrón saw the aesthetic of *Quetzalcoatl* as being complicit with and even dependent on the preexisting graffiti text that was already up on the wall.[48] He understood that murals and graffiti were sharing the same urban spaces and thus there needed to be a relationship of mutual respect between the two. As a matter of fact, soon after completing the mural, he invited local youth to incorporate *placas* into the overall design. *Quetzalcoatl* was then dedicated to Geraghty Loma, one of the most visible gangs in City Terrace.[49]

The choice of using Quetzalcoatl as the mural's central figure speaks to both the Indigenist and the graffiti aesthetics that informed this work by Herrón. Quetzalcoatl was indeed an important figure in Chicano nationalist thought and, as such, was a common sight in community murals, as previously discussed in Chapter 2 of this book. But the simple forms that composed this figure in Mesoamerican representations attracted graffiti writers and crews as well. Quetzalcoatl's popular though disputed representation in Teotihuacán's Temple of the Plumed Serpent was also well known among taggers. The basic shapes that make up this figure lent themselves well to the gestural quality of a lot of graffiti designs. Furthermore, Quetzalcoatl's mythic role in the creation of the world was also critical for muralists and taggers alike, who were concerned with the physical and cultural survival of their communities, whether these were gangs or barrio residents as a whole. But like the role that graffiti played in muralist aesthetics, the role of Quetzalcoatl in indigenous history was equally contested. His figure emerges quite prominently in colonial discourse as well where Spanish chroniclers of the conquest claim that the Aztecs saw the arrival of Hernán Cortés as the second coming of Quetzalcoatl and thus were ready and willing to cede the center of power to him. But the serpent god, as Davíd Carrasco explains, was also associated with the rise of urban centers throughout Mesoamerica.[50] He further stipulates that indigenous ruling classes often used the figure or symbol of Quetzalcoatl to legitimize their entitlement to power. These connections to urbanism and power through a process of legitimization were also at the core of the work by graffiti writers and muralists, and naturally made Quetzalcoatl an attractive figure.

Shortly after creating *Quetzalcoatl*, Herrón painted *The Wall That Cracked Open* (1972; Figure 3.2), located on the back of the bakery adjoining Hidalgo Market. The artist depicted an illusionistic crack in the wall that revealed various faces trying to break out of the mural's confines; these included, as described by Marcos Sánchez-Tranquilino, "a gang-victimized bleeding young man, fighting youth, and a crying grandmother."[51] The most prominent

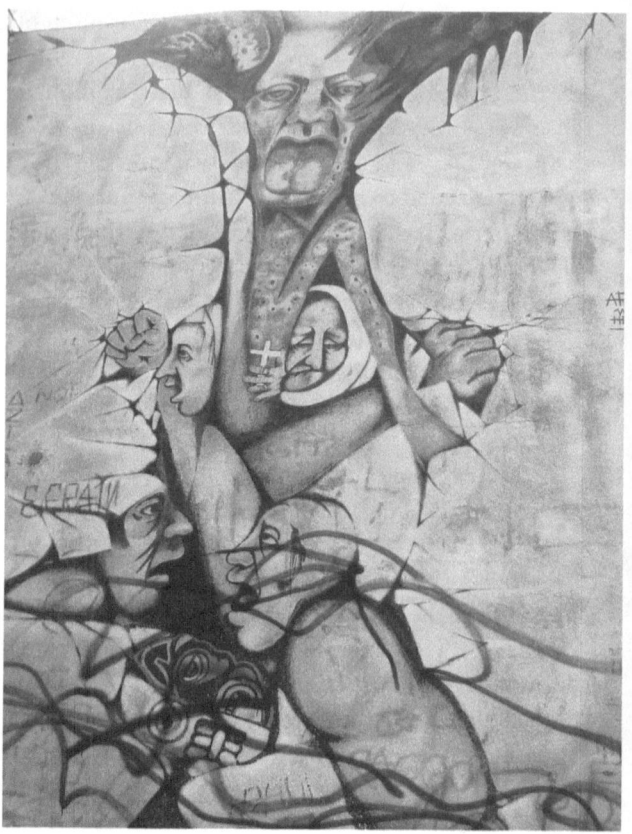

FIGURE 3.2. Willie Herrón, © 1972, *The Wall That Cracked Open*, mural, City Terrace, Los Angeles, California. Courtesy of Willie Herrón.

figure, however, emerges at the top of the composition, and it is a man whose facial expression reflects feelings of despair and anguish, as Herrón himself later explained: "[This figure] looks totally diseased and totally plagued and his tongue's hanging out and it's like he's exhausted and he's tired . . . by everything that has produced him that he almost lacks regurgitation. He almost lacks something coming out of his mouth. It's dry."[52] The highly emotional and urgent facial expressions of the mural's figures are heightened by a sort of Indigenist vanitas symbol placed on the lower portion of the composition: a life/death mask from Tlatilco, an ancient pre-Aztec site near Mexico City. This mask/skull with Mesoamerican features is present to remind the viewer of the fleeting nature of life. Symbolizing the duality of life and death, this particular motif is there to trace the connection between the lives of contemporary Chicanas/os and those of their Mesoamerican ancestors, but also to express a desire for the continuation of the cycles of life in the barrio.

Like with *Quetzalcoatl*, the mural's location, the aforementioned back alley in City Terrace, established a direct connection between muralism and the creative expressions of graffiti artists, or taggers. Furthermore, Herrón created his composition around the preexisting graffiti calligraphy on that wall, and, as a symbol of respect, subsequent taggers inscribed their *placas* around Herrón's design, thereby establishing an informal collaboration between the two. The combination of urgency, indigeneity, and graffiti aesthetics that characterized this mural brought together visual discourses that, in spite of being very much part of Chicana/o culture as a whole, had been segregated from one another.

The artist also painted *The Wall That Cracked Open* as a reaction to his younger brother's brutal stabbing in that very alley, allegedly at the hands of a rival gang, Big Hazard. The mural, then, was the result of the artist's visceral reaction to this near tragedy. Though Herrón's brother survived the attack, the themes of death and despair saturated the mural. In an almost trancelike state, he began to envision ideas for the mural shortly after he and his brother Val found their wounded and bleeding younger brother, John, in the same alley where Willie had painted *Quetzalcoatl*:

> I noticed that he had several ice pick wounds in his neck. . . . [When the ambulance arrived,] I got in and I rode with him and the paramedics to the General Hospital. And on my way, I started to sketch. I had my sketch pad with me. I know it sounds corny and all that. I'm an artist and I carry a sketch pad around. But I flipped it open and just started to sketch and stuff. And I was really influenced by all my senses [, which] were like on high gear and they were like this huge vacuum just sucking everything in. The sound of my brother breathing out loud. I would turn back and see him with the mask and still see him without the shirt and stuff. I just saw all these little holes. And there were like membranes coming out of these little holes that were like sort of—without getting really graphic—I could see in the little membranes like the little bit of blood collected in them.[53]

Later that evening, while the gut-wrenching emotions of the event were still fresh in his psyche, Herrón went home to pick up his paints and returned to the scene of the crime to create *The Wall That Cracked Open* right above the location of the attack.

The Wall That Cracked Open was indeed an unconventional mural for its time due to the artist's use of graffiti aesthetics and to the boldness of its visual vocabulary. But Herrón's unorthodox approach to muralism proved to be controversial, even more than two decades after its creation. In 1999, the mural became the target of the Los Angeles Department of Public Works Graffiti Abatement Program, a city initiative that sought to refurbish the urban environment by ridding it of "vandalistic" effacement such as graffiti. The city assured artists that legitimate artwork such as community murals would be spared. But sometime in the late spring or early summer of 1999, this mural was covered up with gray paint. All the evidence pointed to county contractors associated with the Abatement Program as the responsible parties. Though they denied any involvement, Valerie Hill, supervisor of the program, explained their rationale for judging what is up on a wall: "What I consider a mural may be different to what someone else considers a mural. When I see something covered with graffiti, the historical value is gone to me."[54] The Graffiti Abatement Program put the city in the troublesome position of deciding which wall designs and markings possessed artistic or historical value. Herrón sued the city for the damages done to his work and was awarded a generous financial compensation to repaint *The Wall That Cracked Open*. Battling with the city of Los Angeles and repainting his mural, however, made him feel, as he would later remark, "like my brother got stabbed all over again."[55] Unlike most Chicana/o murals, *The Wall That Cracked Open* hovered within that uncertain territory between muralism and graffiti and, consequently, between established artistic practices and street youth culture.

As in Los Angeles, the city-sponsored anti-graffiti programs in San Diego were equally if not more derisive and virulent. The surveillance systems put in place to discourage and criminalize graffiti have functioned in many ways as an extension of the systems of control that police border crossings and hunt down undocumented immigrants. The city even maintains a Web site where users can log in to report "illegal graffiti" activity, thus encouraging the public at large to become vigilantes of a sort. In spite of this atmosphere, or perhaps because of it, San Diego has emerged as an important site of Chicana/o/Latina/o public art. The mural environment known as Chicano Park emerged in large part as a reaction to the city's increasingly oppressive policies against Mexican/Chicana/o communities. Though Chicano Park is discussed in greater detail in Chapter 4, it is relevant here to point out that the spontaneity, looseness, and creative abandon that characterized the early stages of mural production there reflected the same spirit that informed graffiti aesthetics, including the practice of "bombing" walls often enacted by taggers. Salvador Torres, a Chicano artist and community activist at the time, said that those early murals were "done spontaneously; we exploded onto the walls,"[56] while another participating Chicano artist, Guillermo Aranda, declared that "permission or not, we were going to

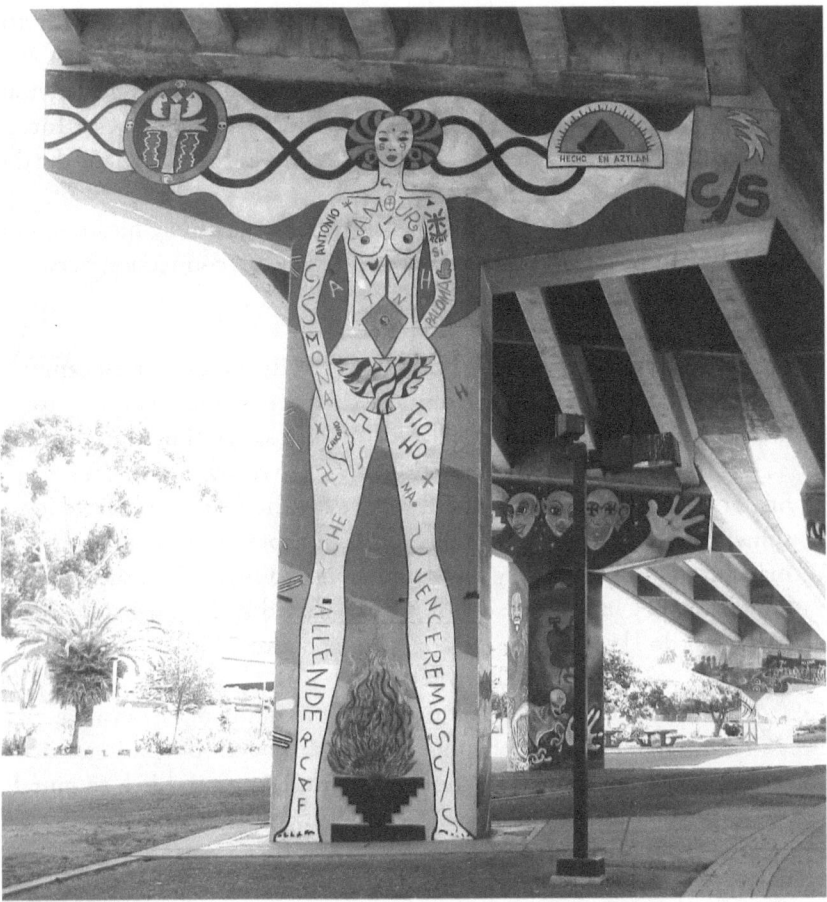

FIGURE 3.3. Esteban Villa and Ricardo Favela, © 1974, *Mujer Cósmica/Cosmic Woman*, mural, Chicano Park, San Diego, California. Courtesy of Esteban Villa.

paint."[57] While the methods of mural making at the site resembled graffiti creative strategies, few murals in Chicano Park displayed the direct stylistic and iconographic influence of the taggings and *plaqueasos* that also defined San Diego's urban environment. An exception to this trend, however, was Esteban Villa and Ricardo Favela's mural *Mujer Cósmica/Cosmic Woman* (1974; Figure 3.3), which, in many ways epitomized the coming together of muralism, Indigenism, and graffiti. Villa and Favela, along with other members of RCAF, had been invited to participate in the mural initiatives taking place in Chicano Park shortly after the park had been taken over by Barrio Logan residents from the city.[58] José Montoya, one of the other founding members of the RCAF, and Villa had been classmates with Salvador Torres while attending college in Oakland. When the three graduated with art degrees and teaching credentials in 1961, Torres returned to his hometown of San Diego, where he would eventually spearhead the mural initiative at Chicano Park. Given the college connection that the RCAF had with Torres, they were delighted with the invitation and stayed in San Diego for the duration of the mural work.

Like Herrón, Villa was one of the few artists on the early Chicana/o mural scene who understood the intimate and dialectic connection between graffiti and muralism:

> From a Chicano viewpoint, graffiti was the birth of murals. First came the graffiti and then came the murals. Then the murals went back to artistic graffiti. Now, in cities like New York, it's a legitimate art form. ... If it's done well, if it's done artistically, it can really turn into a very fine art form. To me, it's a desperate cry for the youth to believe in something, find a means of self-expression: spray can painting, felt marker pens, anything they could find, house paint, to paint the town. Graffiti is very important; I'm not embarrassed by it or ashamed of it ... [nor do I] try to hide it or tell people not to do it.[59]

Like other muralists, Villa did see an evolution taking place between graffiti and murals, but he did not conceptualize this development in a strictly linear fashion. Even though he thought graffiti had given birth to murals, the relationship did not end there. As graffiti became more elaborate, the influence on muralism persisted.

In *Mujer Cósmica* at Chicano Park, Villa and Favela filled the vertical space of the freeway pylon with the elongated body of an allegorical female figure they called "the cosmic woman," undoubtedly borrowed from Mexican philosopher José Vasconcelos's concept of the *raza cósmica,* which stipulated that the world's ethnicities would one day come together to form a "cosmic race." Indigenous peoples, Vasconcelos argued, would form a critical component of this *raza cósmica* and needed to be included in the new nation-state that emerged after the Revolution of 1910. For many artists and thinkers, the *mestizaje* that writers like Vasconcelos championed in their nationalist treatises provided models for Chicanas/os to incorporate indigenous identity into the heterogeneity that defined their experience. But aside from the indigeneity that underlies Villa and Favela's *Mujer Cósmica*, the artists were seeking to create a more universal symbol that was also steeped in European visual culture. "My mural was just a universal Mother Earth metaphor," Villa asserted. "Mother Earth, *la mujer*, has always been symbolically used by the French artists during the French Revolution, the Russians, and in just about every country," he continued. Earth goddess figures, of course, also figured prominently in Mesoamerican pantheons with Aztec deities like Coatlicue and Tlazolteotl.

What differentiated the *Mujer Cósmica* in Chicano Park from other earth goddess figures, however, are the various markings and inscriptions written all over her body, which Villa himself called tattoos. Tattoos were one of the many forms of creative expression that characterized Chicana/o youth culture, in particular gang culture. Tattoos were also closely related to the practice of graffiti among these young people; like graffiti, tattoos could also publicly demonstrate affiliation and loyalty to a particular neighborhood or clique, as Susan Phillips tells us: "Graffiti and tattooing often overlap in the contexts of their use—people use each medium to position individual and group identities at different scales toward different audiences."[60] The organic relationship that exists between the two practices speaks volumes about the blurred distinction between personal and public space in certain barrio settings. Villa and Favela use the personal space of this woman's body to make a public statement, and thus her body markings function both as tattoos and as graffiti tags. While I do not want to overlook the problematic and patriarchal implications of male muralists inscribing signs on a woman's body, it is also relevant to point out that the markings on her body are highly coded and encrypted, much like gang graffiti. Villa used this coded language in many of his murals to avoid the scrutiny and even censorship that city officials often imposed on muralists and public artists. Many of the codes and tags inscribed upon *Mujer Cósmica*'s body are references to the UFW and Communism, both of which were highly influential to his political consciousness at the time.[61] The numbers "5" and "6" on her face are coded representations of the hammer and sickle symbols associated with Communism (as a matter of fact, two lone sickles can be found, one on her neck and one on her left knee). The inscriptions "Tio Ho" (Uncle Ho) and "Allende," inscribed on her left thigh and right shin respectively, were references to Ho Chi Minh, founder of the Indochina Communist Party and former president of the Democratic Republic of Vietnam, and Salvador Allende, the socialist president of Chile who had been slain during a military coup just a year earlier. These codes were then complemented by the symbol of the UFW, placed between her feet, with its characteristic "stepped" eagle, which here also contains the burning blaze of Aztlán. Another stylized UFW eagle can be found covering the *Mujer Cósmica*'s pelvic region. While fairly coded, these symbols could still be recognized by a relatively observant and intuitive mainstream audience. Nevertheless, other codes in the mural required a more Chicana/o insider sensibility to crack. Villa and Favela's inclusion of the swastika on her right thigh reflected a trend among Chicano Park muralists to recover the Native American roots of this motif from its association with Nazi Germany. This was a practice borrowed from gang graffiti writers, who, according to Jerry and Sally Romotsky, "relate these decorations to pre-Columbian Mexican culture."[62] Both muralists and graffiti writers, however, tilt the motif slightly to one side so the arms of the swastika are in a diagonal position. Another common motif in both murals and graffiti is the "C/S" inscription, which in the *Mujer Cósmica* is located on the figure's right elbow and left ankle. "C/S" is, of course, an acronym for the expression *con safos* (with respect), originally used in Chicana/o gang graffiti but that later became popular among muralists and literary writers. "*Con safos* functions as a guardian to the inscription," Sally and Jerry Romotsky explained, "simultaneously protecting and challenging."[63] Indeed, *con safos* is an expression of self-protection often utilized by gang writers wishing to protect their tags from other gangs' *placas*. It also carries a warning with it, "same to you," in other words, those who deface, cross out, or disrespect a given tag or *placa* can expect a similar fate. For Chicana/o nationalists and radicals, *con safos* took on a larger metaphorical meaning; it signified the protection of Chicana/o culture from the forces of assimilation and hegemony but was also a challenge to U.S. dominant society to not deter the development of Chicana/o cultural nationalism. Villa and Favela's inclusion of the acronym in *Mujer Cósmica* symbolically protected the mural from effacement, but also proclaimed a sense of Chicana/o civic pride through a deeply coded insider language.

In spite of the influence of artists like Willie Herrón and Esteban Villa within the Chicana/o arts movement, the practices of graffiti and muralism continued to function as two distinct political factions within the public art scene during the early to mid-1970s. As muralists, all Herrón and Villa could do was to acknowledge and embrace the influence and importance of graffiti in their work, yet the fact that they took concerted efforts to do so also underscored the sustained cultural and political abyss that separated the two art forms at the time. A number of events and phenomena in California in the mid seventies and beyond would, however, bring graffiti and muralism closer together while at the same time disrupt time-honored definitions and established boundaries between the two practices. What seemed to persist, however, was the recognition on the part of some muralists and street writers that graffiti, like indigenous glyphs, existed within the aesthetic borderland between text and image.

Los Four at LACMA and Charles "Chaz" Bojórquez

Two important happenings greatly contributed to the formation of a more symbiotic and conciliatory relationship between muralism and graffiti. One of these events was the 1974 exhibition of Los Four in the Los Angeles County Museum of Art, the first Chicana/o art show hosted by a major museum.[64] Los Four was composed of Chicana/o artists Frank Romero, Gilbert Luján, Carlos Almaraz, Roberto de la Rocha, and Judithe Hernández (added to the group for this LACMA show), most of whom were experienced muralists as well as painters. Much of the work they exhibited in this historic show was saturated with graffiti designs, texts, and motifs. De la Rocha went as far as spray-painting a tagger's "piece" on the very walls of the museum.[65] The reason for their use of the graffiti was twofold: on the one hand, they wanted to use a mode of expression that could embody the Chicana/o experience, and, on the other, they sought to bring a marginalized form of creative expression into the exclusive and elitist space of the museum.

The second important event that galvanized and legitimized the graffiti influence on Chicana/o art was the emergence of Charles "Chaz" Bojórquez as an important figure in the contemporary art scene. Though he was not a muralist, Bojórquez started his career as a young tagger in the streets of Los Angeles but later attended art school and became a respected artist. He is often regarded as a figure who reconciled "counterculture" aesthetics with the visual discourses of European and North American modernism.[66] While Willie Herrón would argue that the presence of graffiti in museums as well as in the art market goes against the very spirit of the practice and thus, in such places, ceases to be graffiti altogether, I would contend that the likes of Los Four and Bojórquez, who introduced the aesthetic to the mainstream art world, disrupted the reductive and exclusive definitions of modern visual vocabularies. At any rate, to some artists, the acceptance of graffiti into the museum space meant the co-optation of its urban and irrepressible spirit, whereas for others, it signified a dissolution of monolithic notions about modernism.

But Bojórquez's influence encompassed more than a mere reconciliation between graffiti and contemporary art; he was also a crucial proponent of establishing a connection between graffiti calligraphy and indigenous glyphs, though his interest in Asian writing has received more attention in the arts literature. Much of his work in the eighties and nineties reflected said connection. For instance, in *Placa/Roll Call* (1980; Figure 3.4), Bojórquez fills the entire canvas with the names of friends and families close

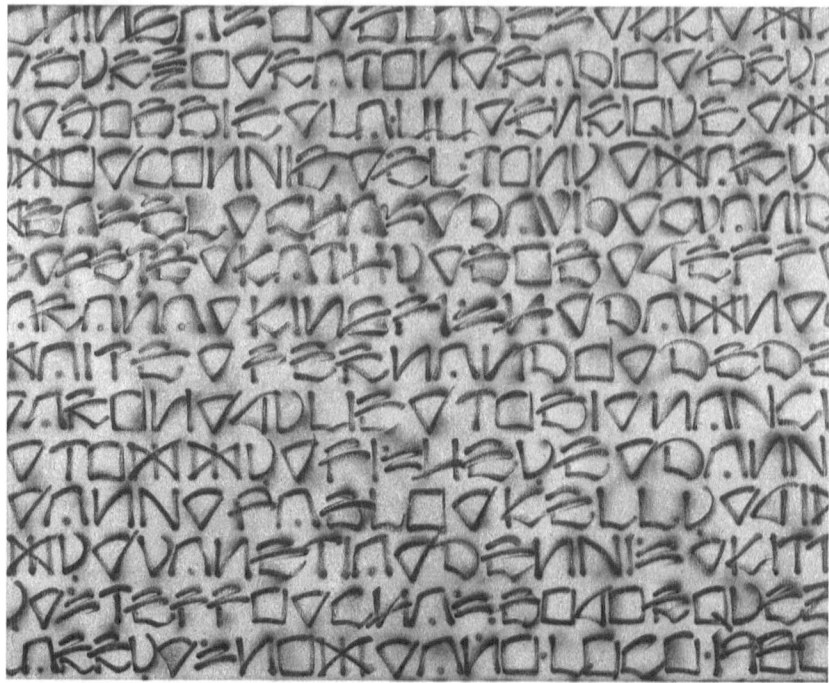

FIGURE 3.4. Charles "Chaz" Bojórquez, © 1980, *Placa/Roll Call*, acrylic on canvas. Collection of the Smithsonian Institution, Washington, D.C. Courtesy of Charles "Chaz" Bojórquez.

to him, emulating the "roll calls" often written by Chicana/o gang members to define, as Susan Phillips explains, "who does and does not belong to a gang or clique."[67] The names are written in characteristic L.A. "*cholo*" writing style, and Bojórquez's use of acrylic and canvas to create his own personal roll call naturally and intentionally blurs the boundary between "fine" and "popular" art. The muted color scheme also gives the painting the appearance of a glyph-filled ancient parchment, thus connecting graffiti text with non-European forms of writing. However, in *Por Dios y Oro* (*For God and Gold*, 1992) by Bojórquez, graffiti and Mesoamerican aesthetics and glyphs share the same pictorial space. One of his few sculptural works, this piece was created in the year of the five-hundredth anniversary of Columbus's arrival in the American continent, which, for many indigenous peoples throughout the Americas, was a day of hemispheric mourning rather than celebration. Bojórquez produced his own Mesoamerican stela made of wood, using stylistic elements from various Mesoamerican visual traditions in sculpture and architecture.[68] He then proceeded to tag it with various markings: a cross,

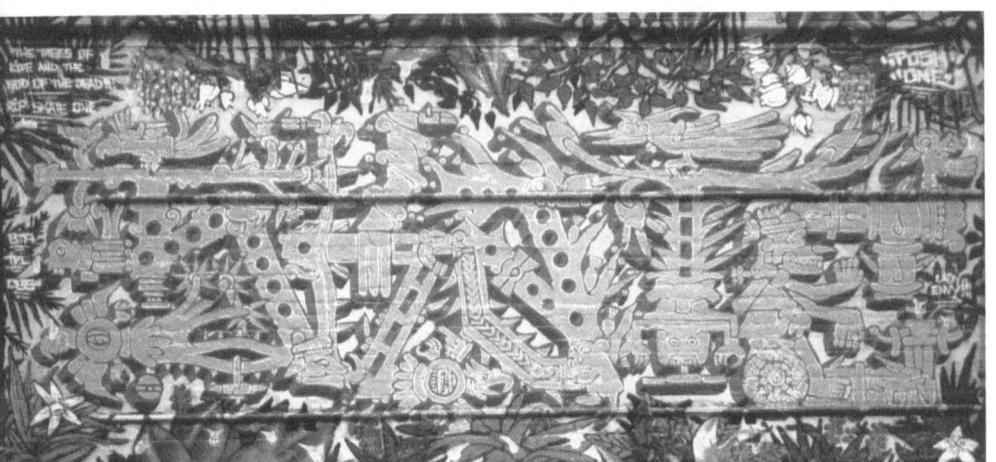

FIGURE 3.5. Posh One, © 1997, *Skate One*, graffiti mural, Fullerton Road and Melrose Avenues, Hollywood, California. Courtesy of Alan Barasch.

the year 1492 in Roman and Latin numerals, and a series of *cholo*-style graffiti inscriptions. These taggings represent, as Bojórquez himself remarked, "how a European gang... [came] into another culture's territory and claimed it as their own."[69] While the artist was utilizing a reversal of codes to subvert colonial discourse by imposing the criminalizing connotations attached to graffiti upon European culture itself, the taggings on this piece not only denote the "vandalism" enacted on indigenous cultures through conquest and colonialism but also establish a stylistic connection between the two. The undulation and sinuous form of the "serpent" heads at the top of the stela echo similar stylizations in the graffiti text. Moreover, given that claiming territory is an important component of graffiti, *Por Dios y Oro* can also be read as a statement of reclamation; graffiti artists, many of whom see themselves as contemporary glyph makers, are thus reclaiming preconquest indigenous culture for themselves.

Graffiti Crews, the 1980s, and the East Coast Influence

Until the 1970s, Chicana/o muralists turning to graffiti for inspiration were primarily looking at East Coast gang graffiti, as opposed to the crew graffiti phenomena that took place later on in California. The styles associated with these two groups of writers are actually quite distinct. Gang graffiti in California is usually characterized by lettering done in single strokes drawn with spray paint or marker in a single color. While gang graffiti can become extremely stylized and elaborate, it is often more simple in design than the writing done by graffiti crews. The extremely elaborate and colorful calligraphy, the "wild style" designs, and the use of "characters" (drawn figures or objects)—all characteristics of crew graffiti in New York—were introduced to Los Angeles in the 1980s. But while New York writers became known for the work they did in subway trains, L.A. crews introduced new elements to the genre, as Posh One explained: "Emulating the New York styles of trains and all that really started to blow up [in 1987, 1988], but all we had [in L.A. were] freeways and yards, and by a yard I mean abandoned tunnels, abandoned lots, broken-down buildings, wherever you could find a place to paint . . . [In the end], we showed New York what you could do with a wall."[70] Many artists who came on the scene as taggers and graffiti artists, not necessarily muralists, would inadvertently contribute to the history of Indigenist murals in California by making their "pieces" and "masterpieces" increasingly elaborate and by interjecting indigenous aesthetics into their designs.

Graffiti artists' influence on the California public art scene additionally contributed to the growing cultural diversity of wall writers in the area, as Sherri Cavan states: "The young (mostly) males involved in [graffiti] represent every race, every ethnicity, and every social class."[71] The practice of creating graffiti functioned for many taggers and writers as an identity in itself, as the practitioners often referred to themselves as belonging to an "aerosol nation." Nevertheless, artists like Posh One do acknowledge that there are identity politics centered on ethnicity and race within the graffiti scene:

> A lot of kids got started [in graffiti] because they were of a certain ethnicity so they hooked up, or they were from a similar neighborhood so they hooked up, but there is also a group of people who disavow that and hook up with anybody, and their group of friends is made up of anybody, so I think it's a mixed bag. You end up with people who are very ethnocentric and you end up with people who aren't. . . . You can [also] have people whose only bond is the fact that they do [graffiti].[72]

Though mainstream culture has often stereotyped graffiti as a localized phenomenon within any given urban setting, many writers argue that graffiti has introduced them to an increasingly globalized worldview, as Man One explains:

> To me, graffiti is a very unifying culture. I can go to any country in the world for vacation or a visit, and it will probably take me a couple

of e-mails or a couple of phone calls and I'll have a place to stay, I'll
have somebody to paint with, I'll have somebody to show me around
town. . . . We might not even speak the same language, but graffiti is
very unifying that way; it makes the world really small if you're in the
culture.[73]

Nevertheless, Ivor Miller contends that "urban writers from all ethnic groups
have a common history of dislocation from their ancestral lands and cultural
fabric."[74] Moreover, while there is an inherent heterogeneity and legitimate
multiculturalism that defines graffiti culture, the contribution of Chicana/o
writers has been critical for the development of the form and, in many ways,
has further enriched graffiti visual vocabulary. Though many artists from a
variety of social and cultural backgrounds find a voice and a space within
graffiti culture, some Chicanas/os who are part of the scene, like Man One,
find connections between graffiti and the Chicano Movement:

What is going on with graffiti art right now is just an extension of
the Chicano Movement. To me, we're the new Chicanos taking on the
movement. It's more than just the Chicano Movement, it's an inter-
cultural movement now, so I think it's even stronger because more
people are fighting the cause. In the seventies, the Chicano Movement
was happening because everything that was happening against Chicanos was very blatant, and it was pretty easy to single it out. But now,
the racism is so hidden in the culture that it is not as easy to detect
anymore. Things like graffiti push the bottoms of [the mainstream]
and [the prejudice and racism] comes out as a result of that. To me, it's
totally an extension of the Chicano Movement. . . . For example, it's
a felony now to do graffiti. To me, that's a direct attack on minority
groups in the state. What a bigger cause than to fight against youth
being criminalized?[75]

Whether or not the contemporary graffiti art scene is truly a transformed
version of the Chicano Movement, the intersections and connections between the two are indeed compelling and palpable.

The Contemporary Graffiti Scene

L.A. graffiti artist Posh One's throw-ups, pieces, and masterpieces have gained
much fame and recognition in the graffiti and public art scene of Southern
California. Though not a Chicano artist in the cultural and ethnic sense, Posh
outwardly rejects the labels "white" or "European-descent American," along

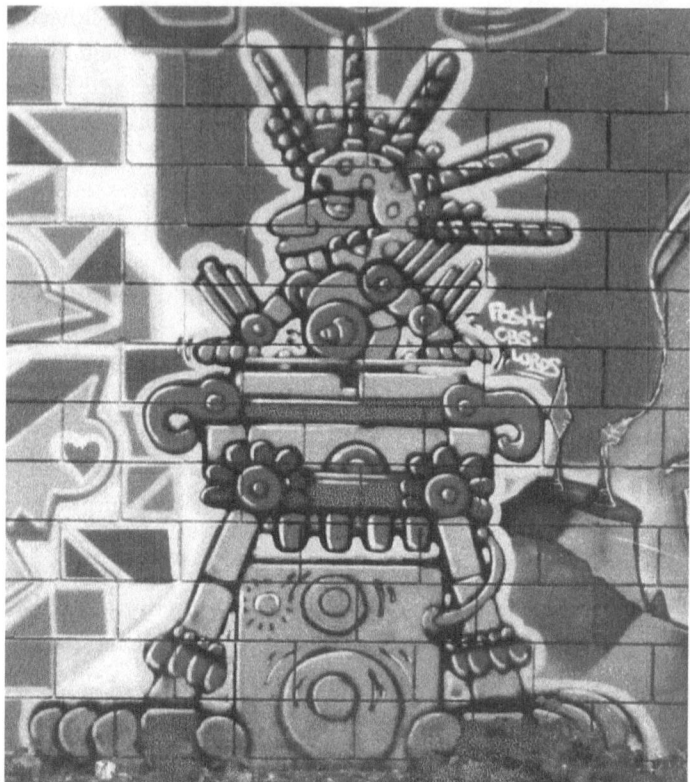

FIGURE 3.6. Posh One, © 2003, *DJ Quetzal*, graffiti mural, East Los Angeles, California. Courtesy of Alan Barasch.

with the implications of privilege that often accompany them. Identifying both a Jewish and a Scottish family heritage, Posh cites his ancestors' history of migration, displacement, discrimination, and violence as important self-identity markers that define his present-day experiences.[76] Moreover, through his engagement and contact with Chicana/o/Latina/o culture in the city as well as his own intellectual interest in European and non-European aesthetic traditions, the artist has incorporated indigenous iconographic motifs into a number of his graffiti murals. In 1992, the graffiti scene in Los Angeles was shaken by the untimely death of Skate One, a prominent graffiti artist who was killed by a train while practicing his craft. In his memory, Posh, who was a close friend of Skate's, created a piece entitled *Skate One* (1997; Figure 3.5), located at Fullerton Road and Melrose Avenue in Hollywood. This mural exemplified how graffiti writing and indigenous aesthetics could be intertwined with one another in deeply organic and symbiotic ways. *Skate One* is also representative of the aforementioned graffiti tradition of taking writing into the realm of the aesthetic. The entire composition here revolves around the extremely stylized and intricately decorated inscription of the word "Skate." Using earth tones to render the writing, Posh makes the letters in this piece take on the attributes of both text and image. The wild style that is characteristic of street art, with its intentional illegibility and radical stylization, is here complemented by the busy and highly ornamental design styles of Mesoamerican art found in Maya stelae and Aztec codices. Posh interweaves recognizable indigenous motifs such as birds, jaguars, skulls, plants, and deities into the various curves and angles of the text.

Of course, the tradition of doing memorial pieces for departed individuals dates back millennia in many cultures, including Mexico. Memorial pieces were also part of graffiti culture. On the East Coast in particular, individuals often commissioned graffiti artists to create memorial murals for departed loved ones who lost their lives to gang violence.[77] So in accordance with both Mesoamerican funerary art and graffiti memorial walls, in *Skate One,* Posh puts emphasis not so much on his friend's life as on his desire to perpetuate a kind of afterlife for his departed comrade, for Skate's legacy is still felt among L.A. taggers who either learned from him directly or were influenced by his style. Posh here provides a lush afterlife setting for Skate, with luxurious foliage and vegetation resembling environments associated with Maya territories. Moreover, the theme of transformation seems to saturate the entire composition. Death, as Mesoamericanist Esther Pasztory argues, is a metaphor for the transformations and cycles that nature undergoes and thus is intimately connected to life itself.[78] The cyclical and transformative nature of death is underscored in *Skate One* by the continuous back-and-forth transformations that the letters and images undergo in this particular piece, but also by the metaphorical transformation of Skate One himself through this commemorative piece.

As explained earlier, the introduction of characters into the graffiti aesthetic was ushered in by the influence of East Coast styles on California. The most recurring of these character figures was the B-boy or break-boy, which was a kind of archetypal figure that usually accompanied graffiti murals there. The B-boy, usually drawn in comic book–style, personified the fashion and attitude of the urban hip-hop hero, with baggy trousers, sportswear, and an irreverent attitude to match. Given that the characteristics and features of the B-boy reflected East Coast hip-hop culture, L.A. graffiti artists often altered this figure to fit the social context of Southern California. For Posh One, for example, these figures needed to reflect not only his own interests as an artist but also the cultural makeup of the community where he tagged his work. In 2003, working with other taggers, the artist collaborated in a piece on a

wall located in East Los Angeles that reflected the influence of Mesoamerican art in his work, but also the ways in which graffiti characters are made to
reflect the largely Mexican and Chicana/o community there. Amid text created by other artists, Posh included two characters, *DJ Quetzal* and *Grafteka*
(Figures 3.6 and 3.7), both of which exhibited characteristics of hip-hop and
indigenous culture, as he explained: "I did the characters that way because
I was looking for a good way to mix the cultural imagery of traditional indigenous art with the current culture of the people living in East L.A., [that
is,] a youth culture heavily influenced by graffiti and DJs/Hip-Hop."[79] *DJ
Quetzal* stands before a turntable as he is mixing and "scratching" tunes that
flare out of the speaker below him. Posh here reminds the public of the historical connection between graffiti and hip-hop music and also appeals to
the growing interest in rap and R & B among Chicana/o youth in areas like
East L.A.[80] The figure also wears a jaguarlike helmet with colorful spikelike
elements protruding from its surface. His turntable, the medium of choice
for the DJ, resembles a Mesoamerican structure made of stone slabs and

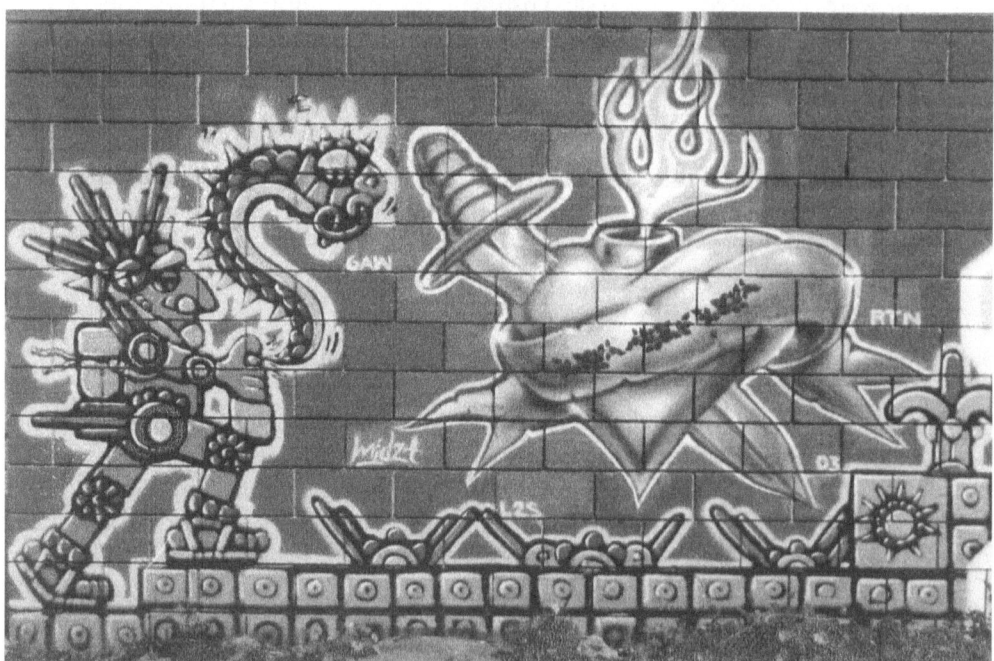

FIGURE 3.7. Posh One, © 2003, *Grafteka*, graffiti mural, East Los Angeles, California.
Courtesy of Alan Barasch.

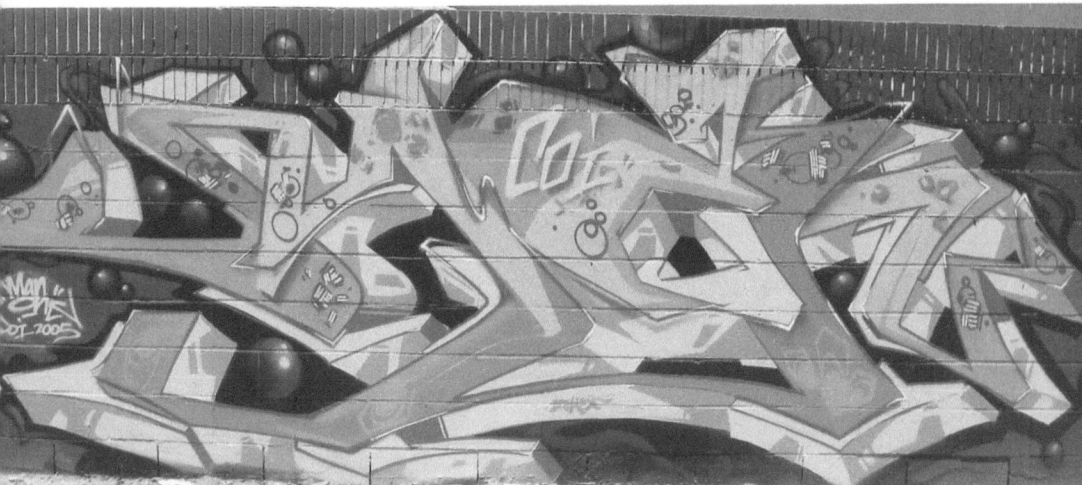

FIGURE 3.8. Man One, © 2005, *Coral on Indigo*, graffiti mural, East Los Angeles, California. Courtesy of Man One.

decorated with colorful glyphs. Nearby, we find the figure of the *Grafteka*, a graffiti-writing *"azteca,"* who is stepping into what looks like a temple. His body's anatomy seems almost architectural in design, echoing the angularity of the temple building before him. Like his colleague, *DJ Quetzal*, he also wears a highly ornate headdress, but in addition, he sports a pair of *chanclas* (sandals) to complete his *azteca* ensemble. In his hand, however, he holds a spray can, which unequivocally identifies him as a graffiti writer. But rather than paint coming out of the can, a twisting serpent resembling the Aztec deity Quetzalcoatl sprays out. In this way, the artist likens the Mesoamerican glyph writer or artist to the contemporary graffiti tagger. In other words, the creativity of the graffiti writer, namely *Grafteka*, is heightened by his invest-ment in the cultural capital of his indigenous identity.

Posh's representation of indigenous culture through *DJ Quetzal* and *Grafteka* is clever in its use of wit and humor, but the artist does not seek to poke fun at the prevailing Indigenist aesthetics in the barrio. With this piece, he pays respect to the recurrent indigeneity that has saturated East Los Angeles wall paintings for nearly three decades while also underscoring the similarities between graffiti and indigenous aesthetics. In the process, Posh One disrupts any hierarchical categorization between these and blurs clear distinctions between different forms of creative expression. Graffiti itself, as both Posh One and Man One explained to me, is characterized

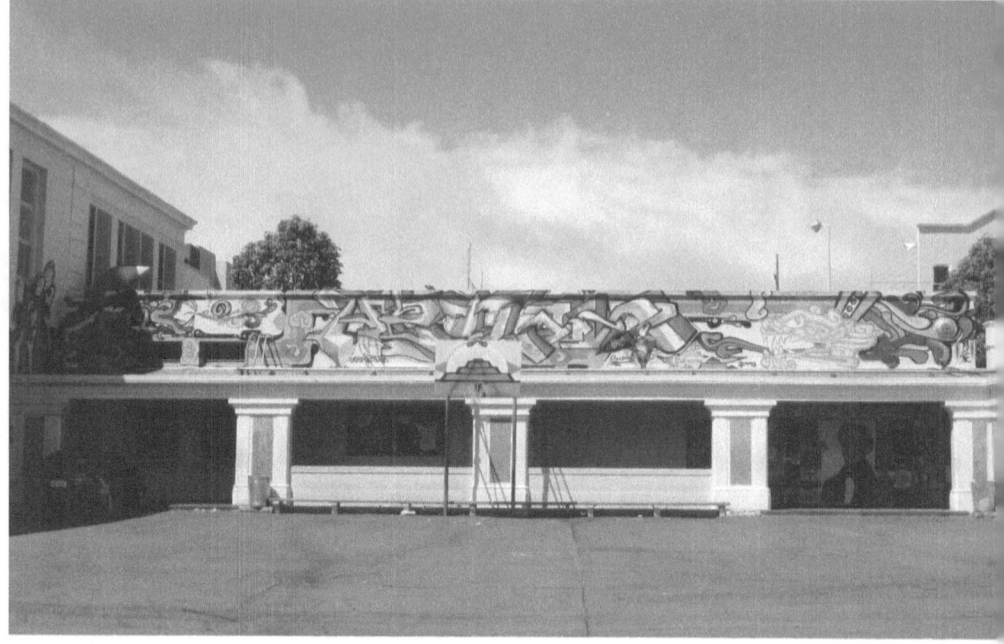

FIGURE 3.9. Spie, © 1998, *Aztlán*, graffiti mural, San Francisco, California. Courtesy of Eric Norberg.

by the lack of stable definitions and by the refusal on the part of its practitioners to abide by established rules and regulations.

Like Posh's work, that of Los Angeles graffiti artist Man One also focuses on the aestheticization of text and on the pictorial qualities of calligraphy, though without any of the overt and clearly discernible references to indigenous culture. During a visit by two prominent New York graffiti artists to the Los Angeles area, Man One was invited to work side by side with them on a wall in East L.A. The result was a striking and bold piece the artist entitled *Coral on Indigo* (2005; Figure 3.8). Part of the motivation behind the work of graffiti artists is the achievement of fame and street credibility and the desire to earn respect among their peers in the scene. Such a motivation was heightened for Man One in the presence of these East Coast artists. "I think the competitiveness and ego comes to play when painting alongside such well-respected artists," Man One explained "You want your piece to shine, maybe even outshine the others."[81] So Man One put particular emphasis on himself as an artist in this piece, making his signature style and technical skill the subject matter of *Coral on Indigo*. The artist here tagged his name, "Man," using wildly stylized and abstracted text spread over a darkened background. "The names by which individuals are known in the streets serve as prestigious labels," Sally and Jerry Romotsky have argued.[82] The elaboration of the text in *Coral on Indigo* was further accentuated by a three-dimensional effect and by bubblelike motifs surrounding the letters. The artist's use of this almost-flamboyant calligraphy makes his name legible mostly to graffiti connoisseurs and practitioners and not to the lay public, so to speak (though Man also included a traditional and readily legible signature for the untrained eye on the left-hand side of the composition). *Coral on Indigo* can therefore be interpreted as a gigantic signature that celebrates Man's creative genius and underscores his authorship of this particular piece.

The tradition among graffiti writers to tag or sign their names throughout the city has implications that go beyond their desire for fame and street credibility. The practice is also a reaction to the attacks against their individuality and humanity that indigenous and African-descent peoples have historically suffered as a result of colonial, expansionist, and capitalist projects; it is a practice of naming those who have been either rendered invisible or subhuman by systems of power. For many street writers, seeing their names rendered in large letters along freeways, train cars, or elsewhere in the public sphere offered a therapeutic and even spiritual remedy to this history of erasure: "It is a way of meditation," explained San Francisco muralist and graffiti artist Fred Alvarado: "It's not just about people knowing who you are, but also about learning who you are. I am as important as anything else I can say. I'm a valid thing in the universe."[83] For many of the graffiti artists who personally identified with the experiences of marginalization and displacement—as many indigenous peoples of the Americas do—the act of inscribing their names upon the urban landscape signified a radical and defiant proclamation of decolonization.

The importance of the artist and his/her individual style within the graffiti scene in many ways seemed to counter the spirit of collectivity that characterized Chicana/o muralism as well as other forms of indigenous art in the Americas. In most indigenous cultures, an artist's style can simply function as his/her signature. Among contemporary Maya weavers in Guatemala, for instance, a subtle personal style often functions as an individual artist's signature.[84] The tradition of artists signing artwork is, for the most part, a modern Western European practice that marks a shift in social attitudes toward the artist: from anonymous worker/laborer to individual creative genius. Some preconquest Maya pottery painters, however, represent an exception to this trend. As the Maya reached what is called the Classic Period (AD 250–850), with a highly complex and urbanized society, the social importance of the artist changed, particularly for those individuals working closely with the nobility. Dorie Reents-Budet argues that representations of artists dressed in elaborate attire while sitting next to important rulers, as seen on many Classic Maya ceramic vessels, indicated the high social status they enjoyed.[85] Furthermore, the technical and intellectual skill required to make this pottery suggests that Maya artists were among the most highly educated in society, with profound knowledge about history, cosmology, and science.[86] It is in this context that we see numerous examples of artists signing their work in glyphic form on ceramic vessels. These signatures place emphasis on individual rather than collective authorship and often serve to further reiterate the social standing of an artist.

Graffiti artists like Man One understood the function of the artist's signature in both European and indigenous traditions, but they also understood their own complex social position in the art world. While graffiti is generally a marginalized art form, artists can gain status among their peers in the scene. They can also achieve fame by accessing the mainstream art world, as Charles "Chaz" Bojórquez and other writers have done. In many cases, status is also accomplished through public displays of skill and technical mastery in the streets. Designs that showcased elaborate and monumental artists' signatures were in many ways self-promotion pieces that lauded a particular writer's artistic genius before a larger community of taggers. The signature itself, in these cases, became the artwork and the focus of aesthetic endeavor. It would seem, then, that graffiti artists took the whole practice to an extreme by focusing solely on the signature as a marker of artistic legitimacy and self-advancement. Yet the very fact that these artists have insisted on remaining true to an art form that is closely associated with the streets and with group rather than individual aesthetics speaks of the tension between the individual and collective concerns that drive the graffiti writer. Like the Classic Maya ceramic artists who were compelled to maintain their social status as artists by signing their work, but who were also responsible for the documentation of the collective histories belonging to the nobilities they served, graffiti artists are caught between the quest for individual artistic validation within a social system that often criminalizes them and the accountability to their crews or to the communities where they tag.

San Francisco, though not as prominent as Los Angeles, has also emerged as an important graffiti site on the West Coast. The prevalence of graffiti there, of course, also coincides with its importance as a hub of mural activity. The meteoric artistic success of graffiti-writer-turned-fine-artist Twist (aka Barry McGee) from San Francisco has also helped to put the city on the graffiti map. But nowhere in the city does the hybridization between graffiti and murals become more evident than in the Mission District. The murals located in Balmy Alley and Clarion Alley, for example, have exemplified the ways in which these two art forms have intersected in almost symbiotic fashion in the Mission. The Balmy Alley murals are discussed in Chapter 4, but it should be noted here that Clarion Alley hosted an important mural initiative called the Clarion Alley Mural Project in the early 1990s, which included a number of spray-painted pieces, thus putting murals and graffiti on the same plane of existence.

The graffiti pieces found in the Mission District epitomized the ways these artists addressed the intersection between their desire for community engagement and their individual artistic concerns. In 1998, local community muralist and street writer Spie (Eric Norberg) was approached by the staff of Horace Mann Middle School to design a mural on its premises, which became *Aztlán* (Figure 3.9). While many graffiti artists do "illegal" walls—that is, they appropriate spaces without city or patron sanction— this piece was created with the school administration's approval. As a community artist with knowledge and experience in graffiti aesthetics, Spie sought to bring out his own individual style in *Aztlán* while also reflecting the cultural and political makeup of the community in the Mission District. Spie came from a politically active family of Nordic and Chinese cultural background, but he was particularly knowledgeable about Chicana/o history and culture. He had also traveled to Mexico and had studied indigenous art forms, and he told me that he found that graffiti text resembled "carved-out glyphs."[87] He was also aware that 1998, the year when this mural was made, marked the sesquicentennial anniversary of the Treaty of Guadalupe Hidalgo. Spie was conscious that this treaty signified for Chicana/o and Mexican communities the beginning of a prolonged history of dispossession and disenfranchisement that has continued to the present. To reflect the school's Chicana/o/Latina/o student population, the artist created a piece that combined contemporary aesthetics with indigenous themes specific to Chicana/o culture. The horizontally oriented composition revolved around the word "Aztlán" written in the characteristic wild-style lettering while still remaining legible to a wider public. Rendered predominantly in browns and reds to reflect earth tones, "Aztlán" is inscribed on the wall in block lettering that turns and twists in surprising and unexpected angles. Like other graffiti text, the typography of this piece achieves a certain degree of three-dimensionality, for the letters appear to recede into an illusionistic space. But Spie complicated this three-dimensionality by purposely creating overlapping planes and inconsistent linear perspectives that disrupted traditionally Western notions of receding space. Beneath the first letter *A* of "Aztlán,"

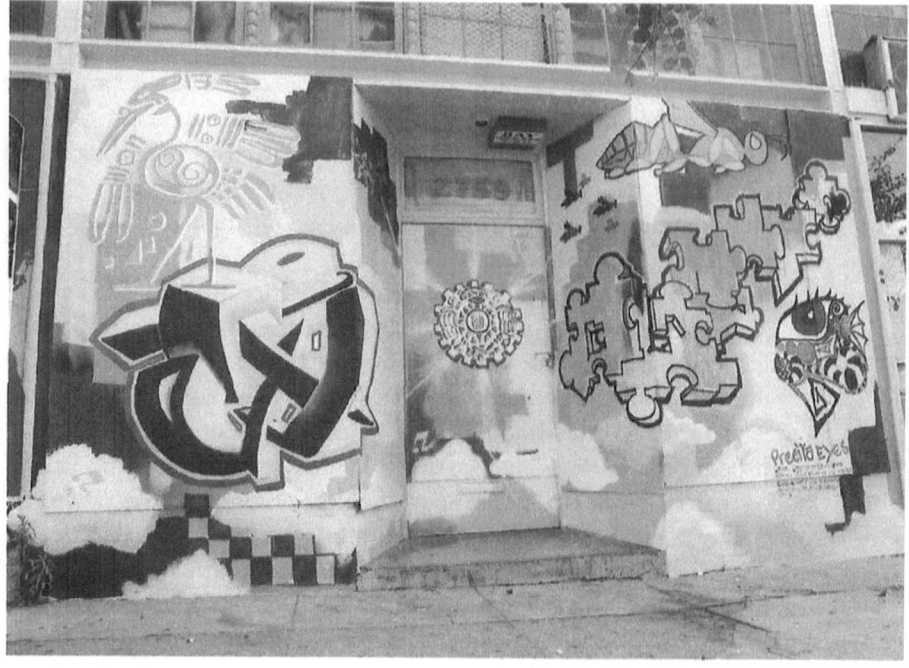

FIGURE 3.10. Precita Eyes Muralist Urban Youth Arts Program, © 2005, *Untitled*, mural, Twenty-first and Bryant Streets, San Francisco, California. Designed by Frederick Alvarado, Josh Stevenson, and students. Courtesy of Precita Eyes and Frederick Alvarado.

we find a smaller and simplified inscription of the word "Califaztlán," with the map of the U.S. Southwest drawn directly behind it. With such an inscription, the artist is providing the spectator with a geographical location for Aztlán, namely, the U.S. Southwest, with California at its center. Spie then weaves a ribbonlike visual device through the last two letters of the larger inscription of "Aztlán." This device ends in an arrow point, very much like the arrows used by Native American groups in the United States. The year 1848, along with the copyright symbol (©), is written on the arrow in a clearly legible white font. While the "Califaztlán" inscription and the U.S. Southwest map operate as indicators of Aztlán's physical locality, this arrow with the year 1848 speaks of the chronological origins of this mythohistorical homeland. The artist traces the birth of Aztlán not to the era of the preconquest Aztecs, but to 1848, the signing of the Treaty of Guadalupe Hidalgo between the United States and Mexico. So the origins of Aztlán, indicated here by the copyright symbol next to the year 1848, take place during the quintessential moment of dispossession for the Mexican-turned-Chicana/o population of Mexico's northern provinces, soon to become the U.S. Southwest. With this definition of Aztlán, it is clear that the artist defines Chicana/o indigenous consciousness according to the population's history of disenfranchisement and loss, a history that is symbolically overturned by the recovery and repossession of space metaphorically claimed by this mural. The central inscription of "Aztlán" in the mural is then flanked by the figure of a Quetzalcoatl-like dragon[88] on the right and a charging serpent on the left. Spie actually based the latter figure, the serpent, on a sketch made by local Chicano elder artist Johnny Hernández. The stylization and busy ornamentation of both figures reflect the general design of the graffiti text in the composition. The overt and clearly political Indigenist aesthetic of the mural is further radicalized by the graffiti elements in the piece. The artist seems to imply that an indigenous consciousness is not unlike the oppositional politics of the graffiti lifestyle.

Spie is part of a generation of young muralists in the Mission District who trace their artistic origins to their youth as taggers. Many of these artists went on to attend art school and work in community settings while still pursuing their love for graffiti. Such was also the case of Fred Alvarado, who was raised in various urban settings that included Long Beach, Chicago, Houston, and Guatemala City. After earning his art degree from the San Francisco Art Institute, he settled in the Bay Area and currently works there as a community artist. Though Alvarado is of Guatemalan descent, his cultural experiences are indeed heterogeneous and diverse, since he grew up in such different geographical areas. Nevertheless, hip-hop culture and graffiti were present in all these environments and were critical components of his social and political consciousness. In collaboration with Josh Stevenson, another local community artist, Alvarado created an untitled mural (2005; Figure 3.10) in the Mission District at Twenty-first and Bryant Streets with a group of students whose ages ranged from eleven to twenty-three. The cultural makeup of the students was fairly heterogeneous as well; it included two Latinos, an Asian American, and a European American student. The result was a mural that combined indigenous glyphs and graffiti iconography and thus established an intimate connection between the two; it seemed as if the graffiti and indigenous language utilized in the mural spoke to the diverse experiences of the group. The artists approached the wall with few premeditated ideas about the imagery that would be used, save for the background, which included clouds and abstracted color: "This mural project was a spontaneous mural. When we set out to start, we had a small idea of what the background would be like, but nothing was really planned out."[89] This fairly neutral background provided a starting point for the artists without seriously conditioning their individual creative sensibilities. But the mural was in part conditioned by an event affecting the public art scene in the Mission District, namely, the untimely death of Luis Cervantes, a renowned Chicano artist in the area. Cervantes was like a community elder among Mission muralists, so Alvarado, Stevenson, and company sought to acknowledge his legacy with this wall painting:

> At the time when this mural was painted, one of the founders of the Precita Eyes Mural Center had passed away. Luis Cervantes was an artist in San Francisco practicing his art since the fifties. He died at the age of eighty-two. He was very much into studying Mayan and Aztec imagery as well as sharing his knowledge of those cultures. The day we painted that mural Josh [Stevenson] stumbled upon one of the books that Luis Cervantes had shared with us. We read through it and chose some imagery from the book, in his honor.[90]

The book that Alvarado and Stevenson borrowed from Cervantes's personal collection was Jorge Enciso's *Design Motifs of Ancient Mexico* (1953), which is a kind of catalogue of basic indigenous forms and figures from Mexico, categorized by type, such as geometric forms, natural forms, human figures, etc. These were all based on actual stamp designs from various indigenous cultures in Mexico. Stamps, as Enciso explains in his book, are generally made of clay and used to imprint designs, mostly on pottery, though some are also used to print motifs on skin, cloth, or paper.[91] While these are most common among Mexican indigenous cultures, stamps were utilized by native peoples throughout the Americas, from the U.S. Southwest to South America, including the Caribbean. These stamps also typify the kinds of cultural exchanges that occurred between indigenous communities, for these were seen as articles of trade and economic transaction among different preconquest nations.

Most images in *Design Motifs of Ancient Mexico* displayed the boldness and profound stylization that characterizes much indigenous art, elements that were particularly attractive to Alvarado and company, whose aesthetic sensibilities were heavily shaped by the boldness and stylization of graffiti. Their mural at Twenty-first and Bryant in the Mission brought together these two aesthetics within the same composition. The mural was composed of floating icons or motifs reflecting the individual artists' creative interests as well as the indigenous knowledge that Cervantes had passed on to them. Painted over a doorway entrance, the mural's largest images are two graffiti pieces with the names of two of the participating artists. On the left-hand side of the composition, the name "Neto" emerges quite prominently and is written in three-dimensional text, yet the different letters that compose the name are tightly wrapped around one another, thus endowing this word with a clusterlike appearance that ultimately compromises its readability to those unfamiliar with graffiti aesthetics. Directly above this text, the stylized figure of a crane seems to stand on the surface of this three-dimensional graffiti piece. The flatness and linearity of this figure counter the illusion of depth exemplified by the text below. Inspired in design by indigenous pottery motifs from Mexico and the U.S. Southwest, the crane symbolized "travel of long distances," according to Alvarado.[92] Indeed, cranes are known for their ability to fly across long distances in their migrations from one place to another. It could be said, therefore, that the participating artists' diasporic consciousness was embodied through the crane's connection to movement and migration. Moreover, cranes carry significant symbolism in cultures throughout the world, including European and native peoples of the Americas. In the U.S. Southwest, the Hopi and the Zuni organized around clans named after the crane, while Crow and Cheyenne warriors associated themselves with the sandhill crane. The Mimbres people of New Mexico, whose culture reached its height between AD 1000 and AD 1500, featured cranes prominently in their pottery designs; these figures symbolized the lunar eclipse, which formed part of a larger pantheon of animal motifs connected to celestial occurrences among the Mimbres. The crane thus operated as a symbol that spoke simultaneously of an indigenous and a global consciousness. But the direct source for the mural was an indigenous Mexican stamp found in Mexico City that depicted not a crane, but a heron, a related bird species. Various Mesoamericanists, including Hernando Alvarado Tezozómoc and José Rubén Romero Galván, argue that the heron as a symbol is connected to the Aztec homeland of Aztlán.[93] The Nahuatl word for heron is *aztatl,* and the word for place is *tlan,* thus "Aztlán" can literally be translated as the "place of herons" or the "place of whiteness," given the white plumage of the heron.[94] So the significance of travel that Alvarado and the others connected to this bird motif can also refer to the ancient migration of the Aztecs from Aztlán to Tenochtitlán,[95] and to the general idea that diasporic cultures are formed through the experience of movement as much as they are through the subjectivity of static place and space.

Another indigenous symbol that figures prominently in this unnamed mural created by Alvarado, Stevenson, and the others is a round seal-like motif painted right on the door of the entrance. The seal was inspired by some of the floral stamp patterns that appear in Enciso's *Design Motifs of Ancient Mexico*. At the center of the seal, Alvarado painted a hand motif based on a stamp design from San Andrés, Tuxtla (Mexico). The artist was primarily attracted to the formal qualities of these motifs while taking considerable liberties with the design. For the participating artists, this seal lent a paradisiacal quality to the entire mural and simultaneously acted as a sun image with rays extending outward. While not permeated with the symbolic significance carried by the crane/heron motif, this indigenous seal functions as a decorative motif that helped the artists in this mural make stylistic connections between preconquest indigenous imagery and contemporary graffiti, as Alvarado explained: "Now, we chose these ancient symbols to co-exist with what one could call modern glyphs to show some connection of our roots to ancient artists."[96] By making these connections, Alvarado, Stevenson, and the rest of the artists who worked on this mural were legitimizing graffiti as an art form by connecting it to indigenous motifs while at the same time making these motifs current for the local youth in the Mission District via their association with graffiti.

Conclusion

Whether we talk about graffiti and murals as being distinct and individual art forms, in California it became increasingly difficult to establish clear demarcations between the two. Ultimately, these were two art forms that were necessarily defined by their oppositional posture toward the systems of power that dominated city spaces. The aesthetics created by these visual practices represented the subjectivities of communities who lived in these spaces yet possessed little to no power to affect their own surroundings. While murals enjoyed a greater degree of public approval and sanction than graffiti, both sought to reclaim the spaces traditionally denied to disenfranchised communities. For this reason, the reclamation of space becomes a critical component of the public art produced by Chicanas/os.

In Chapter 4, I introduce the various politics of space that have traditionally informed the practice of mural making by Chicanas/os. Of particular importance to this next chapter is the emergence of a phenomenon that I call *mural environments*, that is, the creation not just of single murals but rather of groups of murals that are bound together by the same location, initiative, and spirit.

CHAPTER FOUR

The Chicana/o Mural Environment
Indigenist Aesthetics and Urban Spaces

Chicana/o Murals and Social Spaces

As I stipulated in the introduction to this volume, Indigenist imagery in muralism was meant to function as a metaphorical and tangible platform where Chicana/o artists could carve out spaces for the articulation of cultural citizenship and decolonizing creative expressions. The space, site, and location of a mural were as critical to its production as its style, iconography, and subject matter. These elements are so important that Chicana artist Judy Baca once stated that when preparing to make a new mural, she always carefully surveys the space where the work of art will reside. She takes into consideration the space's topography, spirit, and people before she ever puts up scaffolding.[1] Knowledge about the physical and metaphysical power contained within a particular space, Baca argues, leads to the creation of a mural that has a more organic and sensitive relationship to its environment. Nevertheless, murals must not only reflect the energy of their location; they must also have the power to positively transform it. Psychologist Robert Sommer, whose thoughts on the psychological effects of murals were elicited by the editorial board of *Community Murals Magazine* in 1982, also underscored the importance of site for murals:

> The community muralist knows in advance where the work will go and who will see it. Before the work is started, the artist is obliged to study the site, talk with the residents about their concerns in general, and about the artwork in particular. *The community artist is obliged to undertake this research on site and audience.*[2]

The visionary ideals that Chicana/o muralists like Baca and observers like Sommer held about the ways in which murals reflected and transformed the spaces around them were often counteracted by the politics involved in the creation of public art. Community mural painting constituted an artistic practice that required a complex negotiation with city officials or other potential patrons for the public space in which it was located. In some instances,

the successful procurement of the space for the mural signified for the artists and their communities an empowering victory over the marginalizing
politics of federal urban initiatives. In other instances, securing said spaces
required artists to reach a certain degree of compromise with their political
and social consciousness. In either case, however, Chicana/o artists were underscoring the profound importance of the site for the creation of a mural,
thus acknowledging that, as Erika Suderburg stipulates, "'site' in and of itself
is part of the experience of the work of art."[3] The site specificity of murals
implied that the space was a critical component of the artwork to the degree
that the mural would be incomplete without it. The practice of mural making for many Chicana/o artists was deeply dependent on their understanding of space as a social construct. In other words, the Chicana/o experience
of marginalization and displacement proved to them that urban space was
never neutral or devoid of meaning and, furthermore, that it was a result of
a complex history of labor and social production. These attitudes toward
space in many ways reflected Henri Lefebvre's definition of social space:

> They [social spaces] are products of an activity which involves the eco-
> nomic and technical realms but which extends well beyond them, for
> these are also political products, and strategic spaces. . . . The state and
> each of its constituent institutions call for spaces—but spaces which
> they can then organize according to their specific requirements. . . .
> Thus this means of production, produced as such, cannot be separated
> either from the productive forces, including technology and knowl-
> edge, or from the social division of labor which shapes it, or from the
> state and the superstructures of society.[4]

While murals reclaimed *physical* spaces on behalf of the Chicana/o community, Indigenism asserted *metaphorical* spaces for said population. The
Indigenist aesthetic that many California muralists generated was indeed
the symbolic counterpart to the more concrete claims for public space that
their work required. The images of indigenous America being deployed in
these wall paintings operated as visual signifiers for the mythical homeland
of Aztlán. Indeed, Chicana/o cultural producers as a whole were conscious
that Aztlán, as Rafael Pérez-Torres explained, made "claims to a political and
economic self-determination not dissimilar to claims asserted by indigenous
populations throughout the world."[5] After identifying the entire U.S. Southwest as a possible location for this Aztec homeland, Chicana/o artists and
intellectuals sought tangible ways through which to lay claim to U.S. territory, as explained by American studies scholar George Vargas: "[Chicana/o

artists] hoped to reclaim a place of honor in the American landscape on behalf of dispossessed Mexicans and Chicanos, who at one time dominated much of the Mexican territory now known as the U.S. Southwest."[6] Virginia M. Fields and Victor Zamudio-Taylor further argued that Aztlán became a symbol of legitimization for Chicanas/os: "The concept of Aztlán served a legitimizing strategy, enabling Chicanos to assert an indigenous identity and fostering a sense of belonging."[7]

Discourses about the reclaiming of metaphorical spaces in Chicana/o activist thought were common during the Chicano Movement of the 1960s and beyond. But the gap between metaphorical discourses and the immediate need of the Chicana/o community for more appropriate spaces in which to live often did not correspond to one another. Chicana/o activists needed to find a way to mesh their needs as a disenfranchised community with the symbolic language they formulated. Indigenist imagery, coupled with the public nature of the community mural, addressed both the pragmatic and conceptual concerns and presented a solution to the disparity between abstract ideals and immediate needs.

Rather than discussing the spatial qualities inherent in the iconography and physical location of *individual* Indigenist murals, I focus in this chapter on the phenomenon of *mural environments* as they present themselves in the cities of Los Angeles, San Diego, and San Francisco. As I define them, these environments consist of initiatives to create a series of murals in close proximity to one another and within a defined and limited space. These murals are not supposed to be seen as single works of art, but rather, their position and iconography should be understood in function of the surrounding murals and in relation to the space in which they reside. The ultimate purpose of these environments is to create or transform particular urban spaces so that they become more attractive and livable for the communities that inhabit them. I will be looking at three specific instances of this phenomenon in Southern and Northern California, namely, the murals of Chicano Park in San Diego, Estrada Courts in East Los Angeles, and Balmy Alley in San Francisco. Though these are by no means the sole examples of these phenomena in California, they are representative of the general form these environments take.

Finally, I conclude my analysis with a general discussion of yet another phenomenon related to muralist production that functions in a very similar way to the mural environment. Mural dedications are usually celebratory events that take place around the creation of a new community mural. These celebrations require a symbolic "takeover" of the immediate area where the mural is located. Art historian Oscar Vásquez also suggested to me that these "performative" mural environments functioned as symbolic recolonizations or reterritorializations of the site where they are located. Public speeches, concerts, poetry readings, and, most prominently, Aztec dances are enacted in this space and usually form part of the mural dedication. As collective expressions of identity with Indigenist overtones, and as symbolic claims over the surrounding area around the mural in which both the artist and community participate, these dedications act as the performative counterparts to the mural environment. Given that witnessing one of these dedications is perhaps one of the most effective ways to truly understand how claims for space are made during these events, I also recount my own experience while attending the dedication for Paul Botello's *Inner Resources* in City Terrace, Los Angeles, on July 22, 2000.

In light of the history of marginalization, dislocation, displacement, and forced migration suffered by Chicana/o and Mexican populations in the United States, these mural environments not only provide ideal sites for the creation of autonomous spaces within the urban landscape, but they also furnish the artists and their communities with platforms through which to critique and contest this very history. Raúl Homero Villa, in his book *Barrio-Logos* (2000), explains the various processes by which the spatial designation of the barrio was imposed on Mexican and Chicana/o residents in California but was nevertheless also utilized by these communities as a space for cultural and political expression. Villa asserts that the barrio, then, becomes a phenomenon created by opposing external and internal forces that come together to create a unique cultural landscape:

> With their complicated conjuncture of internal and external forces, the barrios of Los Angeles and other California cities have been real and rhetorical locations from which, and about which, to enact ideologically expressive critiques of domination, whether this comes from within or from outside their social spaces. The collective Chicano [community—activists, writers, and artists] are ... intervening in this intimate social space while interrogating the larger landscapes of power through the political culture of their expressive works.[8]

Urban planning scholar David R. Diaz also recognized the barrio space as "a zone of segregation and repression." Nevertheless, he argued that this realm represented "the reaffirmation of culture, a defense of space, an ethnically bounded sanctuary, and the spiritual zone of Chicana/o and Mexicana/o identity."[9] Diaz further maintained that barrios held an important significance to Chicanas/os not only because they are fairly protected cultural enclaves but also because they function in a manner similar to preconquest indigenous cities and first-nation settlements throughout the Southwest, where the social structure is highly dependent on *mutualista, compadrazgo,* and *comadrazgo* kinship ties that place particular importance on nonfamilial relations like the mutualist and godparent networks.

Mural environments act as perhaps one of the most monumental examples of the creative expressions enacted within the barrio space by Chicana/o artists and communities generally. The reputation of the barrio as a dangerous and undesirable place to live is challenged by the creation of these mural environments. Chicana/o artists created these environments with the express purpose of transforming increasingly deteriorating barrio spaces (usually due to city initiatives), and others were erected to change the predominantly negative attitudes about the spaces inhabited by Mexican and Chicana/o communities. In both cases, however, mural environments function as emblems and physical markers of a space exclusively allocated or altered for the needs of the Chicana/o community. While David R. Diaz contends that resistance within the barrio waged "a battle against mainstream planning, urban renewal, and modern urban restructuring,"[10] I would argue that the public mural became an important tool in this bitter and arduous battle. But though muralism was crucial in celebrating and strengthening the political viability of Mexican/Chicana/o neighborhoods, these public works of art did not necessarily have to be located in barrios to articulate a radical critique of the urban policies of space in California and elsewhere.

Cultural Citizenship, the Treaty of Guadalupe Hidalgo, and Aztlán

The struggle over space often waged by Chicana/o and Mexican communities has been a crucial component in their quest to attain proper *cultural citizenship*, a term coined by Renato Rosaldo in 1987. The term defined "citizenship" beyond its legalistic implications and, according to William V. Flores and Rina Benmayor, included "a range of social practices which, taken together, claim and establish a distinct social *space* for Latinos in this country."[11] Flores and Benmayor, as well as Rosaldo before them, defined social space as both a metaphorical *and* a physical space where cultural citizenship can be achieved. These writers further established a direct link between an identity established at a community level and the need for spatial autonomy:

> For Latinos, community is essential to survival, not only in terms of neighborhood or geographic locale, but also in terms of collective identity. The struggle for the right to control space and to establish

community is a central one. . . . This has been especially true for Latinos, whose neighborhoods are routinely cut up by freeways or demolished under the aegis of redevelopment.[12]

Keeping Flores and Benmayor's description in mind, then, mural environments represent perhaps one of the most overt expressions of cultural citizenship enacted in public spaces.

Chicana/o artists since the late 1960s have been responding to a U.S. history in which identity politics and struggles over territory and space have been closely linked. A pivotal moment in that history was undoubtedly the signing of the Treaty of Guadalupe Hidalgo and the subsequent annexation of the northern Mexican territories by the United States in 1848, which Raúl Homero Villa identified as "the originary moment in the general subordination of *mexicanos*-cum–Mexican Americans."[13] But this event for Chicana/o artists, activists, and intellectuals not only signified a moment of material and territorial dispossession for the former Mexican nationals living in these provinces; it also gave rise to the racialization and proletarization of Mexicans living in U.S. territory, a situation still suffered by Chicanas/os to this day. The concepts of Manifest Destiny and westward expansion—prevalent U.S. nationalist ideologies in the nineteenth century—also covertly associated the right to possess land and territory with the category of "whiteness." In many ways, the events of the nineteenth century established a social order and a spatial politics that would remain in place in areas like California well into the twentieth and twenty-first centuries.

If the signing of the Treaty of Guadalupe Hidalgo and all its implications signified for Chicana/o artists and activists a particularly pernicious moment in Mexican American history, then the period of the Aztec Empire functioned as an ideal historical moment that worked as a metaphor for the events surrounding the Chicano Movement of the sixties and seventies. By citing the existence of the ancient homeland of Aztlán—the Mexica place of origin according to their mythohistorical accounts—Chicanas/os found a way to retake the territory lost in the nineteenth century while adhering to Indigenist aesthetics in the process. According to this myth, the Aztecs left Aztlán guided by Huitzilopochtli and migrated south, where they founded their empire in Tenochtitlán, a story told as far back as 1610 by Gaspar Pérez de Villagrá in his *Historia de la Nueva México*. Chicana/o intellectuals later embarked on a quest to seek out Aztlán, as indicated by Michael Pina in 1989: "The most recent search for Aztlán occurred within the decades of the nineteen sixties and seventies as Chicano nationalists sought Aztlán as a spiritual homeland and the object of nation-building."[14] Prominent literary scholars like Luis Leal and Francisco Lomelí began to take an interest in Aztlán not so much as a historical or geographical reality but rather as part of a "mythic system" that was specifically Chicana/o.[15] Instead of searching for its location somewhere in the U.S. Southwest, they began to look for it within the creative expressions that came out of the Chicano Movement. Interestingly enough, though they found many instances of the concept in literature and political activism, no one recognized that perhaps one of the most ubiquitous examples of creative expressions that attempted to reconstruct the lost homeland of Aztlán was the very act of mural making, in particular that of the mural environment. I am arguing that Chicana/o artists took to the streets not to *search* for Aztlán, but instead to *re-create* it with the aid of the public mural. It also seems fitting to underscore that both concepts— Aztlán and the mural—have roots in Mesoamerican indigenous culture and history.

Estrada Courts, East Los Angeles

The murals that graced the walls of Estrada Courts, a predominantly Chicana/o and Mexican housing project in East Los Angeles, were created with the purpose of beautifying the barrio space[16] and counteracting the graffiti markings that had previously dominated the apartment buildings there. In his master's thesis about the social phenomenon that surrounded the mural production in Estrada Courts, Chicana/o studies scholar Marcos Sánchez-Tranquilino described how these graffiti taggings and subsequent wall paintings were played off by residents and artists alike as "contesting systems of signification" that supposedly operated in opposition to one another.[17] Under the direction of self-taught Chicano artist and community organizer Charles "Gato" Félix, and with funding from the Los Angeles Housing Authority, the Estrada Courts wall paintings composed a mural environment that, on the one hand, sought to empower the residents of this housing project through its various images about cultural and ethnic pride and, on the other, to show to the outside world that Estrada Courts was a desirable place to live. The murals here can be spatially divided into two distinct categories: those facing the interior spaces of the complex, which were produced primarily by Estrada residents, along with members of the local youth gang Varrio Nuevo Estrada (VNE), and those facing Olympic Boulevard, which were created by relatively established Chicana/o artists from Los Angeles and elsewhere in California. With the majority of the murals in Estrada being created between 1973 and 1978,[18] the works facing Olympic Boulevard that were executed by the practicing artists represent some of the most important examples of early Chicana/o muralist production. For example, the site included the *Black and White Mural* (1973–1980) by Willie Herrón and Gronk, and *We Are Not a Minority* (1978–1996) by the Congreso de Artistas Chicanos de Aztlán (CACA), an artists collective headed by San Diego–based artist Mario Torero. The images in these murals would become signifiers of Chicana/o resistance aesthetics and marked Estrada Courts as a quintessential mural site in California. Nevertheless, Sánchez-Tranquilino noted that the residents and the artists there had different criteria and motivations in mind. Residents and local youth who worked on murals there regarded the intervention of the invited artists as somewhat of an infringement on their territory, and as recounted by Estrada resident Alex Maya, they resented that "artists from San Diego, San Francisco, the long-hairs from City Terrace who made those weird murals [Gronk and Willie Herrón] . . . have all these good walls."[19] In spite of this, most individuals who painted a mural here were conscious that they were executing not a single work of art but rather a visual component that formed part of a larger initiative to transform the space in Estrada Courts through artistic means.

The layout of the Estrada Courts murals followed the interior/exterior dynamic that defined the spatial organization of Estrada Courts itself, in which the inner spaces represented the domain populated by the residents themselves, and the outer or peripheral areas were those frequented by a larger constituency. The apartment buildings of Estrada Courts are laid out on a basic grid system within an L-shaped city block contained by Grande Vista Avenue, Glenn Avenue, Concord Street, Hunter Street, Lorena Street, and the very busy Olympic Boulevard. Most buildings are placed parallel to one another, with few structures aligned perpendicularly to one another. It seems fitting here to address Gaston Bachelard's ideas about the paradoxical intimacy that exists between inside and outside spaces. Even though outside and inside are always interrelated and inform one another, the gap that separates them constitutes a space of violent rupture: "Outside and inside are both intimate—they are always ready to be reversed, to exchange their hostility. If there exists a border line between such an inside, the surface is painful on both sides."[20] Like border theory, which often describes the border as a wound or a scar located between established spaces, the transition between the interior and exterior space in Estrada is also a disjunctive and disorienting one.

The interior/exterior dynamic at Estrada Courts also implies that this mural environment was, intentionally or not, created not only by two different groups of muralists but also with two different audiences in mind. This phenomenon in Estrada Courts is similar to the ways in which cultural production often functions among historically disenfranchised indigenous communities in the Americas. Creative activities among such communities generally have internal and external expressions whereby their members allow certain practices to be exposed to the outside world while others remain part of their internal cultural practices. In such cases, there is a clear distinction between public and private forms of expression, which allows these communities to exert a certain degree of control over their cultural product as well as over the impressions that mainstream society possesses about them.

Estrada Courts was not an Indigenist mural environment only because it reclaimed and transformed the barrio space on behalf of its residents. The recurring indigenous motifs that appeared in the Estrada murals further underscored the Indigenist spirit of the whole initiative. These motifs emerged in both the interior and the exterior spaces of the complex and served to transform the domestic environment that formed part of the everyday lives of the residents there while also altering the broader landscape in which this housing project is located. As pointed out by Sánchez-Tranquilino, the murals managed to address the site-specific concerns that affected Estrada residents while also generating broader statements about Chicana/o and Mexican identity. Indigenist images and symbols provided artists and residents with a sort of template to simultaneously address the local and the universal; it allowed them to articulate concerns that were "indigenous" to the area while also dealing with questions about their identity within a wide-ranging spectrum. The Indigenist imagery in mural environments like the one in Estrada Courts established an indirect link between Estrada Courts as a disadvantaged community within the United States and the various enclaves of native populations that have struggled for autonomous spaces throughout the Americas. The Indigenist murals that so deeply affected the urban environment within and outside this housing complex established Estrada Courts precisely as an autonomous space where cultural difference and affirmation were articulated in their most public form.

The Indigenist murals that would saturate the more private areas of Estrada Courts were not easily visible to the general public, and they usually possessed a highly schematized and simplified visual vocabulary. Sánchez-Tranquilino speculated that the aesthetic expounded in murals from these interior spaces surely appealed to the inhabitants of this housing complex because it was reminiscent of the flatness and straightforward quality of

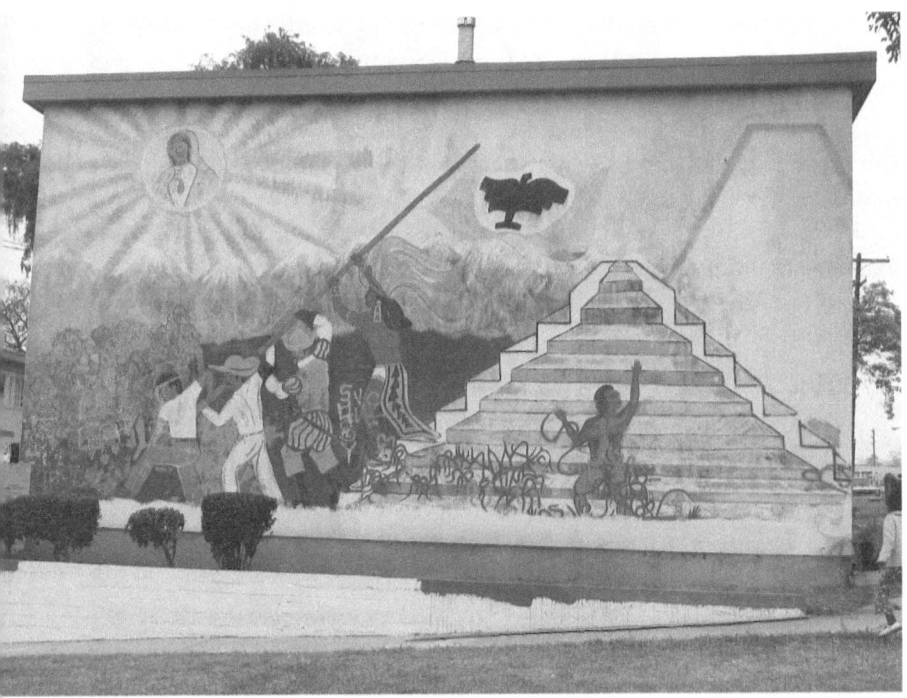

FIGURE 4.1. Alex Maya, © 1973–1975, *Tribute to the Farmworkers*, mural, Estrada Courts, East Los Angeles, California. Photograph by Guisela Latorre.

graffiti calligraphy and design, an urban aesthetic that was already familiar to this community. The often highly stylized and almost coded motifs found within the inner areas of Estrada provided residents with images that carried a highly iconic quality wherein the simplification and flattening of the form contributed to the directness of the message—a message that clearly stipulated, in this case, that the residents of this complex had branded and declared this space an Indigenist domain. Within the more intimate interior spaces of Estrada Courts, images like these were encoded with an Indigenist meaning that could easily be understood and engaged in by those who lived within the boundaries of this housing project.

In spite of the simplified quality that defined a great deal of the mural imagery within the residential spaces of Estrada Courts, a number of images in these areas carried a more narrative theme. Alex Maya, in his *Tribute to the Farmworkers* (1973–1975; Figure 4.1), constructed an imaginary scene that tapped into the collective cultural consciousness of his audience. Within an intuitively rendered mountainous landscape, four figures hoist up the flag of the UFW as they descend from a Mesoamerican pyramid: a pre-Columbian Indian, a Spanish conquistador, a Mexican peasant, and an urban Chicano. Floating above them, an apparition of the Virgin of Guadalupe seems to indicate that the entire scene has been blessed with divine benediction. In spite of the relatively intuitive and seemingly spontaneous execution of the mural, this image cites two important visual sources that were probably readily familiar to the residents of Estrada Courts. The inclusion of a holy figure overlooking an earthly event and the depiction of a shallow receding space echoes the *retablo* tradition that harked back to the colonial period in Mexico, including its northern provinces like Alta California. *Retablo* scenes are usually painted on small tin plaques and are often commissioned by patrons who had been spared from a near tragedy in their lives as a form of gratitude to a holy figure responsible for their salvation. While Maya has replaced the tragic event with a scene of Chicana/o cultural affirmation and monumentalized the reduced scale of the *retablo*, he retained the personalized quality of this folk art form by placing the mural within the more intimate interior spaces of Estrada Courts.

Another important source that informed the iconography of Maya's *Tribute to the Farmworkers* mural was, of course, the Iwo Jima national memorial in Arlington National Cemetery, a bronze statue based on a 1945 photograph by Joe Rosenthal. Like the *retablo* tradition, this monument also formed part of a repertoire of recognizable imagery to a general public. Unlike the *retablos*, however, the Iwo Jima memorial—which depicted a group of soldiers planting a U.S. flag on top of Mount Suribachi in Iwo Jima, Japan, as a symbol of military victory—represented a nationalist canon that did not include the contribution of minorities in this institutionalized version of U.S. history. Employing the familiarity of the image but omitting its exclusionary nationalist tone, Maya here subverted the meaning of the Arlington monument to accommodate a specifically Chicana/o nationalist theme. The artist here demonstrated to the public in Estrada Courts that U.S. nationalism can take various forms and that it can include the participation of both Mexican and Chicana/o communities. By the inclusion of the pyramid and the Mesoamerican Indian, Maya also shows that Indigenist symbols can speak to a nationalism that transcends specific places and moments in history.

As stated earlier, the murals facing Olympic Boulevard in Estrada Courts displayed a somewhat different aesthetic than the ones hidden from the general public. David Botello's *Dreams of Flight* (1973–1975, restored in 1996),[21] for instance, betrayed the characteristics of a more established and seasoned form of public art with its use of linear perspective and overlapping planes.

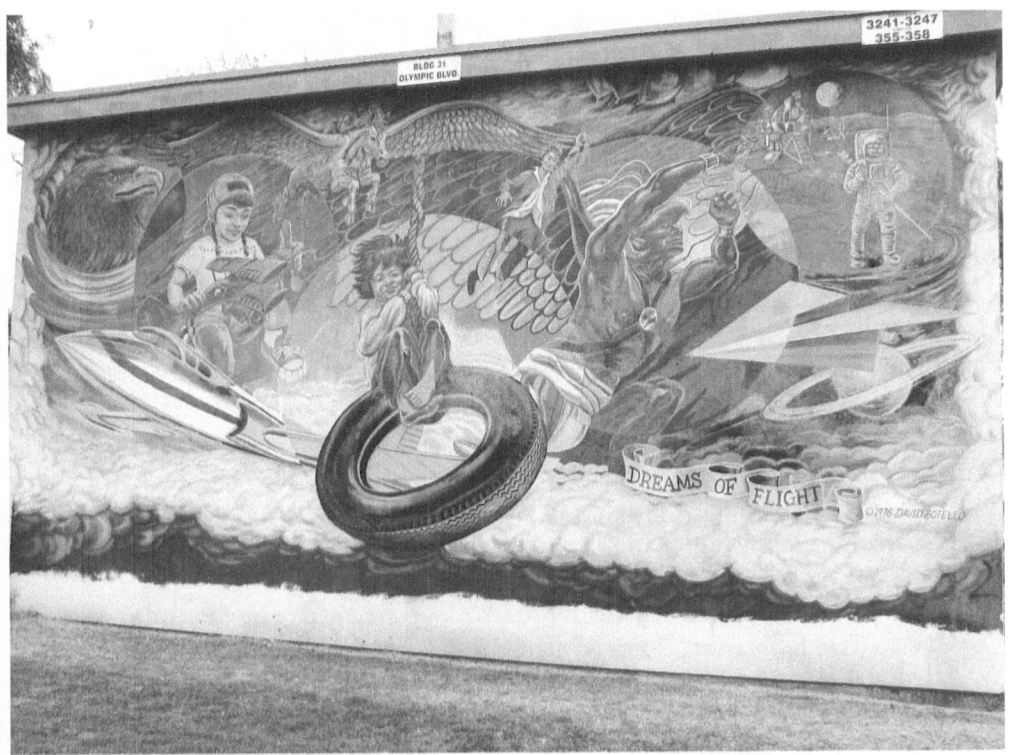

FIGURE 4.2. David Botello, © 1973–1975 (restored in 1996), *Dreams of Flight*, mural, East Los Angeles, California. Courtesy of David Botello.

By the time he began working on this wall, his first solo mural project, Botello had already gained extensive experience in the medium after he, along with Joe and John González, founded in 1969 the Goez Gallery, a commercial gallery and mural workshop in the heart of East Los Angeles.[22] Botello had also received some artistic training, albeit scattered and incomplete, in high school and at California State University, Los Angeles, and East Los Angeles College. By 1970, he had familiarized himself with the Mexican mural movement when he traveled to Mexico City to see and photograph public works by the likes of Rivera, Orozco, and Siqueiros.[23] His mural in Estrada Courts wove together his background as a muralist with the site-specific concerns of the broader mural initiative in this housing complex.

In *Dreams of Flight* (Figure 4.2), Botello created a sort of fantasy scene that would appeal to the children from Estrada Courts and the nearby area. At the center of the composition we see a child soaring through the air as he swings on a tire. While he is engaged in this exhilarating activity, his imagination conjures up all kinds of images related to the theme of flight, from a simple paper airplane gliding across the picture plane to a group of astronauts exploring the moon's surface. The notion of flight then metaphorically stands for the aspirations and dreams that have traditionally been denied to Mexican and Chicana/o children from areas like East Los Angeles. Even though Botello claimed that when he was making this mural he actually wanted to get away from the Indigenist themes that had saturated Chicana/o art up to that point, one of the most prominent figures in the mural's iconography is that of a winged-eagle knight/warrior who seems to fly up toward the sky. While this figure contributes to the general theme of flight in the mural, it also functions as the only signifier of cultural identity in the composition, thereby grounding the imagery within a specifically Chicana/o context. By the early 1970s, the figure of the Aztec warrior was so highly coded with Chicano nationalist thinking that it had become synonymous with the politicized consciousness associated with *el movimiento*.

Though mural production in Estrada Courts seemed to be clearly demarcated by the interior/exterior dynamic that defined the overall construction of the complex, Charles "Gato" Félix's contributions to this mural environment attempted to unify the two aesthetics that were operating on the inside and outside spaces of the courts. As the organizer and mastermind of the entire mural initiative there, his role was more than that of an artist and a community advocate; he was also there to mediate between the concerns of the Estrada Courts residents and the regulations of the city of Los Angeles. Sánchez-Tranquilino discussed how Félix himself held a unique position within the Estrada Courts community in that he was not a resident of the complex but, unlike the other visiting artists, was considered an insider to the community due to his *compadrazgo* ties with one of the residents there.[24] The collaborative murals he would undertake with the help of various individuals living there would also express a kind of conciliatory tone amid the almost dichotomous nature of the muralist production in Estrada Courts.

The location of *Sacrifice Wall* (1974; Figure 4.3), a mural executed by Félix with the help of the Varrio Nuevo Estrada gang, was perhaps the most immediate indicator that the artists were seeking a middle ground between the interior and exterior aesthetics of the Estrada Courts murals. Situated right at the main entrance of the complex, also facing Olympic Boulevard, this mural occupied the threshold between the two spaces that separated the mural work in the housing complex. It possesses both the flat Mesoamerican design elements that characterized some of the interior works as

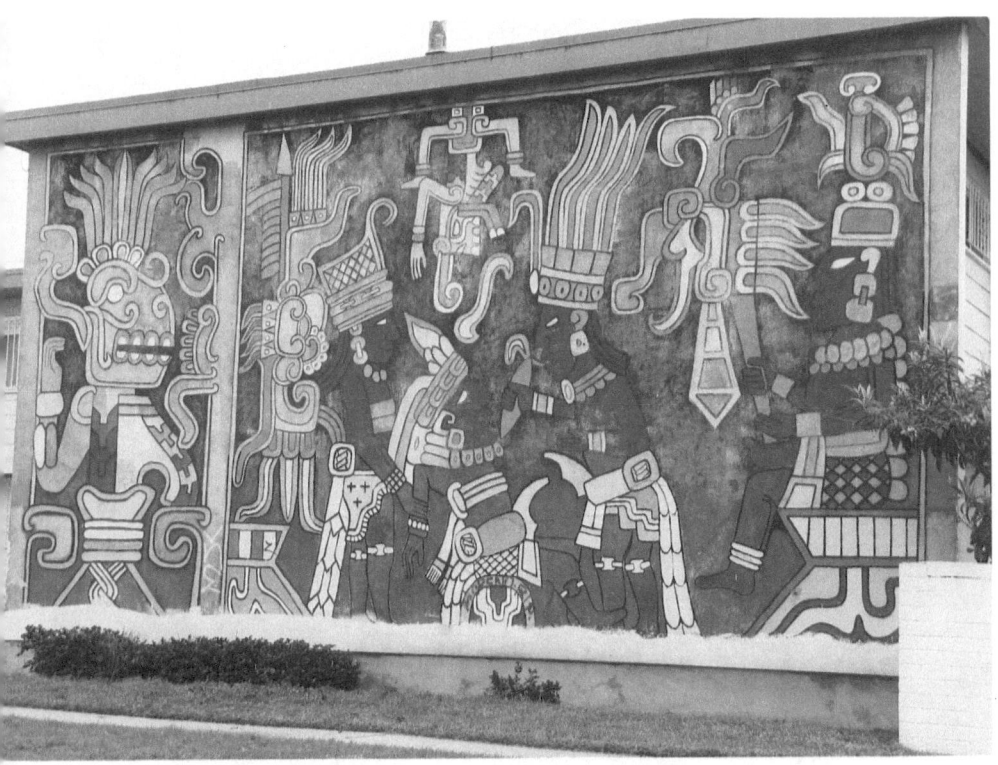

FIGURE 4.3. Charles "Gato" Félix and Varrio Nuevo Estrada (VNE) Gang, © 1974, *Sacrifice Wall*, mural, Estrada Courts, East Los Angeles, California. Photograph by Guisela Latorre.

well as the rather finished and polished quality of the other murals facing the boulevard. Félix and his colleagues drew direct inspiration for this work from the northeast sculptural relief panel found in the South Ballcourt of El Tajín in Veracruz, Mexico, a Huastec site in Mesoamerica (Figure 4.4).[25] What this ancient scene depicts is a human sacrifice occurring after a ritual ball game played between different members of ruling kingdoms at El Tajín. While scholars like S. Jeffrey K. Wilkerson argued that pre-Columbian ball games had very profound religious significance because the participants often impersonated gods engaged in cosmic struggles for dominance, they also pointed out that these rituals functioned "to allow public reaffirmation of power and to demonstrate the prerogatives of status [of a particular Maya ruler]."[26] What the artist of the northeast relief in the South Ballcourt depicts is the sacrificial demise of one of the ball-game participants. While another participant restrains him, a priest-looking player holds a flint knife

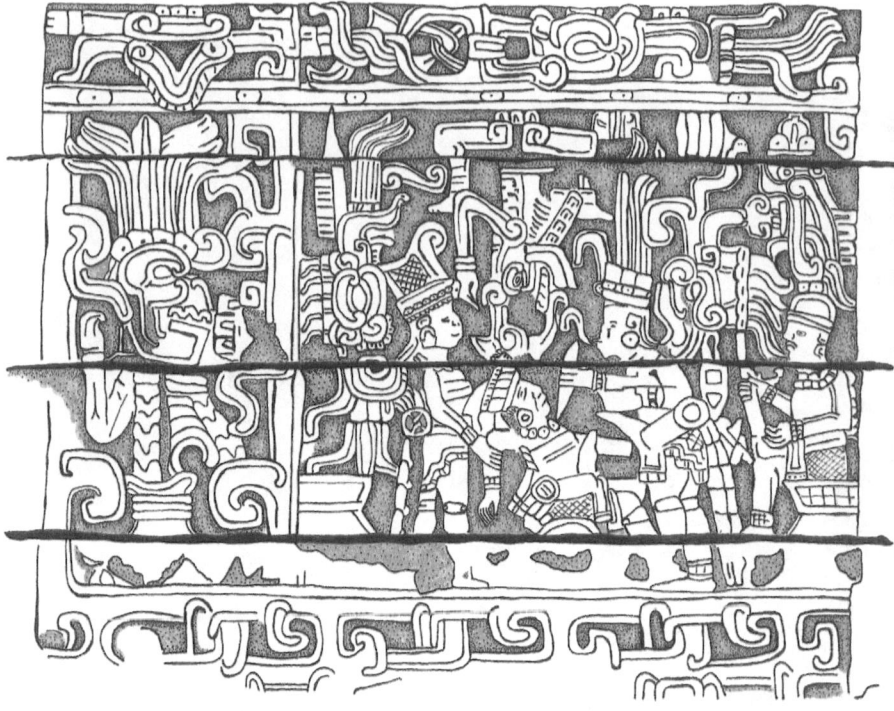

FIGURE 4.4. Ballcourt relief (Late Classic, AD 600), El Tajín, Veracruz, Mexico. Pen-and-ink drawing by Guisela Latorre.

as he prepares to decapitate his victim.[27] The whole scene is meant to occur within both an earthly and a divine setting.

Sánchez-Tranquilino explains that Félix had left the choice of subject matter up to the VNE gang members who had participated in *Sacrifice Wall* at Estrada Courts. He stated that these young men wanted to work with an image with which they could identify. They saw the El Tajín figures as highly decorated warriors whose status was indicated by the clothing they wore—not unlike themselves within their own gang affiliations.[28] While this explains some of the motivations behind the use of the Maya relief, it doesn't really address the image's possible meanings beyond the intentions of the artists. What seems anachronistic about the iconography in *Sacrifice Wall* is that it portrays an image of—as the title directly states—*sacrifice*, a somewhat odd choice of subject matter, given that the purpose behind the whole mural project in Estrada Courts was to provide a more positive and nonviolent view of Mexican and Chicana/o youth culture. Within the Mesoamerican context, however, the concept of sacrifice was associated not so much with death and violence as with the continuation of life itself, for it was believed that the gods required sacrifices in order to perpetuate human existence and other forms of life on earth. Taking into consideration that the threat of gang violence affected the lives of most young people in Estrada Courts, an image that indirectly alluded to the continuation of life seemed a fitting symbol to make for a group of gang members who wished to improve their image in the eyes of the larger community. Moreover, the notion of sacrifice here must have mirrored the importance placed by gangs on dying for *familia* or for allegiance to a particular neighborhood. Furthermore, in the same manner in which depictions of sacrifice in the Mesoamerican world served as a means to legitimize the power of a Maya ruler, in the context of 1970s East Los Angeles, it functioned as a way to affirm Chicana/o cultural agency in a visibly public way.

The Indigenist aesthetic that *Sacrifice Wall* presented also greatly contributed to the transformation of space sought by artists and community members in Estrada Courts. The El Tajín wall relief was situated within a ballcourt, a space that held deep ritualistic and religious meanings for the Maya people. This space was either fully or partially sectioned off by walls and buildings to distinguish it from more mundane and secular areas in El Tajín. The courtyards that surrounded the wall reliefs at this pre-Columbian site were thus not unlike the courtyards that divided the space in Estrada Courts. As such, the Indigenist imagery in *Sacrifice Wall* served the purpose of associating the contemporary architecture of this housing project with the ancient ruins of El Tajín. Moreover, this mural signaled the existence of sacred spaces within what was previously considered to be a run-down and depreciated area where Mexican and Chicana/o communities lived.

Chicano Park, Barrio Logan, San Diego

While the Indigenist wall paintings in Estrada Courts were created with the purpose of beautifying the spaces allotted to Mexican and Chicana/o communities, the ones in San Diego's Chicano Park functioned as testaments to the struggles the community underwent to protect and preserve those very spaces. Chicano Park, perhaps the site of one of the most ambitious community mural environments of our era, was precisely the result of the community's resistance toward urban development initiatives that threatened to displace and destroy San Diego's Barrio Logan neighborhood, a predominantly Chicana/o and Mexican area. In her seminal essay "The Story of Chicano Park," Eva Cockcroft recounted the complex negotiations that barrio residents and artists went through with city officials in order to protect the neighborhood from San Diego's growing industrialization and urban renewal.[29] For many decades, Barrio Logan had been an area used by the city of San Diego to allocate junkyards (called "yonkes" by barrio residents) and later became a site for the construction of a major freeway intersection. The community's efforts to protect their residential neighborhood led them in the late 1960s to pressure the city to construct a park precisely underneath the intersection between Interstate 5 and the on-ramp leading to the Coronado Bridge. Community activists were well aware that the need for a park in Logan transcended mere concerns over leisure activities. Open space and recreation, as stipulated by David R. Diaz, are cornerstones for Mexican/Chicana/o culture that "form an essential arena of communal discourse and cultural sharing." Moreover, the need for park space is heightened in barrios like Logan where residents usually live in crowded and crammed quarters and need a public space that does not further confine them in any way.[30]

The proposed location for Chicano Park was rather unorthodox, given that it would be built in the middle of a series of highway pylons, with all the noise of the freeway traffic coming from above. Nevertheless, it would be a space that unequivocally belonged to the residents of Barrio Logan. The city, however, went back on its promise to build a park for the community and unexpectedly began construction of a highway police station on the site. When the bulldozers arrived on April 22, 1970, to begin this undertaking, Logan residents and other supporters took the matter into their own hands, blocked the passage of construction crews with human chains, and began work on the park themselves, thereby making one of the most powerful statements of political resistance and civil disobedience the city of San Diego had ever seen.[31]

Though mural production in Chicano Park did not begin until 1973, the images artists and community members would create functioned as a visual reminder and documentation of the efforts that ultimately led to the construction of the park (Figure 4.5). In her now-famous essay on Chicano Park, Eva Cockcroft provided a rigorous account of the different phases of mural work that took place there and even described the contesting ideologies that informed the iconographic program of the murals. Both she and Raúl Homero Villa agree that it was Salvador "Queso" Torres, an artist and longtime Logan resident, who first saw the gray highway pylons interspersed throughout the park and envisioned the creative possibilities that these concrete structures presented. He soon began to make sketches of the pylons with designs painted all over them, which eventually led to the now-legendary mural initiative that flooded Chicano Park. The use of the pylons as canvases for the murals points to a common strategy that has characterized Chicana/o artistic production since the late 1960s. Using elements imposed by institutions of power—such as the pylons constructed by the city of San

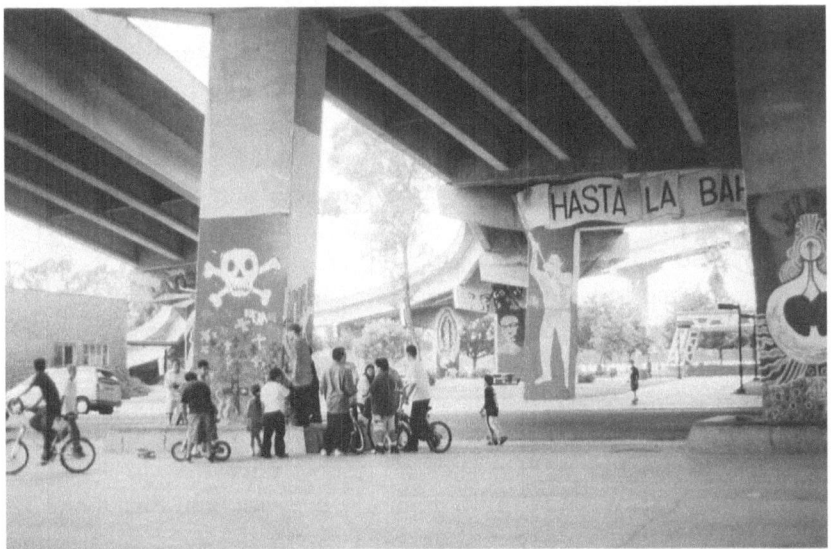

FIGURE 4.5. General view of Chicano Park, San Diego, California. Photograph by
Guisela Latorre.

Diego in Logan Heights—and transforming them into assets that benefit
marginalized communities became a recurring strategy by Chicana/o artists
who sought alternative venues for their work. In this respect, Chicano Park
was no exception, but it was unique in that nowhere else had art and community activism worked so closely to contest hegemonic control.

Coincidentally, artists who participated in the mural efforts undertaken
in Chicano Park—especially in its earlier phases—were affected by the
growing Indigenist consciousness that informed the Chicano Movement
as a whole. Guillermo Aranda, a local artist and organizer of many of the
mural initiatives there, made a clear connection between his own personal
quest for a new cultural identity and the message he was trying to convey
as an artist in Chicano Park: "I just like to think of myself as indigenous. I
wanted to give pride and identity to my own people. I wanted them to realize that they have roots in this continent."[32] For artists like Aranda, Indigenism provided a system of signifiers that functioned on various levels. On
the one hand, it provided Chicanas/os a means by which to think of their
identity as intrinsically indigenous both in an individual and a collective
mode. On the other hand, by embracing such a consciousness, Chicanas/os
were making strong connections to the land they inhabited in the United
States, directly proclaiming their entitlement to the spaces previously denied

to them. For this reason, it was particularly fitting that artists and community members would create a mural environment in the contested site of San Diego, just a few miles from the U.S.-Mexico border. The repossession of the land for the park and the creation of the mostly Indigenist murals within it consolidated both the pragmatic and the symbolic language that formed part of Chicana/o activist discourse. As Marilyn Mulford—director of the documentary film *Chicano Park* (1988)—would later remark, "the ancient prophecy of a new Aztlán was answered [in Chicano Park]."[33]

Although the park is visible to a wider audience from Interstate 5 and Coronado Bridge, direct access to it is somewhat more difficult, as it requires the potential visitor to drive through a complex network of intersections and freeway exits to get there. Though Chicano Park itself may seem at first glance to be somewhat overshadowed by the freeway ramps above it, the power of the park's presence in the middle of Barrio Logan draws its visual strength from the collective aesthetic of its murals. While each individual mural has a very distinct style and content, there is a certain degree of unity among them, perhaps due to the fact that most artists in Chicano Park had to conform to the T shape of the highway pylons. But more than that, the energy that somehow bound the murals together has more to do with the common impetus that propelled artistic production at the site. Every artist and community member who secured wall space for a mural was conscious of the incredible importance of the park as a site of cultural and political resistance. Furthermore, the community's triumph after the struggle for space indirectly signified a symbolic return to Aztlán, which elicited an Indigenist aesthetic that unified the mural environment in Chicano Park.

Aside from operating as an aesthetic that supported ideologies of space, Indigenism in Chicano Park also acted as a binding agent that unified local concerns with more universal concepts about cultural identity. Certainly, the murals were the result of the very site-specific reality in Logan Heights, but they were also part of the broader concerns that informed the artistic renaissance associated with the Chicano Movement. The events surrounding the construction of the park attracted the attention of artists and activists all over California. For example, the Chicano Park mural project counted on the contributions of artists like Rupert García from the San Francisco Bay Area, the members of the Royal Chicano Air Force from Sacramento, and, in its later phases of mural production, it even included works by non-Chicana/o artists like Michael Schnorr and Susan Yamagata. Indigenist thinking recognized the local spaces that belonged to Chicanas/os' indigenous history, and it also linked those spaces to the more conceptual and transcendental ideas about the nature of this history. Many Chicana/o activists and thinkers believed that if change were to occur for Chicanas/os at

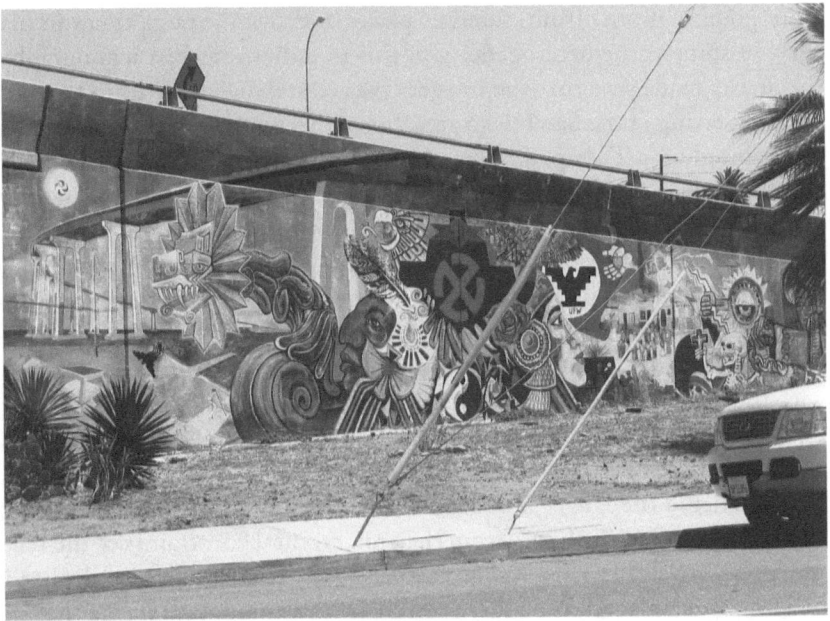

FIGURE 4.6. Guillermo Aranda, Mario Acevedo, Víctor Ochoa, Salvador Torres, José Cervantes, Tomás Castañeda, Guillermo Rosete, and others, © 1971, *Quetzalcoatl*, mural, Chicano Park, San Diego, California. Courtesy of Víctor Ochoa.

the local level, it needed to be accompanied by a discourse that legitimized their presence in transhistorical spaces. Indigenism, both as an aesthetic and as an ideology, provided an appropriate framework to articulate all these concerns. For this reason, Indigenism figures prominently in the park's iconography and its general planning.

Without a doubt, it was the iconographic program in Chicano Park that most immediately identified the site as an Indigenist mural environment par excellence. Recurring images of monumental Aztec warriors and grandiose Mesoamerican architecture and sculpture were meant to transform the otherwise mundane urban environment that surrounded the murals while reminding the spectator that this space was once the ancient homeland of Aztlán. The iconography in these works also created the effect of an expanded space beyond the actual tract of land encompassed by the park. Such was the case of the *Quetzalcoatl* mural on ramp 1B (Figure 4.6), executed by a team of mural painters and barrio residents that included Guillermo Aranda, Mario Acevedo, Víctor Ochoa, Salvador Torres, José Cervantes, Tomás Castañeda, and Guillermo Rosete. Originally created in 1971, and renovated in 1987, the ramp 1B mural compiled many Indigenist iconographic motifs from different places and from various times in history. In spite of the heterogeneity of this mural's Indigenist iconography, the artists made sure that the imagery was contextualized within the site-specific setting of the San Diego area. Since this was one of the few murals *not* painted on a T-shaped highway pylon, the artists had relatively more compositional freedom than most of their peers. Using the triangular shape of the ramp, the muralists included in the foreground a crowded group of figures and objects, most of which form an important part of the Chicana/o iconographic nationalist pantheon. To the left we see Quetzalcoatl, the plumed-serpent deity in Aztec cosmology, whose body undulates upward as his features display the traditional attributes associated with this god in pre-Columbian representations. The artists' source for this figure was, most likely, the serpent-head sculptures attached to the Temple of the Feathered Serpent at the ancient site of Teotihuacán. The muralists here emulated the fanged muzzle and feathered headdress of these sculptures, but released the figure from the architectural constraints of the temple; they even fashioned a stylized serpent body to go along with the head. Next to Quetzalcoatl, the muralists rendered a compound image that included a male and a female figure wearing a traditional Maya headdress, an eagle warrior with a speech scroll, and various symbols that appealed to Chicanas/os' political consciousness. Among the most prominent of these symbols was a swastika that the muralists placed between the two Maya figures, but rather than making references to Nazism and anti-Semitism with its inclusion, the artists of this mural were seeking to reclaim the symbol from its infamous past and recall its original meaning of prosperity and good fortune that originated in India. The symbol also occurred in the Americas and was often used by the Maya and the Diné (Navajo). Below the swastika, a Chinese yin/yang sphere floats between the male and female Maya figures, reminding the viewer that the world is made of a balance of dualities. Behind them, the United Farm Workers' flag displays its identifying symbol, the stylized "stepped" eagle, a contemporary motif with ancient indigenous roots. In the background, a re-creation of the San Diego Bay with the Coronado Bridge looming above stretches into the horizon. Directly beneath the bridge, the muralists included a simplified representation of Chicano Park, identified by the pyramid kiosk that is located at the center of the park. A Chicana/o family then stands nearby overlooking the bay while they cast the shadow of the UFW eagle.

The muralists responsible for *Quetzalcoatl* on ramp 1B were seeking a visual language that defined the many facets of Chicana/o identity. They provided a pantheon of figures and symbols that conveyed an Indigenist past and present. By juxtaposing a recognizable representation of San Diego with these Indigenist motifs, these artists carved a metaphorical space within the city's urban landscape that allowed for the articulation of an empowering cultural citizenship for the Chicana/o and Mexican residents of Barrio Logan. Moreover, the fact that *Quetzalcoatl* was not located within the park itself but rather in an area directly adjacent to it suggested that the muralists were also seeking to expand the tract of land originally allotted to Chicano Park.[34] One important function of the murals was that they indirectly advocated for increased space and territory for Chicanas/os, not just in the park and Barrio Logan, but also in every place in the country where Latinas/os have been displaced or marginalized, and they did this merely by proclaiming an Indigenist aesthetic at a very public level.

Raising public consciousness about Chicano Park's history and social importance within the urban landscape of San Diego inspired the work of numerous muralists working there. In 1978, local Chicano artists Tomás Castañeda and Roger Lucero painted their mural entitled *Chicano Park Takeover* (Figure 4.7), which would function as a commemorating monument to the site's historic takeover and to the city's indigenous heritage. The mural was then renovated in 1991 by Guillermo Rosete, Felipe Adame,

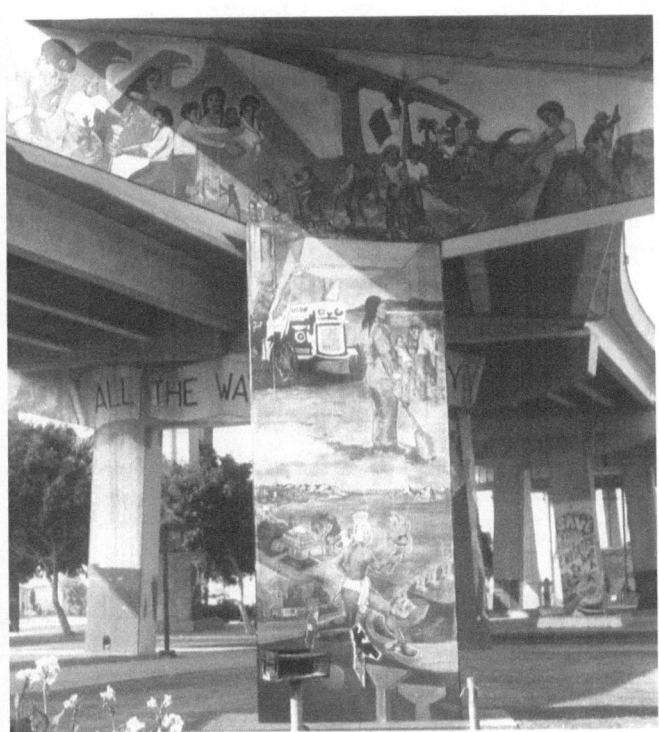

FIGURE 4.7. Tomás Castañeda and Roger Lucero, © 1978–1991, *Chicano Park Takeover*, mural, Chicano Park, San Diego, California. Photograph by Guisela Latorre.

Octavio González, and Vidal Aguirre. The narrative of this work could be read from top to bottom or bottom to top, depending on the viewer's approach to this T-shaped mural. If viewed from top to bottom, the mural began by illustrating the park's takeover, and the artists based their composition on photographs of the actual events. In this upper section of the mural, we see barrio residents—men, women, and children—with gardening and landscaping tools as they work on the land that they had reclaimed from the city of San Diego. Behind them, the Coronado Bridge rises from the bay while the silhouettes of eagles emerge from the ocean, a reference to Aztec eagle warriors whose spirits here are guiding the barrio residents. At the center of the composition, the artists painted the figure of a child climbing a lamppost as he proudly hoists the flag of Aztlán displaying the mestizo, tripartite face,[35] an important symbol of Chicana/o Indigenist identity, as explained in Chapter 2. This detail not only reflected a real occurrence during the park's historic takeover but also demonstrated how the residents themselves regarded the reclamation of this land as a political act deeply embedded in an indigenous consciousness. As we move down the composition, we again see the figures of local residents working the land, but this time they stand in front of the bulldozers contracted by the city of San Diego to build the infamous highway patrol station. The central figure in this section of the mural is a woman dressed in overalls, standing as an allegory of the proletarian worker who rejects the forces of capitalist "progress" by turning her back to the bulldozers. Below this scene in the mural, the artists moved away from the somewhat documentary approach to the subject matter to a more mystical rendering of the events surrounding the takeover. Here we see an aerial view of San Diego where Chicano Park is featured prominently and where the city's architecture has both Mesoamerican and modern Western features, reflections of the area's indigenous and colonial history. Running across this hybrid urban landscape is the figure of a Tarahumara male with a torch in his hand, a reference to the world-renowned reputation of the Tarahumara or Rarámuri peoples of the Sierra Madre Occidental (Mexico) as long-distance runners. This image also refers to a similar tradition that is revived in San Diego among its Chicana/o and indigenous communities every year. What this mural crystallized for the residents of Barrio Logan was that an indigenous identity necessarily implied a reclamation of land and space, as we see this Tarahumara figure appropriating San Diego's urban territories to symbolically overturn the deterritorialization and dispossession of colonization. This mural, then, clearly illustrated the role Chicano Park's mural environment played in the effort to reclaim this urban space on behalf of the Mexican,

Chicana/o, and indigenous peoples of San Diego. Moreover, if the viewer read the mural from bottom to top, she/he would first see the Tarahumara, who is situated at eye level, and then understand the rest of the park's history through an indigenous lens.

In addition to the discourses about space and cultural citizenship that the murals expounded, another purpose of the iconographic project in Chicano Park was to provide the community with a pantheon of heroes with whom the Logan community could identify. As explained in Chapter 2, these heroes, of course, would be protagonists of a revised version of U.S. history that included the participation of Mexican and Chicana/o figures. Those figures, however, could be either historical or mythical entities that formed part of this Chicana/o mythohistorical repertoire. Muralist Víctor Ochoa discussed the importance of portraiture in Chicano Park: "We thought that it was very important that our community realize that we had very important people in our history, and we did a series of portraits to have more role models or heroes."[36] Ochoa's statement seems to suggest that the very act of making portraits is synonymous with that of creating the role models and heroes themselves. Indeed, many Chicana/o artists and writers were conscious of the "constructedness" of history and sought to reconfigure its narrative and main characters. Compositionally, the freeway pylons in Chicano Park were particularly fitting for the depiction of full-body figures rendered on a monumental scale. Such was the case of Felipe Adame's *Cuauhtémoc* (1978) and Vidal Aguirre's *Aztec Archer* (1978–1980). Directly borrowing figures from the Mexican home calendars (see below) and the chromo-print tradition, Adame elevated his Cuauhtémoc to the height of national hero worship, endowing him with all the proper attributes and military decorations. Though Adame was working with preexisting images that were probably already familiar to most Logan residents through mass-produced calendars and posters purchased for homes or local businesses, the location and scale of these figures transforms their status from domestic bric-a-brac curiosities to majestic cultural icons. This shift from the private to the public sphere legitimized this imagery associated with Mexican culture. While Cuauhtémoc was an identifiable historical figure who epitomized resistance against the Spanish invader during the conquest, *both* Adame's and Aguirre's heroes in Chicano Park can be regarded as generalized symbols of an Indigenist pride in which spectators were supposed to partake. These figures with idealized physiques and poses acted as allegories of indigenous culture, history, land, and people.

Certainly, contesting ideologies that also went into the creation of Chicano Park often sidelined the rather utopian ideals behind its creation.

Many of the individuals who participated in its mural initiatives lauded the early stages of artistic production in the park as an "explosion" of creative energy in which artists and community alike literally "attacked" the walls with paint and color. In the latter stages, however, it seemed that before anything could go up on the walls, a long and complex process of submitting proposals and sketches was required in order to paint a mural in Chicano Park. It appeared to many artists and community members that mural production there had become an institutionalized endeavor. Furthermore, artists such as José Montoya cited the growing divisions within the Chicano Movement as a threat to the initial ideological unity and integrity they felt defined the early work at Chicano Park.[37] Whether or not this mural environment truly represented a consolidation of Chicana/o activist thinking since the park's inception in the early 1970s, the claim over the urban space it occupied remains one of its most powerful attributes. In spite of the contesting ideologies and the contrasting aesthetics that defined the mural production at the park, there was nevertheless a sense of collectivity in the way each of the murals contributed to carving out a metaphorical Aztlán in the middle of Barrio Logan.

The Balmy Alley Murals, Mission District, San Francisco

As a later though equally important mural environment, the Balmy Alley murals emerged within the heart of the predominantly Latina/o neighborhood of San Francisco's Mission District during the 1970s. Balmy Alley is a short and narrow street that stretches from Twenty-fourth to Twenty-fifth Street in the Mission, sandwiched between Harrison Street and Treat Avenue. Balmy is lined primarily by garage doors and backyard fences belonging to private homes and thus tends to attract mostly local traffic. Compared to the other sites discussed here, Balmy Alley is relatively small and narrow.[38] Nevertheless, its location adjacent to Twenty-fourth Street, where the Galería de la Raza and the Precita Eyes Mural Arts center are located, situates this particular mural environment within a culturally charged location where Chicana/o/Latina/o art has traditionally flourished. With its close proximity to other arts organizations, Balmy Alley contributes to a visibly significant reclamation of the urban space. While they do not encompass the breadth of space that the murals at Estrada Courts and Chicano Park command, the Balmy murals hold a power that transcends quantifiable space. For more than thirty years, this environment has been an important monument to the local community, particularly to the residents who have a mural painted on their fence, wall, or garage door, but Balmy Alley has also become a sought-after location for visitors coming to the city of San

Francisco. Various travel and leisure Web sites now advertise Balmy Alley as one of the many tourist attractions in the city. Although this kind of attention given to a mural environment could potentially make it vulnerable to co-optation, depoliticization, and city control, the Balmy murals continue to be, for the most part, testaments of oppositional consciousness and Indigenist aesthetics that reflect the still predominantly Chicana/o/Latina/o cultural makeup of the Mission District.

Balmy Alley differs from both Estrada Courts and Chicano Park in that its origins are profoundly connected to the history of women artists in the community mural movement, including Chicanas. The first mural phase that took place there in the 1970s was led by women artists and educators. For instance, in 1972, Mia Gonzalez and Susan Kelk Cervantes directed a group of preschool children to carry out a collective mural project in Balmy. A year later, Patricia Rodríguez and Graciela Carrillo painted two decorative murals on a nearby wall. Rodríguez, Carrillo, and Cervantes all went on to become prominent muralists in the Mission District. Rodríguez and Carrillo would later found the seminal artists collective Las Mujeres Muralistas, and Cervantes would produce some of the most ambitious and elaborate mural cycles in the Mission District. A few years later, Chicano artist René Yáñez would establish the Neighborhood Arts Program, which would fund various mural projects throughout Balmy.

Nevertheless, Balmy Alley's status as a mural environment was enhanced and heightened when Chicago-based muralist Ray Patlán moved to the San Francisco Bay Area in the 1980s and joined forces with Rodríguez to lead a project called PLACA that they carried out with a grant from the Zellerbach Family Fund. Patlán explained the project as follows:

> Patricia Rodríguez and I were very good friends since I moved into the area. During nine months in 1984, we organized 36 artists, some working collaboratively and some working as individuals, to do 25 murals on Balmy Street. We called ourselves PLACA, which means the mark kids make on the walls. Our thrust was peace in Central America.[39]

The inception of PLACA in Balmy led to a sustained proliferation of mural production there that continues to this day, a phenomenon that transformed this small barrio street into a full-fledged mural environment. PLACA was innovative on many fronts. The artists chose as the project name the word *placa,* which, as explained in Chapter 3, was a term that referred to graffiti tagging, a practice that many muralists wanted to distance themselves from, yet Patlán and Rodríguez chose to reiterate the connection between murals and graffiti with this name. The innovative character of the PLACA project also rested on the fact that it counted on the active participation of women, and it brought to the forefront the hardships and abuses that Central American countries like El Salvador, Guatemala, and Nicaragua, and especially their indigenous communities, were suffering under both long-term and newly constituted right-wing regimes heavily controlled or influenced by U.S. policies. These circumstances ushered in a new influx of immigrants to the United States, namely, the many refugees and exiles who were escaping the violence and political persecution in their home countries. The Mission District became an important destination in Northern California for many of these Central American newcomers. Chicana/o activists and community organizers found a common cause between their struggles and those of the growing Central American diaspora living in the urban areas of California, and as a result, established critical counterhegemonic alliances with them. The horrific violence, forced displacement, and brutal migration that the mostly Maya populations there were subjected to echoed the similar histories experienced by Mexican and North American indigenous communities as a result of colonization and westward expansion. Like Chicanas/os, the Maya had a history of migration going back millennia that was even recorded in their sacred texts like the *Popol Vuh*.[40] Thus, Balmy Alley became one of the first mural sites to expound an Indigenist aesthetic that transcended a Chicana/o-centric Indigenism while simultaneously making meaningful connections between the Central American struggle and the Chicano Movement's indigenous consciousness.

Chicana artist Juana Alicia was among the thirty-six artists that Patlán and Rodríguez invited to Balmy for the creation of this important mural environment. The New Jersey–born and Detroit-raised artist had moved to the San Francisco Bay Area in the 1980s and quickly became involved in the Chicana/o/Latina/o community mural movement in the area. For her first contribution to Balmy, Juana Alicia painted an image entitled *Te Oímos Guatemala/We Hear You Guatemala* (1985; Figure 4.8).[41] This mural was meant to raise awareness among the local community about the systematic violence targeted at Guatemala's Maya communities at that time. By the 1980s, the military government in Guatemala embarked on a campaign to crush what they regarded as guerrilla warfare among indigenous and rural communities in the country. The attacks directed at the Maya were swift and unusually brutal, traumatizing these communities for years to come. This state of terror that gripped the country in the 1980s came to be known as "la violencia"; genocide would probably not be an inappropriate word to describe what was being done to the Maya at this time:

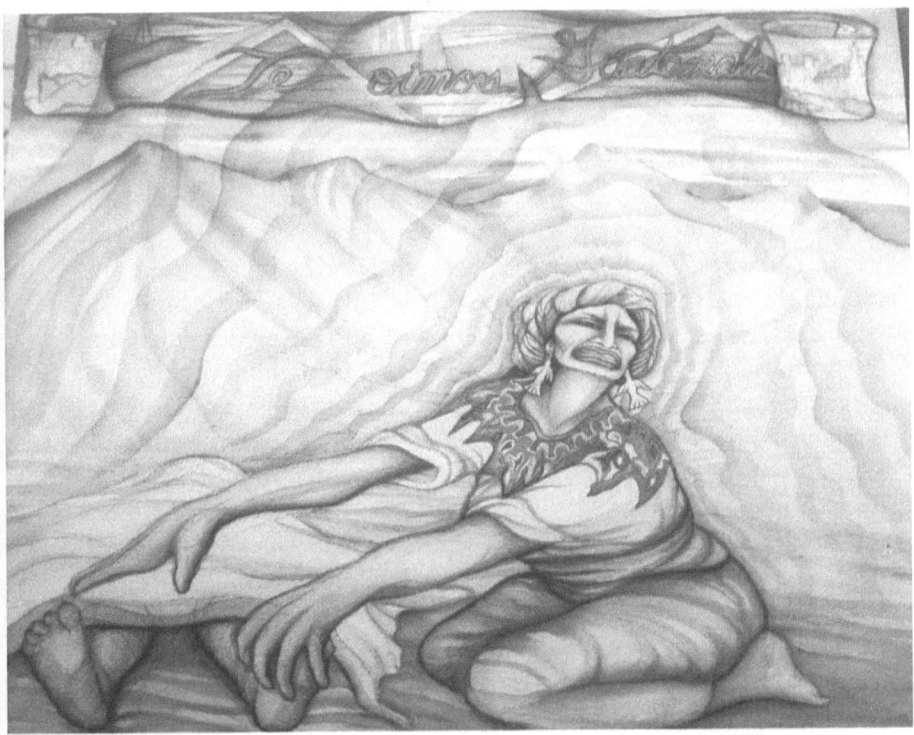

FIGURE 4.8. Juana Alicia, © 1985, *Te Oímos Guatemala/We Hear You Guatemala*, preparatory drawing for mural located in Balmy Alley, San Francisco, California. Courtesy of Juana Alicia.

Some 440 villages by the army's own count, 626 according to the Comisión de Esclaramiento Histórico statistics, were totally destroyed. The Maya as a group were identified by the army as insurgent allies and targeted for elimination without regard to their civilian status. One hundred-fifty thousand Maya were killed during this period. The horror of the massacres, the brutality of the torture and murder, the pervasive fear that engulfed the Maya communities . . . remain vivid to this day among those who lived through that time.[42]

For Chicana/o artists like Juana Alicia, the plight of the Maya was not just an internal matter affecting Guatemala, but was directly related to the current political and social situation in the United States. U.S. government officials, concerned with the spread of dangerous insurgency and Communism so close to home, and seeking new cheap labor markets to exploit in an ongoing push for international control, intervened in various Central American internal affairs in the 1980s. In Guatemala, for instance, many of the troops that carried out the attacks on the Maya had been trained under the U.S. Alliance for Progress program.[43] Moreover, the perilous situation in the country forced the Maya to migrate to urban centers within Guatemala itself, to Mexico, and to the United States and Canada. Nevertheless, most of the immigrants who came to the United States from Central America were denied asylum by the Immigration and Naturalization Service (INS) because it claimed that they were "economic," not political refugees. As a result, much of the Central American diaspora in the United States lived and worked in the country without the benefits of "legal" status. The parallels between the Chicana/o/Mexican and Central American experience, including that of the Maya, were not lost on Chicana/o artists and activists and, in many ways, further galvanized the legitimacy of *la causa*.

In *Te Oímos Guatemala*, Juana Alicia depicts the figure of a kneeling Maya woman, clothed in the traditional indigenous headdress and *huipil* (blouse), as she tragically mourns over the body of a victim of political violence covered in a white bed sheet, undoubtedly a murdered loved one. In the background, we see a mountainous landscape and a banner that bears the words "Te oímos Guatemala." The anonymity of the dead figure is counteracted by the raw and poignant emotion that the Maya woman is expressing. Her arms are extended over the body as she throws her head back, letting out an agonizing wail of grief and despair. Her scream is so loud and sweeping that it creates "sound ripples" that engulf her body and the landscape behind her. The title, "We Hear You Guatemala," suggests that the cries of anguish and suffering of the Maya people can be heard all the way to the Mission District and its community, where Chicanas/os and Guatemalan exiles now share the same contested urban space and many realities. While the scene reflects the indigenous consciousness of the Central American community, the position of these two figures is reminiscent of Judeo-Christian lamentation scenes where the Virgin Mary mourns over the body of Christ. Such an association would then endow this indigenous victim with the status of saintly martyrdom and this Maya woman with an aura of holiness. In spite of the despair and hopelessness of the scene, Juana Alicia renders this female figure as an allegory of the collective anguish suffered by the Maya but also as the hope for a peaceful resolution to this horrific violence, for she wears two doves of peace as earrings. This detail proved to be almost prophetic in its vision, given that Rigoberta Menchú, a Quiché Maya woman, would emerge a few years later as one of the most prominent peace activists of our time. Juana Alicia then signed the mural with her name and the words "para PLACA y todos los varrios" ("for PLACA and all the barrios"), implying that she was directing the message of this mural to the largely Chicana/o/Latina/o community of the Mission District.

As stated earlier, one of the most positive outcomes of the PLACA project in Balmy Alley was that it ushered in sustained mural production in that location. Whenever murals there deteriorated or were destroyed, new ones would soon be created to take their place. In 1990, Ray Patlán and his colleagues realized that many of the murals from the mid-1980s had indeed deteriorated considerably, so they led an initiative to restore and, in some cases, replace the ailing murals from the original PLACA project. Such was the case with Nicole Emanuel's mural *Indigenous Beauty* (1984), which was mostly destroyed when the garage door it was painted on was in need of replacement. In *Indigenous Beauty,* Emanuel painted a lush and expansive landscape that is being planted and harvested by its largely Maya population. In the foreground, we see groups of indigenous women engaged in a variety of activities that relate to their reproductive, productive, and creative abilities: breast-feeding, agricultural harvesting, and pottery making. A child sits next to them holding the globe of the world showing the Americas, a reference to the hemispheric consciousness shared by all indigenous peoples. As the landscape stretches to the right-hand side of the composition, it turns into an urban setting, which refers to the escape into cities that many of the Maya were forced to make. *Indigenous Beauty* was then replaced by Susan Kelk Cervantes's *Indigenous Eyes: War or Peace* in 1990 (Figure 4.9). Though not a Chicana per se, Cervantes—through her prominence as a muralist and community leader in the Mission District and through her marriage to the late Chicano artist Luis Cervantes—acquired a heightened sensitivity about the issues that affected the local Chicana/o/Latina/o population in and beyond the San Francisco Bay Area. She also understood the cultural, social, and political dimensions of the indigenous consciousness within this community. In addition, she was not only the collective and individual author of various murals in the Mission, but she was also the founder of Precita Eyes Mural Arts center. In *Indigenous Eyes*, she used Emanuel's landscape imagery that still survived on the adjoining walls to the garage door and created a more simplified yet equally powerful image. The harvest fields that Emanuel had created now stretched into the mural's foreground to form a pair of large indigenous eyes that stare directly at the viewer. On the pupil of the left eye we see a skeletal figure dressed as a soldier, an iconographic motif that was present in Emanuel's original mural and that Cervantes chose to preserve in *Indigenous Eyes*. In the right eye, we find the dove of peace flying toward

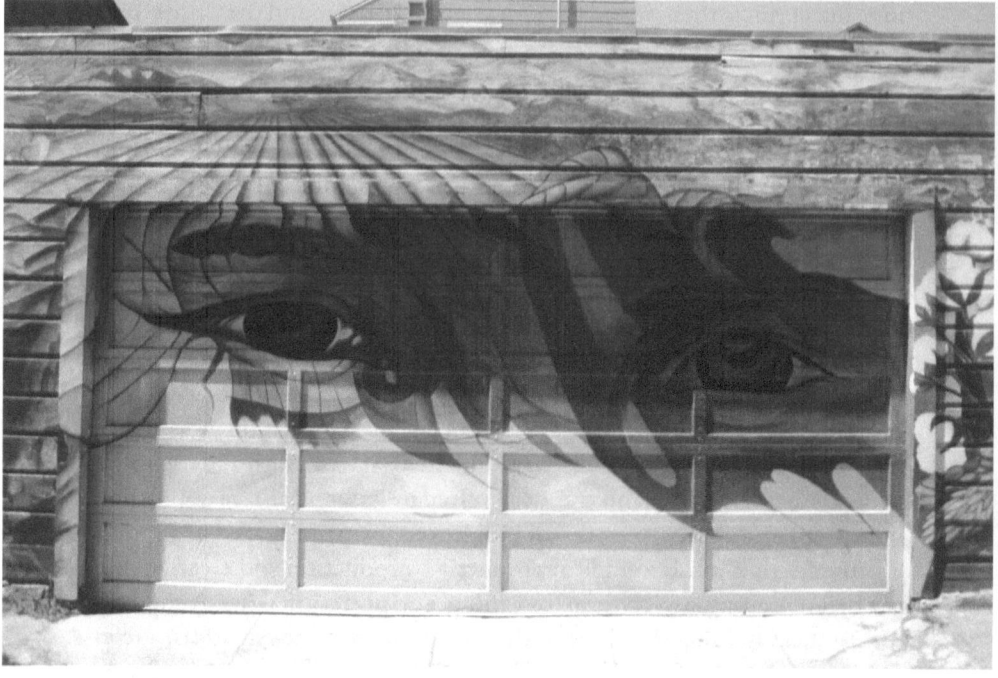

FIGURE 4.9. Susan Kelk Cervantes, © 1990, *Indigenous Eyes: War or Peace*, mural, Balmy Alley, San Francisco, California. Courtesy of Susan Kelk Cervantes.

the sky. These two motifs reflect the contradictory life of the contemporary Maya people, who are caught between the violence of state repression and the peacefulness of their cultural practices. But the large-scale and confrontational quality of these two eyes compel the spectator to look at the world through indigenous eyes, so to speak, and bear witness to the same horrors and abuses endured by the Maya and other populations. Here, Cervantes is depicting an indigenous consciousness that is not the sole purview of indigenous peoples themselves.

Balmy Alley's Indigenist aesthetic effectively transformed the social spaces of the Mission District and beyond. It proved that the power of mural environments transcended the limits of their physical locations. Moreover, the high visibility that Chicana artists enjoyed in the creation of this environment operated as an indicator of the prominence they would gain within the mural movement in California, thus challenging the male domination of the medium, as elaborated in greater detail in Chapter 5. But these public works of art in Balmy and elsewhere in the Mission District are currently being threatened by the very forces that Chicana/o muralists sought to battle with their work, namely, gentrification and the insatiable real estate market that has historically displaced and marginalized people of color. In the past ten years, the price of rent and property there has soared as wealthier sectors of society have become attracted to the Mission because of its cultural richness and "charm." As a result, many Chicana/o/Latina/o residents whose families have lived there for generations can no longer afford the cost of living and have been forced to leave. The same holds true for the community of artists responsible for most of the murals there. Ironically, gentrification in the Mission is driving out the very people who are responsible for the cultural richness that the new residents so crave. If murals were created to make barrios into desirable places to live, those in the Mission perhaps succeeded too well. Only time will tell what will happen to the Mission murals or its Chicana/o/Latina/o community, including the artists.[44]

The Mural Dedication as Environment:
Paul Botello's *Inner Resources*

Mural environments like Estrada Courts, Chicano Park, and Balmy Alley provided physical and tangible means by which communities could reclaim or transform urban spaces to fit their needs, and the phenomenon of the mural dedication operated as a more *performative* form of mural environment. A critical part of almost every Chicana/o mural in California, the dedication is enacted to introduce the community to a new mural erected in a particular area or neighborhood of the city. The dedication also becomes a kind of extension of the mural's visual discourse beyond the confines of the walls on which it is painted; it provides a discursive three-dimensionality to the message being conveyed in the iconography. Like environments such as Estrada Courts, Chicano Park, and Balmy Alley, dedications also carve out an Indigenist space in which the community can exercise a greater degree of cultural citizenship. The mural dedication, however, takes on both a celebratory and a ritualistic form in which the different activities that are part of the event establish a prescribed order in which a collective identity is to be articulated. The Aztec dances that are often part of the mural dedication serve to remind the community not only that the practice of mural painting has ancient roots in indigenous America but also that the space they inhabit used to form part of the indigenous homeland of Aztlán.

Paul Botello's dedication for his mural *Inner Resources* (Figure 4.10) on July 22, 2000, included all the elements that usually characterize such festivities. Even though the event was dedicated as much to Botello's work as it was to the construction of the new gymnasium where the mural was painted, the power of the visual images that saturated the space of the celebrations seemed to take on greater importance. Taking place in East L.A.'s City Terrace Park, where the mural is located, this particular dedication brought together different elements of the community that supported the creation of this work. The dedication began with the traditional Aztec dances in the immediate area in front of the mural (Figure 4.11). The majority of the members of this dance troupe were children from the community who had been trained to perform in such events. Following the performance, one of the principal dancers of the group led a ritual blessing of the mural and of the muralist himself (Figure 4.12). The blessing was then followed by a series of public speeches conducted by city park and recreation officials, a local radio DJ, the pastor from the nearby Our Lady of Guadalupe church, and Paul Botello, who concluded this portion of the event with descriptions of the mural's iconography and with comments about his role as a community artist. Next there was a session of poetry readings by various Chicana/o students from UCLA and a live appearance by Act of Faith, a Chicana/o rock group that had made quite a name for itself in the East Los Angeles music scene during the 1980s.

The mixture of celebratory zeal and civic pride that distinguished Botello's mural dedication was mirrored by the iconographic program of *Inner Resources*, a mural inspired by the ideas community members gave to the artist. The composition revolves around a central group that Botello described during the dedication as "a global family" that has kinship ties not only with all of humanity but also with the animal kingdom, as indicated by the various figures that surround them. The central focus of this family is a female figure who displays maternal attributes. This global family resides within a generalized setting that displays both rural and urban characteristics coexisting in a harmonious environment. Botello has commented that while community muralists from the 1960s and 1970s were interested in issues about cultural nationalism, members of his generation of the 1980s, 1990s, and the turn of the century have been more concerned with heterogeneous notions about collective spirituality.[45] In spite of this desire to break away from the rigid articulations of identity that defined the earlier phases of Chicana/o muralism, Botello's *Inner Resources* does betray vestiges of the Indigenist iconography that characterized earlier permutations of the medium. For instance, the central "mother" figure sports a necklace composed of human hands, hearts, and

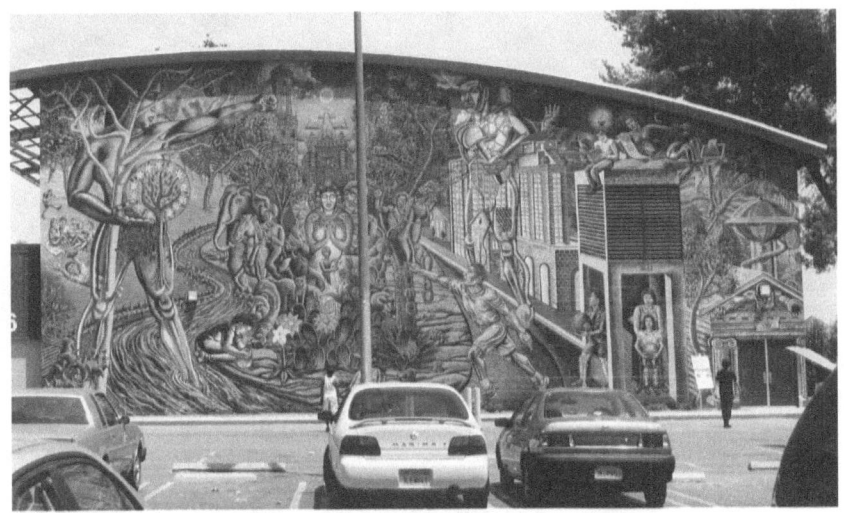

FIGURE 4.10. Paul Botello, © 2000, *Inner Resources*, mural, City Terrace, East Los Angeles, California. Courtesy of Paul Botello.

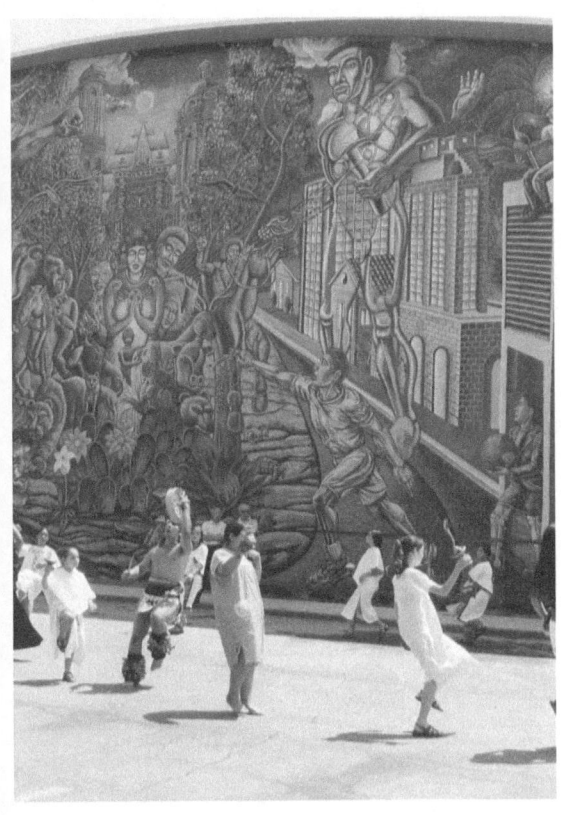

FIGURE 4.11. Aztec dances at the *Inner Resources* mural dedication, July 22, 2000. Photograph by Guisela Latorre.

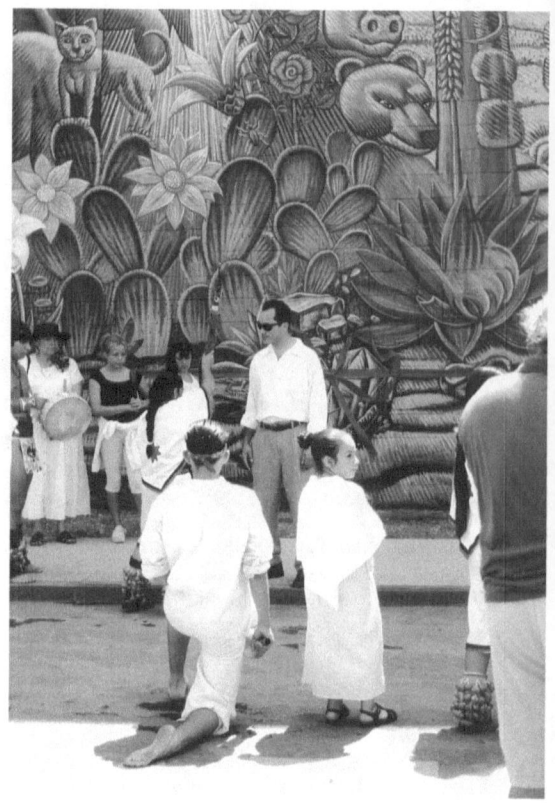

FIGURE 4.12. Blessing at the *Inner Resources* mural dedication, July 22, 2000. Photograph by Guisela Latorre.

a skull, a direct reference to the Coatlicue sculpture from Tenochtitlán mentioned earlier in this chapter. Far into the background, we get a glimpse of four different buildings, three colonial-style structures and a Mesoamerican pyramid looming behind them. The inclusion of these Indigenist elements, coupled with the dedication's Aztec dances, permeated the atmosphere with vestiges of an indigenous past that made itself palpable and relevant in the present. In spite of the fleeting nature of mural dedications, they have the ability to transform the space in a permanent manner. The actual mural remains as the testament to the collective and performative expressions of identity that were enacted in the area adjacent to this public work of art.

Conclusion

If community murals can be regarded as highly effective strategies for articulating a collective Indigenist identity at a public level, then mural environments become the ultimate means by which to carve out a metaphorical and physical space for this identity. The physical space that these environments occupy and the figurative space that the images themselves convey enable the community to exercise their right to cultural citizenship. But despite the seemingly democratizing way in which community murals reconfigured public space, this space remained highly gendered. Women were traditionally excluded from these spaces and were certainly not expected to exercise any form of cultural citizenship, especially in the form of creative expressions. Chapter 5 recounts how Chicana muralists challenged the exclusions that traditionally informed the muralist praxis.

CHAPTER FIVE

Gender, Indigenism, and Chicana Muralists

The Gendering of Murals and Nationalism

The chosen medium for the politically engaged Chicana/o artist in the 1970s was undoubtedly the public mural.[1] Indeed, the public mural was deeply saturated with a powerful history of politicization as well as a profound connection to indigenous artistic traditions. But murals also possessed a gendered history that historically and discursively relegated women to the margins and subsequently rendered them completely invisible, thus mirroring the dynamics of the Chicano Movement itself.[2] Chicano writers and activists from the 1970s, such as Rodolfo "Corky" Gonzales and the leaders of the militant group the Brown Berets, regarded the participation of women within *el movimiento* as supportive and secondary to that of the men. The Chicana/o arts renaissance that emerged on the coattails of the movement would re-create the gendered hierarchies that existed within the ranks of Chicana/o activist circles. Just as many male Chicano militants constructed the very notion of empowerment along masculinist lines, the Chicano mural, with its public character and its connections to the Mexican School, was strictly defined as a male art form. During the early to mid-1970s, not only did Chicana mural work go largely unrecognized, but the presence of Chicanas in the iconographic programs of these public works was omitted, sexualized, or circumscribed.

The Indigenist aesthetic that defined much of Chicana/o decolonized consciousness was also strongly male identified. The radical and nationalist language of foundational Chicano texts such as Alurista's "El Plan Espiritual de Aztlán"—drafted in 1969 at the Chicano Liberation Youth Conference in Denver attended mostly by Chicanos from California—bolstered an Indigenism defined by manhood:

> *Brotherhood* unites us, and love for our *brothers* makes us a people whose time has come and who struggle against the foreigner "gabacho" who exploits our riches and destroys our culture. ... Before the world, before all of North America, before all our *brothers* in the

bronze continent, we are a nation, we are a union of free pueblos, we are *Aztlán*.[3]

The unambiguous connection between the male-identified concept of brotherhood (or *carnalismo,* as it is referred to in other contexts) and the "bronze continent" (i.e., Aztlán or the indigenous Americas) articulated in "El Plan" allowed little or no room for the expressions of woman-centered subjectivities. Chicano identity, as initially defined by *el movimiento,* was static, finite, and clearly delineated along masculinist lines. As writers like Ana Nieto Gómez, Cherríe Moraga, Alicia Gaspar de Alba, and others tell us, Chicanas were expected to play a pivotal role in the creation of Chicano cultural nationalism, but this participation needed to happen on the sidelines of this project. While the men fashioned themselves as the intellectual architects of this new consciousness, the women were to stand by their side and assist them in this task. Many Chicano radicals and Chicana loyalists[4] saw any articulation of difference within this nationalist paradigm as an attempt at divisiveness and ideological treason. Given the subordination of their positions within *el movimiento,* most Chicana feminists saw no other alternative but to construct their own discursive and physical spaces.

In the visual program of the Chicana/o arts movement, iconography that alluded to women's experiences or, worse, feminist concerns would inevitably decenter Chicano nationalist aesthetics by mere virtue of its content. The Indigenist imagery that so eloquently spoke of decolonization in community murals illustrated utopian indigenous realms largely decreed by a patriarchal order. But in spite of the blatant exclusion of women within this nationalist aesthetic, many Chicanas who came of age as artists during the early phases of the Chicano Movement were not necessarily compelled to work independently of their male peers. In fact, Judy Baca and Patssi Valdez, for example, initially forged many alliances with male Chicano artists as part of the general desire of these cultural producers to create community among Chicana/o artists. During her early years as a community artist, Baca recalls that her initial artistic associations occurred primarily with male artists who were doing murals at the time, like Manuel Cruz and Leonardo Castellanos,[5] director of the Mechicano Art Center, one of the earliest Chicano cultural centers founded in Los Angeles. Given that the majority of the women associated with Chicano artistic circles in Los Angeles at the time were the wives or girlfriends of the male artists, Baca found it difficult to relate to them.[6] In the case of painter Patssi Valdez, she came onto the art scene also in the early seventies as a member of the now-legendary Chicano performance art group Asco, along with

Harry Gamboa, Willie Herrón, and Gronk. Judithe Hernández came into prominence as the sole female member of the artists collective Los Four, which also included male Chicano artists Frank Romero, Carlos Almaraz, Gilbert Luján, and Roberto de la Rocha. "I was literally the ONLY female at meetings who was NOT a girlfriend or wife, but an active artist participant," Hernández would later explain to me.[7] Many Chicana artists began their careers at a time when there were very few women artists active in the Chicano Movement, which made it difficult for them to create feminine or feminist affiliations. Moreover, in relation to dominant artistic currents in the United States, and specifically California, both Chicana *and* Chicano artists, with a few exceptions,[8] were not widely recognized or exhibited by mainstream galleries and museums in the country.

While Chicana feminist writers and activists were directly calling out Chicanos' notions of male privilege and sexism within the movement, Chicana artists were challenging masculinist aesthetics not by direct militant action but rather through the introduction of new iconography that placed women at the center of the decolonization process. While Chicana cultural producers came out of the political effervescence of the Chicano Movement just as the male artists did, their artistic contribution would assert itself as an alternative aesthetic that in some instances intersected nationalist iconography and in others steered clear of it. Chicana artists transformed Indigenism in ways that reflected their experiences as women of color residing on the margins of nationalist movements. Chicana artists who engaged in muralism, like Judithe Hernández, Yreina Cervántez, Judy Baca, and Las Mujeres Muralistas, not only produced an Indigenist imagery that allowed for an inclusion of gender, but also created a visual vocabulary that embraced many other intersecting identities (African American, Central American, lesbian, etc.). Chicana artists, unlike their male contemporaries, attached increasingly multiple meanings to the figure and culture of the Indian in the Americas. Within Chicana/o art history, women pioneered in using Indigenism for reasons that ventured beyond the nationalist paradigm of *el movimiento,* and they did so by revealing a spiritual component behind Chicanas/os' own indigenous heritage.

Masculinity and Femininity in Murals

Various Indigenist murals produced by male artists effectively masculinized nationalist discourses and thus relegated women and issues of gender to the margins. These images were meant to function as discourses of liberation for the Chicana/o community as a whole, yet women were often rendered

invisible within these public works of art. While issues of agency and empowerment had everything to do with the fact that women artists chose to
participate in such a public way within the Chicano mural initiative, their
contribution to the existing Indigenist visual vocabulary had even more to
do with a spontaneous and instinctive desire to loosen the rigidity of the
cultural nationalism being disseminated in the barrios and other public
spaces via the community mural. It ultimately became quite self-evident
that both men and women were active participants within the urban settings where murals reside. Yet much of the patriarchal thinking that saturated the Chicano Movement assumed that a woman's place was private
and domestic spaces, in spite of the fact that many working-class Chicanas,
whether feminist-identified or not, have long had no choice but to venture
into public arenas in order to provide for themselves and their families. If
the Chicano Movement strove to formulate a concept of U.S. history and
culture that was more inclusive of historically marginalized communities, it
would then follow that women would be fundamental players within this
new formulation. Chicano cultural nationalism, however, fostered prescriptive ideologies that called for an Indigenist iconography devised according
to predominantly male principles of desire. Chicana feminists soon found
that there was an inherent contradiction in the discourses of liberation stemming from the Chicano Movement. So, in reality, Chicanas were physically
present and active in the public spaces of muralism but discursively absent
in its iconography. It was because of this paradoxical situation that Chicanas
soon began to produce a feminine or feminist iconography that redefined
how gender was negotiated in a public setting. Chicanas' contribution to
mural history is critical not only because women were up on scaffolding doing public art,[9] but also because their work lent a more heterogeneous character to the community mural, allowing for a greater diversity in the style
and subject matter. Moreover, Chicana artists were the first to introduce an
Indigenist aesthetic that operated on multiple levels, thereby becoming a
powerful vehicle for social and political mobilization as well as an effective
tool for gender and patriarchal critique.

Similarly to the way Indigenism provided Chicanos a model for inclusion
into U.S. history and culture, it also inadvertently facilitated the exclusion of
women within its nationalist canon. Furthermore, Mexican mural imagery
during the twenties, thirties, and forties certainly provided a precedent for
a male-centered Indigenist iconography to the Chicano artists working in
the seventies and beyond. As a consequence, many male Chicano muralists
produced a masculinist image of Mesoamerican native culture and history.
Murals such as Felipe Adame's *Cuauhtémoc* (1978) in San Diego's Chicano

Park, for instance, monumentalized and glorified the indigenous male to the point of overstatement. Directly appropriating an older image made in the mid-1940s by Mexican almanac and calendar illustrator and painter Jesús Helguera, Adame bypassed the small-scale format and private nature of Helguera's compositions by presenting this Aztec warrior larger than life. Helguera's work in general was extremely influential to many Chicano artists seeking to create Indigenist aesthetics, as Tere Romo explains:

> The Mexican calendar became another source Chicano artists tapped to explore their identity and history. But whereas these calendar images had been used in Mexico to "Europeanize" the national identity, Chicanos used the very same images to "indigenize" a Mexican American self-image. It was a significant tenet of the "I'm brown and I'm proud" movement of the Brown Berets, as well as of nationalist *indigenistas*.[10]

Helguera was also an important source, primarily to male Chicano artists, because his work fit so well with the *machista* sensibilities of *el movimiento*. In the case of Adame's *Aztec Warrior*, all the artist had to do to his "adaptation" was to slightly adjust the original composition to the T shape of the highway pylon in Chicano Park. Emulating Helguera's academic style learned at the San Fernando Academy of Fine Arts in Spain,[11] Adame capitalized on the warrior's classicist anatomy and highly decorated attire to accentuate and complement his monumentality. The overt and prominent glorification of indigenous male figures in many of these murals, whether historical or allegorical, pointed to the general assumption that all native cultures in the Americas were patriarchal and patrilineal. Moreover, all the attributes conferred on this Aztec warrior were indicative that masculinity was carefully crafted and manipulated during the Chicano Movement, demonstrating that gender was performed and enacted in conscientious ways.[12]

Adame's work and that of other Chicano muralists illustrated an Indigenist project dedicated to the recovery and revitalization of the Chicano male's masculinity. This masculinity, from the male radical perspective, had been undermined by decades of racism, oppression, and marginalization. Nowhere was this sentiment more apparent than in the importance placed on the Zoot Suit Riots by Chicano writers and artists. The Zoot Suit Riots occurred in 1943, when a mob of servicemen and civilians assaulted a group of East Los Angeles Mexican American youth and stripped them of their pachuco attire. This dark episode in Mexican American history exemplified a pernicious incident in which the Chicano male was symbolically stripped of his identity. Marcos Sánchez-Tranquilino and John Tagg argued that the pachucos' zoot suit "made them visible in a way that had to be denied."[13]

The riots, however, also signaled an implied feminization of the pachuco's oppositional cultural posture, which was highly dependent on his masculine persona. Some of the images depicting scenes from this incident that would later circulate would further underscore the pachuco's damaged masculinity, such as the actual press photographs that documented this incident and Judy Baca's own 1981 rendition of the Zoot Suit Riots in *The Great Wall of Los Angeles* (see Figure 1.4). Though the *Great Wall* is discussed in more detail later in this chapter, suffice it to say here that the body of the pachuco in both these images is reduced to a fetuslike state, the epitome of disempowered masculinity. Moreover, this image of the emasculated pachuco allegorized that of the fallen Aztec warrior after conquest, as disclosed in Luis Valdez's 1978 play *Zoot Suit*. Thus nostalgic figures like Felipe Adame's *Cuauhtémoc* in Chicano Park pointed not only to the performative aspect of Chicano masculine identity but also to a certain sense of melancholy that becomes part of masculinist constructions, a phenomenon defined by feminist critic Judith Butler as that "unfinished process of grieving,"[14] a nostalgic longing for something that never existed.

In the few instances where the figures of women were included in Indigenist mural imagery, they were configured according to the gender expectations and roles outlined by *el movimiento's* ideologies. Women were indeed present within these murals' iconographic programs, but this visual presence functioned as a device that would further render them invisible. *Read Between the Lines* (1975; Figure 5.1) by David Botello, a member of the mural collective the East Los Streetscapers, depicted a kind of panoptic space where the ill effects on Chicano culture of assimilation into U.S. culture were illustrated in the middle of the busy intersection of Ford and Olympic Boulevards in East Los Angeles. Mural historian Alan W. Barnett observed that in this image we see "a Chicano worker who has been uprooted from the *campesino's* way of life and is chained to machinery and tangled in cables like Laocoon while his heart [and brain are] being monitored."[15] While this male Chicano worker offers physical and psychological resistance to the forces and tools of assimilation, other members of the nuclear Chicano family, on the right half of the composition, have been completely lured in by the seductive images of the manipulative U.S. mass media. Watching in surveillance over this entire scene are a large microscope and a camera, fixing their lenses not only on these figures below but also on the spectator. In spite of the seeming hopelessness of the situation, Botello offers an allegorical solution to this cultural, social, and political predicament in the two central figures who act as agents of salvation, namely, the figure of an intervening Quetzalcoatl descending from above, epitomizing Mexican culture, and that of the boy reading a book on Mexican history, symbolizing the next generation

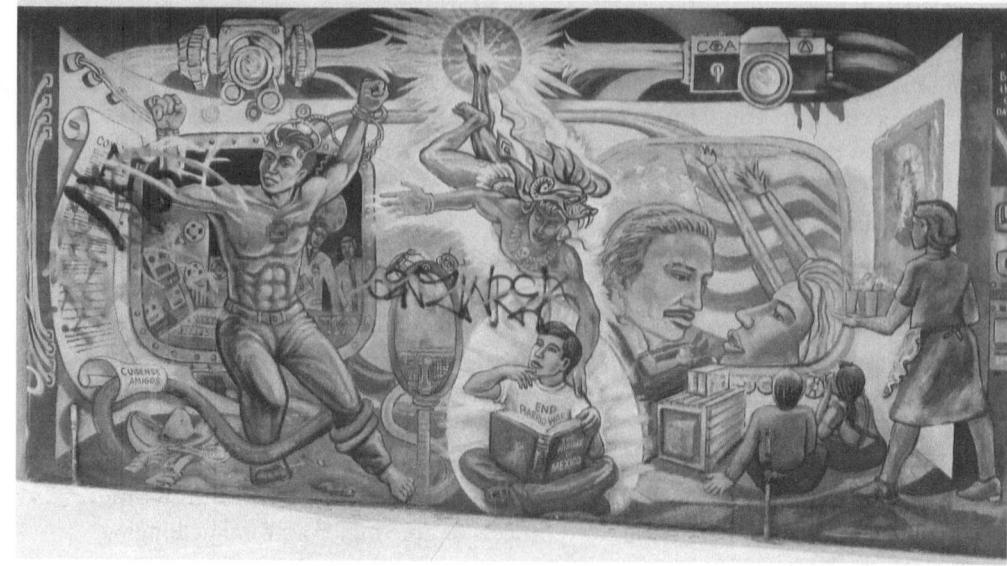

FIGURE 5.1. David Botello, © 1975, *Read Between the Lines*, mural, East Los Angeles, California. Courtesy of David Botello.

of Chicanos. Though Botello opted to include an indigenous figure in this scene, Quetzalcoatl here operates as a syncretic device, for he also resembles a Judeo-Christian saint interceding in earthly affairs, reminiscent of Mexican *retablo* paintings. The "enlightened" male child displays the same holy attributes of the Virgin of Guadalupe as rays of light emanate from his body. Here the artist illustrates how assimilation can be avoided by embracing the indigenous element of the Chicano being. Oblivious to both the processes of assimilation and salvation, however, is the dutiful and anonymous Chicana—tied to her apron strings and to the kitchen—who stands to the right of the composition while attending to her domestic chores as she gives her back to the viewer. She is not part of the process of political awareness that the male child experiences, nor is she deserving of the Indigenist attributes that he possesses; in other words, she exists outside of the paradigm of liberation that allows Chicano males to resist assimilation.

The silencing of women's agency during the early stages of the Chicano Movement did not preclude some muralists from also creating Indigenist scenes that eroticized the female presence. Juan Garduño's *Aztec Mural* (1977), located inside Victor Clothing Company in downtown Los Angeles, managed to combine the taste for Indigenist imagery with a glimpse of what

Garduño imagined to be preconquest everyday life, that is, a genre scene of sorts. The interior setting of this work, a rare occurrence among Chicana/o community murals, lends a more intimate quality to the image, offering the pleasure of a more private viewing. From left to right, we see three scenes separated by colorful stone stelae. On the left, Aztec architects and artisans are working to construct and decorate the amazing architectural structures that would even astound their own future colonizers, and, to the left, we see a group of Mesoamerican farmers working the land by planting the seeds of their civilization. The central scene, however, presents us with a strange ritual where a female dancer, whose voluptuous and well-rendered body shows through her light drapery, performs before an enthroned Aztec ruler. Garduño reconstructs the pre-Columbian world as a civilized yet still idyllic paradise undisturbed by European contact or even by Western codes of "morality." Rather than trying to completely subvert the primitivising language traditionally used to represent the culture of the Other, Garduño seems to be striking a compromise whereby the men in the scene represent the "civilized" element of the pre-Columbian world while the women remain the object of an exoticizing gaze. Chicano Indigenism opened the doors for a reinterpretation of American indigenous culture, yet this new reading failed to liberate women from the "noble savage" paradigm.

Chicana Muralists Challenging the Nationalist Canon

While the celebration of Indigenism was taking place in the streets and public spaces of California via the community mural, Chicana artists were almost inconspicuously beginning to assert their position within these spaces at the same time that Chicano nationalism was still developing. Judy Baca's 1971 mural entitled *Mi Abuelita* (Figure 5.2), located in East L.A.'s Hollenbeck Park, was one of the first community murals created by a Chicana artist and, as such, it introduced numerous innovations to the genre. As Alan Barnett remarked, it was the first time in Los Angeles that a muralist recruited the collaboration of gang members for the creation of a wall painting.[16] Working under the auspices of the city's Department of Recreation and Parks, Baca discovered that her role was as much that of an artist as it was that of community organizer. The innovations of this mural resided not only in its mode of production but also in its subject matter and Indigenist aesthetic. *Mi Abuelita*'s iconography introduced a new way to synthesize the Indigenist discourse that Chicana/o artists elaborated in other murals with the gender concerns preoccupying Chicanas. Using an old photograph of the artist's grandmother as a basis for the features and color of the central figure, Baca

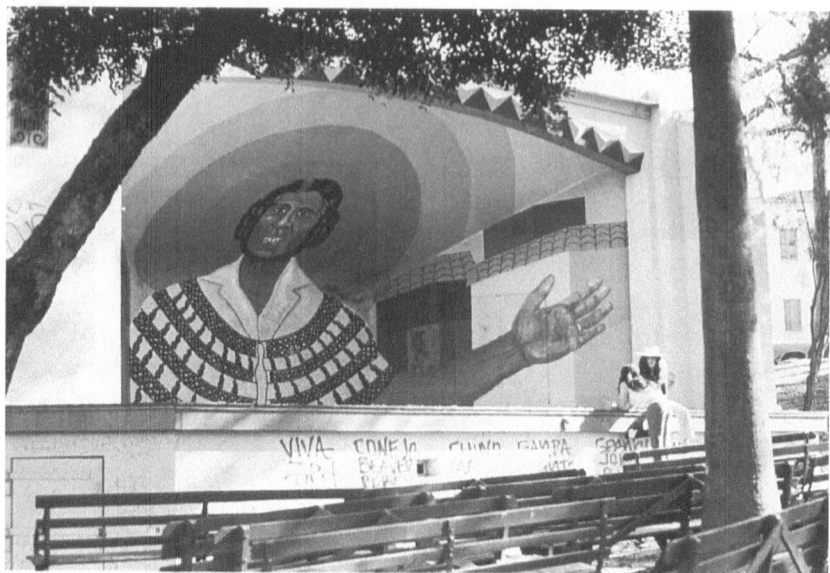

FIGURE 5.2. Judy Baca, © 1971, *Mi Abuelita*, mural, Hollenbeck Park, East Los Angeles, California. © SPARC (www.sparcmurals.org).

and the local youth created an image meant to represent the archetypal Chicana grandmother. She extends her arms in an embracing fashion resembling a Byzantine apse painting, an effect that is accentuated by the concave shape of the band shell where Baca painted the image.

This mural also formed part of a series entitled *Nuevas Vistas,* done by Baca in Hollenbeck Park, which included images that graced the park's gang rehabilitation and recreation centers, such as the Aztec Calendar Stone, representations of the Popocatépetl and Ixtaccihuatl legend, and codex figures, among other pre-Columbian motifs. So it was in this Indigenist context that the community's collective consciousness was expected to absorb *Mi Abuelita*'s indigenous features, dark skin, and colorful dress rendered in warm tones. When Baca worked on this project, she had just graduated from California State University in Northridge, where she had acquired a general knowledge of art history, but it was limited to, according to her, "the Greeks and the Romans... and Western Europeans."[17] It would not be until 1972 that she read the Mexican Muralists' Manifesto, and not until 1977 that she would travel to Mexico and participate in the Taller Siqueiros in Cuernavaca. It is evident, then, that in *Mi Abuelita* she seems to be drawing primarily from Western iconographic traditions, yet her contact with Chicana/o youth in the city's

east side as well as with the budding Chicano Movement was already beginning to shape her political and cultural consciousness. Nevertheless, the
artist's choice to use her own grandmother distanced this mural from that of
other male muralists. Baca used an element from her personal life to address
a collective consciousness. Most of the Chicano murals at the time avoided
any references to the artists' personal lives because these signaled self-cen-
tered and individualistic concerns that went against ideals of collectivity
connected to the Chicano Movement. The use of one's personal experience
as a springboard to address broader issues of social and political concern was
a characteristic element of Chicana feminist consciousness. Moreover, the
act of tracing Chicanas/os' indigenous roots through the female lineage in
la familia also became an important cornerstone of Chicana feminist praxis.
Later, in 1978, Chicana painter Yolanda López would pick up on this theme
when she traced her own cultural identity through herself, her mother, and
her grandmother as she cast them all in the likeness of the Virgin of Guadalupe in her now-classic *Guadalupe Series*.

Cultural studies scholar Jeffrey Rangel maintains that Baca's efforts in
community organizing and in "the cultivation of 'indigenous' art forms"
in Hollenbeck Park faced considerable opposition from members of the
community and fellow Chicano artists alike,[18] something that further
stressed her sense of isolation as a woman artist working in Los Angeles.
Chicanas would not make significant contributions to community mural
history until 1973, when the artists collective of Las Mujeres Muralistas
would come together. Composed by Chicanas Patricia Rodríguez, Irene
Pérez, and Graciela Carrillo and Venezuelan Consuelo Méndez, Las Mujeres Muralistas established a model for collaborative and collective activity
among community artists, particularly women of color. Rodríguez herself
was conscious of their unique position within the urban art scene as well
as their role as trailblazers:

> We have pioneered, initiated something that had not been done be-
> fore. In other words, a group of Chicanas actually put up scaffolding
> as men do. . . . I think Mujeres Muralistas [are] very important be-
> cause we [represent the] beginning of an art movement for women.
> . . . At this point in history our work is important because there are
> no other Chicana artists who have done such extensive work on the
> community on such a large scale and without pay.[19]

In the middle of the frenzied hustle and bustle of San Francisco's Mission
District, and in close proximity to the radically nationalist murals created

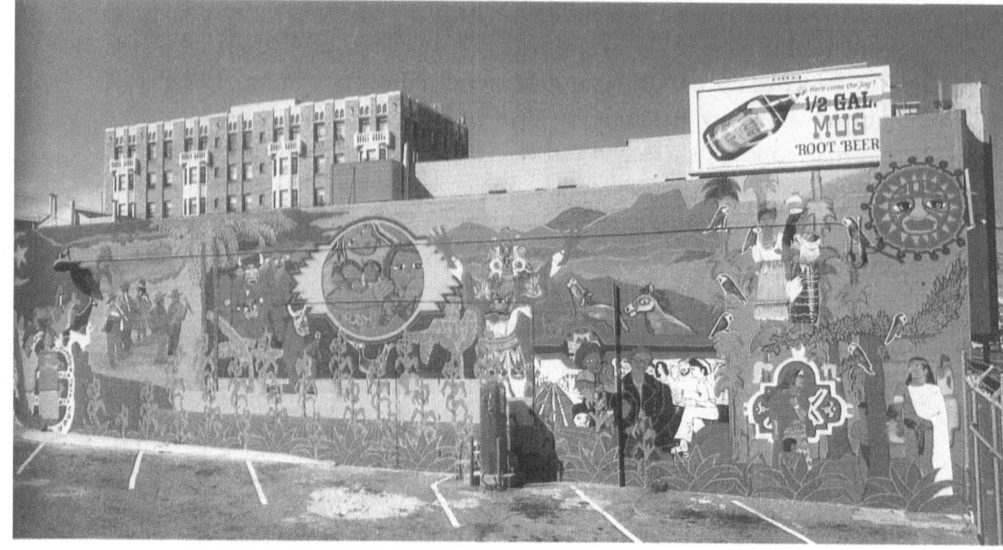

FIGURE 5.3. Las Mujeres Muralistas, © 1974, *Latinoamérica*, mural, San Francisco, California. Courtesy of Timothy Drescher.

by their male counterparts, Las Mujeres Muralistas produced a new visual vocabulary that almost inadvertently introduced issues of gender within the Chicano nationalist paradigm that saturated most community murals at the time. Their now-destroyed mural entitled *Latinoamérica* (1974; Figure 5.3), originally painted in the district's Mission Street, extolled an Indigenist aesthetic that superficially seemed less militant than that of their male colleagues, for this mural made no overt references to issues of social justice or colonization suffered by indigenous peoples. With *Latinoamérica,* the artists chose instead to focus more on the lushness and sensuality of the natural environments in the Americas while celebrating the richness of the continent's indigenous cultures.

Stretching horizontally in a composition that spanned approximately seventy feet, the mural depicted a utopian natural environment containing various plants, animals, and peoples from different regions of the Americas. Using vegetation motifs like cornstalks, maguey plants, and banana trees to divide and organize the pictorial space into different registers,[20] the artists depicted both female and male Indian figures sharing this idyllic realm. In the lower-left corner, two Zapotec women dressed in traditional headdress and attire stand beside a cactus plant while gazing at the next register, where a group of Peruvian Indians are playing flutes. The iconography in the central and largest register revolves around a Zia, a Navajo motif signi-fying the sun,[21] that contains the figures of an archetypal Latina/o family; the parents are embracing their children while the mother reveals a fetus showing through her womb. Flanking this roundel, to the right, is a group of four Venezuelan devil-mask performers, and, to the left, a Bolivian dancer engages in a ritual ceremony. All these figures seem to be honoring the La-tina/o family, as they direct their gestures and movements toward the Zia. Almost as a disjunctive element, a depiction of a contemporary Chicana/o family, with scenes of modern urban life behind them, occupies the lower-right corner of this central register. In the last and concluding register, a group of Guatemalan women are absorbed by their cooking as they tend to their children while a group of male Guatemalans are hunting and gather-ing for food, an illustration of the division of domestic labor among Meso-american cultures.[22] The entire composition is flanked by representations of the sun and the moon, which function as visual devices that contain the entire mural iconography. The sun and moon motifs, however, additionally operate as signifiers of the importance placed on cyclical time among many indigenous cultures, as well as the series of dualities that define the nature of the universe. The recurring use of vibrant reds, greens, and blues that create flat areas of unmodulated color defines the mural's entire color scheme. In addition, Las Mujeres Muralistas used black outlines for most figures and objects in *Latinoamérica* to facilitate the reading of the mural.

As far as its subject matter was concerned, *Latinoamérica* seemed less politically engaged than the works by the other, mostly-male muralists in San Francisco. Quite the contrary, the mural appeared to present a more accommodationist, conciliatory, and apolitical vision of Latin American indigenous culture, almost in keeping with colonial constructions of the exotic noble savage. However, when art historian Shifra Goldman asked member Irene Pérez about this assessment in 1982, the artist responded that, as an artists collective, Las Mujeres Muralistas sought to provide an alterna-tive visual language to the "blood and guts" aesthetics upheld by the more militant Chicano muralists.[23] Moreover, in their artistic manifesto, they even provided a utopian response to this charge:

A lot of people have told us that our work is pretty and colorful, but that it is not political enough. They ask us why we don't represent the starvation and death going on in Latin America or even the oppres-sion of women . . . our interest as artists is to put art close to where it needs to be. Close to the children, close to the old people who often wander the streets alone . . . We feel it is important that the atmosphere of the world be surrounded with life: WE OFFER YOU COLORS WE MAKE.[24]

In many respects, however, Las Mujeres Muralistas' murals were perhaps among the most radical of their time. I contend that the activities of this artists collective during the midseventies—perhaps the height of Chicano cultural nationalism—can be situated within what historian and cultural critic Emma Pérez termed third-space feminism. Using the concept of the "decolonial imaginary," which refers to "that interstitial space where differential politics and social dilemmas are negotiated,"[25] Pérez discusses examples of third-space feminism where Chicana and Mexican women asserted agency from within nationalist movements by taking on postures that reproduced dominant masculinist positions while simultaneously negotiating for an independent voice, a strategy she calls "dialectics of doubling." In that respect, Las Mujeres Muralistas were "doubling" the efforts of their Chicano colleagues by using *their* medium of choice, muralism, while also inadvertently challenging various paradigms in the process. Not only was their mere presence up on scaffolding a threat to the male dominance of muralism, but their Indigenist themes presented an important point of departure from the nationalist models previously seen. Now indigenous women[26] and children, not just Aztec warriors and their scantily clad female companions, inhabited these pictorial landscapes. By depicting indigenous figures from various regions in Latin America, Las Mujeres Muralistas pushed the limits of the Indigenist vocabulary utilized by Chicano artists by creating imagery that not only transcended Aztec/Maya archetypes more commonly seen in California community murals, but also gave greater agency to the role women played in indigenous cultures.[27]

Back in Los Angeles, other Chicana artists would further reinforce a strong female presence in the community mural art scene. Judithe Hernández, whose work could also be placed within Pérez's third-space feminist model, created several murals during the 1970s that eventually defined the urban aesthetics of areas like East Los Angeles. She was deeply invested in the ideals of the Chicano Movement, which often led her to produce imagery that seemed to unproblematically uphold male-centered nationalism. As far as feminism was concerned, she shared the same tentative views that other Chicana activists held, as Hernández explained in 1979: "The feminist movement has made significant strides for women, but it addresses issues that are not relevant to the barrio. . . . I don't really feel a part of it. I find it basically an upper middle class, white woman's movement."[28]

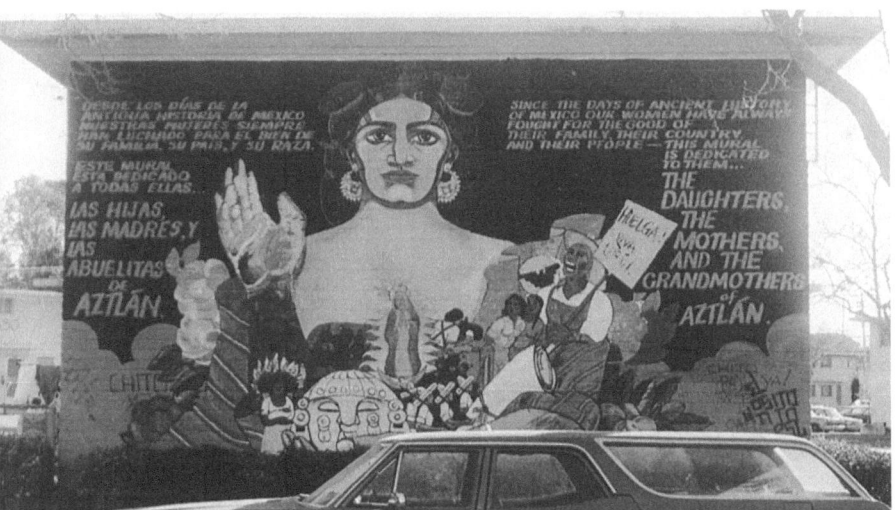

FIGURE 5.4. Judithe Hernández, © 1976, *Mujeres de Aztlán*, mural, Ramona Gardens, East Los Angeles. Courtesy of Judithe Hernández.

Nevertheless, Hernández's 1976 mural entitled *Mujeres de Aztlán* (Figure 5.4) accomplished a third-space position between the emerging feminist movement and the still radically masculinist postures of the Chicano men. As part of a mural project organized by the Mechicano Art Center with funds from the National Endowment for the Arts, *Mujeres de Aztlán* reminded viewers of the roles Chicanas had played historically and needed to play again in support of *el movimiento*. Similarly to Baca's *Mi Abuelita*, Hernández's mural presents the viewer with an archetypal image of the Chicana woman while explaining her role in the forging of Aztlán. Exhibiting indigenous-like hair, earrings, and facial features, this central figure raises her right hand in an oathlike gesture while holding a number of figures and objects that allude to her various roles as a Chicana within the movement. On either side of this figure, we find an inscription, in both English and Spanish, that refers to a Mexican or Chicana woman's importance within *la familia*, the basic unit of the Chicano nation, as expressed by several Chicano militants: "Since the days of ancient history of Mexico our women have always fought for the good of their family, their country, and their people—this mural is dedicated to them ... the daughters, the mothers, and the grandmothers of Aztlán."

In many ways, this mural mirrored the sentiments among many male

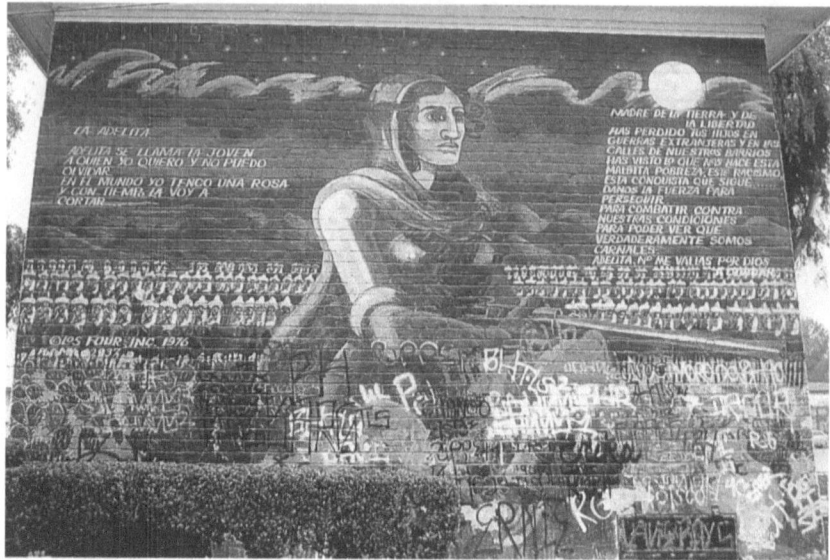

FIGURE 5.5. Carlos Almaraz, © 1976, *Adelita*, mural, Ramona Gardens, East Los Angeles. Courtesy of Elsa Flores Almaraz.

Chicano artists and activists that women should not disrupt the Mexican American family structure. *Mujeres de Aztlán* also echoed many of the aesthetic elements employed in the Ramona Gardens murals by acting as a visual complement to Carlos Almaraz's *Adelita* (Figure 5.5), a work painted in the same year, just down the street and around a few corners from Hernández's mural. Actually, the two artists helped one another in completing the murals, yet Hernández was never able to fully complete her wall, as she later recounted: "Ramona Gardens was a very violent housing project at the time. As Carlos and I neared completion of my mural, we were caught in the crossfire of a gang gunfight one afternoon. We decided that trying to complete the mural was going to be too dangerous. I later learned that the mural was finally finished sometime later by residents."[29] Almaraz's mural also made reference to a woman's role as a pillar of the Chicano family by referring to her in the mural's text as "Madre de la tierra y de la libertad [quien] has perdido tus hijos en guerras extranjeras y en las calles de nuestros barrios" (Mother of earth and liberty [who] has lost your children in foreign wars and in the streets of our barrios). His mural, however, cast the archetypal Chicana more specifically in the role of Adelita/*soldadera*, the anonymous yet loyal female camp follower, usually of indigenous background, who aided male soldiers during the Mexican

Revolution of 1910. Although Chicana artists and feminists did not necessarily view the Adelita/*soldadera* as a liberating figure, Hernández accepts that characterization in *Mujeres de Aztlán* but also provides an array of additional roles for Chicanas to undertake as means to achieve liberation and decolonization. Acting as visual affirmation of the mural's inscription, the figures and objects that Hernández's woman holds in her left arm speak of the multiple achievements that Mexican and Chicana women can and have accomplished throughout history. While we do see the motif of the Adelita/*soldadera* here, represented by the women holding rifles and standing in a military lineup below, the figure of the female member of the United Farm Workers (UFW) holding a picket sign is there as well. Allusions to both working-class and college-educated Chicanas are also made by the inclusion of a garment worker and an actual college diploma leaning on this large woman's forearm. Hernández even cites women's roles as purveyors of spiritual power during the colonial and pre-Columbian eras by including the image of the Virgin de Guadalupe and that of the maligned Aztec goddess Coyolxauhqui, identified by the bells on her cheeks (the importance of this deity to Chicanas is discussed below).

Hernández and Almaraz, as members of the influential artists collective Los Four, joined forces in a unique partnership to pay homage to the Chicana's role in *el movimiento* and to begin the redefinition of that role, as Hernández later explained: "Carlos and I actually conceived our murals as something of a 'diptych.' We discussed designing murals that specifically paid homage to the role of women in our cultural past, present, and hopefully future, as a direct counterresponse to the endless male-dominated, *machismo*-celebrating murals that were the norm at the time."[30] By the mid-1970s, Chicanos had already firmly established a male-centered nationalist paradigm supported by an Indigenist aesthetic, so the attempt to liberate that aesthetic from this pattern would involve a gradual process.

Gender, Multiple Subjectivities, and Spirituality

During the same year that Hernández completed her mural in Ramona Gardens, Judy Baca began her work on what would become perhaps the most ambitious mural project in California to date, namely, *The Great Wall of Los Angeles* (1976–1983), painted on the wall of the Tujunga Wash drainage canal in the San Fernando Valley. The project began when the Army Corps of Engineers contacted Baca about making a mural in this location as part of a larger effort to develop and beautify the area. After much planning, fund-raising, and coordinating, the work for the mural began two years later and took place during the summer months between 1976 and 1983. Having gained ample experience in community organizing while working on the Hollenbeck Park murals, Baca once again recruited young people for the completion of this gargantuan project. Stretching half a mile and lauded as the longest mural in the world, *The Great Wall* documented the history of Los Angeles from the perspective of social, racial, gender, and even sexual minorities, as Baca would later recount:

> When I first saw the wall, I envisioned a long narrative of another history of California; one which included ethnic peoples, women and minorities who were so invisible in conventional textbook accounts. The discovery of the history of California's multicultural peoples was a revelation to me as well as to the members of my teams.[31]

The Great Wall's counterhistory began with the prehistoric era and concluded with the 1950s and with a panel on the 1984 Olympics.[32] During the span of the production process, Baca employed over four hundred young adults and teenagers to work on the mural, many of whom were considered to be at-risk youth. A number of these young participants, by their own accounts, found their lives completely transformed by the experience. In addition, a team of artists, scholars, historians, and community members also participated in the creation of the mural. *The Great Wall* epitomized how the process of creating a mural was just as important as the finished product. Many of the mostly Chicana/o and Black young people who participated in the project felt themselves empowered by becoming agents in the process of writing history and by seeing themselves reflected in that history. For many of them, their experience of marginalization, exclusion, and invisibility was overturned, or at least momentarily suspended, during their involvement with *The Great Wall*.

The historical importance of *The Great Wall* was also that never in the global history of muralism had a woman, least of all a woman of color, directed such a complex and large-scale mural project. The public role that Baca took on as artist, teacher, and community organizer was literally unheard of for a Chicana in the 1970s. *The Great Wall* definitely made her into a prominent and important figure within the history of community muralism and public art in the United States. Her historical importance was further underscored by her efforts to foster mural activity in the Los Angeles area. The creation of *The Great Wall* led to the foundation of the Social and Public Art Resource Center, better known as SPARC. Founded by Baca, along with painter Christina Schlesinger and filmmaker Donna

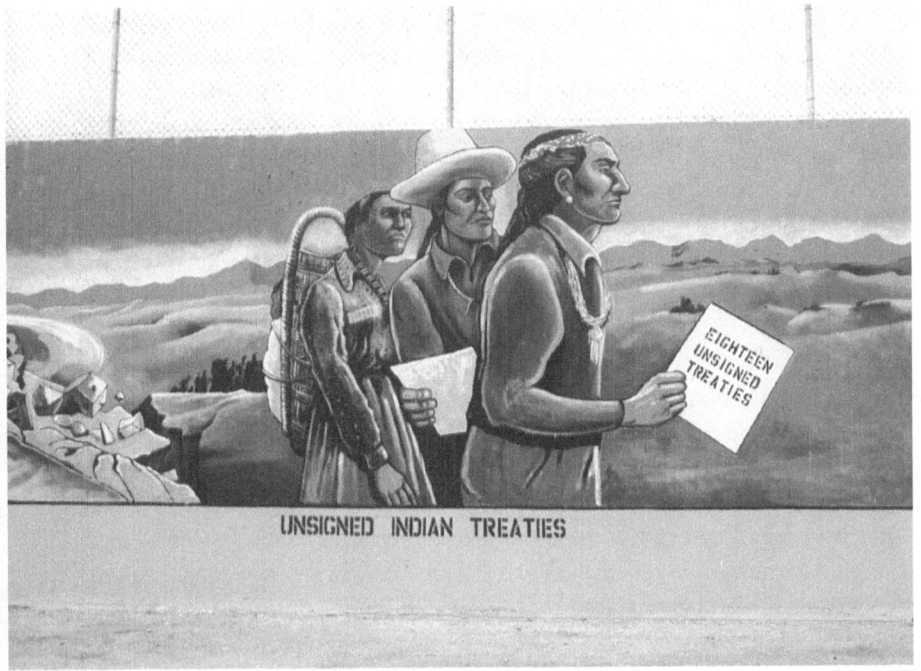

FIGURE 5.6. Judy Baca, © 1980, *Unsigned Indian Treaties* panel from *The Great Wall of Los Angeles*, mural, Tujunga Wash, San Fernando Valley, Los Angeles. © SPARC (www.sparcmurals.org)

Deitch, in 1976, this organization has sponsored numerous mural and public art projects throughout Los Angeles for over thirty years. Baca and the staff at SPARC created three overarching areas of activity within the organization: production, education, and preservation as they relate to mural and public art production.[33] So Baca's contribution to mural history does not only rest on her role as an artist and organizer, but also on her capacity as sponsor and patron of the arts.[34]

Given that Baca and her assistants were seeking to uncover a hidden history in *The Great Wall*, the contribution of indigenous peoples figured prominently in the mural's iconography. The first panel, entitled *Pre-Historic California* (1976), depicts the Chumash people as the founding pillars of civilization in California. Several feet along the mural, we also see a scene from the 1950s entitled *Indian Assimilation* (1983), which depicts the "Americanization" and displacement from ancestral lands of Native American communities in the United States. But Baca and her fellow mural makers were also cognizant of the importance of women in California's indigenous history. The panel entitled *Unsigned Indian Treaties* (Figure 5.6), completed during the summer of 1980, makes reference to the period during the Great Depression and the New Deal in the 1930s when several Native Americans were "forced to sell two thirds of their land to developers at 45 cents an acre."[35] Native American communities sought redress for lands that, according to their interpretation of the Treaty of Guadalupe Hidalgo, signed between Mexico and the United States in 1848, were rightfully theirs.[36] These efforts were largely ignored by the U.S. judicial system, thereby undermining the spirit of the treaty. Baca and her assistants illustrated the reaction of several Native Americans after being repeatedly disenfranchised and dispossessed by the U.S. government. In this scene, we see a group of three Native American people holding a copy of all the unsigned articles appended to the Treaty of Guadalupe Hidalgo regarding indigenous land rights. All facing the same direction, these individuals seem to be addressing an invisible authority figure, a symbol of the lack of Native American representation at a federal level. The presence in the group of a Native American woman who is carrying her baby in a woven cradle board while carefully overseeing the proceedings before her points to the duality of her role as a mother and an activist within a specific moment in U.S. history, namely, the 1930s, a period when her contribution as a woman of color would have gone completely unnoticed. Baca also makes a clear connection between the Native American plight of that era and that of Mexican Americans by placing this scene right next to *The Great Wall*'s panel entitled *350,000 Mexican-Americans Deported* (1980), which depicts the mass deportations of Mexicans and Mexican Americans coordinated by the U.S. government to alleviate the economic devastation of the Depression. Not only do Mexicans and Native Americans have common Mesoamerican ancestors, but they possess a shared colonial experience. By charting a common history of dispossession and displacement between the two groups, Baca was making connections between events previously ignored or unconnected by dominant narratives about the city of Los Angeles.

By the early 1980s, the presence of women within the Chicano community mural movement had ceased to be an exception to the rule as Chicanas gradually became a common sight up on mural scaffoldings. Even the *Community Murals Magazine*, a publication produced from 1978 to 1985 through an editorial board headed by Tim Drescher and Miranda Bergman in the Bay Area, dedicated to community public arts, took notice of the changes happening in the streets when they published a cartoon in 1983 entitled "So Much for Macho..." that indirectly lauded the prominence of women artists engaged in these activities. In the first frame of the strip, we see two male muralists taking a break as they drink beers. A male barrio resident approaches them saying: "Y'know, you muralists are all right—nothin' artsy-fartsy about a job like this! You're just typical workin' men like us!" In the second frame, however, a group of women muralists descend from scaffolding in the background chastising the men: "Hey, Mike, you wanna cut the bullshittin' and get back to work? Let's try to get done by lunch so we can varnish it tomorrow!" While the cartoonist was poking fun at the *machismo* and working-class sensibilities associated with mural making, he was also taking notice of a gendered shift in cultural production within the public spaces of California's urban centers. The role of women as muralists within these spaces was becoming normalized. This is not to say that Chicana muralists had exactly received full respect and recognition from their male peers and the rest of the art world, but it did mean that they had definitely carved out a niche for themselves within the communities in which they worked. Simultaneously, the 1980s saw the emergence of Chicana feminist writers such as Gloria Anzaldúa and Cherríe Moraga, who were proposing oppositional ways of thinking and acting vis-à-vis systems of power. Chicana muralists, for their part, deployed Indigenist aesthetics, not as static signifiers of cultural identity, but rather as springboards for the understanding of more complex notions about space, place, and time as they applied to Chicanas/os as a neocolonized people. This new feminist consciousness was increasingly mobile and dynamic, capable of constantly shifting and moving according to the continuously changing nature of reality, as theorist Chela Sandoval explains: "I think of this activity of consciousness as the 'differential,' insofar as it enables movement 'between and among' ideological positionings ... considered as variables."[37] This movement "between and among" consequently allowed Chicana artists to work not only with members of their own community and with each other, but also with artists not belonging to the Mexican American sphere and even with individuals who were not associated with the visual arts, such as writers and activists.

Though active as an artist since the 1970s, Yreina Cervántez would not become a prominent figure in the Los Angeles mural scene until the late 1980s when she created her mural *La Ofrenda* (1989; Figure 5.7), located in Toluca Street near downtown and completed with the help of assistants Claudia Escobedo, Erick "Duke" Montenegro, Vladimir "Dracer" Morales, and Sonia Ramos. Created as her MFA thesis at UCLA, the mural added a decisively feminist dimension to the prevailing Indigenist aesthetic by showcasing women as the principal protagonists in the construction of a collective cultural identity and social consciousness. As Cervántez herself

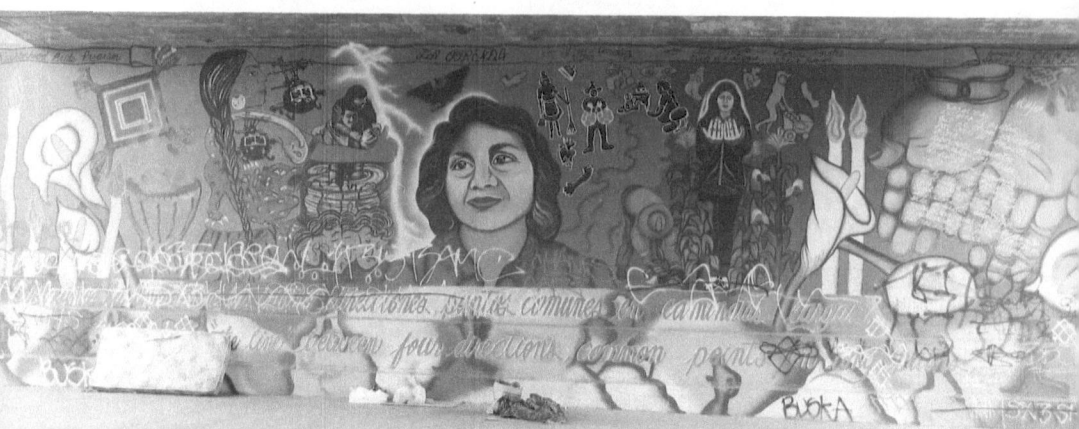

FIGURE 5.7. Yreina D. Cervántez, assisted by Claudia Escobedo, Erick "Duke" Montenegro, Vladimir "Dracer" Morales, and Sonia Ramos; © 1989, *La Ofrenda*, mural, First and Toluca Streets, Los Angeles, California. Courtesy of Yreina D. Cervántez.

conveyed in her artist's statement, the iconography in the mural makes reference to "themes of culture, spirituality, war and the power of women—represented by a portrait of Dolores Huerta, the co-founder and vice-president of the United Farm Workers."[38] In this respect, *La Ofrenda* departs from usual Chicano mural iconography in that the artist chooses to focus on Huerta rather than UFW founder César Chávez, a more common sight in Los Angeles's east side.

In addition to placing these female figures in central positions in *La Ofrenda*, Cervántez opted not to create a concretely illusionistic space for her figures in the mural, thus somewhat departing from the strictly social-realist style prevalent in most Los Angeles murals. The ambiguity of the pictorial space here thus operates metaphorically as the bordered, ambivalent, and fluid social spaces inhabited by women of color. I have also indicated elsewhere how this ambiguity in *La Ofrenda* can be interpreted as a metaphorical obliteration of the boundaries drawn by patriarchal orders between domestic and public spheres:

> Latinas have fought for a more important role within the private sphere of the home and the family, as well as for the right to work or earn an education.... Cervántez's images in *La Ofrenda* suggest she intended to establish a strong foothold for Latinas in both spaces. The iconography of the mural includes elements commonly seen in both spheres.

The viewer can readily link the candles, the calla lilies and the craft elements to private domains, for many home altars include these objects. The word "ofrenda" (offering) suggests that the artists intended the entire mural to be a gigantic altar[39] dedicated to Dolores Huerta. . . . The very inclusion of Huerta's figure and her obvious links to both the UFW and the civil rights movement implies that the lessons to be learned from *La Ofrenda* also belong to the public domain.[40]

Though the mural's iconography revolves around this central figure of Huerta, her presence here, however, is more spiritual than concretely historical. While some of the figures and objects around her do refer to her role as a labor organizer and activist, others speak more broadly of other historical and even spiritual realities. As a matter of fact, much of the iconography actually alludes to the plight of undocumented immigrants, the sorrows of war in Central America, and the hardships of migrant farmworkers. With the exception of the latter, many of these themes relate to Dolores Huerta only insofar as they all form part of a larger matrix of domination and decolonization. What these figures and objects do accomplish, however, is that they act as spiritual counterparts to Huerta's person. Cervántez is then visually articulating the idea that Chicana feminist consciousness is constructed through the dialectic relations and exchanges that women of color have with various and simultaneous historical, cultural, and political phenomena, many of which may seem wholly unrelated and even contradictory to one another.

But *La Ofrenda*'s Indigenist imagery most succinctly expresses a notion of spirituality that is strongly tied to cultural, political, and gender identity. Citing elements from Mesoamerican indigenous cultures, Cervántez evokes an Indigenist spirituality that is both personal and collective. Among the most prominent figures that surround Dolores Huerta in this mural is that of an indigenous woman whose body transforms into a leopard with a serpent tail. Cervántez has often spoken about the importance of *nahuals*, animal spirits, in her work's iconography. At a personal level, she strongly identifies with the jaguar and recognizes it as *her* animal spirit.[41] In that respect, this particular figure in the mural personifies the artist's individual spirituality, but also allegorizes broader social and political concerns, as she is depicted embracing a group of war victims from the Central American wars.

Cervántez also carries the Indigenist theme over to the mural's stylistic and formal elements. Directly behind the Huerta figure we find a group of pre-Columbian-like pictographs, which, on closer inspection, are actually representations of more contemporary figures whose presence is common nowadays on both sides of the U.S.-Mexico border, as recounted by the artist herself:

> They are *El Naranjero*, the orange vendor at the freeway exit, *La Costurera*, the seamstress in the sweatshop who sews designer clothes, *La Criada*, the maid who cleans or sometimes helps to raise someone else's children, *El Paletero*, the ice cream man who travels miles on foot in the course of one day, and the farm laborer who picks the food we eat on our tables.[42]

Though figures such as these speak of concrete and tangible social conditions, Cervántez also connects this politically charged Indigenist vocabulary to spiritually charged connotations. For this, she collaborates with Chicana poet and writer Gloria Enedina Alvarez in the textual inscription running along the horizontal band supporting the mural's composition. These are the opening verses of Alvarez's bilingual poem entitled "Vende Futuro," a piece she wrote about the life of undocumented workers, with particular emphasis on the freeway orange seller, mirroring Cervántez's own iconography above: "Cruzamos la 'línea' entre las cuatro direcciones, puntos comunes en caminatas largas. We crossed the 'line' between four directions, common points on long paths."[43] Subsequent verses in the poem deal more overtly with the everyday reality of these migrant workers, yet the artist chooses the lines that allude to the mythical origins of a migrant's transnational journeys today. The wording of this excerpt from "Vende Futuro" bears a striking resemblance to passages of the *Popol Vuh*, the Quiché Maya sacred book of creation. Among the numerous mythical characters in this book, we find the twins Hunahpú and Ixbalanqué who, upon reaching the end of their own journeys, arrive, in the words of the *Popol Vuh*'s text, "where the four roads converge, there they were defeated, at the cross of the four roads." As in the *Popol Vuh*, the "four directions" in Alvarez's text and Cervántez's mural signify a new beginning, fresh cultural possibilities, especially for Chicanas/os. Here both artists trace the current migrations of undocumented workers and immigrants to mythical beginnings.

According to Chicana cultural critic Laura Pérez, expressions of spirituality, especially in the creative work by Chicanas, are a means by which these artists assert agency in male-centered Judeo-Christian societies that would never grant them such transcendental capabilities.[44] But rather than using codes and tropes from dominant religious practices, artists such as Cervántez opt to employ elements from indigenous America, for these spiritualities, as explained by Pérez, lend themselves more effectively to the creation of "egalitarian world views that are inseparable from questions of social justice, with respect to class, gender, sexuality, culture, 'race,' and environmental welfare."[45]

Articulating their sociopolitical identity as an issue of both political *and* spiritual significance was, in essence, nothing new for Chicana artists and writers. After all, two years prior to the completion of Cervántez's *La Ofrenda,* Gloria Anzaldúa had published her seminal text *Borderlands/La Frontera* (1987), in which she not only established the multilayered nature of the mestiza's identity that embraced issues of personal spirituality, but also employed ancient indigenous ideas and myths to explain this heterogeneity (such as the Nahuatl concept of *nepantla* and the myth of Coyolxauhqui). Cervántez's contribution lies in her incorporation of these ideas into the large-scale and public format of the mural. With *La Ofrenda,* the artist obscured the distinctions between social spheres that have traditionally undermined the role of women, such as the separation between domestic and public spaces or between individual and collective concerns, using spirituality as a vehicle to move across these domains. Unlike traditional public monuments dedicated to Western forms of religious devotion, this mural proposed a nonoppressive and secular form of spirituality that allows for free movement across Judeo-Christian and indigenous belief systems. *La Ofrenda* offered a way by which the Echo Park community as a whole could empower itself politically, socially, and spiritually by either participating in its creation, as Cervántez's assistants did, or by partaking of its collective interaction as spectators.

By the onset of the 1990s, Chicana/o community murals had become increasingly heterogeneous in character, with artists of all backgrounds collaborating in these projects and dealing with a variety of issues that did not necessarily pertain exclusively to the Chicana/o community.[46] By then, Judy Baca had already started work in Los Angeles on what could be regarded as the first international mural project, *The World Wall* (1987–1991), a portable mural structure that consisted of six ten-by-thirty-foot canvas panels mounted on a system of poles and guywires that eventually traveled the globe and featured the participation of several artists from around the world. Baca explained that *The World Wall* was meant to "examine contemporary issues of global importance: war, peace, cooperation, interdependence and spiritual growth."[47] The highly utopian and universalized ideals behind the creation of this project were, nevertheless, based on more culturally specific ideas about ethnic identity. In the particular case of the panel entitled *Triumph of the Heart* (1991; Figure 5.8), the artist created an image that represents "the beginnings of the transformation towards peace, where individuals of all races

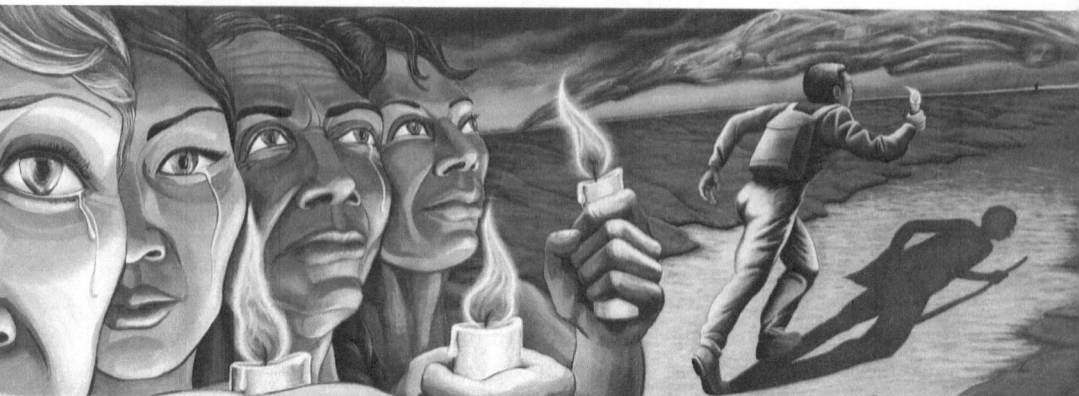

FIGURE 5.8. Judy Baca, © 1991, *Triumph of the Heart* panel from *The World Wall*, portable mural. © SPARC (www.sparcmurals.org).

make a conscious choice to take action together."[48] Baca here utilized five archetypal figures representing the world's ethnicities, a device used nearly sixty years earlier (1932–1933) by Diego Rivera in his Detroit Institute of Arts cycle, where he rendered four monumental figures, two male and two female, representing the Caucasian, Asian, African, and Native American populations.[49] Baca, however, departed from this pictorial convention by making all the figures female, with the exception of the young Black man who breaks away from the main group in an active search for peace while casting the shadow of Mahatma Gandhi.[50] The predominance of the female figures in this panel not only put women at the forefront of cultural production but also positioned them prominently within global processes. Moreover, Baca's addition of a mestiza or Latina figure, placed fourth from the left, incorporates an added Indigenist dimension to that racial paradigm, placing particular emphasis on the ethnic and cultural makeup of the Americas. By placing the Native American and mestiza/Latina figure right next to one another, Baca just reinforced what Chicana/o activists and thinkers had already reiterated in the early years of *el movimiento*, namely, that Chicanas/os are inherently an indigenous community and that, as such, they have numerous cultural, historical, and political experiences in common with Native Americans. This Indigenist imagery also extends to some of the symbolic vocabulary embedded in *Triumph of the Heart*. The vessel-shaped pupils in these figures' eyes represent an individual's heart among various Native American groups.[51] With this panel, Baca sought to propose an allegorical and conceptual resolution to the issues of social and political strife in the world while also pointing to a desire to take Chicana/o muralism beyond the local context.

The conceptualization of this mural, and of the *World Wall* project as a whole, derived from the ideological and visual development that the Indigenist mural aesthetic had been undergoing since the late 1960s. Indigenism had served as an effective tool to address issues of local concern, such as the specific problems that affected the residents of the barrio where a particular mural might be located. These site-specific themes that were articulated through Indigenist iconography would then take on a national character, as they alluded to the marginalized position of Chicanas/os and other minorities in the United States. Baca took this thematic progression a step further by employing an Indigenist aesthetic *with* feminist overtones that was meant to have an international appeal and to visually render concepts of universal and cosmic proportions.

While Baca had established by the early 1990s a precedent for collaborative work across the racial divide and had pioneered in universalist themes within community muralism in Southern California, similar practices by Chicana muralists in the San Francisco Bay Area had already been in place for several years. This tradition facilitated the creation of what could be considered the most ambitious collectively produced women's muralist project ever, *Maestrapeace* (1994), located on Lapidge and Eighteenth Streets in San Francisco's Mission District. Since this mural will be discussed at length in Chapter 6, the focus in this chapter will be on a distinct Indigenist element in the mural's iconographic program and on the particular contribution of Chicana artist Irene Pérez. The figure of Coyolxauhqui (Figure 5.9), the so-called Aztec moon goddess, created by Pérez and located on the Lapidge Street façade of the mural, allegorized Chicanas' indigenous *and* gender consciousness. Using the ancient stone relief carving of this deity in Mexico City's Templo Mayor museum as a model for her own image (Figure 5.10), Irene Pérez purposely toyed with the iconography of the original and subverted its meaning. According to Aztec myth, Coyolxauhqui's ultimate demise was prompted by her own treachery, as retold by Mesoamerican art historian Mary Ellen Miller:

> Coatlicue [Coyolxauhqui's mother] kept a temple shrine on a hill near Tula called Coatepec, or "hill of snakes." After tucking a ball of down feathers in her bosom, she became pregnant with Huitzilopochtli. Repelled by her condition, her children, especially her daughter Coyolxauhqui, plotted her death. When Coatlicue's enemies attacked her

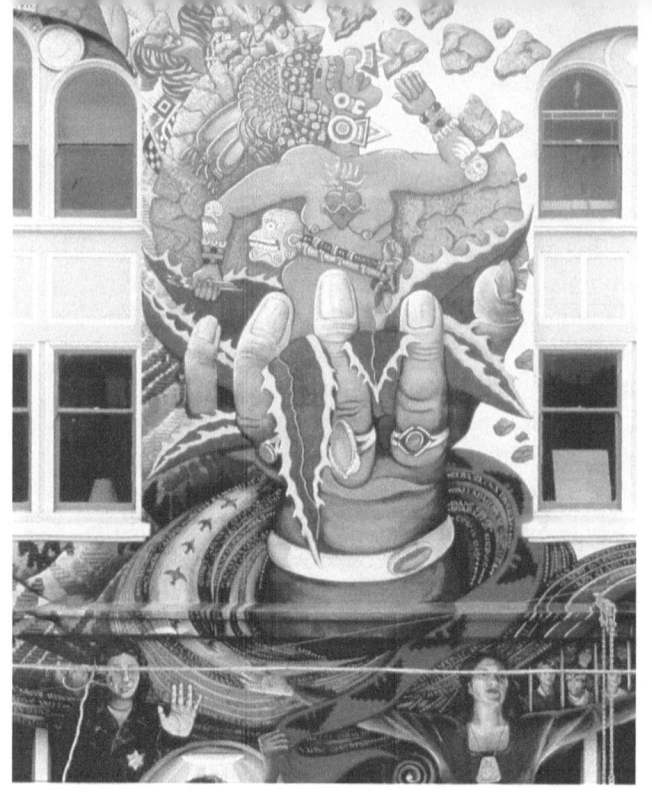

FIGURE 5.9. Juana Alicia, Miranda Bergman, Irene Pérez, Yvonne Littleton, Meera Desai, Edythe Boone, and Susan Kelk Cervantes, © 1994, *Maestrapeace*, detail, mural, Lapidge Street façade, San Francisco California. Photograph by César Rubio. Courtesy of Meera Desai.

FIGURE 5.10. Coyolxauhqui, c. 1519, relief sculpture, Templo Mayor, Mexico City. Pen-and-ink drawing by Guisela Latorre.

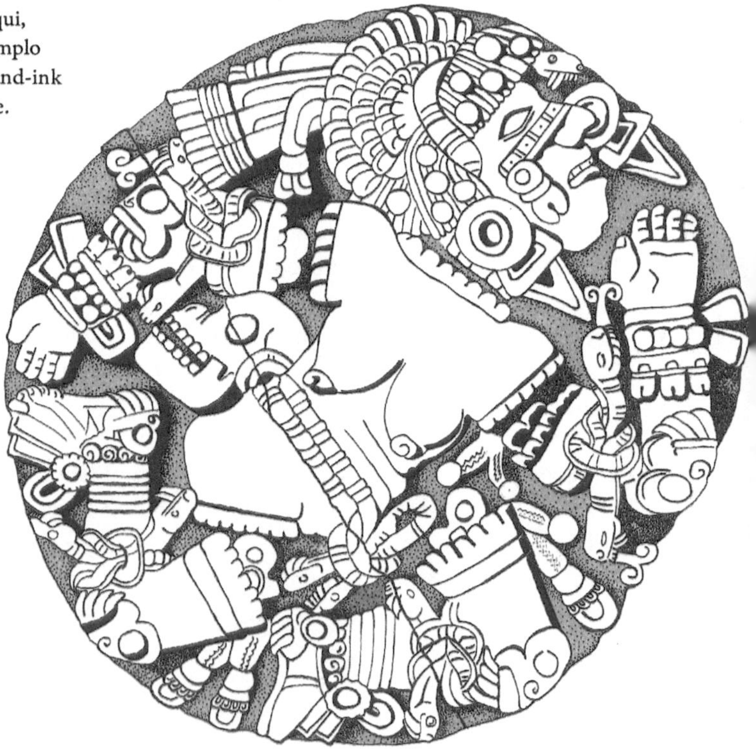

and sliced off her head, Huitzilopochtli rose from her severed trunk fully grown and armed. He banished his attackers and mutilated his evil sister, severing her extremities, so that she collapsed at the base of the shrine.[52]

It is the aftermath of this occurrence that is depicted in the Tenochtitlán stone relief and it is also the scene to which Pérez alludes in *Maestrapeace*. The artist not only pieces the goddess back together, but also shows her breaking away from the constraints of the stone itself. Pérez empowers Coyolxauhqui not only through the subversion of the ancient text and image, but also by depicting her with paintbrushes in hand, an indication of the artist's self-identification with this tarnished figure of Mexica cosmology. Pérez was not alone in this representation of Coyolxauhqui, who, like La Malinche, had become an icon for Chicana feminists. Chicanas, like these indigenous women in Mexican history and myth, had felt the stigma of being labeled *traidoras* (traitors) for having strayed away from the Chicano nationalist cause. Artist and writer Gloria Anzaldúa put into words her own perspective on Coyolxauhqui for the La Frontera/The Border (1993) exhibition in San Diego, in a statement that in many ways echoed Pérez's own reconceptualization of this deity:

> I stop before the dismembered body of *la diosa de la luna*, Coyolxauhqui, bones jutting from sockets. The warrior goddess, with bells on her cheeks and serpent belt, calls to mind the dominant culture's repeated attempts to tear Mexican culture in the U.S. apart and scatter the fragments to the winds. . . . I stare at the huge round stone of *la diosa*. To me, she also embodies the resistance and vitality of the Chicana/*mexicana* writer/artist. . . . [Representations of Coyolxauhqui by Chicanas signify] the cultural rebirth of the Chicana struggling to free herself from oppressive gender roles.[53]

Likewise, Cherríe Moraga understood the figure of Coyolxauhqui as an allegory of the violence suffered by Chicanas at the intersection of race, class, gender, and sexuality. In her renowned collection of poetry and fiction *The Last Generation* (1993), Moraga regarded this brutal encounter between siblings as the symbolic reconfiguration of power from matriarchal to patriarchal rule:

> Here mother and daughter are pitted against each other and daughter must kill male-defined motherhood in order to save the culture from misogyny, war and greed. But el hijo [the son] comes to the defense

of patriarchal motherhood, kills la mujer rebelde [the rebel woman], and female power is eclipsed by the rising light of the Sun/Son. This machista myth is enacted every day of our lives, every day that the sun (Huitzilopochtli) rises from the horizon and the moon (Coyolxauhqui) is obliterated by his light.[54]

In spite of her tragic fate, Coyolxauhqui also embodied women's strength in a misogynist and hostile world; she epitomized the reconstitution and "remembering" of the fragmented female body and consciousness.

As an Indigenist motif, the figure of Coyolxauhqui in *Maestrapeace* articulates a discourse within the mural's general theme that eloquently epitomizes the idea of empowerment from the margins. This figure also helped prevent the privileging within the mural of feminist concerns over issues of class and race and vice versa, thereby establishing a balanced synthesis that had been difficult to achieve in the past. While Pérez's Coyolxauhqui holds a prominent position within the mural's iconographic program, this Chicana artist's contribution, nevertheless, is tempered and complemented by that of her colleagues, who brought in their own complex and pressing preoccupations into the making of *Maestrapeace*.

Back in Los Angeles, Chicana artists continued to experiment with new collaborative projects, innovative uses of artistic media, and creative juxtapositions of imagery. This has been particularly true about younger artists who witnessed the Chicano Movement but were too young to actively participate in it. Alma López, whose work is characterized by the use of digital technology to articulate often controversial issues about sexuality, has emerged as a rising star in the Los Angeles artistic scene. The artist is perhaps best known for her digital image entitled *Our Lady* (1999), which depicted performance artist Raquel Salinas wearing a rose bikini while cast in the role of the Virgin of Guadalupe. In February of 2001, López showed this work in the Museum of Folk Art in Santa Fe, New Mexico, as part of their Cyber Arte: Tradition Meets Technology exhibition. The image sparked heated objections from a mob of protesters led by community activist José Villegas and New Mexico archbishop Michael J. Sheehan, who called for its removal from the museum.

Back in 1997, however, López made a series of digital murals while working in the Social and Public Art Resource Center's Digital Mural Lab,[55] some of which, like *Our Lady*, also proved to be controversial. Of particular relevance to the continuing interest in Indigenist imagery on the part of Chicana artists is López's digital mural entitled *Las Four* (1997) (Figure 5.11),

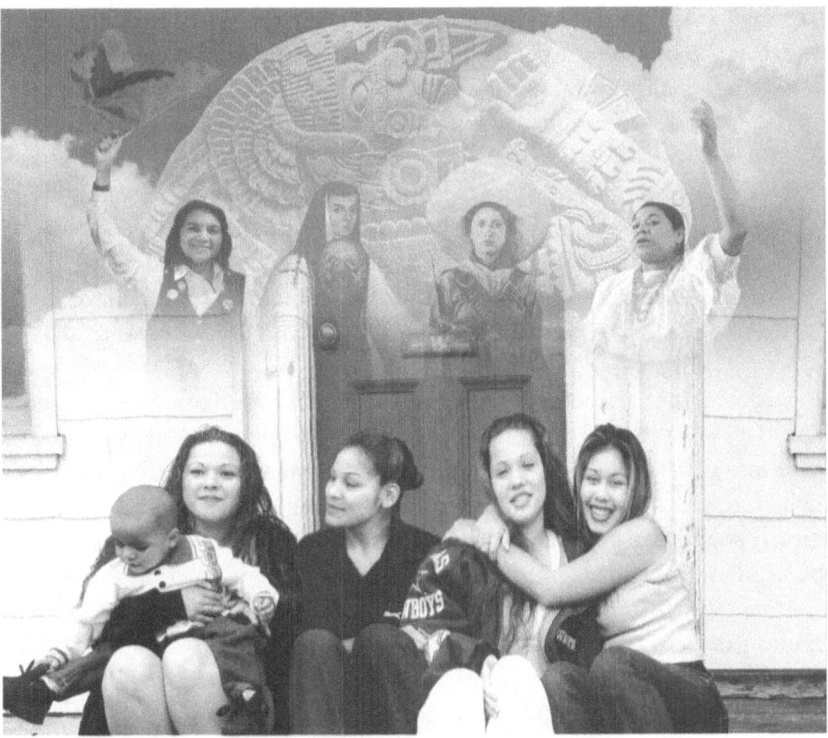

FIGURE 5.11. Alma López, © 1997, *Las Four*, digital mural, Estrada Courts, East Los Angeles, California. Courtesy of Alma López.

installed in Estrada Courts, the East Los Angeles housing project discussed in Chapter 4 where Charles "Gato" Félix and other well-known Chicano muralists painted a series of murals in the early seventies. López was keenly aware of the importance of Estrada Courts as a major mural site on the West Coast, and she fashioned her imagery as a form of feminist dialogue with the predominantly masculinist aesthetics surrounding her. López made *Las Four*, in part, as a response to another mural in Estrada, namely Ernesto de la Loza's *Los Cuatro Grandes* (1993), which celebrates the historical and political contributions of four male heroes, who are, from left to right, César Chávez, Emiliano Zapata, Francisco Villa, and Mario Moreno Cantinflas—all of whom stand as prominent architects of Chicano/Mexican culture. López's reaction to this type of imagery forced her to reevaluate the icons of Chicana/o identity with which she was raised:

I grew up in northeast Los Angeles . . . during the Chicano Mural Renaissance of the 1970s and early 80s. My visual world included: wall
size, meticulously spray painted black, old English, graffiti lettering;
bakery and market calendars of sexy Ixta draped over the lap of strong
Popo; tattoos of voluptuous bare breasted women with long feathered hair, burgundy lips, and raccoon eyes; painted cholas; and murals
mostly depicting Emiliano Zapata, Francisco Villa, and Aztec warriors. . . . To this visual world, my contribution would go beyond the
sexualized images of Ixta and the tattoo women; to create images of
women parallel in presence to Zapata, Villa, and the Aztec warriors.[56]

Indeed, standing in the place of Villa, Zapata, and the like are four eminent
Latinas whose historical significance has long been recognized by other Chicana muralists: Dolores Huerta, who is waving the UFW flag; Sor Juana Inés
de la Cruz, the seventeenth-century Mexican nun whose poems and plays
greatly shaped baroque/colonial literature; a Mexican *soldadera*; and Rigoberta Menchú, whose oratorical gesture echoes that of Huerta. As a compositional mechanism, the two raised arms of Huerta and Menchú then act as
framing devices around the image of Coyolxauhqui, who also appears in this
mural as an icon of Chicana admiration. Like Pérez's Coyolxauhqui in *Maestrapeace*, this particular Indigenist motif holds great metaphorical meaning
for López, who interprets the violent act directed at her by Huitzilopochtli
as that "of a brother towards his sister, as the murder of male and female
duality and balance, and the violent birth of a patriarchal system."[57] But unlike the representations by other Chicana muralists of these charismatic figures, López chooses to downplay the importance of Huerta, Sor Juana, the
soldadera, Menchú, and Coyolxauhqui by placing them in the background as
entities of a meaningful yet bygone era. In the foreground we see the image of
four young Chicanas, actual residents of Estrada Courts. Their relationship
to the figures in the background, explains López, is one of "spiritual leaders
nourishing a future generation of young women who can claim an ancestral
legacy as ancient as [that of] the pre-Columbian goddess Coyolxauhqui."[58]
For López, establishing a historical and spiritual continuity between indigenous figures like Coyolxauhqui and contemporary Chicanas promotes an
indigenous consciousness that is relevant to the average young Chicana living in the barrio. Learning about the story of Coyolxauhqui, in particular,
helped these women understand the historical dimensions of their own gender oppression. But López's use of real-life women in her work is precisely
what seems to stir controversy among the communities that see her work.
Shortly after its installation in Estrada Courts, *Las Four* was vandalized and

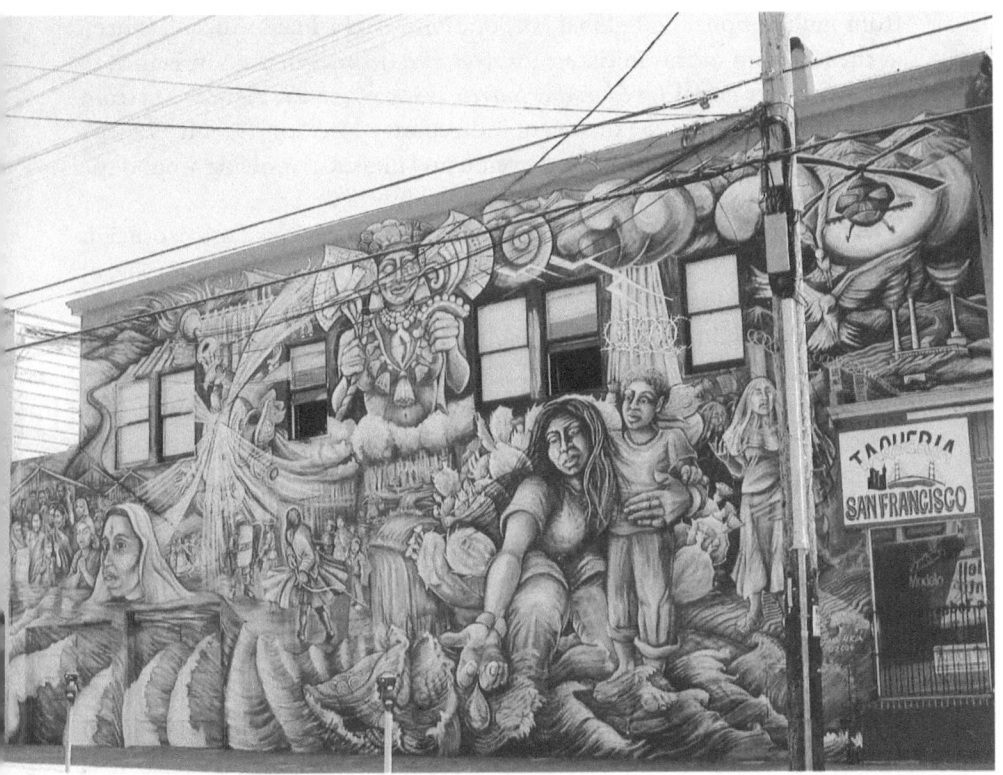

FIGURE 5.12. Juana Alicia, © 2004, *La Llorona's Sacred Waters*, mural, San Francisco, California. Courtesy of Juana Alicia.

damaged by a group of young men from Estrada who disliked one of the women in the mural because she dated a man from a different neighborhood/gang, so they objected to her representation. This episode proved that images of women's empowerment and agency were still regarded as threatening and even offensive to some sectors of the Chicana/o community.

The decades of the 1990s and 2000s have been marked by a growing interest among Chicana/o muralists in the intersection between indigenous consciousness and environmental concerns, as can be appreciated in Ernesto de la Loza's 1990–1991 mural, *Resurrection of a Green Planet*, discussed in Chapter 1 of this book. After all, the same colonialist enterprises that violently decimated indigenous communities in the Americas and elsewhere also eventually devastated the natural environments and ecosystems of these locations. Chicana muralists, however, have placed women at the center of the activism seeking to demand social and environmental justice from multinational and global corporations. Artist Juana Alicia has been at the forefront of this initiative for over two decades in the San Francisco Bay Area. Her mural *La Llorona's Sacred Waters*[59] (2004; Figure 5.12) seamlessly brings together the themes of indigenous consciousness and women's activist response to social and environmental injustice revolving around the allegorical figures of La Llorona and Chalchiuhtlicue.

A well-known figure to the predominantly Chicana/o/Latina/o neighborhood of the Mission District where the mural is located, La Llorona, or the weeping woman, is a legendary figure in Mexican lore who allegedly drowned her children as revenge against her unfaithful, philandering, and abusive husband. As punishment, she was condemned to forever wander and weep in search of her lost children. While her legend has multiple incarnations, meanings, and interpretations, La Llorona has come to epitomize bad motherhood, a kind of antimodel for women's behavior or, as Alfredo Mirandé and Evangelina Enríquez have commented, "[La Llorona is] an image of a woman who willingly or unwillingly fails to comply with feminine imperatives."[60] Almost paradoxically, however, this figure has also come to allegorize women's angst against the oppressive mandate of a patriarchal society, for the act of infanticide she commits, anthropologist José Limón contends, is "the symbolic destruction of the nuclear family at one stage, and the later possible restoration of her maternal bonds from the waters of rebirth as a second stage."[61]

Though a hybrid postconquest figure, La Llorona is connected to Meso-american nature goddesses through her association with water—the very site of the tragic drowning. Literary scholar Ana María Carbonell, for instance, recognizes the connection between La Llorona and Cihuacoatl, the Aztec goddess of childbirth and fertility, who in turn is also a mythical descendant of the powerful earth goddess Coatlicue.[62] Chicana feminist writers like Gloria Anzaldúa[63] as well as artists like Alma López and Rosa M.[64] have all made the association between La Llorona and Cihuacoatl. These Chicana cultural producers invoke this hybrid figure's indigenous roots as a symbol of La Llorona's empowering feminine attributes. In keeping with this Chicana feminist tradition, Juana Alicia, in her mural *La Llorona's Sacred Waters,* alludes to the indigenous and powerful elements of this figure but also transforms her into a symbol of global women's struggles against oppression, as Leticia Hernández indicates:

> In addition to Mexican and Aztec female archetypes, [Juana Alicia's] mural highlights Bolivians in Cochabamba who have fought to keep

Bechtel Corporation from buying the water rights in their country; Indian farm workers in the Narmada Valley protesting in the flooded waters of their homes against their government's irresponsible dam projects; and the women in black protesting the unsolved murders of women in Juarez, in the shadow of the Rio Bravo and the maquiladoras.[65]

Indeed, the theme of water becomes a leitmotif throughout *La Llorona's Sacred Waters,* both in its content as well as its form.[66] Juana Alicia uses varying hues of blue as the predominating color palette of the mural. Much of the composition revolves around the figure of Chalchiuhtlicue, the Mexica goddess of lakes and streams who is often depicted wearing a jade skirt in Mesoamerican representations, such as the Teotihuacán monumental sculpture from the Early Classic Period in pre-Columbian Mexico. In the Codex Ríos, Chalchiuhtlicue is shown with a stream of water flowing beneath her body.[67] In Juana Alicia's representation, she also wears the jade skirt, yet here the skirt also becomes a series of plentiful waterfalls and torrents that irrigate the land around her. Nevertheless, Chalchiuhtlicue is seen here weeping before the scenes of social injustice and violence happening around her as a Mesoamerican speech scroll emanates from her mouth, implying she is speaking against these social conditions. Directly next to her, we see the figure of La Llorona herself, who also weeps as she holds a young child close to her body while reaching out to Chalchiuhtlicue's sacred waters. La Llorona's proximity to the mourning women of Ciudad Juárez suggests that she is weeping for her children killed not by her own hand—as the popular legend recounts—but rather by the mysterious culprits of *femicidio* (femicide) in the Ciudad Juárez–El Paso border region, where the murders of over four hundred women since 1994 remain largely unsolved. While Chalchiuhtlicue is a preconquest figure and La Llorona is often associated with Mexico's Spanish colonial period, in *La Llorona's Sacred Waters,* Juana Alicia makes them both relevant to contemporary events and current social conditions. These two figures here also transcend the specificity of the Mexican/Chicana/o experience, for Chalchiuhtlicue's waters extend to the women protesters in Bolivia as they confront riot police in Cochabamba. These waters even reach the female demonstrators in India who oppose the building of numerous dams on the River Narmada. These dams would have negative effects on the riverine environment as well as on the local populations of the Narmada Valley who depend on the river's resources and who would be forcibly displaced by the construction of the dams.

Juana Alicia in *La Llorona's Sacred Waters* utilizes two powerful female indigenous figures, namely Chalchiuhtlicue and La Llorona, to underscore the negative effects of globalization on marginalized communities around the globe, not just among Mexicans and Chicanas/os. The onset of globalization, however, has ushered in the realization among many Chicana feminist artists that the struggles of the Third World and of women of color around the world bear striking similarities; thus, their approaches to activism and resistance are also comparable. The figures of Chalchiuhtlicue and La Llorona, then, function as recognizable or familiar symbols to the local Latina/o community in the Mission District, drawing them into the struggles of the women in Ciudad Juárez, Cochabamba, and Narmada as well.

Conclusion

The relevance of documenting and historicizing the contribution of Chicanas to muralism while simultaneously accounting for the recurrence of Indigenist motifs in their work goes beyond the necessity to construct a revisionist history based on feminist principles. Indigenist iconography, for both Chicana *and* Chicano muralists, became a sort of fertile ground where articulations of cultural and gendered identity were played out in a public setting. As a result, the direct and indirect statements Chicana muralists made about gender oppression were not just the concern of women but of the community as a whole. Furthermore, the contribution of women in the Chicana/o mural scene marked an important milestone in the medium's history. Chicana artists' challenge to the male-centered visual vocabulary prevalent in community murals led to a general loosening of strict and static representations of Chicana/o culture in these public works of art.

In the next chapter, we will explore the fragmentation and dissolution of monolithic definitions of both muralism and its accompanying Indigenist aesthetic in the hands of artists who, for a variety of reasons, have a conflicted and complex relationship with the ideals of *el movimiento*. This seeming disintegration, as we shall see, did not threaten the political viability of either muralism or Indigenism as vehicles for social empowerment, but it did define these cultural practices as necessarily postmodern and heterogeneous.

CHAPTER SIX

Murals and Postmodernism

Post-*movimiento*, Heterogeneity, and
New Media in Chicana/o Indigenism

The Postmodern Aesthetic in Indigenist Murals

The changes in the Chicana/o mural scene and its accompanying Indigenist vocabulary ushered in by individuals like graffiti artists, Chicana muralists, and others greatly contributed to a breaking down of some of the monolithic notions of identity that at times defined these public works of art. The new visual vocabularies that these artists were introducing, however, were part of a broader trend among urban artists to loosen static definitions of muralism. From its very inception, Chicana/o muralism in California possessed a postmodern quality whereby new aesthetics were constantly being erected and broken down almost simultaneously. Moreover, muralism's goal to write alternative histories of marginalized communities led to a general deconstruction, or at least suspicion, of master narratives on the part of many muralists. Literary scholar Rafael Pérez-Torres has argued that "Chicano cultural production provides a counterdiscourse that draws on history and simultaneously interrogates it."[1] The spirit of collectivity and community involvement that defined the medium was also coupled with a persistent attitude of self-critique and redefinition among muralism's practitioners. Furthermore, the ideals that informed muralism and Indigenism, as well as the intersection of the two, though seemingly unified, did not really represent a single ideological project. Although muralism emerged as an apparently cohesive artistic project that represented the spirit of the Chicano Movement, in actuality, mural history developed unevenly through the fragmented subject positions of the artists and the communities they served. There is no *one* mural Indigenist aesthetic but rather a multiplicity of complementary, overlapping, and contesting aesthetics. In this chapter, we will discuss the nature of this postmodern aesthetic by examining various examples of Indigenist murals throughout California that for numerous reasons challenge traditional and time-honored notions about muralism. For instance, we will analyze examples of works that challenge and question the ideals of *el movimiento* and its budding Indigenism as well as murals that utilized Indigenist themes as a springboard for a greater heterogeneity. New and innovative media utilized to create murals, such as recycled materials, performance, and digital technology, will also be discussed here. In addition, I argue that the indigenous iconography in many of these murals often operated as a catalyst for articulations of postmodern social realities. These murals, I contend, fall under three categories that heighten their postmodern status: post-*movimiento*, heterogeneity, and new media.

The use of muralism as a viable form for political and cultural expression certainly was not an unquestionable creative choice for Chicana/o artists. While this particular art form seemed to most appropriately fit the ideals of the Chicano Movement, the notion that all Chicana/o artists painted murals with Indigenist motifs became increasingly contested as early as the 1970s. When I spoke to Chicana artist Yreina Cervántez in the fall of 2000, she voiced to me her concern about what she saw as a backlash against muralism carried out by many Chicana/o artists who felt their own artistic production had become a cliché. Though it is true that most of these artists worked in a variety of forms, murals seemed to be the identifying artistic vehicle to generate a political consciousness during the Chicano Movement. The questioning of the Indigenist mural aesthetic ushered in a general attitude of self-critique and contemplation on the part of Chicana/o artists regarding the validity of their creative endeavors. Simultaneously, the mural's form and content were inadvertently pushed to a greater diversification in the atmosphere of growing transnationalism and globalization that characterized the last three decades of the twentieth century. Responding to the postmodern predicaments of the actual urban environments that inspired the early Indigenist murals associated with *el movimiento*, Chicana/o artists had to modify the medium so that it could accommodate itself to the ever-changing reality of these public spheres. This growing fluidity, however, prevented art historians and critics from providing static definitions of Chicana/o muralism that agreed with the preexisting vocabulary formulated around modern and contemporary art. Indigenism, as an aesthetic and an ideology, became the starting point for a greater multiplicity in Chicana/o creative expressions. Drawing from José Vasconcelos's notions about the formation of a cosmic race, Gloria Anzaldúa, for instance, wrote about Indigenist identity as a crucial element of the new mestiza's cultural and social consciousness: "Indigenous like corn, like corn, the *mestiza* is a product of crossbreeding under a variety of conditions."[2] Anzaldúa stripped *mestizaje* of the essentialism that Vasconcelos had advocated and reformulated it to include the previously marginalized experiences of women and lesbians.

The changes in the social and cultural context during the last three decades of the twentieth century also gave rise to a different generation of

Chicana/o artists. Many of the artists who participated in the early phases of the Chicana/o mural movement, like Manuel Cruz and Antonio Bernal, were largely self-taught community artists, whereas many of those who came of age in the 1980s and 1990s had earned BFAs and MFAs from reputable universities, as was the case with Yreina Cervántez and Alma López, both of whom graduated with art degrees, from UCLA and UC Irvine, respectively. Many Chicana/o artists did feel ambivalent and sometimes downright negative about their own education. Judy Baca, for instance, felt that when she returned to East Los Angeles from college, her art degree became irrelevant.[3] Nonetheless, through their education, their worldview was inevitably altered. Their global consciousness was further heightened by their travels abroad. Many Chicana/o artists visited Mexico to study the works of the Mexican muralists, but in the process witnessed the struggles of poor indigenous populations there. In the 1980s, Chicana/o artists from Southern and Northern California, such as Juana Alicia, Yreina Cervántez, and Barbara Carrasco, traveled to Nicaragua to carry out mural work there and to establish ties with the local muralists in the country. The result was an increased understanding on the part of many Chicana/o artists of how the forces of oppression and colonization affect marginalized communities in similar ways across national borders. Another outcome of this new consciousness was the way muralists began to treat local versus global concerns. The site specificity of many community murals was complicated by the broader perspective that these artists acquired in college and in their travels, where they established contact with communities outside the social sphere of the barrio. Their new attitudes did not necessarily do away with the local concerns that affected life in the barrio; quite the contrary, artists were now even more conscious of how national or global phenomena affected the unique experiences of the barrio. Their studies in academia and elsewhere gave them a more comprehensive vision regarding how the local interacted and conversed with the universal.

Post-*movimiento*: Contesting the Mural

Political and cultural currents like the Chicano Movement and its accompanying Indigenist mural renaissance formed part of a dynamic historical process. The rise of cultural phenomena like the Chicano Movement is often characterized by unusually innovative and creative responses to oppressive or marginalizing systems. The often radical character of *el movimiento*, however, prevented other equally disempowered groups from taking part in its activities, thereby creating a phenomenon I call post-*movimiento*.[4] Women were among the first to criticize their marginalization within the Chicano Movement; the Chicana/o queer community would soon follow suit. This post-*movimiento* sought to redefine and contest the goals of the "original" movement, in particular its nationalist proclivities, as explained by Ramón García:

> From traditional Mexican culture, Chicano nationalism extracted the glorious image of the Aztec, the Mexican revolutionary and Aztlán, transforming them into myths. That these mythologies would later reveal themselves as ineffective and politically bankrupt should come as no surprise, for as Roland Barthes has postulated, myth is always on the side of power and ideology, and not on the side of history or reality.[5]

Speaking in more general terms, even though postmovements often propose diametrically opposed discourses to those of the movement itself, their very existence is dependent on or relative to the former. In many cases, postmovements tend to emerge when movements become institutionalized or dogmatic. But certainly the more interesting and cutting-edge examples of postmovements are those that occur almost immediately after the onset of the movements themselves. Such was the case of the Mexican poets Los Contemporáneos, who overtly or covertly questioned and critiqued the work by the likes of Diego Rivera, David Alfaro Siqueiros, and José Clemente Orozco as early as the 1930s. Their choice of poetry as their preferred means of creative expression greatly contrasted with the social-realist style of the muralists and the writers of revolutionary novels like Mariano Azuela. The literary work of individuals like Salvador Novo and Jorge Cuesta, for instance, betrayed a certain anxiety and frustration about being excluded from the nationalist canon of the muralists, that is, about belonging to the margins of the margin.

Those who did not fit the profile of the Chicano radical, like women, gays, bicultural artists, or individuals who simply did not identify with the ideals of *el movimiento,* were the ones who instituted the unofficial Chicana/o post-*movimiento.* Such was the case of Asco, an artists collective from East Los Angeles whose name loosely translates into English as "nausea" or "disgust"[6] and whose primary form of artistic production was the street performance. Founded by Harry Gamboa Jr., Willie Herrón, Patssi Valdez, and Gronk in 1972, Asco, as pointed out by Howard Fox, "operated more or less within the Chicano Movement, but as the enfant terrible of the family."[7] Though they were conversant with artists who were associated with the Chicano Movement, they never really felt part of this phenomenon. Gronk, in particular, expressed his anxiety about the artistic and cultural isolation they felt in East Los Angeles:

> We didn't have the same kind of Marxist agenda or sensibility [that other Chicana/o artists collectives had]. It was more spontaneous [for us]. Instead of having to take [inspiration] from the streets and put it in our work, we were in the streets doing work. . . . We were just a rumor to a lot of people for the longest time, and they sort of thought of us as drug addicts, perverts. All kinds of names were hurled at us by other Chicano artists. . . . But we were not accepted by the mainstream art gallery kind of Westside thing either. So we were on our own to develop our own way.[8]

By the early 1970s, Asco was already contesting what had become the trademark art form of the Chicano Movement, muralism. In a staged interview that took place at the Los Angeles County Museum of Art in 1975, Herrón and Gronk expressed with satiric humor their views on the status of muralism:

> NEWORLD: What's your definition of art?
> GRONK: Antonin Artaud: "No more masterpieces!"
> HERRÓN: I don't have one. I'm not that old.
> NEWORLD: What would you like to see?
> HERRÓN: People taking murals less seriously. I'd like to see Siqueiros come back to life in City Terrace [East Los Angeles].
> GRONK: As a bumblebee.
> HERRÓN: I'd like to receive Orozco's left arm in the mail by Gronk.[9]

The tongue-in-cheek tone of this exchange seemed like blasphemy to those who revered muralism's ostensible ability to politicize a community. Not only were Herrón and Gronk contesting the importance of muralism to Chicana/o artists, but they were also poking fun at the Mexican muralists and their reputation as the predecessors to the current mural movement. They also found the Indigenist aesthetic often attached to muralism to be out of touch with the everyday lived reality of the streets, as explained by Gronk: "I don't do Virgins of Guadalupe. I don't do corn goddesses. I can only do what I'm about, and I'm an urban Chicano living in a city."[10] The members of Asco were not so much seeking to ridicule muralism as to elevate it "from a static medium to one of performance,"[11] as stated by Harry Gamboa himself. The group's irreverent attitude toward the state of artistic

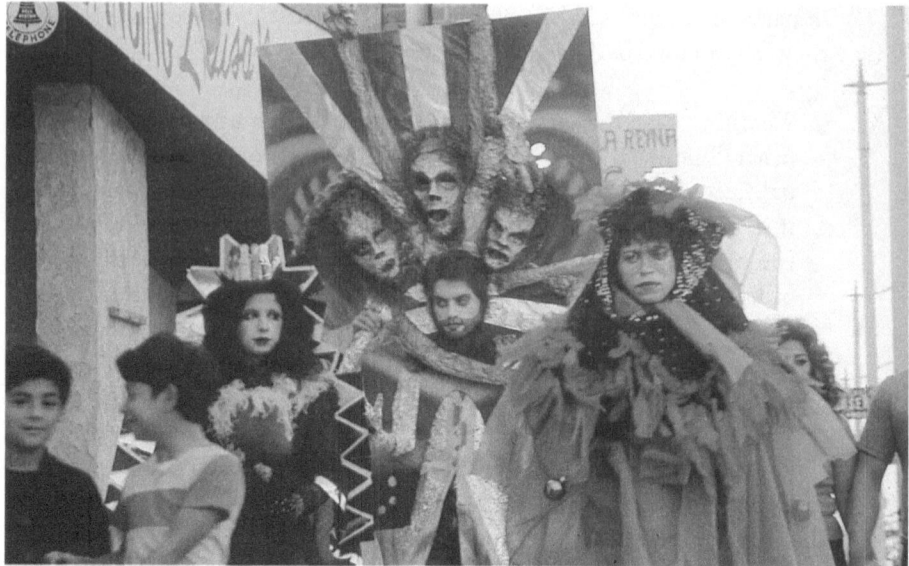

FIGURE 6.1. Harry Gamboa Jr., © 1972, *Walking Mural,* photograph of public performance, East Los Angeles, California. Courtesy of Harry Gamboa Jr.

production in East Los Angeles made them perhaps some of the most astute critics of an art form they themselves had practiced (both Gronk and Willie Herrón had executed murals prior to and after joining Asco).

On Christmas Eve, 1972, Herrón, Valdez, Gronk, and Gamboa took to the streets of East Los Angeles to stage their performance later titled *Walking Mural* (Figure 6.1). On Whittier Boulevard, three members of Asco paraded down the street in very distinct guises: Valdez was dressed as the Virgin of Guadalupe, Gronk as a Christmas tree, and Herrón as a "multi-faced mural that had become bored with its environment and left," as described by Gamboa, who photographed and filmed the event.[12] Aside from lamenting a mural's perceived physical and discursive stagnation, in this particular performance the members of Asco removed the mural from its site specificity and turned it into yet another icon (or cliché) associated with the Chicana/o culture, along with the Virgin of Guadalupe and the Christmas tree. To further transgress muralism as a consecrated art form, the group included three protruding heads on the surface of this walking mural, one of which was Herrón's own; the effect lent a sculptural quality to the piece that defied the flatness commonly associated with murals. These faces also rather humorously resembled the tripartite or mestizo face that symbolized *mestizaje,* an image often seen in Chicana/o community murals.[13] With this street intervention, Asco had lampooned various icons that were dear to the Chicano Movement and its accompanying artistic renaissance. Though performance art would be championed by the likes of the Border Arts Workshop/Taller de Arte Fronterizo from the Tijuana/San Diego border region later in the 1980s, in the early 1970s, the art form was introduced to the California Chicana/o art scene by Asco. The group articulated performance as the diametrical opposite of muralism. Whereas they saw murals as static, performance was dynamic and fluid; while murals possessed a history that dated back thousands of years, performance, as a *visual* art form, was a relatively new phenomenon. In most aspects, wall paintings were more closely associated with the Chicana/o Indigenist aesthetic, but performance included an element of ritual that seemed not unlike indigenous forms of cultural expression in the Americas.

Two years later, also on Christmas Eve, Asco returned to Whittier Boulevard to enact the *First Supper (After a Major Riot)* (1974). This intervention consisted of the members of the group setting up a dinner table at the intersection of Whittier Boulevard and Arizona Avenue, the site of a police shooting a few years earlier. In the midst of rush-hour traffic, Gamboa, Valdez, Gronk, and this time Humberto Sandoval dined alongside various flamboyant props like a skeleton, a large doll, and paintings depicting torture.[14] At the end of the meal, Gronk, using masking tape, proceeded to attach Valdez's and Sandoval's bodies to the wall of a nearby liquor store, thereby creating their famous *Instant Mural* (Figure 6.2). Gamboa later assessed this street performance in the following manner:

> *Instant Mural* challenged the fragility of social controls. Several anonymous individuals, concerned about their welfare, offered to help Valdez and Sandoval escape the confines of the low-tack masking tape. After an hour of entrapment, Valdez and Sandoval simply walked away from the visually intimidating, yet physically weak lengths of tape.[15]

Though Gamboa was referring to the wall as a metaphor for social control and containment, *Instant Mural* also operated as a commentary on the state of mural production. If imposed on an artist, muralism could be a stifling medium that in certain circumstances could preclude the exercise of free creative expression. Moreover, the action of taping actual human beings to a wall parodied muralism's perceived capacity to capture a slice of real life. Valdez's and Sandoval's subsequent liberation from the wall further contradicted muralism's association with permanence and with the notion that a long and involved process is required to make a wall painting. In many mural

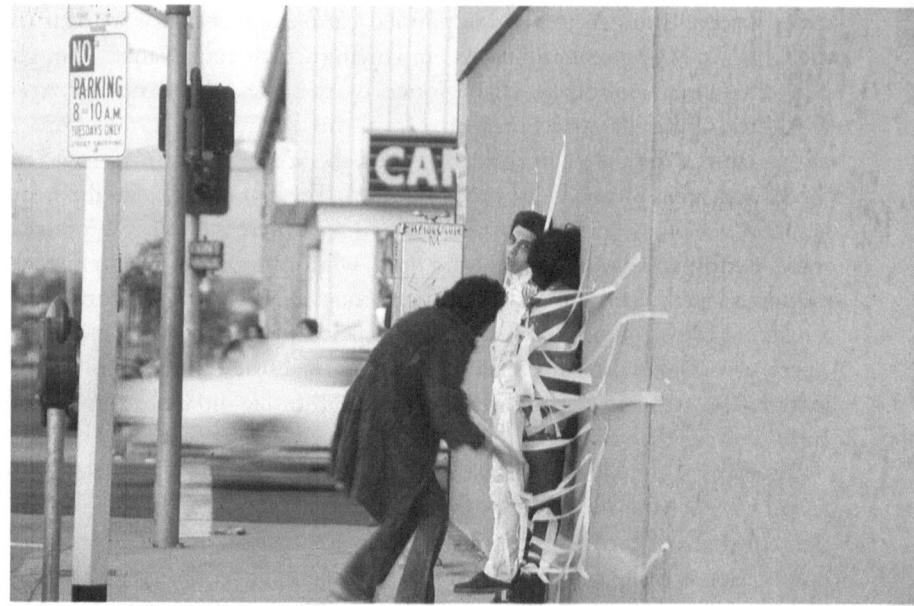

FIGURE 6.2. Harry Gamboa Jr. © 1974, *Instant Mural*, photograph of public performance, East Los Angeles, California. Courtesy of Harry Gamboa Jr.

traditions, wall paintings are considered to be monuments capable of long outlasting the communities that created them—as was the case of the murals in Bonampak or Teotihuacán—but in the Chicana/o and Mexican barrios of California, they became fleeting forms of artistic ventures. Victims of vandalism, city "cleanup" efforts, lack of funding for restoration and protection, among other circumstances, community murals have come and gone along with the changing face of the urban environment (in this respect, murals *do* resemble performance art). Asco's *Instant Mural* made the ephemeral quality of many Chicana/o murals all the more evident.

The critical and self-reflective attitude most of the members of Asco held toward muralism informed their own work. The wall paintings they executed individually or as a group were perhaps some of the most original murals in East Los Angeles. Aside from the seminal importance of Herrón's *The Wall That Cracked Open*—discussed in greater detail in Chapter 3—Gronk and Herrón's contribution to the Estrada Courts murals, the *Black and White Moratorium Mural* (1973), redefined the preexisting mural aesthetic that predominated in East Los Angeles. In this work, the artists recounted the events of the Chicano Moratorium—the 1970 march that took place in

Los Angeles denouncing the disproportionate number of young Chicanos who were being killed in the Vietnam War—by depicting them as images from film stills.

Heterogeneity and the Changing Face of Murals

The postmodern phenomenon in California Chicana/o murals was also influenced by a growing cultural heterogeneity in its iconography and means of production. As early as the 1980s, we begin to see the emergence of murals that articulate the cultural diversity and complexity that make up the urban environment. Originating within the fields of science and technology, the concept of heterogeneity is often defined as the state in which a whole can only exist when different or dissimilar parts hold together its structure. In postcolonial studies, heterogeneity and hybridity have often been used interchangeably or in conjunction with one another. Within this context, the concept refers to the expressions in colonized societies that display elements from multiple cultural origins. Postcolonial writers Bill Ashcroft, Gareth Griffiths, and Helen Tiffin point out how hybridity is "a strength rather than a weakness" and that the phenomenon "stresses the mutuality of the [colonizing] process."[16] But the subtle distinction between hybridity and heterogeneity depends on who exhibits these traits. In other words, hybridity assumes that it is the colonized, *not* the colonizer, who is transformed; heterogeneity, on the other hand, does not imply such an assumption. While hybridity often requires a colonial or postcolonial setting, heterogeneity thrives in more generalized environments of cultural exchange. Heterogeneity is also connected to what Rafael Pérez-Torres calls resistant multiculturalism, an idea diametrically opposed to the melting-pot notion championed by traditional multiculturalism. Resistant multiculturalism, Pérez-Torres contends, "foregrounds a basic inequality within the mosaic of multicultural America."[17]

Michel Foucault has described the nature of knowledge as an intrinsically heterogeneous one. He explained that the breadth of human knowledge, no matter how diverse and seemingly contradictory, is contained within what he called an archive, that is, "a complex volume, in which heterogeneous regions are differentiated or deployed, in accordance with specific rules and practices that cannot be superposed."[18] The ways Chicana/o artists were constructing new knowledge through the public mural reflected this heterogeneous process that Foucault describes. Moreover, cultural critic Néstor García Canclini, though captivated by the presence of hybridity in Latin America, found that "the study of cultural heterogeneity [provided] one of the routes to explain how oblique powers can infiltrate liberal institutions ...

how democratic social movements affect paternalist regimes, and how these transact with one another."[19] Given that using the word *colonization* when discussing the status of Chicanas/os vis-à-vis U.S. dominant culture is often problematic and reductive, speaking of heterogeneity in their work is more suitable when discussing the free flow of cultural capital across different social and cultural spheres.

Though the Indigenism formulated by many Chicana/o artists seemed to be almost synonymous with a specifically Mexican subjectivity, this aesthetic loosened the rigidity of the Chicano nationalist canon. Just as Indigenism offered a kind of springboard for discussions about *mestizaje* for thinkers like José Vasconcelos and Alfonso Caso, for Chicanas/os, Indigenism provided a framework through which to address their simultaneous sensibilities and overlapping identities. As was discussed in Chapter 5, Chicana artists took the lead when it came to pushing muralism and its Indigenist iconography toward an increased diversity as they sought to redress the male-centered discourses of the Chicano Movement. But aside from Chicanas, multifaceted Chicano artists like Willie Herrón and Gronk, who explored creative expressions as diverse as performance art and rock music,[20] saw both the potential qualities but also the limitations of Indigenist mural imagery.

As Chicana/o artists sought increasingly diverse means by which to express themselves, their visual vocabulary became more familiar to a larger community. As I explained for the cases of artists like Posh One, Spie, and Susan Kelk Cervantes in Chapters 3 and 4, there was also a great diversity of individuals who were not Chicanas/os, but were nevertheless familiar with and cognizant of the significance of Chicana/o indigenous culture. The inherent heterogeneity in the mural movement led to the migration of artistic forms, iconographic motifs, and thematic context in and out of the Chicana/o cultural sphere. What were once considered specifically Mexican themes became more general signifiers of universal concerns. These discursive and aesthetic migrations were sometimes the result of counterhegemonic alliances among marginalized or politically conscious groups or just the outcome of the growing diversity within formerly Chicana/o or Mexican urban areas, as in the case of the Mission District in San Francisco. This was true for Josh Sarantis, Isais Mata, and Jan Cook's *The Dreamers among Us Still Look to the Sky* (1997), a Mission District mural that graces the playground of Bryant Elementary School. Painted on two large walls of the school building, this highly utopian work depicts a number of ethnically diverse children engaging in various activities related to science, technology, agriculture, aviation, and transportation. The artists were seeking to stimulate the aspirations and dreams of the children in Bryant by using monumental images of kids like themselves as models. Though the mural celebrates multiculturalism and cultural diversity in a direct and rather uncritical manner, the artists included a very distinct Indigenist motif in its iconographic program, namely the image of Quetzal-coatl. Painted in a dull gray color, this image is both discreet and prominent within the mural's composition. It is placed on a smaller panel between the two main walls of *The Dreamers among Us*. This particular panel depicts a smiling African American girl staring at an atom in the process of forma-tion. The atom obtains its power from a crank below that connects to an underworld presided over by Quetzalcoatl.[21] The Mesoamerican deity here also stands out from the rest of the figures and objects in that it is the only sculptural, three-dimensional motif in the entire composition that is located right on the floor of the playground. Thus, he inhabits the underworld of the mural's iconography, but he also shares the actual space where the children of Bryant play so they can touch and climb over him.

Quetzalcoatl's relationship to the overall theme of *Dreamers among Us* operates on several levels. The muralists honor the tradition in Chicana/o murals of likening the feathered serpent god with the quest for knowledge and education.[22] Quetzalcoatl also appears here as a symbol of *mestizaje* and heterogeneity. According to the conquest chronicles, Hernán Cortés was allegedly thought to be Quetzalcoatl himself, returning after his participa-tion in the Fifth Creation. While this reading of the events surrounding the conquest of Mexico is certainly a colonialist one, it did serve to provide a more heterogeneous interpretation of Quetzalcoatl's historical and cultural importance. In *The Dreamers among Us Still Look to the Sky*, Quetzalcoatl ceases to signal an exclusively Mexican sensibility and points toward a more universalizing subjectivity.

But perhaps one of the murals in San Francisco that most effectively il-lustrates the dissemination of Indigenist Mexican imagery across different cultural and social spheres is *Tonantsin Renace* (*Tonantsin Is Reborn*), a mu-ral executed by Anglo-American artist Colette Crutcher on the corner of Sánchez and Sixteenth Streets (Figure 6.3). The artist first made the mural in 1990 using only two-dimensional media, namely acrylic paint on wood. After a few years of being exposed to the elements, the mural began to de-teriorate. Since this work was so well loved and admired by the local resi-dents, Crutcher decided to restore the mural. While working as an artist in residence for NORCAL Waste Systems, Crutcher took an interest in recycled materials and decided to use them in the restoration of the mural: "My interest in recycled materials stems from an innate thriftiness, disgust of the wastefulness of our society, and a love of the unexpected," she would later explain. Using scrap metal, mosaic, fiberglass, and cast resin, Crutcher

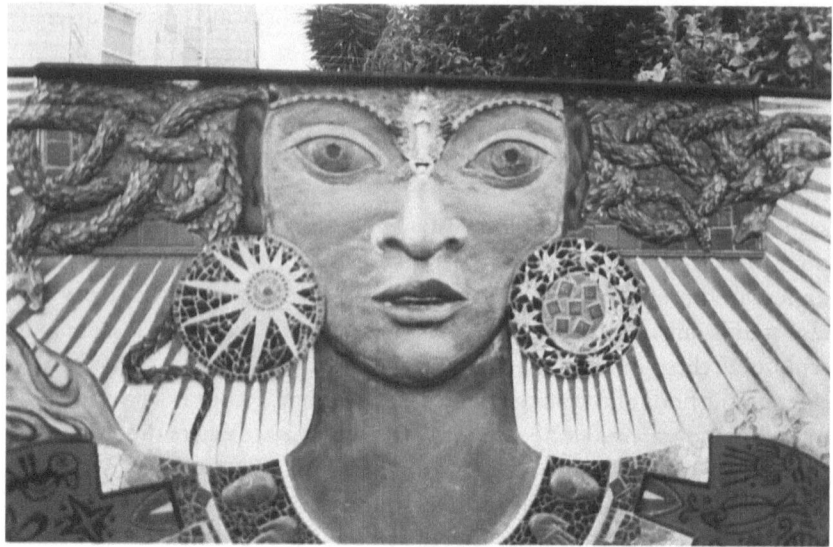

FIGURE 6.3. Colette Crutcher, © 1990; 1997, *Tonantsin Renace,* detail, mural, San Francisco, California. Courtesy of Colette Crutcher.

transformed the flatness of her original design into a three-dimensional and sculptural mural in 1997.[23]

Crutcher has commented that one of the reasons she enjoyed working with recycled materials was that, when reused, these take on a new life. The idea seemed appropriate to the artist, since *Tonantsin Renace* had enjoyed its new life when it was being restored. The theme of new life was also fitting for the mural's subject matter. Tonantsin was the mother of gods to the Aztecs, often evoked during childbirth and healing rituals. A shrine was erected in her honor on the hill of Tepeyac in what is now Mexico City. As is commonly known by Mexicans on both sides of the border, Tepeyac was also the site where, during the colonial era, an Aztec Indian by the name of Juan Diego experienced his legendary vision of the Virgin of Guadalupe, her very first appearance on Mexican soil.[24] Mesoamericanists and colonialists alike observed that Tonantsin and the Virgin of Guadalupe were subsequently evoked interchangeably by the Indians. In the same way that the worship of *orisas* in Cuban *santería* was revived in the veneration of Catholic saints, the Guadalupe's appearance in Tepeyac was regarded by Mexico's indigenous peoples as a second coming of Tonantsin.

Though in the 1960s and 1970s it might have seemed anachronistic for a non-Chicana/o artist to work with themes associated with Mexican culture, the ever-growing heterogeneity that characterized cities like San Francisco during the last decades of the twentieth century made *Tonantsin Renace* the logical consequence of the times. Crutcher was inspired to do a mural about Tonantsin through her contact and counterhegemonic alliances with La-tina/o groups in the area. The artist had been an active member of the Coro Hispano de San Francisco, a chorus dedicated to the performance and dis-semination of Latin American and Iberian music. Her idea for *Tonantsin Re-nace* came from a song the Coro Hispano sang that was written by an Indian who had studied music with Catholic priests in colonial Mexico. The song was dedicated to the Virgin of Guadalupe and Tonantsin simultaneously, and it displayed the musical influence of both Spanish and Mexica cultures; in essence, it was a hybrid and syncretic song. Crutcher sought to achieve a similar aesthetic with her mural. Moreover, the artist created *Tonantsin Renace* with a specific patron in mind, namely Juan Pedro Gaffey, director of the Coro and owner of the house with the wooden fence on which the mural was painted.[25]

Tonantsin Renace's iconography and style represented the combination of the artist's imagination and research—especially during the renovation phase in 1997. Crutcher depicted the Mesoamerican goddess with her arms extended. Here she is in control of the world's four elements: water, earth, fire, and air. With her right arm she commands the flight of birds (air) and the flames of underground molten strata (fire), while with her left she oversees the currents of the marine world (water) and the dynamics of the planet's vegetation (earth). Instead of hair, she has snakes emerg-ing from her head, making Tonantsin look like a cross between Medusa and the Coatlicue sculpture of Tenochtitlán who wore a skirt of writh-ing snakes. The presence of the snakes is also significant because in Me-soamerican iconography these signify fertility, thus echoing the theme of renewed life Crutcher was exploring. Also like the Tenochtitlán Coatlicue, Tonantsin here wears a necklace made of hands, hearts, and skulls. Her mosaic inlaid earrings depict images of the sun and the moon, alluding to the Mesoamerican concern with the duality of day and night. But the art-ist also highlights Tonantsin's connection to colonialism's Christian legacy by placing on her forehead a sculptural image of the *guadalupana* herself being held by the archangel Saint Michael, in keeping with traditional rep-resentations. Crafted from sheets of metal, Tonantsin radiates the same holy rays of light that emanate from the Virgin of Guadalupe. Crutcher, however, heightens this image's heterogeneity by including Oceanic-like pictographs imprinted on her body and by using an overall color scheme reminiscent of Tibetan art.[26]

In addition to the iconography, in *Tonantsin Renace* Crutcher included some textual definitions or English translations of Nahuatl words associated with Tonantsin. These definitions indicate that the artist hoped to educate a broader audience about ancient Mexican culture and spirituality, but they also function as textual complements to the image itself; they extend the meaning of the mural's iconography. The references in the text to other Aztec goddesses like Chicomecohuatl, Coatlicue, or Tlazolteotl speak of their relationship to Tonantsin but also of the importance of female deities in Mesoamerican cultures. The mural's location in a rather ethnically diverse area of San Francisco and the mostly European American cultural background of the artist also make this image a more general statement about women's agency and empowerment in the spiritual world. If heterogeneity refers to those elements that consist or are made up of dissimilar parts, then *Tonantsin Renace* displays a heterogeneous aesthetic because it reflects the coming together of various cultural spheres. Moreover, the mural was constructed with different forms of creative expression, namely, the textual and the visual (and even the visual here is assembled through mixed media). The work's heterogeneity is also representative of a multicultural feminism that has emerged on a global scale. The feminism of the 1960s and 1970s was harshly criticized for excluding the contribution of women of color and of the so-called Third World as well as for collapsing all feminine sensibilities and experiences into one. Multicultural feminism, on the other hand, rises from the real-life social and cultural contacts between different groups, as clarified by Ella Shohat:

> As a situated practice, multicultural feminism takes as its starting point the cultural consequences of the worldwide movements and dislocations of peoples associated with the development of "global" and "transnational" capitalism. . . . The relational feminist approach demands moving beyond nation-bound and discipline-bound teaching, curating, and organizing.[27]

The growing heterogeneous environments of urban centers like San Francisco have fostered multicultural feminist expressions like the one seen in *Tonantsin Renace*. The mural stemmed not from assumptions about the culture of the Other, but rather from the concrete familiarity and contact among different groups, relations that often present themselves in cities like San Francisco. In this mural, Tonantsin becomes a general allegory of cultural survival in the face of adversity. Since she is reincarnated and takes new form in the figure of the Virgin of Guadalupe, she is also an allegory of

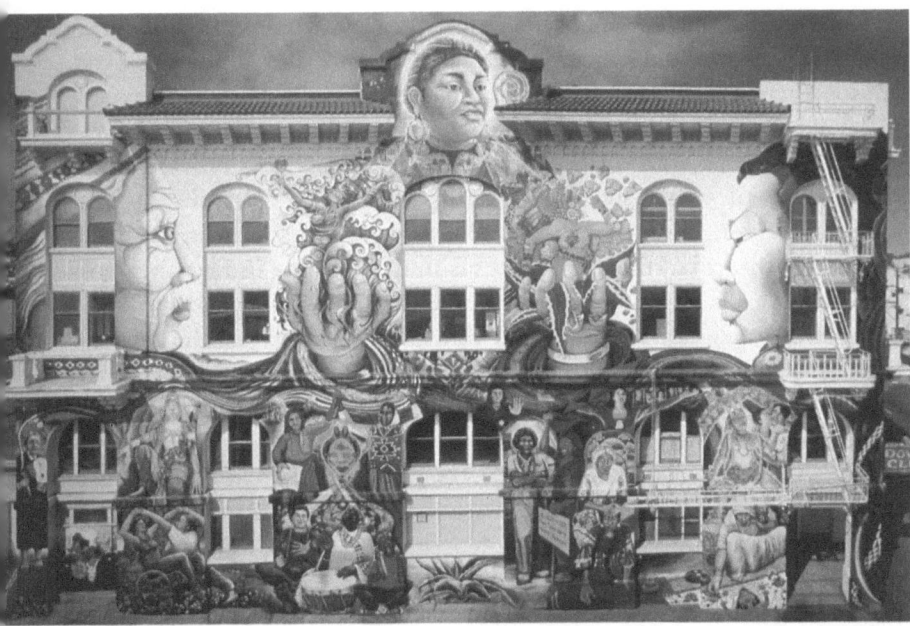

FIGURE 6.4. Juana Alicia, Miranda Bergman, Irene Pérez, Yvonne Littleton, Meera Desai, Edythe Boone, and Susan Kelk Cervantes, © 1994, *Maestrapeace*, mural, Lapidge Street façade, San Francisco, California. Photograph by César Rubio. Courtesy of Meera Desai.

overlapping and fluid identities and thereby appeals to communities other than that of women of color.

But perhaps no other mural in California better exemplifies the heterogeneity and multicultural feminist spirit on the West Coast than *Maestrapeace* (1994), located in San Francisco's Mission District (Lapidge Street façade shown in Figure 6.4). Lauded as a larger-than-life celebration of transnational feminism, *Maestrapeace* symbolizes the heights reached by women artists in the U.S. community mural scene. This mural has come to epitomize what Shohat herself calls multicultural feminism, "where many critical voices engage in a dialogue in which no one voice . . . muffles the others," in other words, a "dissonant polyphony" of types.[28] The mural operates as evidence of the growing cultural heterogeneity that has come to characterize San Francisco's Mission District. The seven visual artists chosen to undertake this project—namely, Chicanas Juana Alicia and Irene Pérez, along with Miranda Bergman, Edythe Boone, Susan Cervantes, Meera Desai, and Yvonne Littleton—sought to depict female figures who represented conciliatory presences amid global struggles and conflicts.

Plans for the mural began back in 1992 when the Women's Building's administrative committee, including then acting director Shoshona Rosenberg, got together to make plans for a mural that would commemorate this organization's fifteenth anniversary.[29] The building's staff disseminated a survey asking the various individuals who visit the organization to provide input about the mural's theme, suggesting that this work's imagery was the result of ideas transcending those of the artists collective that was selected to produce it. Quickly thereafter, the administrators initiated fund-raising campaigns and issued a call for artists who, on the one hand, possessed the skill to carry out such an undertaking and, on the other, aptly represented the cultural heterogeneity of San Francisco and the Bay Area. Artist Miranda Bergman described the chosen group of seven artists, affectionately called the "San Francisco Seven" by certain journalists, in the following manner: "The muralists—Alicia, Bergman, Boone, Cervantes, Desai, Littleton and Pérez—had collectively more than 100 years of mural experience and were an integral part of the San Francisco Bay Area mural movement." The artist also explained that the group was composed of "two African-Americans, two Latinas, one East Indian, and two Caucasians, one Jewish; lesbian, straight, and bisexual."[30] Susan Cervantes, for her part, understood that *Maestrapeace* could not have happened without the strong mural history that the city of San Francisco possessed, a history that included the critical contribution of Mexican muralist Diego Rivera in the 1930s, African American artists such as Dewey Crumpler, and women artists like Las Mujeres Muralistas.[31]

The artists painted *Maestrapeace* over two façades on the four-story Women's Building, a not-for-profit women's advocacy center operating from the heart of San Francisco's Mission District. Viewers are generally introduced to the mural through the façade facing Eighteenth Street, which is a fairly busy avenue. Having to creatively use the space between the many windows of this building, the artists fashioned a symmetrical composition flanked by two archetypal female figures representing the African and Native American ethnicities, who extend their hands toward each other's face. Above them we find the Goddess of Light and Creativity, whose womb reveals a six-month-old fetus of a girl, representing the future generations of enlightened women. The creation of muralist Susan Cervantes, this figure, the artist explained, demonstrates that all "women can learn to have control over their own destinies. She holds the sun [, symbolizing] that potential."[32] This goddess is shown releasing the water of life from her womb. As it descends down the wall of the Women's Building, this stream turns into a Celtic textile to the right and a Samoan fabric to the left. At the spectator's eye level, the muralists placed four figures of children, representing the largest continents of the world: an indigenous (Guatemalan) girl teasingly hiding behind streams of fabric representing the Americas, which the muralists here renamed Aztlán; a Caucasian girl holding an Eastern European Goddess Oracle; a Sri Lankan girl; and a grandmother and granddaughter belonging to the Wodaabe people of Niger. These figures were placed close to the ground level so they would be accessible to the many children who visit the building with their parents. The Eighteenth Street façade functions as a conceptual introduction to the mural's overall theme. The multicultural feminist message behind the imagery is established not only through the diversity of the various allegorical figures in this façade but also through the textile designs running across the pictorial space. These streams of fabric function as binding agents for the mural's composition and as a unifying device for *Maestrapeace*'s subject matter. While conducting research for the creation of this mural, the artists found that textile design and production constituted the one common artistic expression that women traditionally practiced throughout the world. Consequently, they included more than three dozen examples of textile designs, including Zapotec fabrics, Chinese embroidery, and North American quilts. Representing the concept of multicultural feminism furthered by scholars like Ella Shohat, *Maestrapeace* sought to find the commonalities among women without undermining the specificity of their experiences brought about by differences in social class, ethnicity, nationality, sexuality, and other factors.

As the Eighteenth Street façade introduces spectators to the general concepts behind *Maestrapeace*, it also subtly invites them to turn the corner over to Lapidge Street by following the Samoan fabric design that emerges from the water of life. The two façades are adjacent to one another, thereby allowing the muralists to establish a certain continuity between the iconographic programs on both walls. On Eighteenth Street, passersby are presented with more generalized concepts, and then on Lapidge Street, they are provided with specific examples of actual historical and mythical female figures who represent the ideas previously elaborated. The wall on Lapidge provided the muralists with the opportunity to include a denser iconographic program, as there was relatively more wall space on which to paint. By comparison, Lapidge Street is a smaller road, almost an alley, with much less traffic than Eighteenth Street, thus having fewer distractions that might divert the attention of a potential audience from the mural (not to mention that it probably provided the muralists with a calmer environment in which to work). This façade is saturated with images of female historical and mythical figures that have greatly impacted world history, and it not only highlights the contributions of these various women but also explains how they connect with one another across national borders, racial lines, and class hierarchies. For instance, the muralists chose to depict together the figures of former U.S. Surgeon General Joycelyn Elders, UFW activist Jessica Govea, and Mexican *curandera* María Sabrina as examples of how women excel in the health professions in many forms. As viewers turn the corner from Eighteenth to Lapidge Street, they are instructed on how the local engages the universal and vice versa.

The entire composition on the Lapidge Street façade of *Maestrapeace*, however, is presided over by a figural group that possesses powerful indigenous overtones. This group, located in the upper-central portion of the façade, is composed of Guatemalan indigenous rights activist Rigoberta Menchú, who holds in her hands the figures of Yoruba water goddess Yemayá and Aztec deity Coyolxauhqui. The importance of this group within the mural's iconography is further heightened by their comparatively larger scale to the other figures. As discussed in Chapter 5, Irene Pérez was mostly responsible for the figure of Coyolxauhqui, but Juana Alicia did most of the work on Yemayá and the face of Menchú. Susan Cervantes designed Menchú's *huipil* after an arduous process of researching Maya textile designs. Alicia herself, however, was quick to point out that during the creation of *Maestrapeace*, no one artist claimed ownership of any of the images, thus making all the participating women into *dueñas* (owners) of the iconography.[33] These three figures represent perhaps the most common cross-cultural alliance in the Americas, namely, the one between indigenous and African-descent peoples. On a local level, the pairing of the Guatemalan Nobel Peace laureate with these two mythical deities signaled the various contacts between Black and Chicana women artists in the San Francisco community art scene while also revealing the growing closeness between Black and Latina/o communities in the San Francisco Bay Area.

In *Maestrapeace*, Juana Alicia and Susan Cervantes depict Rigoberta Menchú wearing the traditional Quiché Maya *huipil* she's known for, thus making a link to the theme of textile production present throughout the mural. Menchú is here presented in the act of speaking, as a Mesoamerican speech scroll emerges from her mouth. This motif is significant, given Menchú's use of the spoken and written word as means for political, cultural, and gendered empowerment, such as in her seminal testimonial *I, Rigoberta Menchú*. To her right, the Pleiades constellation representing the Seven Sisters oversees Menchú's act of individual and collective emancipation, for when she spoke about her personal experience, Menchú simultaneously spoke for her indigenous community. She wears the medallion of the Nobel Peace Prize as earrings, but the image of the three male figures with interlocked arms that is commonly seen in these medallions is transformed into three women, thus calling into question the gendered iconography associated with the Nobel Prize and the underlying assumption that only men can be peacemakers.

Though Alicia depicts Menchú within the specificity of her historical context, the connections established here to Yemayá and Coyolxauhqui speak of her category as an allegory of women's peaceful yet brave forms of resistance in the Americas. Alicia's rendition of Yemayá[34] echoes the celebratory tone of the entire mural. The artist illustrates this water goddess emerging victorious from within the splash of an ocean wave. Venerated in Nigeria by the Yoruba people for many centuries, Yemayá's worship was transported to the Americas by the African diaspora to countries like Brazil and Cuba, where the syncretic religion of *santería,* or *ifa,* is practiced. Yemayá, a sea and riparian goddess, is considered to be the mother of all *orisas* (spirit deities) and is also associated with the moon.[35] In *Maestrapeace,* Juana Alicia depicts Yemayá with some of her traditional attributes. In her right hand, she holds a so-called round fan, which, according to art historian Robert Farris Thompson, is "an emblem embodying the coolness and command of [the] water spirits."[36] With her left hand, she offers an *okoto,* or seashell, another one of her important emblems. Yemayá's personality is said to mirror the moods of the ocean, as *santería* priest Miguel "Willie" Ramos explains: "She can be as calm as the most serene body of water, yet suddenly she can be devastating as a tidal wave."[37] In *Maestrapeace,* both the impetuous and the peaceful characteristics are evident in the artist's image. Juana Alicia represents her as a beautiful and curvaceous woman whose nude body is elaborately decorated with beads and cowry shells. Her reproductive organs are revealed through her abdomen, in keeping with her role as the *orisa* who controls women's reproductive capabilities. Yemayá oversees women's gestation periods and, after they give birth, makes sure they have plenty of breast milk for their children.[38] Instead of ovaries, however, in *Maestrapeace* Juana Alicia replaces them with seashells.

Like other *santería orisas* and many indigenous figures in the Americas, Yemayá has become a somewhat politicized symbol of resilience and resistance to colonization and slavery. As such, Yemayá shares many characteristics with syncretic figures like the Virgin of Guadalupe/Tonantsin. Many of the West African people who were taken to the so-called New World continued worshipping their *orisas* in the form of Catholic saints. The patron saint of Havana Harbor in Cuba as well as that of fishermen and sailors, Our Lady of Regla, is often regarded as a reincarnation of Yemayá, for both share a most important attribute, water.[39] The connection that Juana Alicia, Irene Pérez, Susan Cervantes, and the other artists of *Maestrapeace* establish between these three figures—Menchú, Yemayá, and Coyolxauhqui—speaks of the historical alliances and associations between Black and Brown/indigenous peoples in the Americas. If a critical component of indigenous consciousness is its element of resistance and decolonization, then Indigenism becomes a necessarily heterogeneous concept; in other words, Indigenism is specific enough to effectively address the struggles of indigenous peoples but sufficiently dynamic and open to establish bridges of communication with other historically aggrieved communities.

Postcolonial critics like Stuart Hall and Homi Bhabha have observed that heterogeneity and hybridity often function as strategies of cultural survival for colonized populations. Artists working within community contexts in California articulated expressions of heterogeneity in their work for these very reasons. Though ideologies like multiculturalism tended to homogenize and do away with cultural specificity, artists engaging in counterhegemonic alliances were seeking to establish social relations in which the different participating entities could function effectively. California's cultural history has been claimed by numerous groups, making the area one of the most politically contested regions in the United States. Given such a history, the state became an ideal platform for heterogeneous relations. But instead of proposing a dominant cultural model to represent California, various community artists pushed a multifaceted and polyvalent image of the state, one that reflected the cross-cultural currents of everyday life.

New Media: Chicana/o Murals in the Age of Digital Technology

Art historians and critics have long recognized that experimentation with new and mixed media is a defining characteristic of a postmodern aesthetic. Chicana/o muralism from the onset has challenged traditional mural techniques. Historically, murals have been produced through the fresco technique, wherein paint was applied to a wet plaster surface. For example, artists from both the Italian Renaissance and the Mexican mural movement used this technique. Nevertheless, Chicana/o artists often opted to use acrylic and even house paints instead, due primarily to financial limitations. Also, acrylics were more time effective because they dried much faster than fresco and even oil painting. In addition, Chicana/o artists who were doing murals mostly in exterior settings found that frescoes did not fare too well in the elements. Their use of new media to create murals, however, was not predicated on pragmatic concerns only. The introduction of performance, sculptural techniques, and other new media into the creation of murals, as we previously saw with the examples of Asco and Colette Crutcher, exemplified the ways in which these artists were constantly seeking to adjust murals to the changing needs and desires of their communities. They were also seeking to challenge static and time-honored definitions of muralism and its means of production.

The introduction of digital media into the practice of mural making among Chicana/o artists was perhaps the most revolutionary innovation during the last decade of the twentieth century. Judy Baca has been at the forefront of this initiative. Her work has been key in reformulating the Chicana/o Indigenist aesthetic commonly seen in murals and in developing new media to make murals. The founding of the UCLA César Chávez Digital Mural Lab within the Social and Public Art Resource Center (SPARC) in 1996 brought computer technology to the practice of community muralism.[40] Functioning in conjunction with the UCLA César E. Chávez Department of Chicana and Chicano Studies, the lab became the site of a class entitled "Beyond the Mexican Mural—Muralism and Community Development," taught by Baca herself. The lab is equipped with high-speed computers, printers, and scanners, and has its own server for the storage of images that can be accessed remotely with a password. The murals are generally created with the latest version of Photoshop, which allows Baca and her students to seamlessly use a combination of preexisting imagery and original artwork in the same composition. The SPARC digital murals are generally printed on Mylar, which makes them easily portable. Many Chicana/o muralists have been concerned about the conservation of their work, and an advantage of a digital mural is that it can be reprinted should it become destroyed. The cost of reprinting a mural, however, usually runs in the thousands of dollars, as explained to me by Enrique Gonzales, the SPARC lab technician.[41]

The addition of digital technology to the community mural scene has, nevertheless, problematized the practice of mural making. From the standpoint of several Chicana/o artists, the power of community muralism is most concretely felt during its actual on-site production when artist and community collaborate and interact. Digital murals, however, are made in the comparatively more isolated environment of a computer lab. Gonzales insisted to me that the SPARC digital murals are also made in a community context. Not only are they produced in collaboration with the UCLA students who take Baca's class, but they are also made in consultation with various community members through the Internet. If modern mural movements came to be synonymous with community making, then digital murals radically redefined concepts of community. The community that came together to create these murals was no longer defined by physical location but rather by their common interest and input into the creation of these computerized images.

Another aspect of digital murals that seems to counter prevailing notions about community muralism is that they are not made *in situ*, that is, they are not created in the space where they will reside, thus complicating the connection with space and place that other murals have. If digital murals have a connection to a particular space, it's a fluid and porous one; it is the shifting place of wherever these murals may be installed or it is the ambiguous domain of digital sites or cyberspace. Most of the digital murals that Baca and her assistants have created have a physical and a cyber location, for many are also prominently featured on SPARC's Web site (www.sparcmurals.org).

By using digital and information technology for community muralism, Baca and her students understood the heterogeneous relationship between the social and the technological to which certain cultural critics alluded. For example, sociologist Mike Michael observed how discussions about technological developments usually ignored the social circumstances that bring them about, subsequently realizing that "the social and the technological cannot be easily disentangled or distinguished . . . [and that] technologies are shot through with social relations, and vice versa."[42] Moreover, Baca's use of this technology can be regarded as the indirect outcome of globalization near the end of the twentieth century. Globalization, which was certainly aided by the advent of information technology, is a result of capitalist and post-colonial institutions of power extending their reach across national borders. David Lyon has argued that these institutions, nevertheless, "tend to have a negative effect on the indigenous development of Third World communities. Their presence all too often benefits only metropolitan elites rather than rural subsistence farmers or migrant shantytown dwellers."[43] In California itself, people of color were often excluded from the benefits of globalization and the information era. In fact, Southern California was the unsuspecting neighbor but also complicit partner of the maquiladora industry in Tijuana, where entire communities still continue to work for meager wages.

With her engagement of digital technology, Baca also challenged the prevailing discourse on the so-called digital divide that emerged in the 1990s during the Bill Clinton administration. Politicians took note of how race, class, and gender affected the level of access to digital technology among U.S. populations, thus effectively creating generations of technology "haves" and "have-nots." Nevertheless, technology studies scholars Alondra Nelson, Thuy Linh N. Tu, and Alicia Headlam Hines observed that more than legitimately providing greater access to minority and working-class communities, the "digital divide" promoted the idea that these communities were culturally and socially disinclined toward the digital:

> The digital divide has become a self-fulfilling prophecy, confirming that people of color can't keep pace in a high-tech world that threatens to

outstrip them. The divide—unbridgeable, unequivocal—unwittingly confirms that poor and working-class people have a technophobia that's hard to shake.[44]

Baca, as a digital user and producer, was also confronting a disturbing history that paired technology and colonization together. Indeed, Nelson, Tu, and Hines astutely observed that "people of color have been casualties of technologically enabled systems of oppression, from colonial expansion, to the racial sciences of craniology and phrenology, to surveillance and information gathering."[45] By using tools that have traditionally been denied to colonized and marginalized communities, Baca turned the tables on the world order ushered in by colonization and, later, globalization. She used the strategies of the oppressor, so to speak, to empower the oppressed. A similar tactic had been used by indigenous Mexican groups like the Zapatistas in Chiapas, whose first communiqués and political manifestos were transmitted via the Internet much before their activities were known to the mainstream press. Baca tapped into a relatively recent yet powerful tradition of indigenous groups utilizing technology to further their political causes and challenge the power dynamics of neocolonization.

One of the first undertakings that Baca embarked on with her students at the Digital Mural Lab was the *Witness to L.A. History* project, begun in 1997. Similar to her *Great Wall of Los Angeles*, this initiative sought to create a series of digital murals dealing with the experiences of cultural minorities during key historical moments of the city. The students were expected to collaborate in producing the imagery as well as in conducting research to obtain material about the different facts of the city's history. One of the most poignant murals of the series is the one that celebrates L.A.'s indigenous history, *Toyporina* (Figure 6.5), which is composed entirely of preexisting imagery. Baca and her students utilized Photoshop to layer together the different levels of history they were seeking to restore. The mural is a tribute to Toyporina, a young Native American woman who, at the age of twenty-three, organized an uprising against the San Gabriel Mission in Southern California during the nineteenth century.[46] Using the image of an anonymous Tongva Indian woman to stand in for Toyporina, Baca and her students placed her centrally in the composition amid a backdrop of Franciscan monks. According to the UCLA students who worked on the project, the friars are there to represent "the constant scrutiny and dehumanization of the native people."[47] Toyporina's body reveals tattoolike images borrowed from a conquest codex showing the hanging bodies of executed Native Americans. Initially, it seemed anachronistic for Baca to create an Indigenist work

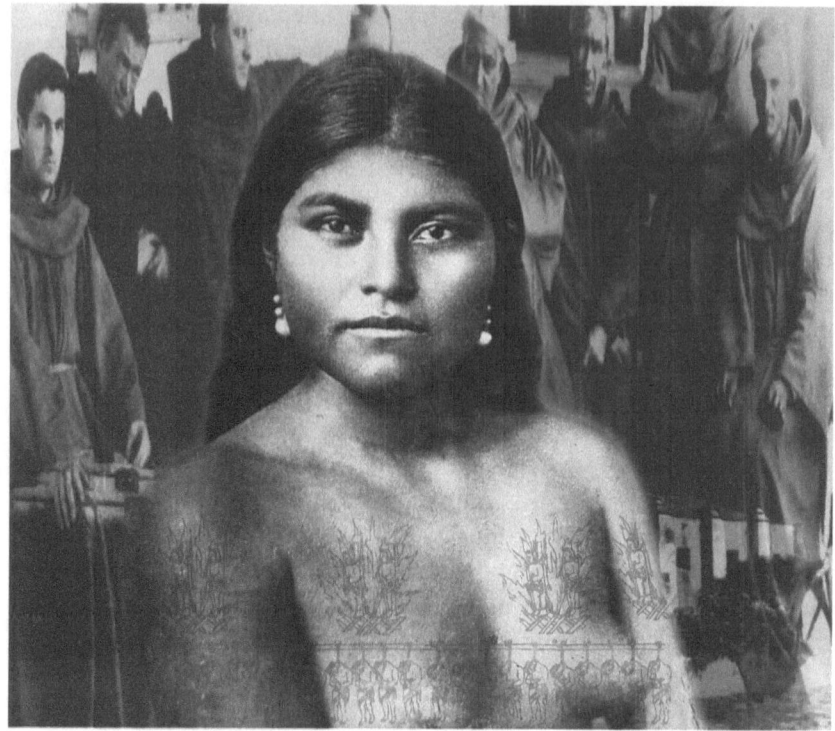

FIGURE 6.5. Judy Baca, © 1997, *Toyporina* panel from *Witness to L.A. History*, a student-produced public art project by the UCLA/SPARC César Chávez Center Digital/Mural Lab and Professor Judith F. Baca. © SPARC (www.sparcmurals.org)

of art utilizing state-of-the-art technology: "The first time she came up on the screen, it just knocked my eyes out. It was so bizarre to see this brown, extremely beautiful woman on the screen, a Tongva woman on the screen in the computer. Why was this so weird?"[48] Baca, in a way, was reacting to the seemingly paradoxical melding of an indigenous *and* digital aesthetic within the same pictorial space.

Another series that came out of the UCLA/SPARC César Chávez Digital/Mural Lab was the *Los Angeles Tropical* project in 1999. The idea for the series emerged out of the continuing efforts to clean and conserve Siqueiros's *La América Tropical* mural on Olvera Street.[49] Baca and her students were cognizant of this particular mural's importance to Mexican American history in Los Angeles. The often-frustrating efforts to renovate the mural, led by the Getty Institute and conscientious conservators and historians like Shifra Goldman, Jesús Salvador Treviño, Jean Bruce Poole, and Luis Garza, echoed the disappointments experienced by the city's Mexican populations. Inaugurated in August of 2000 during the Democratic National Convention,[50] *Los Angeles Tropical* was part of a mural center built at the bottom of the stairway that leads to Siqueiros's famous wall painting, now part of the city's historic downtown area.[51] Wall-size prints of the city were produced and mounted on the walls of the entryway that would lead to *La América Tropical*. The series illustrated not only how Siqueiros's work and activities were intimately connected to the history of Los Angeles but also how Baca's own work belonged to the same artistic genealogy as that of the celebrated Mexican School.[52]

The centerpiece for the *Los Angeles Tropical* series was placed on Wall 1 of the aforementioned entryway and was entitled *Siqueiros* (Figure 6.6). Again utilizing the layering tool of Photoshop along with documentary photographs, Baca and her students took Siqueiros's image of the crucified Indian from *La América Tropical* and presented it as an allegory of the difficulties suffered by the city's ethnic and cultural minorities. Rather than use an older image of the mural, the artists chose to show this section of the mural as it currently appears in its faded and weathered state. Through the magic of digital technology, the silhouette of the Indian here seems to be carved out of the very stone that makes up the wall. The glowing figure of Siqueiros himself appears behind the wall, resembling a sort of secular saint, as he is busy at work on one of his murals, presumably *La América Tropical*. Siqueiros's crucified Indian as well as his contribution as an artist/activist operate here as transnational and transhistorical symbols of cultural and political resistance. The backdrop then reveals an aerial image of Los Angeles with the L.A. River at its center. Scattered through the urban landscape, we find various scenes belonging to the city's past: workers toiling in sweatshops, Mexicans and Mexican Americans being forcibly deported from the United States, crowds standing in breadlines, and others.[53] But amid all the despair, we see a sign of hope: the water of the L.A. River, which is often very dry, has been digitally restored to a deep blue and plentiful stream capable of nurturing the city through its misfortunes.

The decision on the part of several Chicana/o artists to take up the digital medium was necessarily a political one, given that the development of science and technology has been historically complicit with systems of oppression and colonization. Not only have indigenous peoples and other people of color been excluded from discourses about science and technology, but they have also been violently undermined by their rhetoric. One need only look at the guiding principles behind scientific racism and phrenology to understand their destructive power. For this reason, a number of

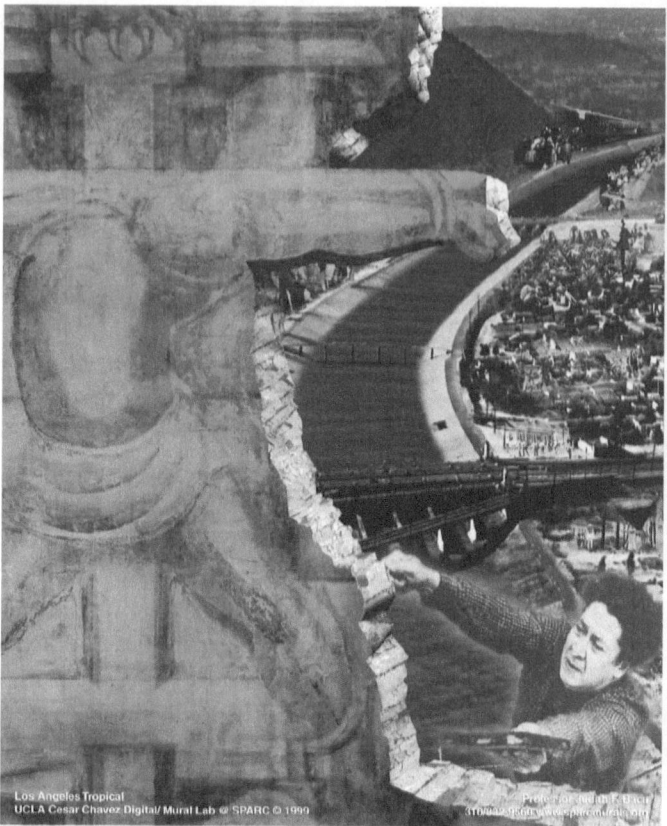

FIGURE 6.6. Judy Baca, © 1999, *Siqueiros* panel from *Los Angeles Tropical*, a student-produced public art project by the UCLA/SPARC César Chávez Digital/Mural Lab and Judith F. Baca. © SPARC (www.sparcmurals.org)

Chicana/o artists have utilized digital media as a tool of creative expression to "appropriate but also resist corporate/colonial culture," as Chicano artist John Jota Leaños explains.[54] Leaños is an Arizona-based artist who, in collaboration with San Francisco's Galería de la Raza, founded the Digital Mural Project (DMP) in 1999. Every year since then the Galería has exhibited digital murals on a billboard placed on its exterior wall.[55] The location of this billboard, however, had a charged history; it had been the site of corporate logos and advertisements for many decades until the 1970s. Local residents and activists grew tired of these images in their neighborhood, namely, the predominantly Latina/o enclave of San Francisco's Mission District. In 1972, they successfully gained control of that billboard from the company that owned it and have used it ever since as an art space. "Artists who were tired of corporate logos in the community," Leaños explained, "created a decolonized space, a contested site that now carries a legacy of continuous mural making."[56] These murals/billboards have tackled issues as diverse and controversial as the Mission District's growing gentrification and Chicana lesbian consciousness.

Seeking to "detonate reality bombs and alarm the public,"[57] Leaños, together with artists René García and Praba Pilar, founded the artists collective known as Los Cybrids, whose work focuses primarily on exposing the effects that digital and information technology have had on colonized or formerly colonized communities. They define the word "cybrid" as "a Latino digi-tech artist from a disproportionately underrepresented demographic in the cyberworld."[58] Together with Los Cybrids, Leaños has been responsible for a number of the digital murals created for the Galería de la Raza's DMP, works that Carolina Ponce de León, executive director of the Galería, described as being "on the cutting edge of muralism and cultural critique."[59] In 2001, the group exhibited a mural there entitled *Humaquina: Manifest Tech-Destiny* (Figure 6.7) with which they sought to explore the ways digital technology was colonizing the "new frontier" of the human body. In their artist statement, Los Cybrids spoke of the new research the U.S. government and large corporations have carried out that seeks to "enhance" the functions of the human body with the help of information technology (IT) and digital devices: "Los Cybrids see this exploration into the body as the latest manifestation of the colonialist ideal of Manifest Destiny."[60] In the absence of other physical spaces to colonize, the artists contend, the human body has become a new site of control and occupation for institutions of power. In the mural, a rather androgynous-looking human figure lies on top of a computer motherboard that seems to be absorbing him/her into its circuitry. The figure's body is attached to and fragmented by various electronic and digital devices. Rather than enhancing his/her biological functions, these devices and implants restrain and undermine the figure's movement and free will. This "humaquina's" thoughts and brain functions are monitored and controlled by two interfaces connected to a pair of headphones; one interface connects to a laptop computer and the other to an orbiting satellite.

In *Humaquina*, Los Cybrids are undoubtedly providing the largely Latina/o community in the Mission District with an image of the cyborg, that is, "the interface of the organic with the technological," according to Tony Fitzpatrick's definition of the term.[61] But for many scholars of cyberculture, the process of "cyborgization" does not just happen through the implantation of actual digital and electronic devices into our bodies, but also through our daily interaction and interface with technology: computers, cell phones, MP3 players, even cars and bicycles.[62] The figure of the cyborg that Los Cybrids illustrate in *Humaquina* is indeed informed by these ideas, yet the "cyborgization" that he/she undergoes is also precipitated by an implied process of colonization. Thus this cyborg figure also becomes an allegory of the

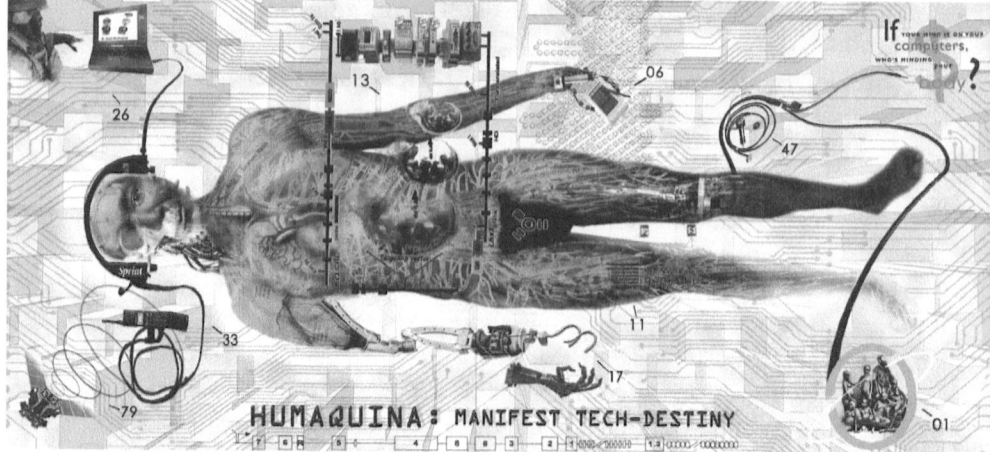

FIGURE 6.7. Los Cybrids, © 2001, *Humaquina: Manifest Tech-Destiny*, digital mural, temporarily installed in the Galería de la Raza, San Francisco, California. Courtesy of John Jota Leaños.

colonized indigenous peoples of the Americas. The artists and their audience alike were conscious that the ideologies and technologies of Manifest Destiny, which are being revisited here with the term "Manifest Tech-Destiny" in the title, most adversely affected the lives and bodies of indigenous peoples in the United States. The mechanization and digitization of this cyborg/indigenous figure are the result of his/her oppression and colonization, but also become the very tools of "humaquina's" empowerment and decolonization. In spite of this cyborg/indigene's decimation and dehumanization in *Humaquina*, his/her centrality in the mural's composition as well as the figure's monumentality of scale disrupt and even overturn the colonizing process. Donna Haraway argues that cyborgs are "the illegitimate offspring of militarism and patriarchal capitalism" and that their illegitimacy makes them "exceedingly unfaithful to their origins."[63] Drawing from Haraway's formulations, Chela Sandoval further maintains that "colonized peoples of the Americas have already developed the cyborg skills required for survival under techno-human conditions as a requisite for survival under domination over the last three hundred years."[64] Rather unexpectedly, the realm of the digital has slipped from the control of hegemonic powers and has traversed and navigated across racial, national, and social boundaries. Art historian Michelle-Lee White, though speaking about the Black community, has convincingly maintained that "electronic technology, especially digital, seems to have pierced the protective bubble of fixed racial and ethnic identity by making it easy for us to create physically detached screen personas that transcend social realities."[65] In Los Cybrids' *Humaquina*, the empowering potential of IT and digital media is also implied in the artists' own choice to use this technology as a tool for creative expression and thus decolonization. In other words, they, too, become cyborgs through their own interface with the digital, thereby, at some level, self-identifying with the mural's cyborg/indigene.

Conclusion

With the increasing postmodernity of Chicana/o Indigenist murals, the history of community muralism in California comes full circle. Though the medium's postmodern aesthetic seemed to dissolve the categories that previously defined muralism, murals underwent a transformation that fulfilled some of the objectives laid out by the Chicano Movement in the 1960s and 1970s. As I explained in previous chapters, Indigenist imagery in Chicana/o murals had two principal goals from the outset: to legitimize the Chicana/o/indigenous presence on U.S. soil, and to assert alternative and oppositional cultural expressions from the margins of dominant society. With the growing transnational and cross-cultural trends that have affected social relations in public urban spaces—where muralism often takes place—the distinction between the margin and the center was obscured. Without denying the existence of inequalities along racial, gender, and class lines, the question of who commands official culture and who resides on the fringes of this culture can no longer be easily determined. In the urban context, the Indigenist murals created primarily by Chicana/o artists greatly contributed to cultural heterogeneity in California. Though Indigenism emerged as a cultural identity that could effectively further the political agenda of the Chicano Movement, it nevertheless helped to establish indigenous culture, be it Mexican or Native American, as a critical component of U.S. dominant culture.

Epilogue

O ne of the most motivating reasons that I took a specific interest in the Indigenist iconography found in California Chicana/o murals was that I immediately understood that the recurrence of this imagery functioned as a sort of chronic symptom of Chicana/o culture at the end of the twentieth century. In many cases, the revelations that these murals uncovered about the state of Chicana/o history, politics, and, of course, culture were just as intriguing as the beauty of the images themselves. Suggesting that one could use Freudian psychoanalysis on culture in general, rather than just on an individual, English literature and cultural studies scholar Marjorie Garber has proposed that it is possible "to read culture as if it were structured like a dream, a network of representations that encodes wishes and fears, projections and identifications, all of whose elements are overdetermined and contingent."[1] But what anxieties, desires, or preoccupations did these Indigwenist murals symptomize? Certainly, many of the early works spoke of the frustrations experienced by Chicanas/os due to their systematic exclusion from practically every institution of power in the United States. Moreover, California contained the historical intersection of many different cultures: Native American, Aztec (Aztlán), Spanish, Mexican, and Anglo-American, just to name a few. While Indigenism reflected a nostalgia for a historical past that could restore Chicanas/os' cultural citizenship in the present, it also signaled a desire to establish a connection with those fragmented histories. But what is more remarkable is how Chicana/o Indigenism also operated as a symptom of U.S. culture and society as a whole. The public setting of these images directly contested the uniformity and impermeability believed to characterize U.S. mainstream culture. In California, for many years, the vision of an idyllic realm that bolstered the country's agricultural economy and provided an ideal setting for the nation's film industry became the official and state-sanctioned image of the state. Indigenist murals signaled how this widely disseminated construction was beginning to lose its coherence during the last decades of the twentieth century.

As I identified important works of art in the history of Chicana/o muralism and developed theoretical frameworks by which to discuss the importance of Indigenist iconography throughout this book, the task of structuring a historical narrative was a cumbersome one. The fluidity of artistic production, the gaps and breaks in the historical record, and the complexity of currents that inform community muralism seriously challenged my training as an art historian. As soon as I established theoretical postures from my findings in the field, I would encounter phenomena that defied or questioned my presumptions. I found myself torn between my responsibility as a scholar—that is, my duty to intellectualize creative expressions—and my personal admiration for the various artists I interviewed and for the work they produced. What I did find was that while Indigenism continues to shape the development of Chicana/o community murals, most artists did not recognize it as a driving energy behind their individual artistic production. So even though Indigenism was not a prevailing element in the work of any one artist, it *was* a ubiquitous phenomenon on a collective level. This collectivity of the Indigenist aesthetic—which was most effectively fostered by community muralism—ultimately allowed this art form to transcend its own limits. After the fervor of the Chicano Movement had waned, Indigenist themes seemed contrived and out of touch with current events, but the pervasiveness of the aesthetic allowed it to modify itself according to the different social, cultural, political, and historical contexts. In essence, Indigenism, especially in the public mural, was never part of the specific agendas or intentions of individual artists or organizations; rather, it was the consequent creative outcome of a historical moment characterized by rapid social changes and activist reactions. Unfortunately, as historians, we often need some chronological distance from our subjects of study in order to properly reflect on them and assess their effects and repercussions. Moreover, we tend to struggle with the creation of theoretical models to explain events that are too current with our own time. As a result, academic production can very rarely catch up with artistic production, especially that which emerges from the community and urban sphere. So even though Indigenism and muralism within the Chicana/o cultural psyche will give way to more heterogeneous and fluid artistic forms in the near future that will further challenge current theoretical formulations, the intersection of the two ultimately functioned as a springboard for the establishment of counterhegemonic alliances.

As I neared the end of my research for this book during the summer of 2005, I visited SPARC in Venice to view some of the recent mural work done right on its premises. It was Labor Day, so I did not expect to find anyone there. Nevertheless, I soon noticed that some work was taking place in the building's back lot. It was Judy Baca herself who, with the help of some of her staff there, was finishing off some projects before leaving town to participate in a number of exhibitions. I approached the artist to greet her and ask her how her mural work was going. Looking somewhat weary yet determined, she lamented that the mural and public art scene in Los Angeles was suffering tremendously under the increasingly repressive city politics of the time. If artists had experienced difficulty getting designs and project proposals passed by city officials before, it was now nearly impossible to get anything by them. Even private commissions now needed to be cleared by the city of Los Angeles as well. In Los Angeles, private individuals need city approval for mural work they commission on *their* property, and in San Francisco, they are required by law to clean up "graffiti" from their property (whether commissioned or not).[2] The aggressive conservative backlash that characterized the turn-of-the-millennium politics in the United States was having direct effects on the practice of mural making in California. Not only was there a sharp decrease in mural commissions, but the monies for restoration of existing murals, scant to begin with, were now simply nonexistent. This signaled for Baca the beginning of the end of an era of mural making, at least in Los Angeles, but surely in the whole of the West Coast as well. "I'm glad someone is *still* doing [academic] work on muralism," she told me, referring to my work on *Walls of Empowerment*. I was perplexed by her comment, given that I always found that the literature on the community mural movement had never come to fruition or done service to the complexity and richness of muralism in California. It was then that I realized that the decline in mural activity—not through the fault of the artists themselves, to be sure—had also led to a decline in the scholarship on the subject. I was deeply saddened but also unwavering in my commitment to carry my project through. In the face of what seemed to be a disappearing art form in California, *Walls of Empowerment* would then document the existence but also the historical importance of an art form that was on its way out, so to speak.

Perhaps it is wishful thinking on my part to hope that the forces that are threatening the continued development of mural art in California during the twenty-first century will not lead to its utter demise, but will instead give way to a process of transformation that will effectively counter the increasing sophistication and complexity in the strategies of marginalization utilized by the current status quo. What initially attracted me to the mural movement as a researcher and as a member of a racialized community was its utter strength and boldness in the face of overwhelming political and social opposition. As a Chilean immigrant to the United States who was raised in the social atmosphere of a right-wing dictatorship during most of her childhood and adolescence, I found that the confrontational and oppositional nature of these murals projected a spirit of courage that I wished my own generation in Chile had possessed. Here was an arts movement, I thought, that emerged and flourished out of the sheer will and determination of its artists and communities who had little or no resources to make it happen. Murals were erected throughout these cities without the support of many of the common arts infrastructures like museums, galleries, and proper arts patronage. Murals, for me, represented the inevitability of decolonizing expressions among ethnoracial minorities in the United States and elsewhere and, in many ways, stood as a model for political resistance applicable to other contexts of social inequality and repression. But I also experienced the Chicana/o mural movement as an art historian who was growing increasingly disillusioned and detached from the U.S. modern and contemporary art scene, struggling to feel passionate about any of the "isms" that defined the North American and European avant-garde. The sterile walls of mainstream museums and galleries represented for me the abyss that existed between this visual vocabulary and my sensibility toward the arts. By contrast, the colorful walls of the various barrios I visited in the course of my research for *Walls of Empowerment* epitomized for me a visual movement—though not unproblematic in its ideals—that sought to reconcile the arts with real-life communities and their needs. All the more reason why I now resist the possibility of an utter decline or definitive end to the mural arts, not just out of wishful thinking but out of a heightened understanding of historical processes. So I turn to perhaps the greatest lesson that history has taught me, and that is that homogeny cannot be maintained indefinitely and that resistance always grows as oppression swells and marginalizes entire sectors of society. As the turn of the millennium sees concerted efforts to overturn the accomplishments and strides made during the civil rights movement, many public works of art will continue to represent the social consciousness of marginalized and neglected communities, not just that of Chicana/o and indigenous populations.

Notes

Introduction

1. Goldman, "How, Why, Where, and When," 23.

2. Bonfil Batalla, *Utopía y revolución*, 13.

3. Native American scholar Angela Cavender Wilson often uses the word *indigenous* as a marker of legitimate native identity because it implies that the person defined by the concept has a symbiotic and inherent connection to the land. Wilson, "Reclaiming Our Humanity," 85. Other writers, like Ward Churchill, define indigenous communities as those groups of peoples or nations that originally inhabited a particular territory prior to the arrival or invasion of what he calls "settler-states." Under this definition, European populations such as the Irish and the Welsh in Britain and the Basques in Spain can be regarded as indigenous groups who have struggled against overpowering nation-states. Churchill, *Struggle for the Land*, 372.

4. See Anzaldúa, "La Herencia de Coatlicue," 63–73.

5. Storey, *Introduction to Cultural Theory*, 3.

6. During the nineteenth century, paintings and sculptures depicting Aztec history and its heroes rendered in a classical style saturated the salons of Mexico City's Academia San Carlos. Moreover, during the Reforma period of this nation, portraits of Zapotec president Benito Juárez and his criolla wife were utilized to encourage national unity by promoting *mestizaje*. For more Juárez imagery and other Indigenist imagery in nineteenth-century Mexico, see Widdifield, *Embodiment of the National*.

7. Scheben, "Indigenismo y modernismo," 115.

8. Castillo, "Postmodern Indigenism," 36.

9. The idea that art can construct its spectators was inspired in this text by Emily Hicks's assertion in 1993 that writing constructs its readers. Hicks, "Textual Migration," 18.

10. The relationship between art and sociopolitical accountability is one that Native American and Chicana/o artists have repeatedly supported and upheld throughout their careers. For example, Hopi filmmaker Victor Masayesva has stated that accountability comes with the territory of being an artist and being in possession of an indigenous identity: "A Native filmmaker has . . . the accountability built onto him. The white man doesn't have that. . . . That's where we're at as Indian filmmakers." Quoted in Leuthold, *Indigenous Aesthetics*, 1.

11. The subfield of *connoisseurship* in art history has often operated jointly with modern art discourses in building up the importance of the artist. The *Grove Dictionary of Art*, published periodically by Oxford University Press, defines *connoisseurship* as a technique of attribution that "involves the evaluation, distinction and appreciation of the

work's quality and, above all, the ability to determine the time and place of its execution and, as far as possible, the identity of the artist." "Connoisseurship," *Grove Art Online* (Oxford University Press, http://www.groveart.com, accessed 6 June 2004). In the absence of a signature or appropriate archival material revealing the name of an artist for any given artwork, a connoisseur may step in and examine formal elements such as the shape of a brushstroke or the way a face is rendered in order to detect a particular artist's "hand." When connoisseurs determine that a work of art was indeed the creation of a famous artist, the historical and monetary value of that piece changes dramatically. In these cases, authorship of an artwork supersedes any intrinsic artistic value the work might have, thus also contributing to the growing commodification of art in the current market system.

12. Ybarra-Frausto, "Arte Chicano," 56.

13. Bonfil Batalla, *Utopía y revolución*, 33.

14. Justice, "Seeing (and Reading) Red," 109.

15. Leuthold, *Indigenous Aesthetics*, 32.

16. Caso, *Indigenismo*, 21. Published during a time when the nationalist project of the Revolution was under public scrutiny and serious criticism, this book can be regarded as a defense of the failed Indigenist projects led by the Mexican government. For example, when addressing the lack of federal attention paid to certain indigenous communities, Caso argued that Indians generally "live in the mountains or in inaccessible places," 22; my translation.

17. Sánchez, *Becoming Mexican American*, 56.

18. During an interview, Chicana artist Yolanda López told me that her grandparents crossed the border between Mexico and the United States in 1918 and that they lost five children to malnutrition and dysentery in the process. It was not until the civil rights era, however, that she realized that millions of Mexican Americans shared that common experience and that her grandparents' ordeal was part of a larger mass migration of Mexicans escaping the instability of the revolutionary period. Though painful, this realization gave many Chicanas/os a sense of solidarity with one another and allowed them to create bonds with other disenfranchised communities in the United States. "It was stunning for us to find out," López later remarked. Interview between Yolanda López and the author, August 20, 1999.

19. Though the Works Progress Administration and the Public Works of Art Project sponsored several murals in California and across the country during the New Deal period (approximately 1934–1946), these murals, most painted by Anglo-American artists, were not nearly as influential to Chicana/o artists as those executed by the Mexican artists. Drescher, *San Francisco Bay Area Murals*, 11.

20. Siqueiros's *Portrait of Present-Day Mexico* was recently moved from its location in Santa Monica and taken several miles north to Santa Barbara's Museum of Art. The mural was restored and unveiled to the public on October 10, 2002.

21. Another painful episode of mass deportation occurred in 1954 when the Immigration and Naturalization Service forcibly deported thousands of undocumented Mexican workers residing in the United States, a procedure dubbed Operation Wetback. The majority of these Mexican nationals had been brought into the country in the 1940s through the Bracero Program, a Mexico-U.S. initiative that allowed lawful passage for numerous Mexican workers into the United States to alleviate the labor shortage during World War II. Rosales, *Chicano!*, 84.

22. Though *La América Tropical* is currently in storage at the Getty

Conservation Institute and is in a terrible state of deterioration, this work still remains a crucial influence to Chicana/o artists. In 1998, muralist Alessandra Moctezuma and the late Eva Cockcroft re-created the mural in East Los Angeles, calling it *Homage to Siqueiros,* which also included documentary scenes representing the events surrounding the making of the mural.

23. Aside from the presence of Mexican artists in California, there were numerous artists from the area who either studied or were influenced by the Mexican muralists. Such was the case with Henrietta Shore, whose work during the 1920s included many Mexican Indigenist elements and whose style greatly resembled that of the Mexican School of painting. Moure, *California Art*, 231.

24. Paz, "Art and Identity," 35.

25. Aside from describing Ramírez's oeuvre as being executed in complete solitary confinement, Octavio Paz likens this artist's schizophrenic condition to his cultural duality after having migrated from Mexico to the United States. Paz's assessment reflects a more general trend among certain critics, that of identifying the liminal spaces inhabited by minorities and immigrants as spaces riddled with insanity and incongruity. Though Paz's writings about Mexican Americans have been widely dismissed as too paternalistic by U.S. Latina/o scholars, Chicana writer Gloria Anzaldúa directly addressed the issue of insanity as it had been ascribed, in particular, to women of color. "I question this," she says, "to be disoriented in space is the 'normal' way for us *mestizas* living on the borderlands . . . To be disoriented in space is to be *en nepantla. Nepantla* is the Nahuatl word for an in-between state, that uncertain territory one crosses when moving from one place to another, when traveling from the present identity to a new identity." Anzaldúa, "Border Arte," 100.

26. Ibid., 33.

27. Bracho, "Mexican Psychotic."

28. Chaffey Community Art Association, *Licón*, 2.

29. Ibid., 7.

30. Given the virtual invisibility of artists like Ramos Martínez, Ramírez, and Licón in the history of modern Mexican and U.S. American art, there is a great need to fill the gap that exists in the literature regarding Mexican and Mexican American artists working in the United States from the 1940s to the early 1960s. Though this project does not seek to shed light on these groups of artists, it should be noted that without a scholarly account of their contribution, the history of Chicana/o art becomes fragmented and largely ahistorical.

31. Nuckolls, *Cultural Dialectics*, xxiv.

32. Baxter and Montgomery, *Relating*, 25.

33. Juan García Ponce, in his book *Imágenes y visiones* (1988), argues that the expression "Mexican School of painting," used by several historians and art historians when discussing the artistic production created by the muralists and their contemporaries, is a bit of a misnomer, given the critical ideological and aesthetic differences that existed between Rivera, Orozco, and Siqueiros, let alone among the other artists of the time. The term "school" implies a certain unity or uniformity that, according to García Ponce, did not exist within the artistic circles that emerged during the postrevolutionary period in Mexico. Nevertheless, I maintain that regardless of the distinctions, these artists were responding to similar historical and cultural stimuli, something that placed them in dialogue rather than in opposition to one another. Several decades later, Chicanas/os saw their artistic initiative as a concerted effort to define the modern Mexican nation.

34. "El Plan Espiritual de Aztlán," as a nationalist manifesto, explicitly

outlined the traits and characteristics
of the politically conscious Chicana/o.
The document also prescribed the roles
that this "new" Chicana/o would play
within U.S. society. One of these critical
roles would be to uplift and celebrate
Mexican/Chicana/o culture, a task charged
primarily to cultural producers, as "El Plan"
specifically stipulates: "We must insure
that our writers, poets, musicians, and
artists produce literature and art that is
appealing to our people and relates to our
revolutionary culture" (3). It was in this
particular section of "El Plan" that Denver
muralist Manuel Martínez assisted Alurista
with the language of this important
document.

35. Pérez-Torres, *Movements in Chicano
Poetry*, 57.

36. Posing the argument that mural
Indigenism held a pivotal role in Chicana/o
identity formation requires a closer
reading of the term *identity* itself. While I
have come to think of identity as a means
by which groups or communities define
themselves vis-à-vis society at large, I
recognize, as many others before me have,
that identity can never be stable, but rather
exists in a constant state of flux. Stuart
Hall's writing on postcolonial debates and
cultural studies greatly influenced my
conceptualization of identity. Hall
characterized identity as "historically in
articulation, in a formation, with other
categories and divisions . . . constantly
crossed and recrossed by the categories of
class, of gender and ethnicity." Hall, "New
Ethnicities," 444. In postcolonial and
capitalist social contexts, identity has
historically fulfilled contesting social
agendas. From the subject position of the
colonizer or hegemonic power, the
creation of fixed and stable identities has
worked to contain, control, and curtail the
social, political, and cultural movement of
colonized peoples and ethnoracial
minorities. Nevertheless, in a process

leading to empowerment, emancipation,
autonomy, or social consciousness, such
disenfranchised communities will liberate
identity from these static models, thus
incorporating it into their decolonizing
methodologies. Rather than replacing one
set of stable identity markers for others,
indigenous peoples have traditionally
sought to define identity as always fluid
and dynamic, thereby allowing for
constant rearticulations in the face of cross-
culturalism, heterogeneity, and historical
change. Indigenous communities in the
Americas have historically subscribed to
these unrestrained notions of identity as
strategies for survival but also as tools to
contest oppressive discourses directed at
the cultural Other. This model of identity
defined by a constant state of flux allows
cultural critics to analytically engage the
different permutations and phases that the
community mural movement has
experienced.

37. R. García, "Chicano
Representation," 33.

38. Ibid., 102.

39. Kwon, "One Place after Another," 39.

40. Leuthold, *Indigenous Aesthetics*, 43.

41. Like Mexico, many indigenous
nations of North America also entered
into treaties with the expanding U.S.
nation-state on issues of land ownership
and sovereignty. While many treaties
granting Native American nations land
rights were signed and ratified, subsequent
manipulations and violations of these
treaties led to the usurpation and pillaging
of Native American territory. Indigenous
studies scholar Ward Churchill argues
that there was an overarching illegality
in the way the United States interpreted
and acted upon these treaties. Although
the United States continually and
systematically denied nation status to
the indigenous peoples, international law
stipulates that treaties can only be signed
between *nations*, thus implying that the

United States recognized this status at some point and then arbitrarily denied it later. Churchill further contends that in much of the legal language, U.S. politicians repeatedly used the word *nation* to refer to Native American peoples. Nevertheless, he ultimately maintains that U.S. policymakers recognized that "indigenous nations were sovereign enough to validate U.S. territorial ambitions through treaties of cession, [but] never sovereign enough to decline them." Churchill, *Struggle for the Land,* 61.

42. Griswold del Castillo, *Treaty of Guadalupe Hidalgo,* 150.

43. For more on the connections between Los Toltecas en Aztlán and Native American groups, see Brookman, "El Centro Cultural de la Raza," 27.

44. Moraga, "Queer Aztlán," 166.

45. Nineteenth-century U.S. politicians often cited the Black Legend to denounce Spain's allegedly corrupt and decadent colonial structures while also legitimizing U.S. entitlement to former Spanish colonial territory in northern Mexico and the Caribbean. The Black Legend consists of a particularly unfavorable view of Spain by mostly British and U.S. Protestant writers who often described the country as being prone to corruption, cruelty, and intolerance. These writers often used Bartolomé de Las Casas's chronicle *Historia de las Indias* (1875) as a basis for these judgments. For more on recent perspectives regarding the Black Legend, see Scheuler, "Revising the Paths of Discovery," 116–122.

46. The phrase "right of discovery" in the statement drafted by the Native American activists who occupied Alcatraz was a reference to the Doctrine of Discovery, a fifteenth-century Spanish decree that allowed Spain to take possession of territory inhabited by non-Christians. In 1823, the doctrine was incorporated by the Supreme Court into official U.S.

policy regarding indigenous lands, which ultimately allowed for the appropriation of Native American territory. While it seems ironic that the United States should adopt a doctrine from Spain, a nation often vilified and discredited by U.S. politicians of the time, indigenous studies scholar Ward Churchill further argued that the notion was simply preposterous, given that the United States could not legitimately claim it had "discovered" any of the indigenous nations it sought to dispossess. Churchill, *Struggle for the Land,* 43.

47. Salomon, "Taking Alcatraz," 32. For a more detailed and rigorous account of the Alcatraz takeover (1969–1970), see Johnson, *Occupation of Alcatraz Island.*

48. Griswold del Castillo, *Treaty of Guadalupe Hidalgo,* 142.

49. Penn-Hilden, "How the Border Lies," 155.

50. Bonfil Batalla, *Utopía y revolución,* 39.

51. I. M. García, *Chicanismo,* 53.

52. Ashcroft, Griffiths, and Tiffin, *Post-Colonial Studies Reader,* 356.

53. J. E. Muñoz, "Memory Performance," 100.

54. Carnero Hoke, "Teoría y práctica de la indianidad," 119.

55. Churchill, *Struggle for the Land,* 390.

56. Bonfil Batalla, *Utopía y revolución,* 50.

57. Bonfil Batalla, *México profundo,* 191.

58. Hall, "Cultural Identity and Diaspora," 229.

59. Coj Ajbalam, "Algo sobre la naturaleza del Ixim," 367.

60. Gaspar de Alba, *Chicano Art,* 121.

61. It should be noted that though Rivera's and Siqueiros's allegations that Izquierdo lacked the experience to execute a mural might have sounded like a convincing argument to deny her the commission, when they were called for the first time by José Vasconcelos to create wall paintings in Mexico's most prominent public building in the early 1920s, the issue of inexperience never

came up. Prior to ushering in the Mexican mural renaissance, Rivera had spent more than a decade in Europe, France in particular, learning Cubism, among other currents of the artistic avant-garde. Siqueiros, on the other hand, remained in Mexico during the tumultuous years of the Revolution. He divided most of his time between the San Carlos Academy of Art in Mexico City, where he received his artistic training, and working as a political activist or revolutionary soldier for the Constitutional Army. Nevertheless, neither man had dabbled in mural painting before Vasconcelos's invitation.

62. The subject matter of this Mexico City mural by Izquierdo dealt with the city's history and development. The composition would have included allegorical figures of music, theater, and dance. After losing her commission, she was offered a less public building on which to paint, a proposition she denied.

63. Lozano, "Maria Izquierdo," 50.

64. Sánchez-Tranquilino, "Mi Casa No Es Su Casa," 32.

65. Sánchez-Tranquilino cites the contributions of at least two other Chicana artists to the making of the Estrada Courts murals: Lydia Dominguez and Norma Montoya. Though he admits that the content of Dominguez's and Montoya's murals was "apparently non-controversial," he connects the censorship of Baca's design with the *machista* proclivities of the organizers, not to the broader male-centered politics of the Chicano Movement as a whole. Sánchez-Tranquilino, "Mi Casa No Es Su Casa," 34.

66. Interview with Judy Baca by Guisela Latorre and Chela Sandoval, Social and Public Art Resource Center, Venice, Calif., July 24, 2006.

67. Goldman, "How, Why, Where, and When," 40.

68. Shohat, *Talking Visions*, 4.

69. Pérez-Torres, *Movements in Chicano Poetry*, 210.

70. Vasconcelos, *The Cosmic Race/La raza cósmica*, 24.

71. While the 1980s ushered in an era of greater heterogeneity in Chicana/o muralism, it should be clarified that it did not happen in all spheres of muralist activity. Simultaneous to the multiethnic and pancultural trends, we can still find creations by Chicano artists working in a more nationalist and militant vein. This demonstrates that Chicana/o art often poses critical challenges to the ways in which intellectuals traditionally historicize, categorize, and reify art and culture.

72. Chabram-Dernersesian, "Chicana! Rican? No, Chicana Riqueña!," 288.

73. Though the Los Angeles graffiti-abatement program was designed to rid the city of graffiti and was restricted from defacing artworks, nevertheless, many murals have been whitewashed, as was the case of works by Willie Herrón and Judy Baca. Moreover, considering the often narrow distinction between Chicana/o muralism and graffiti, city officials have engaged in the thorny practice of determining what is art and what is not. For more on the destruction of Los Angeles community murals, see Lorenza Muñoz, "Distinctive L.A. Art Legacy Under Siege," *Los Angeles Times* (July 23, 1999): A1–A9.

74. Hall, "Ethnicity," 15.

75. Ibid., 12 and 13.

76. Lipsitz, *Dangerous Crossroads*, 4.

77. George Lipsitz is careful not to confuse these cultural transactions with instances of appropriation and co-optation of cultural Otherness by the dominant culture, yet he acknowledges that the distinction can sometimes be difficult to make: "Which kinds of cross-cultural identification advance emancipatory ends and which ones reinforce existing

structures of power and domination? When does identification with the culture of others serve escapist and irresponsible ends and when does it encourage an enhanced understanding of one's experiences and responsibilities?" Lipsitz then maintains that these transactions are most legitimate and effective when different groups articulate them through a common history/experience of grievance and marginalization rather than through a fetishistic desire for Otherness. Ibid., 56 and 62.

78. Graves, *Cultural Democracy*, 80.

79. Lowe, "Creating Community," 374.

Chapter 1

1. Art historian Stacie Widdifield has discussed at length the importance of indigenous imagery in postindependence Mexico during the nineteenth century. She maintains that images of the pre-Columbian past "irrupted in the face of foreign control and foreign intervention as well as when the state needed to cohere its citizens." This period of indigenous imagery in painting and sculpture can be distinguished from the Indigenism of the twentieth-century Mexican muralists in that the former presented indigenous themes within a clearly European framework. Paintings like Juan Cordero's *Columbus before the Catholic Sovereigns* (1850) and José Obregón's *Discovery of Pulque* (1869) depicted indigenous peoples rendered in a European academic style. By contrast, the Mexican muralists were not only interested in indigenous themes, but were also captivated by indigenous aesthetics. Diego Rivera, for instance, was an avid collector of pre-Columbian art and often combined European modern vocabularies with Mesoamerican visual conventions. For more information on nineteenth-century Indigenism in

Mexican art, see Widdifield, *Embodiment of the National*. For further details on Rivera's use of pre-Columbian aesthetics in his work, see Brown, "The Past Idealized."

2. It should be noted that while Chicana/o artists were looking at the modern Mexican mural movement as a model for what they were doing in California's urban spaces, they were also deeply influenced by the mural imagery produced by Mesoamerican civilizations prior to European contact. Of particular importance were the mural cycles in ancient cities like Teotihuacán (Valley of Mexico) and Bonampak (Chiapas).

3. Jean Charlot was a French art historian who wrote extensively about the Mexican School of art. He was a contemporary of artists like Rivera, Orozco, and Siqueiros and met them personally during his numerous travels and visits to Mexico.

4. Avalos, "Pure Mexican Accent," 125.

5. Baca, preface to *Signs from the Heart*, 1.

6. Goldman, "How, Why, Where, and When," 25.

7. Cockcroft and Barnet-Sánchez, *Signs from the Heart*, 9.

8. Karlstrom, "Rivera, Mexico and Modernism," 220.

9. Mesa-Bains, "Quest for Identity," 69.

10. Goldman and Ybarra-Frausto, *Arte Chicano*, 53.

11. Making a similar argument, Judy Baca maintains that from the process of mural making there emerge two cultural products. One is the physical mural itself, and the other is "the interracial harmony between the people who have been involved." Quoted in Mesa-Bains, "Quest for Identity," 81.

12. A number of exhibitions in Europe and North America have been dedicated to the phenomenon of visual quotation in modern and contemporary art in the

1980s and 1990s, none of which, however, have included work by Chicana/o artists. For more information on these shows, see the exhibition catalogs for *Quotation: Re-presenting History* and *Quotations: The Second History of Art.*

13. Madill, Introduction to *Quotation: Re-presenting History*, 7.

14. Sartiliot, *Citation and Modernity*, 16.

15. Bakhtin, *Dialogic Imagination*, 279.

16. Hutcheon, "'Scare Quotes,'" 28.

17. Oguibe, "Appropriation as Nationalism," 245.

18. Siqueiros's influence on Chicana/o artists seemed to dominate their visual vocabulary in the 1970s, but the work of José Clemente Orozco also figured prominently in some of their work. For example, Willie Herrón's mural *La Doliente de Hidalgo* (1976)—a mural painted on Mercado Hidalgo in City Terrace, East Los Angeles—makes a direct reference to Orozco's mural *El Padre Hidalgo* (1936–1939), located in Guadalajara. In his mural, Herrón reproduced Orozco's figure of Father Miguel Hidalgo holding a torch as he thrusts his body forward.

19. Treviño, *América Tropical* (Los Angeles: KCET film, 1971).

20. Ibid.

21. Ibid.

22. Siqueiros, *El nuevo realismo mexicano, 1966*.

23. Siqueiros, *Integración plástica*; my transcription and translation.

24. Luis Garza, interview by the author, July 26, 2000.

25. When interviewed for Jesús Salvador Treviño's documentary film *América Tropical*, Siqueiros conveyed the following words to the Chicana/o community: "I believe the Mexicans of this side of the border have the obligation to lend our most complete, fullest support to our *compañeros* who are struggling in the United States."

26. Emigdio Vasquez, Carlos "Higgy" Vasquez, and Cathy Vasquez, interview by author, Santa Ana, April 14, 2005.

27. For a detailed discussion of the MEChA Mural by Shifra Goldman, see *The MEChA Mural: Twentieth Anniversary 1974–1994* (1994), brochure published by Rancho Santiago [Santa Ana] College, available in Nealley Library.

28. Goldman, *The MEChA Mural*, n.p.

29. *Jesús Campusano*, www.newsport. sfsu.edu/soo/murals/death/death.html (accessed on November 1, 2001).

30. Barnett, *Community Murals*, 141.

31. Ybarra-Frausto, "Arte Chicano," 56.

32. Barnett, *Community Murals*, 145.

33. Timothy Drescher notes that Cortázar, Rios, and Campusano shared the same tense and contentious relationship with the patrons of *Homage to Siqueiros* that Siqueiros had with F. K. Ferenz while making *La América Tropical*. During the dedication of *Homage to Siqueiros*, the muralists handed out flyers to the public exposing Bank of America's policies regarding California's Central Valley agribusiness. See Drescher, *San Francisco Bay Area Murals*, 19–20.

34. For more information on indigenous cultural appropriation, see the essays by Lenore Keeshig-Tobias, Jorge Klor de Alva, Nell Jessup Newton, Deborah Root, James D. Nason, and Naomi Roht-Arriaza in *Borrowed Power: Essays on Cultural Appropriation*, ed. Bruce Ziff and Pratima V. Rao.

35. Edward Fischer argues that the move toward strategic essentialism on the part of indigenous peoples, in particular the Maya of Guatemala, is a function not of their acceptance of stereotypes, but rather of their conscious engagement and response to anthropological literature about them. Fischer, "Cultural Logic and Maya Identity," 473.

36. For a thorough discussion of the WPA murals and other New Deal art projects in the United States, see Hoefer,

A More Abundant Life and Harris, *Federal Art and National Culture.*

37. Daniel Galvez, letter to the author, April 22, 2007.

38. By the 1970s, Daniel Galvez, along with John Valadez in Los Angeles, had emerged as an important figure in the community mural scene and was known for his technical skill and photorealistic imagery.

39. Barnett, *Community Murals*, 269.

40. Rodríguez, *David Alfaro Siqueiros*, 55.

41. Having been created nearly twenty years after the height of the nationalist era in Mexican muralism, Siqueiros's *New Democracy* was ill received at the time of its unveiling. Many felt it was too obvious and stereotypical and insisted the artist was utilizing outmoded, propagandistic, and baroque visual conventions. Siqueiros defended the mural by vehemently denying all these charges: "The art of the future—and my mural painting is in that sense an anticipation of what is to come—will be baroque, or better yet *be* post-baroque, since it will be dynamic." Ibid. Siqueiros's repeated references during the 1960s—a time when murals in Mexico were nearly rendered obsolete—to the future of muralism or to a new phase of mural production possessed a prophetic tone that almost seemed to anticipate the Chicana/o mural movement that was about to emerge.

42. Karlstrom, "Rivera, Mexico and Modernism," 231.

43. Sánchez-Tranquilino and Tagg, "The Pachuco's Flayed Hide," 99.

44. Von Blum, *Other Visions, Other Voices*, 87.

45. Sánchez-Tranquilino, "The Chicano Codices," 18.

46. Almost a decade after Carrasco finished her work on *L.A. History*, she participated in The Chicano Codices exhibition, where she showed a mixed-media collage entitled *Projex* (ca. 1992),

resembling a codex manuscript and using preexisting imagery to narrate her own story of having grown up in a housing project.

47. Jeffrey Rangel, "Interview with Barbara Carrasco" (conducted in the artist's home in Los Angeles), April 13, 1999. Artist Oral History, Archives of American Art, Smithsonian Institution.

48. Von Blum, *Other Visions, Other Voices*, 88.

49. Echeveste and Estolano, "Los Angeles Rejects History," 14.

50. Ibid., 15.

51. For more information on heterogeneity in California community muralism, see Chapter 6 of this volume.

52. Gordon, "A Morning with Ernesto de la Loza," 5.

53. Cardoza y Aragón and Rodríguez, *Diego Rivera*, 113.

54. The Albuquerque Museum Sculpture Garden, Frederico Vigil: *Santa Madre y Su Alma* (mural), www.cabq.gov/museum/sculpture/santamadre.html (accessed on December 3, 2000).

55. *El Quinto Sol* (*The Fifth Sun*), www.lamurals.org/MuralFiles/Westside/FifthSun.html (accessed on December 4, 2000).

56. The importance of Native American fresco traditions for Vigil can also be seen in his wall paintings from New Mexico, where most of his mural oeuvre can be found. He has often used natural pigments from the soils of New Mexico to create his work and to forge a continuity between the artistic traditions of the Southwest and his own art.

57. Museum of New Mexico: Statewide Programs and Education Topic Tours: About the Artist Frederico Vigil, www.museumeducation.org/curricula_frederico_frescoes.html (accessed on November 20, 2000).

58. Schele and Miller, *Blood of Kings*, 268.

59. Coe, *Mexico*, 178.

60. A number of mural projects were carried out in the United States during the 1930s and 1940s under the auspices of the Works Progress Administration (WPA), a New Deal federal program aimed at alleviating the economic hardships of the Great Depression. Created in 1935, the WPA provided employment for millions of workers in the United States. The WPA's Federal Arts Project, partly inspired by the federally funded Mexican mural movement, commissioned various mural projects, many of which addressed issues of social justice, labor struggles, and economic disenfranchisement. Artists such as Bernard B. Zakheim, Millard Sheets, Victor Arnautoff, and Stuart Holmes, among others, created murals in California under the WPA. Though not as critical as the Mexican murals, these public works of art were also influential to Chicana/o muralists. For more information on the WPA murals, see Becker, *Art for the People*, and Boyen, "The WPA Mural Projects."

61. Karlstrom, "Rivera, Mexico and Modernism," 232.

Chapter 2

1. "El Plan Espiritual de Aztlán," 1–5.

2. Padilla, "Myth and Comparative Cultural Nationalism," 114.

3. In spite of the various references in the available archaeological and anthropological literature to Aztlán as the homeland of the Aztecs, there is no evidence indicating the exact location of this homeland. For recent research on Aztlán and its cultural and historical implications, see Fields and Zamudio-Taylor, *Road to Aztlán*.

4. Murphy, "Understanding Indigenous Nationalism," 274.

5. The early manifestations of nationalism and Indigenism tended to overlook or ignore the role that gender oppression played in the marginalization of the Chicana/o community. Indigenism, in particular, would eventually be transformed to accommodate the specificity of the Chicana experience. Chicana feminist writers and artists would take an active role in critiquing the male-dominated vocabulary espoused by Chicano radicals and in formulating an Indigenist vision that would account for women's voices. For more on Chicana feminism, Indigenism, and murals, see Chapter 5 of this volume.

6. Connor, *Ethnonationalism*, 92.

7. Ibid., 94.

8. J. Jorge Klor de Alva has argued that nationalist tones added a sense of urgency to the Chicana/o cause: "When ethnic concerns are considered 'national' concerns, what is usually meant is that they are widespread and in need of the federal government's attention." Klor de Alva, "Aztlán, Borinquen, and Hispanic Nationalism," 67.

9. Padilla, "Myth and Comparative Cultural Nationalism," 114.

10. *Pilots of Aztlán* (video).

11. "El Plan Espiritual de Aztlán," 1.

12. Chicana activists, artists, and intellectuals were among the first to question and contest the *machista* sensibilities of the Chicano Movement. For an analysis of the gendered iconography in Chicano community murals and for a discussion of the work by Chicana muralists, see Chapter 5 of this book.

13. Gamboa, "In the City of Angels," 125. For more on Asco's public performances, see Chapter 6 of this volume.

14. Aside from utilizing posters and murals as a means to create alternative spaces for Chicana/o creativity, these artists were also involved with the creation, usually within the barrio itself, of exhibition venues and cultural centers dedicated to showing the work of Latina/o artists. Such was the case of Galería de la Raza in San Francisco, Centro Cultural

de la Raza in San Diego, and Self-Help Graphics in Los Angeles.

15. For further discussion on the relationship between the concept of space, Indigenism, and the Chicana/o public mural, please see Chapter 4 of this book.

16. See *Con Safos* 2, no. 5 (1970): 38–39.

17. Umberger, "Aztec Sculptures," 193.

18. Leal, "In Search of Aztlán," 11.

19. *Pilots of Aztlán* (video).

20. Pina, "Archaic, Historical and Mythicized Dimensions of Aztlán," 39.

21. For more information on Francisco Eppens's mural at UNAM's School of Medicine, see the mural's description and history on the school's Web site: Facultad de Medicina UNAM, www.facmed.unam. mex/fm/mural/cuerpomural.html (accessed on December 1, 2006).

22. Vasconcelos, *La raza cósmica*, 18.

23. N. F. Juárez, "José Vasconcelos and La Raza Cósmica," 54.

24. Vasconcelos, *La raza cósmica*, 15.

25. Brookman and Gómez-Peña, *Made in Aztlán*, 27.

26. Garza, "Duality in Chicano Poetry," 39.

27. Chicana feminist thinkers and artists would take the notion of duality further by discussing the heterogeneity that formed part of their experience as women of color in the United States. For them, duality constituted a limiting concept because it failed to address the incredible diversity of their overlapping and contesting identities as women and as racialized minorities who were also discriminated against because of their social class. And this doesn't even mention the specific cases of Chicana writers and artists like Gloria Anzaldúa, Cherríe Moraga, and Judy Baca, who also had to negotiate their positions as lesbian women within the cultural-nationalism paradigm of the Chicano Movement.

28. Brookman and Gómez-Peña, *Made in Aztlán*, 25.

29. Barnett, *Community Murals*, 108.

30. Mulford, *Chicano Park*, video.

31. Brookman and Gómez-Peña, *Made in Aztlán*, 26.

32. Rivera's *Psycho-Cybernetics* is featured in Timothy W. Drescher's monograph entitled *San Francisco Bay Area Murals: Communities Create Their Muses, 1904–1997*. Drescher, however, asserts that the mural has been destroyed since its creation. My own findings have revealed that, as of the summer of 2001, the mural was still standing in fairly good condition, though the colors had lost some of their intensity.

33. Mary Ellen Miller, "Image of People and Nature," 168.

34. *Pilots of Aztlán* (video).

35. Ybarra-Frausto, "Rasquachismo," 156.

36. Though Botello recognized the importance of SPARC for the funding of community mural work, there were certainly tensions between him, Healy, and Judy Baca in the 1970s. In 1977, Healy wrote a letter to the Chicana/o art journal *Chismearte*, relating his experience with some scaffolding he had borrowed from SPARC (then called the Mural Resource Center) while working on *Chicano Time Trip*. Healy affirmed that Baca, who was the director of the Center, had not lent him the scaffolding for a sufficient length of time for him to complete the mural. Baca herself, Healy alleged, wanted to get the piece of equipment back so she could work on her own mural project (presumably *The Great Wall of Los Angeles*). When Healy refused to return the scaffolding before he finished *Chicano Time Trip*, he was hit with charges of petty theft. Though the charges were eventually dropped and Healy was allowed to keep the scaffolding until he completed the mural, he accused Baca of acting more for her personal ambition than on her social and political convictions. He closed his letter by asserting that "most of the muralists from East Los Angeles

have a Judy Baca story to tell; and now, so do I." Healy, "Letter to Chismearte," 53.

37. Salas, "Soldadera in the Mexican Revolution," 95.

38. According to historian Elizabeth Salas, *soldaderas* found themselves impoverished and disenfranchised after the Mexican Revolution when they discovered they were not eligible for veteran's benefits from the Mexican government. Ibid., 101.

39. Sorell, "Photograph as a Source for Visual Artists," 19.

40. Klahr, *Jefes, héroes y caudillos*, 102.

41. Santa Barraza, e-mail exchange with the author, March 18, 2001.

42. Grambau, "Mural: *La Revolución Mexicana*," 20.

43. Emigdio Vasquez's interest in social realism stemmed from the influence that the Mexican muralists like Siqueiros and Rivera exerted on his own work. He was also deeply affected by the various social-realist artists of the United States. Painters like Thomas Hart Benton, Ben Shahn, and the artists of the Ash Can School and Works Progress Administration all inspired the artist's choice of preferred style. Emigdio Vasquez and Carlos "Higgy" Vasquez, interview by the author, April 14, 2005, Santa Ana, California.

44. "Emigdio Vasquez, June 15, 1984." Oral History, Emigdio Vasquez Papers, California Ethnic and Multicultural Archive (hereafter CEMA), University of California, Santa Barbara.

45. Emigdio Vasquez and Carlos "Higgy" Vasquez interview.

46. Ibid.

47. Ibid.

48. During my conversation with Vasquez, he explained to me that in his mural *Toward the Twenty-first Century,* he included the following quote by Abraham Lincoln: "The strongest bond of human sympathy outside the family relation should be one uniting working people

of all nations and tongues and kindreds." Vasquez regarded this quote as a radical call to all working-class people to unite against the systems of oppression. In spite of the militant political tone of the statement, the city of Anaheim did not seem to object to it, given that the proclamation came from Lincoln, as he was widely accepted and celebrated as a forefather of the U.S. nation-state. Ibid.

49. Quoted in Dunitz and Prigoff, *Painting the Towns,* 260.

50. "Interview with Emigdio Vasquez" by Gloria Ortiz, March 29, 1995, Emigdio Vasquez Papers, CEMA, University of California, Santa Barbara.

51. Undated artist's statement, Emigdio Vasquez Papers, CEMA, University of California, Santa Barbara.

52. "Emigdio Vasquez, June 15, 1984." Oral History, CEMA, University of California, Santa Barbara.

53. Undated artist's statement, CEMA, University of California, Santa Barbara.

54. Vasquez's interest in working-class struggles and labor history was not limited to the Chicana/o community. As a matter of fact, he was and continues to be a great admirer of figures like Joe Hill and Mother Jones and has even painted their portraits in his work.

55. Goldman, "Hidden Histories," 115.

56. For an in-depth discussion of the *MEChA Mural,* see Chapter 1 of this book.

Chapter 3

1. Ivor L. Miller, *Aerosol Kingdom,* 13.

2. Sánchez-Tranquilino, "Mi Casa No Es Su Casa," 48.

3. J. Romotsky and S. R. Romotsky, *Los Angeles Barrio Calligraphy,* 21.

4. Austin, *Taking the Train,* 34–35.

5. Ibid., 64.

6. Man One, interview by the author, June 15, 2005, Sherman Oaks, California.

7. Austin, *Taking the Train,* 34.

8. J. Romotsky and S. R. Romotsky, "L.A. Human Scale," 655–661.

9. "Chicano Murals," 15.

10. Kim, *Chicano Graffiti and Murals*, 8.

11. Chicana artist Judy Baca also saw muralism as a more evolved art form than graffiti. She often employed young gang members and taggers in her mural projects so that they could learn "a simple step forward to use the walls to speak more articulately," as she explained. Nevertheless, while she discouraged them from writing graffiti, she did not prevent them from being creative. Baca would often empower young gang members by rechanneling their creative needs through public murals. Many youth reacted positively to her influence with comments such as "We want the mural lady over here" or "Hey, art lady, you want to see Juan's drawing?" Adam, "Judy Baca: 'Censorship is rampant,'" 7.

12. Barnett, *Community Murals*, 38.

13. In further establishing distinctions between graffiti and murals, Barnett argues that the development from the former to the latter can also be characterized as a progression from an individualist visual language to a more collective art form. Graffiti, however, can hardly be called "individualistic," given that it comes from a collective sense of belonging among gang members or other urban youth groups.

14. Sánchez-Tranquilino, "Space, Power, and Youth Culture," 64.

15. J. Romotsky and S. R. Romotsky, "Placas and Murals," 291.

16. These remarks were made by William Medina, spokesperson for the LAPD. Cited in Martínez, "Going Up in L.A.," 14.

17. Man One interview.

18. Man One regarded the initial tensions and rivalry between muralists and taggers as a result not only of city officials legitimizing murals more than graffiti, but also of a certain degree of

jealousy on the part of muralists: "I think they [the muralists] were also jealous of us because we were getting a lot of the attention, a lot of the stuff that we were doing in the streets was staying up and was big and we could paint a lot faster than they could and do bigger walls. I think there was some jealousy; at least, that's what I perceive." Ibid.

19. Esteban Villa, phone interview by the author, June 24, 2005, Santa Barbara, California.

20. Phillips, *Wallbangin'*, 197.

21. Austin, *Taking the Train*, 6.

22. Miller, *Aerosol Kingdom*, 18.

23. Herring, *Art and Writing*, 25.

24. Coe and Van Stone, *Reading the Maya Glyphs*, 14. By the same token, Chicano graffiti artist Charles "Chaz" Bojórquez explains that with his work he is not "trying to write something for people to understand [but rather] to write something for street people to understand." Durland, "Charles 'Chaz' Bojórquez," 49.

25. J. Romotsky and S. R. Romotsky, *Los Angeles Barrio Calligraphy*, 43.

26. Sánchez-Tranquilino, "Space, Power, and Youth Culture," 59.

27. Reents-Budet, *Painting the Maya Universe*, 8.

28. Herring, *Art and Writing*, 9.

29. Cowgill, "Teotihuacan Glyphs and Imagery," 240.

30. Gates, *Outline Dictionary of Maya Glyphs*, v.

31. Miller, *Aerosol Kingdom*, 74.

32. Austin, *Taking the Train*, 112–113.

33. Crispin Sartwell, "Graffiti and Language." Paper posted on author's personal Web site: www.crispinsartwell.com (accessed on September 1, 2005).

34. Esteban Villa interview.

35. Phillips, *Wallbangin'*, 39.

36. Man One interview.

37. Aside from his travels, Bojórquez studied Asian calligraphy under Master Yun Chung Chiang at the Pasadena

Pacific Asia Museum. Prior to that, he had attended the Universidad de Artes Plásticas in Guadalajara, where he investigated Mesoamerican arts. K. Johnson, "Charles 'Chaz' Bojórquez," 74.

38. Paraphrased in Gary Keller, "Esteban Villa," 294–295.

39. Posh One, interview by the author, June 2, 2005, Culver City, California.

40. Ganz, *Graffiti Women*, 66, 76.

41. Man One interview.

42. Lachmann, "Graffiti as Career and Ideology," 235.

43. Phillips, *Wallbangin'*, 34.

44. Willie Herrón, Oral History conducted by Jeffrey Rangel, Oral History Program, Archives of American Art, Smithsonian Institution, February 5, 2006.

45. Ibid.

46. Sánchez-Tranquilino, "Murales del Movimiento," 97.

47. J. Romotsky and S. R. Romotsky, "Placas and Murals," 296.

48. Various artists would later follow Herrón's example of acknowledging graffiti as a form of urban creative expression. While painting *A People's History of Telegraph Avenue* (1976) in Berkeley, Daniel Galvez and his fellow muralists distributed flyers to the local community explaining the content of the mural and apologizing to the graffiti writers and taggers whose *placas* were being displaced by this mural. Barnett, *Community Murals*, 38.

49. Ibid.

50. Carrasco contends that the rise of cities like Teotihuacán, Cholollan, Tula, Xochicalco, Chichén Itzá, and Tenochtitlán was deeply connected to the cult of Quetzalcoatl. Carrasco, *Quetzalcoatl and the Irony of Empire*, 2.

51. Sánchez-Tranquilino, "Murales del Movimiento," 97.

52. Willie Herrón, Oral History.

53. Ibid.

54. Lorenza Muñoz, "Distinctive L.A. Legacy Under Siege," A-1.

55. This comment was made by Willie Herrón during the Asco panel discussion that took place in SPARC on July 20, 2000, Venice, California.

56. Mulford, *Chicano Park*, video.

57. Ibid.

58. For more information on the Chicano Park murals, see Chapter 4 of this book.

59. Esteban Villa interview.

60. Phillips, *Wallbangin'*, 137.

61. Villa—who admired figures like Che Guevara, Fidel Castro, Vladimir Lenin, and Karl Marx—took an interest in Communism in the 1960s and 1970s but soon found himself disenchanted with the Communist Party in the United States and never actually joined. He was taken aback by the financial demands on Party members and by their desire to politically empower themselves rather than solve social problems. The predominantly European-American cultural makeup of the Party's membership also discouraged the young Villa from joining. Nowadays, Villa subscribes to a more policy-oriented brand of socialism in which the emphasis is on pragmatic social change. Esteban Villa interview.

62. J. Romotsky and S. R. Romotsky, *Los Angeles Barrio Calligraphy*, 53.

63. S. R. Romotsky and J. Romotsky, "Plaqueaso on the Wall," 68.

64. The Los Four exhibition at LACMA came only three years after the infamous "piece" done in that same location by the members of the performance collective Asco. In 1971, the members of Asco approached the curators of modern art at LACMA and asked them if they would be willing to exhibit Chicana/o art in the museum. The artists were dismissed when the curators responded that Chicanas/os do not do art, but graffiti. Soon thereafter, Asco approached the museum grounds and proceeded to tag their names in spray paint throughout the museum, thus inaugurating

the self-proclaimed "first Chicana/o art exhibition in LACMA." When LACMA finally did host a Chicana/o art show with the Los Four exhibition three years later, Willie Herrón, who was one of the founding members of Asco and who attended the opening reception of the show, found the whole affair contradictory to the spirit of graffiti: "It was very difficult for me at that time to look at [the show] and for me to accept it in the same way that I accepted the existing graffiti that was already part of the landscape. This was so because [the Los Four artwork] was created consciously for the purpose of exhibition." Willie Herrón, Oral History.

65. *Piece* is the word taggers use for the more elaborate graffiti designs they do.

66. Rocío Aranda-Alvarado argued that Bojórquez's graffiti motifs "participate in the art-historical debates about the legacy of modernism in late-twentieth-century painting and about the influence of movements ranging from pop and abstract expressionism in the United States to informalism in Spain." Aranda-Alvarado, "Charles Bojórquez," 88.

67. Phillips, *Wallbangin',* 144.

68. In a conversation with Professor Gerardo Aldana, a Mesoamerican specialist at the University of California, Santa Barbara, he explained to me that Bojórquez's re-creation of an indigenous stela in *Por Dios y Oro* possessed characteristics from numerous stylistic traditions in diverse areas such as the Puuc region (Maya Gulf Coast) and Xochicalco. With this combination of indigenous styles, Bojórquez was seeking to create what he called "a New World Aztec stella [*sic*]" that incorporated a variety of indigenous aesthetics, including contemporary graffiti. "Charles 'Chaz' Bojórquez," *Chicana/o Art Book,* http://latinoartcommunity.org/community/ChicArt/ArtistDir/ChaBoj.html (accessed on June 9, 2005).

69. Ibid.

70. Posh One interview.

71. Sherri Cavan, "The Great Graffiti Wars of the Late Twentieth Century," unpublished academic paper presented at the Pacific Sociological Association Conference (1995) and posted on the Web site Art Crimes: www.graffiti.org (accessed on June 13, 2005).

72. Posh One interview.

73. Man One interview.

74. Miller, *Aerosol Kingdom,* 36.

75. Man One interview.

76. Posh One, e-mail message to the author, September 21, 2005.

77. For more information on graffiti memorials, see Cooper and Sciorra, *R.I.P. Memorial Wall Art.*

78. Pasztory, *Aztec Art,* 57.

79. Posh One, e-mail message to the author, September 3, 2005.

80. Crispin Sartwell argued that the relationship between graffiti and hip-hop music on the East Coast is deeply organic and intimate: "Graffiti is joined to hip hop at the hip and rose with it in New York and Philadelphia. It represents many of the same impulses and techniques visually that hip hop represents in sound. The idea of using prerecorded tracks and rapping over them (a technique that originates in Jamaica) is a cheap and relatively simple way to make music: analogous to spray paint. And the rapper repeating his name and bragging on his abilities and threatening his enemies in crews: all that is analogous to the tag." Sartwell, untitled essay posted on his personal Web site: www.crispinsartwell.com (accessed on September 1, 2005).

81. Man One, e-mail message to the author, September 12, 2005.

82. S. R. Romotsky and J. Romotsky, "Plaqueaso on the Wall," 69.

83. Fred Alvarado, phone interview by the author, October 10, 2005, Santa Barbara, California.

84. Cerny, "Thoughts on Anonymity," 35.

85. Reents-Budet, *Painting the Maya Universe*, 47.

86. Ibid., 6.

87. Spie explained to me that a number of years ago he directed an art workshop in Albuquerque, New Mexico, working primarily with Pueblo indigenous children. In their activities and conversations, they discussed how the designs on Pueblo pottery could reveal the geographical location where the vessel was made. Spie realized that the same was true of graffiti; distinct design idiosyncrasies and details could indicate whether a particular piece was done on the East Coast, in the Southwest, or on the West Coast. Spie (Eric Norberg), phone interview by author, September 12, 2005, Santa Barbara, California.

88. Spie made Quetzalcoatl with dragonlike characteristics because the mascot of Horace Mann Middle School is a dragon. Spie (Eric Norberg), e-mail message to the author, April 27, 2007.

89. Fred Alvarado, e-mail message to the author, May 21, 2006.

90. Ibid.

91. Enciso, *Design Motifs of Ancient Mexico*, iii.

92. Alvarado e-mail message.

93. For more information on the meanings of Aztlán, see Romero Galván, "La ciudad de Mexico," 13–32, and Alvarado Tezozómoc, *Crónica mexicayotl.*

94. I thank Professor Gerardo Aldana of the University of California, Santa Barbara, for his assistance in interpreting this crane/heron motif in the mural by Alvarado and company.

95. For more information on the Chicana/o significance of Aztlán, see Chapter 4 of this book.

96. Alvarado e-mail message.

Chapter 4

1. This information was obtained from a presentation delivered by Judy Baca at the University of Southern Indiana, Evansville, on April 20, 2002.

2. Sommer, "Some Psychological Aspects," 50; italics mine.

3. Suderburg, *Space, Site, Intervention*, 4.

4. Lefebvre, *Production of Space*, 85.

5. Pérez-Torres, *Movements in Chicano Poetry*, 59.

6. Vargas, "Historical Overview/ Update," 198.

7. Fields and Zamudio-Taylor, "Aztlán," 39.

8. Villa, *Barrio-Logos*, 15.

9. Diaz, *Barrio Urbanism*, 3.

10. Ibid., 4.

11. Flores and Benmayor, *Latino Cultural Citizenship*, i; italics mine.

12. Ibid., 16.

13. Villa, *Barrio-Logos*, 1.

14. Pina, "Archaic, Historical and Mythicized Dimensions," 15.

15. Leal, "In Search of Aztlán," 8.

16. Lopez, "Estrada Murals," 21.

17. Sánchez-Tranquilino argues that in Estrada Courts there was a concerted effort to clearly distinguish graffiti from murals, where the former was associated with gang activity and vandalism and the latter with more positive and pro-active community initiatives. In the course of mural production there, however, Sánchez-Tranquilino observed that said distinction was difficult to uphold and that both currents often informed one another in nonlinear and dynamic ways. Sánchez-Tranquilino, "Mi Casa No Es Su Casa," x.

18. Other murals in Estrada Courts created during the 1990s, such as Ernesto de la Loza's *Los Cuatro Grandes* (1993) and Alma López's *Las Four* (1997), did not actually form part of the original initiatives to transform the urban environment in Estrada. For a detailed discussion of de la Loza's and López's murals, see Chapter 5 of this book.

19. Quoted in Sánchez-Tranquilino, "Mi Casa No Es Su Casa," 71.

20. Bachelard, *The Poetics of Space*, 218.

21. David Botello first painted *Dreams of Flight* in 1973, but in 1996 he repainted it with funding from the Social and Public Arts Resource Center (SPARC). It was then that he changed the central figure on the mural from a boy to a *girl* holding an airplane.

22. Lugo Saavedra, "Arte de 'East Los,'" 123.

23. David Botello interview, August 10, 1983, transcribed in *Califas, Chicano Art and Culture in California*.

24. Sánchez-Tranquilino, "Mi Casa No Es Su Casa," 26.

25. In conversations with Gerardo Aldana, a Maya specialist at the University of California, Santa Barbara, I learned that the Huastec language is often considered a Mayan language, but given El Tajín's removed location from principal Maya sites, it should be considered distinct from them.

26. Wilkerson, "And Then They Were Sacrificed," 51.

27. Ibid., 62.

28. Sánchez-Tranquilino, "Mi Casa No Es Su Casa," 73.

29. Cockcroft, "The Story of Chicano Park," 145–163.

30. Diaz, *Barrio Urbanism,* 145.

31. Villa, *Barrio-Logos,* 172.

32. Mulford, *Chicano Park,* video.

33. Ibid.

34. Aside from using the murals as a way to symbolically expand the area of Chicano Park, artists and community residents have been constantly pressuring city officials to allow the park to be extended to the bay. To this day, they have not been able to succeed in that effort, and the access to the ocean is still blocked by the various junkyards that surround the park.

35. Chicano Park/Murals/Chicano Park Takeover Mural: http://www.chicanoparksandiego.com/murals/takeover.html.

36. Mulford, *Chicano Park,* video.

37. The intervention of many Chicana feminist activists, thinkers, and artists was often cited as one of the divisive elements that affected the Chicano Movement. In the case of the Chicano Park murals themselves, the participation of women was often viewed with at least some level of reservation on the part of their male colleagues. For example, the female members of the Royal Chicano Air Force (RCAF)—the legendary artists collective from Sacramento—who participated in the mural initiative at Chicano Park arrived at the park to paint their mural earlier than was expected by their RCAF *compañeros.* José Montoya, one of the founders of this artists collective, was clearly taken aback by their actions: "I think the [RCAF] women messed up by jumping the gun. See, they took off without letting us know, so it was a solo fly that usually in the RCAF is a court-martial, man. Again, it's the old *machismo* coming out. But they did a very beautiful pillar." Mulford, *Chicano Park,* video.

38. The relatively small size of Balmy Alley as a mural environment is probably the result of the way urban spaces are laid out in San Francisco, where larger environments are simply not possible. Whereas Los Angeles and San Diego are spread out over large areas, San Francisco is comparatively smaller and more densely laid out. Though securing space for community murals has always been challenging for artists, space in the Bay Area has become increasingly commodified, especially in San Francisco's Mission District, which is predominantly a Latina/o area and a major mural site. Nevertheless, the Mission has recently become increasingly gentrified, with rising real estate and rent prices, thus effectively driving out many of the Latina/o and working-class families who have lived there for decades.

39. Quoted in Dunitz and Prigoff, *Painting the Towns,* 65.

40. In their essay "Survivors on the Move: Maya Migration in Time

and Space," Christopher Lutz and W. George Lovell contextualize recent Maya migrations within older historical patterns: "Archaeologically, Maya origins begin with migrations, the most distant ancestors being among the nomadic bands that trekked across the Bering Land Bridge millennia ago to enter the New World from the Old. Ethnohistorically, the *Popol Vuh* tells us of what might best be thought of as semi-mythic migrations on the part of more recent ancestors, who are said to have entered Guatemala from the Gulf Coast of Mexico." In Loucky and Moors, *The Maya Diaspora*, 11–34.

41. By 1990, *Te Oímos Guatemala* had been completely destroyed. Juana Alicia replaced it with another mural, this one entitled *Una Ley Immoral, Nadie Tiene Que Cumplirla (No One Should Comply with an Immoral Law)* and honoring slain Salvadoran archbishop and human rights activist Óscar Romero.

42. Loucky and Moors, *The Maya Diaspora*, 3.

43. Ibid.

44. I thank Chicana muralist Juana Alicia for her comments and suggestions for this chapter, in particular the section on Balmy Alley and her mural *Te Oímos Guatemala/We Hear You Guatemala*.

45. Paul Botello, phone conversation with the author, July 15, 2000. Botello is the younger brother of David Rivas Botello, member of the legendary mural collective called the East Los Streetscapers, founded in the early 1970s. Botello feels that between his work and that of his older brother it is possible to get a glimpse of the major trends in the history of the community mural movement in Los Angeles.

Chapter 5

1. Posters were also regarded as an important medium for Chicana artists, who looked upon both murals and posters as more democratic forms of art that did not require the exclusive spaces of museums and galleries in order to thrive. While the Mexican School was an important precedent for Chicana/o muralists, artists producing posters through silkscreening, woodcutting, and other printmaking media were looking to Mexican printmaker José Guadalupe Posada and the Cuban poster movement for inspiration. For recent information on Chicana/o poster art, see Goldman, "A Public Voice," 50–57. As in muralism, Chicana artists also became prominent figures in the production of posters, though their contribution was not as readily recognized as that of their male peers. For more on the participation of women in the Chicana/o poster movement, see Barnet-Sánchez, "Presence and Absence," 117–149.

2. Chicana artist Judithe Hernández pointed out to me that the gendered exclusions of the Chicana/o arts movements were no different from the exclusions found in other mural movements and in the art world in general: "In fairness, the Chicano mural movement was not that different from other visual arts movements. How many of the American murals painted for the WPA [Works Progress Administration] were painted by or celebrated women? In the western world, the business of ART has always been male and still is to a large degree." Judithe Hernández, e-mail message to the author, April 24, 2007.

3. Text cited in Anaya and Lomelí, *Aztlán*, 1–5; italics mine.

4. "Chicana loyalist" was a term used for the women in the Chicano Movement who disavowed feminist concerns and who believed in standing by their men, so to speak, by privileging race over gender identity. Women who identified as loyalists harshly criticized feminists, whom they felt were straying from the "real" issues

that affected the Chicana/o community, none of which directly related to gender. For more on the distinctions between Chicana loyalists and feminists, see Maylei Blackwell, "Contested Histories," 59–89.

5. Baca's first artistic collaborations did not occur with artists at all but with barrio youth and gang members while working with the Los Angeles Parks District in the late sixties and early seventies. This experience would be a crucial one when, a few years later, she began work for *The Great Wall of Los Angeles,* a mural project in which she solicited the help of many young people. Regarding her work with community youth, Baca has remarked that, nevertheless, the majority of those who participated were boys and young men. Latina girls usually did not have access to the public spheres where her projects took place.

6. Judith Baca, Oral History, interview by Amalia Mesa-Bains, August 5 and 6, 1986, in Venice, California, Archives of American Art, Smithsonian Institution.

7. Judithe Hernández, e-mail message to author.

8. One exception to the general trend of Chicana/o artists being left out of major galleries and museums in the 1970s was the artists collective of Los Four, who in 1974 became the first group of Chicana/o artists to have an exhibition in the Los Angeles County Museum of Art. "Although I would agree that museums during this period were not beating down our door to offer us shows," Judithe Hernández explained, "there was the beginning of interest in what we were doing and a desire to begin diversifying the art seen in mainstream institutions." Ibid.

9. In the past, I have argued that Chicana artists who have put together a substantial mural oeuvre can be regarded as pioneers in their fields because they lack a historical precedence for their endeavors (i.e., other women doing

murals). Latorre, "Latina Feminism and Visual Discourse," 101. While I don't want to take anything away from the critical contributions of Chicanas to the history of mural art, it can be argued that the spaces in which their works have appeared, namely, the walls of barrio and community architecture, were not as contested and exclusive as those utilized, for example, by the Mexican muralists during the first half of the twentieth century (like government and public buildings). While this argument may provide a partial explanation on this issue, it does not explain how a number of Chicana artists have in recent years secured commissions outside the sphere of the barrio environment, such as Juana Alicia's completion in 2000 of her mural *Santuario* (*Sanctuary*) at the San Francisco International Airport and Judy Baca's mural at the Denver International Airport.

10. Romo, "Chicanization of Mexican Calendar Art," November 20–23, 2002. The presentation text was downloaded from the Smithsonian Center for Latino Initiatives (latino.si.edu) on September 1, 2006.

11. Museo Soumaya, Mexico City, and Mexican Fine Arts Center Museum, Chicago, *La Patria Portátil,* 39.

12. For more on gender as performance, see Garber, *Vested Interests.*

13. Sánchez-Tranquilino and Tagg, "The Pachuco's Flayed Hide," 101.

14. Butler, *Constructing Masculinity,* 23.

15. Barnett, *Community Murals,* 179.

16. Ibid., 109. During the making of *Mi Abuelita,* Baca realized many of the dangers of working collectively and publicly on a community mural, and she assigned one of the young people assisting in the project to act as a lookout in case dangerous gang activity erupted in the area.

17. Baca, Oral History, interview, Archives of American Art, Smithsonian Institution.

18. Rangel, "Art and Activism," 230.

19. University Art Museum, Berkeley, *The Fifth Sun*, 15.

20. The different registers in *Latinoamérica* were created so each member of Las Mujeres Muralistas could work individually on her own section of the mural. With regard to this, Patricia Rodríguez explained that "Irene Pérez painted the magueys and the maize. Graciela Carrillo painted Guatemala. Consuelo Méndez painted the center of the mural, which is the family unit, and Venezuela. I painted Bolivia and Peru." University Art Museum, Berkeley, *The Fifth Sun*, 14. In spite of this, they insisted that their work was the result of a completely collective effort and never discussed who worked on which register.

21. Ochoa, "Creative Collectives," 159.

22. For more information on *Latinoamérica*'s iconographic program, see Barnett, *Community Murals*, 136.

23. Goldman, "How, Why, Where, and When," 40.

24. Manifesto published in *Imagine: International Chicano Poetry Journal* 3, nos. 1 and 2 (Summer/Winter 1986), 148.

25. Pérez, *Decolonial Imaginary*, 6.

26. In her doctoral dissertation, María Ochoa interpreted the presence of some of the women in *Latinoamérica* as "a muted representation of lesbians," often seen when women are depicted standing "a little too close together." Ochoa, "Creative Collectives," 162. Though Ochoa merely brings out the point as a possible reading of the mural, there is no evidence that Las Mujeres Muralistas were intending to incorporate a lesbian subtext to the iconography of this work. Nevertheless, the solidarity and mutual support Chicana artists have found in one another has created a tight-knit camaraderie among them that often elicits recurring images in their work of women in the company of other women. Some Chicana artists

also cite this kind of iconography as the result of the influence that women in their families have bestowed on them.

27. One of the reasons why Las Mujeres Muralistas chose to include images from various Latin American countries was to reflect the diversity of the Mission District's Latina/o population, which was not exclusively Chicano or Mexican American.

28. Kim, "Judithe Hernández," 10.

29. Judithe Hernández, e-mail message to author.

30. Ibid.

31. Social and Public Art Resource Center (SPARC) Web site: www.sparcmurals.org (accessed on September 12, 2005).

32. The concluding panel in *The Great Wall of Los Angeles* depicted the participation of athletes of color in the Olympic Games that took place in Los Angeles in 1984. Nevertheless, Baca and her assistants have plans to expand *The Great Wall* and include panels depicting events from the 1960s to the 1990s. These scenes are projected to include the UFW struggles, the East Los Angeles School Blowouts, Central American immigration to California, the effects of Propositions 209 and 227, and the advent of digital technology, among other historical events. Even though *The Great Wall* began nearly twenty years ago, Baca still speaks of it as a "work in progress." Ibid.

33. Ibid.

34. SPARC's role as an organization that fosters and disseminates mural production is further heightened by its sophisticated Web site. With digitized images, animation, streaming video, interactive features, and archival material, this Web site has become an important tool for researchers and individuals from around the world who are seeking information on Southern California's mural history.

35. SPARC Web site.

36. Griswold del Castillo, *Treaty of Guadalupe Hidalgo*, 99.

37. Sandoval, *Methodology of the Oppressed*, 57.

38. Cervántez, "*La Ofrenda* Artist Statement."

39. While not denying the characterization of *La Ofrenda* as a sort of "mural altar," Cervántez has also asserted in her artist's statement that this mural was for her like an "'offering' to my people."

40. Latorre, "Latina Feminism and Visual Discourse," 97.

41. Healey, "Kahlo Redux," 93.

42. Cervántez, "La *Ofrenda* Artist Statement."

43. While it would seem that Cervántez in *La Ofrenda* is providing the original and a translated version of Alvarez's "Vende Futuro," in reality *both* lines are part of the poem. Gloria Alvarez actually uses translation as a creative tool in her work. As she told me in 1999, she initially began translating her work to expand her audience and as a challenge to herself, but soon the process for her took on a life of its own. She challenges the claims of objectivity and literalness associated with the procedure by using translation in unexpected and innovative ways.

44. Laura Pérez, "Spirit Glyphs," 38.

45. Ibid., 39.

46. For more on the heterogeneous character of community muralism in California, see Chapter 6 of this volume.

47. Social and Public Art Resource Center, *World Wall*.

48. Ibid.

49. The representation of archetypal figures such as the ones seen in Baca's *World Wall* (1990) would emerge once again in the collaborative women's mural *Maestrapeace* (1994) in San Francisco's Mission District. For a detailed description of *Maestrapeace*, see Chapter 6.

50. SPARC, *World Wall: A Vision of the Future without Fear*, http://www.

sparcmurals.org/worldwall/phil.html (accessed on May 10, 2000).

51. Ibid.

52. M. E. Miller, *Art of Mesoamerica*, 209.

53. Anzaldúa, "Border Arte," 108.

54. Moraga, *The Last Generation*, 73.

55. For more information on digital murals, SPARC's Digital Mural Lab, and the controversies regarding the use of this medium for making murals, see Chapter 6 of this volume.

56. Alma López, "Las Four," www.almalopez.net (accessed on August 6, 2001).

57. Ibid.

58. Ibid.

59. The mural *La Llorona's Sacred Waters* by Juana Alicia was painted over the wall where the artist's celebrated mural *Las Lechugueras* (1983) was once located. *Las Lechugueras* focused on the negative effects of harmful pesticides on women farmworkers. Leticia Hernández, "Juana Alicia: A Muralist Takes a Global Look at the Spirit of Women," essay published on Juana Alicia's Web site: http://www.juanaalicia.com/sections/recently-completed/ (accessed on May 21, 2007).

60. Mirandé and Enríquez, *La Chicana*, 33.

61. Limón, "La Llorona," 416. Limón further argues that La Llorona as a cultural figure "remains largely *in the hands of women*," for his field research in areas like South Texas has indicated that it is primarily women who narrate and disseminate this story. Ibid., 417.

62. Carbonell, "From Llorona to Gritona," 53.

63. For a discussion about the connection between La Llorona and Cihuacoatl, see Anzaldúa, *Borderlands/La Frontera*, 35.

64. Rosa M.'s aquatint *Cihuacoatl, la Llorona* (1996) and Alma López's silkscreen *La Llorona Desperately Seeking*

Coyolxauhqui (2003) both make reference to La Llorona in her connection to Mesoamerican deities like Cihuacoatl and Coatlicue.

65. L. Hernández, "Juana Alicia," Web site.

66. In her essay, Leticia Hernández also points to the appropriateness or irony of the water theme in *La Llorona's Sacred Waters,* given that Juana Alicia painted the mural as a result of the irreversible water damage that *Las Lechugueras* had sustained. Given the choice of whitewashing the older mural or repainting it, the artist opted instead to execute a completely different piece, thus preferring to create, as she herself indicated, "from where I am now." Ibid.

67. For further discussions and representations of Chalchiuhtlicue, see Taube, *Aztec and Maya Myths.*

Chapter 6

1. Pérez-Torres, *Movements in Chicano Poetry,* 210.

2. Anzaldúa, *Borderlands/La Frontera,* 103.

3. Information taken from a presentation delivered by Judy Baca at the University of Southern Indiana (Evansville, Indiana), April 20, 2002.

4. The concept of the post-*movimiento* was first introduced to me by Rolando Romero, a scholar of U.S. Latina/o literature.

5. R. García, "Against *Rasquache,*" 3.

6. The idea for Asco's name came from a joint exhibition Gronk, Willie Herrón, and Patssi Valdez put together. In it, they showed what they considered their worst work and appropriately titled it Asco. They kept the name for the artists collective they would later form. Gamboa, *Urban Exile,* 32.

7. Fox, "Tremors in Paradise, 1960–1980," 227.

8. Gronk, Oral History interview by Jeffrey Rangel, Los Angeles, January 20 and 23, 1997, Archives of American Art, Smithsonian Institution.

9. Gamboa, *Urban Exile,* 33.

10. Gronk, Oral History interview.

11. Gamboa, *Urban Exile,* 32.

12. Ibid., 79.

13. For a more detailed discussion of the tripartite face in Chicana/o community murals, see Chapter 2 of this volume.

14. Chavoya, "Orphans of Modernism," 241.

15. Gamboa, "In the City of Angels," 127.

16. Ashcroft, Griffiths, and Tiffin, *Post-Colonial Studies Reader,* 183.

17. Pérez-Torres, *Movements in Chicano Poetry,* 15.

18. Foucault, *Archaeology of Knowledge,* 128.

19. García Canclini, *Culturas híbridas,* 15; my translation.

20. In the late 1970s, Herrón joined Jesús Velo, Bill Reyes, Manuel Valdez, and Antonio Valdez to form the Chicano rock band Los Illegals. For information on this band, see Villa, *Barrio-Logos,* 134–139.

21. The presence of Quetzalcoatl within this underground realm in *Dreamers among Us* is consistent with the Mexica creation myth that recounts how this entity entered the underworld to obtain the bones of the ancestors in order to create the world.

22. For more on the relationship between the image of Quetzalcoatl and the importance of knowledge and education in Chicana/o muralism, see my discussion of David Botello's *Read Between the Lines* mural in Chapter 5. Also, Rafaela G. Castro, author of *Chicano Folklore,* discussed how in 1970 Deganawidah-Quetzalcoatl College was founded in Northern California, an institution created for the educational needs of both Native American and Chicana/o students.

23. All the information in this paragraph was obtained from a phone

conversation held between the author and Colette Crutcher on June 15, 2002.

24. Castro, *Chicano Folklore,* 230.

25. Conversation with Crutcher. Since its execution, *Tonantsin Renace* has become the image that graces the main page of the Coro Hispano's Web site (www.corohispano.org).

26. Crutcher had come in contact with Tibetan art through an exhibition that had made its way to San Francisco while she was painting *Tonantsin Renace.*

27. Shohat, *Talking Visions,* 1.

28. Ibid., 2.

29. Scott, "Unfurling a Maestrapeace," 45.

30. Bergman, "Big Women," 44–45.

31. Scott, "Unfurling a Maestrapeace," 45.

32. Ibid.

33. Juana Alicia, phone conversation with the author, January 25, 2003.

34. There are variations in the spelling of this Yoruba goddess's name. Among these variations we find Yemoja, Yamayah, and Yemalla. The spelling of her name usually depends on the country where she is venerated.

35. Jacob, "Ashé in the Art of Ana Mendieta," 195.

36. Thompson, *Flash of the Spirit,* 72.

37. Ramos, "Afro-Cuban Orisha Worship," 67.

38. Ibid.

39. Lawal, "From Africa to the Americas," 3–37.

40. Baca has finished establishing a digital mural lab in Durango, Colorado, and is beginning the motions to found one in Guadalupe, California, the site of her 1990 *Guadalupe Mural.*

41. All the general information about the SPARC Digital Mural Lab was furnished by Enrique Gonzales during a conversation with the author at SPARC on July 25, 2000.

42. Michael, *Reconnecting Culture,* 18.

43. Lyon, "The Information Society," 205.

44. Nelson, Tu, and Hines, *Technicolor,* 2.

45. Ibid., 3.

46. The UCLA/SPARC César Chávez Digital/Mural Lab Web site: www.sparcmurals.org.

47. Ibid.

48. Judy Baca, interview by Guisela Latorre and Chela Sandoval, July 24, 2006, Social and Public Art Resource Center, Venice, California.

49. For more information on David Alfaro Siqueiros's *América Tropical,* see Chapter 1.

50. Enrique Gonzales, conversation with the author.

51. Lee, "The Writing on the Wall," 3.

52. To view how *Los Angeles Tropical* was laid out inside the entryway leading to *La América Tropical,* see the SPARC Web site at www.sparcmurals.org to download a QuickTime movie re-creating the setup (last accessed on December 20, 2002).

53. Lee, "The Writing on the Wall," 4.

54. John Jota Leaños, "Imperial Silences," presentation delivered at the University of California, Santa Barbara, May 17, 2006.

55. This billboard on the Galería de la Raza was the site of previous murals done by artists such as Michael Rios, Graciela Carrillo, and Derrick O'Keeffe, among others.

56. Leaños presentation.

57. Ibid.

58. This definition was posted on Los Cybrids' Web site: www.cybrids.com (accessed on September 7, 2005).

59. Quote was obtained from the Galería de la Raza's official Web site: www.galeriadelaraza.org (accessed September 7, 2005).

60. *Humaquina: Manifest Tech-Destiny,* Artist Statement, www.galeriadelaraza.org (accessed on September 8, 2005).

61. Fitzpatrick, "Social Policy for Cyborgs," 97.

62. Bell, "Cybercultures Reader: A User's Guide," 6.

63. Haraway, "A Cyborg Manifesto," 293.

64. Sandoval, "New Sciences," 375.

65. White, "Afrotech and Outer Spaces," 91.

Epilogue

1. Garber, *Symptoms of Culture*, 9.

2. For more information on these city ordinances in Los Angeles and San Francisco, see Hernández, "Mural of Graffiti?," A1, and Radin, "Tag! S.F. Property Owners Are It," F2.

Bibliography

Secondary Source Material

Adam, Michelle. "Judy Baca: 'Censorship Is Rampant,' Says Renowned Muralist." *The His-panic Outlook in Higher Education* 2, no. 22 (August 13, 2001): 7.

Aldrich Museum of Contemporary Art. *Quotations: The Second History of Art.* Ridgefield, Conn.: Aldrich Museum of Contemporary Art, 1992.

Alvarado Tezozómoc, Hernando. *Crónica mexicayotl.* Mexico City: Impresora Universitaria, 1949.

Anaya, Rudolfo A., and Francisco Lomelí, eds. *Aztlán: Essays on the Chicano Homeland.* Albu-querque: University of New Mexico Press, 1989.

Anzaldúa, Gloria. "Border Arte: Nepantla, el lugar de la frontera." In *La Frontera = The Border: Art about the Mexico/United States Border Experience,* ed. Kathryn Kanjo, 107–114. San Diego: Centro Cultural de la Raza, 1993.

———. *Borderlands/La Frontera: The New Mestiza.* 2nd ed. San Francisco: Aunt Lute Books, 1999.

———. "La Herencia de Coatlicue: The Coatlicue State." In *Borderlands/La Frontera: The New Mestiza,* 2nd ed., 63–73. San Francisco: Aunt Lute Books, 1999.

Aranda-Alvarado, Rocio. "Charles Bojórquez: Taking 'Old School' Further." *American Art* 18, no. 3 (Fall 2004): 88–91.

Ashcroft, Bill, Gareth Griffiths, and Helen Tiffin, eds. *The Post-Colonial Studies Reader.* Lon-don: Routledge, 1995.

Austin, Joe. *Taking the Train: How Graffiti Art Became an Urban Crisis in New York City.* New York: Columbia University Press, 2001.

Austin, Joe, and Michael Nevin Willard. *Generations of Youth: Youth Cultures and History in Twentieth-Century America.* New York: New York University Press, 1998.

Avalos, David. "A Pure Mexican Accent: The Popular Engravings of José Guadalupe Posada." *Proceedings of the Pacific Coast Council on Latin American Studies* 7 (1980–1981): 123–138.

Baca, Judy. Preface to *Signs from the Heart: California Chicano Murals,* ed. Eva Sperling Cock-croft and Holly Barnet-Sánchez, 1–3. Albuquerque: University of New Mexico Press, 1993.

Bachelard, Gaston. *The Poetics of Space.* Boston: Beacon Press, 1964.

Bakhtin, Mikhail. *The Dialogic Imagination: Four Essays.* Austin: University of Texas Press, 1981.

Barnet-Sánchez, Holly. "Presence and Absence in the Work of Chicana Artists of the Movi-miento = ¿Dónde están las grabadistas chicanas? Presencia y ausencia de la obra de las artistas chicanas en el movimiento chicano." In *Just Another Poster? Chicano Graphic Arts in California,* ed. Chon Noriega, 117–149. Santa Barbara: University Art Museum, Uni-versity of California, Santa Barbara; Seattle: Distributed by University of Washington Press, 2001.

Barnett, Alan W. *Community Murals: The People's Art.* Philadelphia: Art Alliance Press, 1984.

Barron, Stephanie, ed. *Made in California: Art, Image, and Identity, 1900–2000.* Berkeley: University of California Press, 2000.

Baxandall, Michael. *Patterns of Intention: On the Historical Explanation of Pictures.* New Haven: Yale University Press, 1985.

Baxter, Leslie A., and Barbara M. Montgomery. *Relating: Dialogues and Dialectics.* New York: Guilford Press, 1996.

Becker, Heather. *Art for the People: The Discovery and Preservation of Progressive and WPA-Era Murals in Chicago Public Schools, 1904–1943.* San Francisco: Chronicle Books, 2002.

Bell, David. "Cybercultures Reader: A User's Guide." In *The Cybercultures Reader,* ed. David Bell and Barbara M. Kennedy, 1–12. London: Routledge, 2000.

Bell, David, and Barbara M. Kennedy, eds. *The Cybercultures Reader.* London: Routledge, 2000.

Bergman, Miranda. "Big Women: Monumental Mural on San Francisco's Women's Building." *Public Art Review* 6 (Spring/Summer 1995): 44–45.

Berlo, Janet Catherine. *Art, Ideology, and the City of Teotihuacan.* Washington, D.C.: Dumbarton Oaks Research Library and Collection, 1992.

Beynon, John, and David Dunkerley. *Globalization: The Reader.* New York: Routledge, 2000.

Blackwell, Maylei. "Contested Histories: Las Hijas de Cuautémoc/Chicana Feminisms and Print Culture in the Chicano Movement, 1968–1973." In *Chicana Feminisms: A Critical Reader,* ed. Gabriela F. Arredondo, Aída Hurtado, Norma Klahn, Olga Nájera-Ramírez, and Patricia Zavella, 59–89. Durham: Duke University Press, 2003.

Bonfil Batalla, Guillermo. *México profundo: Una civilización negada.* Mexico City: Secretaría de Educación Pública, 1987.

———, ed. *Utopía y revolución: El pensamiento político contemporáneo de los indios en América Latina.* 2nd ed. Mexico City: Editorial Nueva Imagen, 1988.

Boyen, Charles Williams. "The WPA Mural Projects: The Effects of Constraints on Artistic Freedom." Ph.D. diss., Columbia University, New York, 1988.

Bracho, Ricardo. "Mexican Psychotic." Unpublished play proposal submitted to the Center for Chicano Studies, University of California, Santa Barbara, 2004.

Bright, Brenda Jo, and Liza Bakwell. *Looking High and Low: Art and Cultural Identity.* Tucson: University of Arizona Press, 1995.

Brook, James, Chris Carlsson, and Nancy J. Peters. *Reclaiming San Francisco: History, Politics, Culture.* San Francisco: City Lights Books, 1998.

Brookman, Philip. "El Centro Cultural de la Raza: Fifteen Years." In *Made in Aztlán,* ed. Philip Brookman and Guillermo Gómez-Peña, 20. San Diego: Centro Cultural de la Raza, 1986.

Brookman, Philip, and Guillermo Gómez-Peña, eds. *Made in Aztlán.* San Diego: Centro Cultural de la Raza, 1986.

Brown, Betty Anne. "The Past Idealized: Diego Rivera's Use of Pre-Columbian Imagery." In *Diego Rivera: A Retrospective,* ed. Cynthia Newman Helms, 139–156. Detroit: Detroit Institute of Arts, 1986.

Bruce-Novoa, Juan. *RetroSpace: Collected Essays on Chicano Literature, Theory, and History.* Houston: Arte Público Press, 1990.

Butler, Judith. *Constructing Masculinity.* New York: Routledge, 1995.

Carbonell, Ana María. "From Llorona to Gritona: Coatlicue in Feminist Tales by Viramontes and Cisneros." *Melus* 24, no. 2 (Summer 1999): 53–74.

Cardoza y Aragón, Luis, and Antonio Rodríguez. *Diego Rivera: Los murales en la Secretaría de Educación Pública*. Mexico City: Consejo Nacional de Fomento Educativo, 1986.

Carnero Hoke, Guillermo. "Teoría y práctica de la indianidad." In *Utopía y revolución,* ed. Guillermo Bonfil Batalla, 111–125. Mexico City: Editorial Nueva Imagen, 1988.

Carrasco, Davíd. *Quetzalcoatl and the Irony of Empire: Myths and Prophesies in the Aztec Tradition*. Chicago and London: University of Chicago Press, 1982.

Caso, Alfonso. *Indigenismo*. Mexico City: Instituto Nacional Indigenista, 1958.

Castillo, Debora. "Postmodern Indigenism: 'Quetzalcoatl and All That.'" *Modern Fiction Studies* 41, no. 1 (Spring 1995): 35–73.

Castro, Rafaela G. *Chicano Folklore: A Guise to the Folktales, Traditions, Rituals and Religious Practices of Mexican-Americans*. New York: Oxford University Press, 2000.

Cerny, Charlene. "Thoughts on Anonymity and Signature in Folk Art." *El Palacio* 90, no. 1 (Spring 1984): 34–37.

Chabram-Dernersesian, Angie. "Chicana! Rican? No, Chicana Riqueña! Refashioning the Transnational Connection." In *Between Woman and Nation: Nationalisms, Transnationalism Feminisms, and the State*, ed. Caren Kaplan, Norma Alarcón, and Minoo Moallem, 264–295. Durham: Duke University Press, 1999.

Chaffey Community Art Association. *Licón: A Memorial Retrospective*. Ontario, Calif.: Museum of History and Art, 1985.

Chavoya, C. Odine. "Orphans of Modernism: The Performance Art of Asco." In *Corpus Delecti: Performance Art of the Americas*, ed. Coco Fusco, 240–263. London: Routledge, 2000.

"Chicano Murals Making Definite Mark on Art Scene." *Community Murals* (Fall 1984): 15.

Churchill, Ward. *Struggle for the Land: Native North American Resistance to Genocide, Ecocide, and Colonization*. San Francisco: City Lights Books, 2002.

Cockcroft, Eva. "The Story of Chicano Park." In *Chicano Border: Culture and Folklore*, ed. José Villarino and Arturo Ramírez, 145–163. San Diego: Marion Publications, 1992.

———. "Women in the Community Mural Movement." *Heresies* 1 (January 1997): 14–22.

Cockcroft, Eva Sperling, and Holly Barnet-Sánchez, eds. *Signs from the Heart: California Chicano Murals*. Albuquerque: University of New Mexico Press, 1993.

Cockcroft, Eva, John Pitman Weber, and James Cockcroft. *Toward a People's Art: The Contemporary Mural Movement*. Albuquerque: University of New Mexico Press, 1998.

Cockcroft, Eva, and Robert Pierson. *Walking Tour and Guide to the Great Wall of Los Angeles*. Venice, Calif.: Social and Public Art and Resource Center and the U.S. Army Corps of Engineers, 1983.

Coe, Michael D. *Mexico: From the Olmecs to the Aztecs*. London: Thames and Hudson, 1994.

Coe, Michael D., and Mark Van Stone. *Reading the Maya Glyphs*. New York: Thames and Hudson, 2001.

Coj Ajbalam, Pedro. "Algo sobre la naturaleza del Ixim." In *Utopía y revolución*, ed. Guillermo Bonfil Batalla, 366–370. Mexico City: Editorial Nueva Imagen, 1988.

Connor, Walker. *Ethnonationalism: The Quest for Understanding*. Princeton: Princeton University Press, 1994.

Consejo Nacional para la Cultura y las Artes, ed. *Diego Rivera: Art and Revolution*. Mexico City: Landucci Editores, 1999.

Cooper, Martha, and Joseph Sciorra. *R.I.P. Memorial Wall Art*. London: Thames and Hudson, 1994.

Cowgill, George. "Teotihuacan Glyphs and Imagery in the Light of Some Early Colonial

Texts." In *Art, Ideology, and the City of Teotihuacan*, ed. Janet Catherine Berlo, 231–246. Washington, D.C.: Dumbarton Oaks Research Library and Collection, 1992.

Däniken, Erich von. *Chariots of the Gods? Unsolved Mysteries of the Past*. London: Souvenir Press, 1968.

Darder, Antonia, and Rodolfo D. Torres, eds. *The Latino Studies Reader: Culture, Economy, and Society*. Malden, Mass.: Blackwell Publishers, 1998.

Detroit Institute of Arts. *Diego Rivera: A Retrospective*. Detroit: Detroit Institute of Arts, 1986.

Diaz, David R. *Barrio Urbanism*. New York: Routledge, 2005.

Draher, Patricia, ed. *The Chicano Codices: Encountering the Art of the Americas*. San Francisco: Mexican Museum, 1992.

Drescher, Timothy W. *San Francisco Bay Area Murals: Communities Create Their Muses, 1904–1997*. St. Paul, Minn.: Pogo Press, 1998.

Drescher, Tim, and Rupert García. "Recent Raza Murals in the U.S." *Radical America* 17, no. 2 (March–April 1978): 15–32.

Dunitz, Robin J. *Street Gallery: Guide to Over 1000 Los Angeles Murals*. 2nd ed. Los Angeles: RJD Enterprises, 1998.

Dunitz, Robin J., and James Prigoff. *Painting the Towns: Murals of California*. Los Angeles: RJD Enterprises, 1997.

Durland, Steve. "Charles 'Chaz' Bojórquez." *High Performance* 9, no. 3 (1986): 49.

Echeveste, Beatriz, and Gloria Estolano. "Los Angeles Rejects History: Barbara Carrasco Mural." *Community Murals* 9, no. 3 (Summer 1984): 14–15.

"El Plan Espiritual de Aztlán." In *Aztlán: Essays on the Chicano Homeland*, ed. Rudolfo A. Anaya and Francisco A. Lomelí, 1–5. Albuquerque: University of New Mexico Press, 1989.

Enciso, Jorge. *Design Motifs of Ancient Mexico*. New York: Dover Publications, 1953.

Fields, Virginia M., and Victor Zamudio-Taylor. "Aztlán: Destination and Point of Departure." In *The Road to Aztlán: Art from a Mythic Homeland*, ed. Virginia Fields and Victor Zamudio-Taylor, 38–77. Los Angeles: Los Angeles Country Museum of Art, 2002.

———, eds. *The Road to Aztlán: Art from a Mythic Homeland*. Los Angeles: Los Angeles County Museum of Art, 2002.

Fischer, Edward F. "Cultural Logic and Maya Identity: Rethinking Constructivism and Essentialism." *Current Anthropology* 40, no. 4 (August–October 1999): 473–499.

Fitzpatrick, Tony. "Social Policy for Cyborgs." *Body & Society* 5, no. 1 (1999): 93–116.

Flores, William V., and Rina Benmayor. *Latino Cultural Citizenship: Claiming Identity, Space, and Rights*. Boston: Beacon Press, 1997.

Fondo Casasola, ed. *The World of Agustín Víctor Casasola, Mexico: 1900–1938*. Washington, D.C.: Fondo del Sol Visual Arts and Media Center, 1984.

Foucault, Michel. *The Archaeology of Knowledge*. New York: Tavistock Publications Limited, 1972.

Fowler-Salamini, Heather, and Mary Kay Vaughan, eds. *Women in the Mexican Countryside, 1850–1990*. Tucson and London: University of Arizona Press, 1994.

Fox, Howard N. "Tremors in Paradise, 1960–1980." In *Made in California: Art, Image, and Identity, 1900–2000*, ed. Stephanie Barron, 193–233. Berkeley: University of California Press, 2000.

Friedman, Jonathan. "Myth, History, and Political Identity." *Cultural Anthropology* 7, no. 2 (May 1992): 194–210.

Frings, Graciela. "Impulso a la esperanza en el movimiento del mural chicano." *Replica* 20, no. 877 (November 1989): 22–25.

Fusco, Coco, ed. *Corpus Delecti: Performance Art of the Americas.* London and New York: Routledge, 2000.

Gamboa, Harry, Jr. "In the City of Angels, Chameleons, and Phantoms: Asco, a Case Study of Chicano Art in Urban Tones (or Asco Was a Four-Member Word)." In *CARA. Chicano Art: Resistance and Affirmation,* ed. Richard Griswold del Castillo, Teresa McKenna, and Yvonne Yarbro-Bejarano, 121–130. Los Angeles: Wight Art Gallery, University of California, 1991.

———. *Urban Exile: Collected Writings of Harry Gamboa Jr.* Minneapolis: University of Minnesota Press, 1998.

Ganz, Nicholas. *Graffiti Women: Street Art from Five Continents.* New York: Abrams, 2006.

Garber, Marjorie. *Symptoms of Culture.* New York: Routledge, 2000.

———. *Vested Interests: Cross-Dressing and Cultural Anxiety.* New York: Routledge, 1992.

García, Ignacio M. *Chicanismo: The Forging of a Militant Ethos among Mexican Americans.* Tucson: University of Arizona Press, 1997.

García, Marshall Rupert. "The Raza Murals of California, 1963–1970: A Period of Social Change and Protest." Master's thesis, Art History Dept., University of California, Berkeley, 1981.

García, Ramón. "Against *Rasquache*: Chicano Identity and the Politics of Popular Culture in Los Angeles." *Critica: A Journal of Critical Essays* (Spring 1998): 1–26.

———. "Chicano Representation and the Strategies of Modernism." Ph.D. diss., University of California, San Diego, 1997.

García Canclini, Néstor. *Culturas híbridas: Estrategias para entrar y salir de la modernidad.* Mexico City: Grijalbo, 1989.

García Ponce, Juan. *Imágenes y visiones.* Mexico City: Vuelta, 1988.

Garza, Mario. "Duality in Chicano Poetry." *De Colores* 3, no. 4 (1977): 39–45.

Gaspar de Alba, Alicia. *Chicano Art Inside/Outside the Master's House: Cultural Politics and the CARA Exhibition.* Austin: University of Texas Press, 1998.

Gates, William. *An Outline Dictionary of Maya Glyphs with a Concordance and Analysis of Their Relationships.* New York: Dove Publications, 1978.

Goldman, Shifra. "Affirmation of Existence: Barrio Murals of Los Angeles." *Revista Chicano-Riqueña* 4, no. 4 (Fall 1976): 73–76.

———. "Hidden Histories: The Chicano Experience." In *Redefining American History Painting,* ed. Patricia Mullan Burnham and Lucretia H. Giese, 101–119. Cambridge: Cambridge University Press, 1995.

———. "How, Why, Where, and When It All Happened: Chicano Murals of California." In *Signs from the Heart: California Chicano Murals,* ed. Eva Sperling Cockcroft and Holly Barnet-Sánchez, 22–53. Albuquerque: University of New Mexico Press, 1993.

———. *The MEChA Mural: Twentieth Anniversary 1974–1994.* Brochure published by Santa Ana College; available in Nealley Library.

———. "Mexican Muralism: Its Social-Educative Roles in Latin America and the United States." *Aztlán: International Journal of Chicano Studies Research* 13, nos. 1–2 (Spring/Fall 1982): 111–133.

———. "A Public Voice: Fifteen Years of Chicano Posters." *Art Journal* 44 (Spring 1984): 50–57.

———. "Resistencia e identidad: Los murales callejeros de Aztlán, la ciudad ocupada." *Artes Visuales* 16 (Winter 1977): 22–25.

———. "Siqueiros' America in 1978." *Somos* 1, no. 6 (November 1978): 26–27.

————. "Siqueiros and Three Early Murals in Los Angeles." *Art Journal* 33, no. 4 (Summer 1974): 321–327.

Goldman, Shifra, and Tomás Ybarra-Frausto. *Arte Chicano: A Comprehensive Annotated Bibliography of Chicano Art, 1965–1981.* Berkeley: Chicano Studies Library Publications Unit, University of California, 1985.

González, Alicia María. "Murals: Fine, Popular, or Folk Art?" *Aztlán: International Journal of Chicano Studies Research* 13, nos. 1–2 (Spring/Fall 1982): 149–164.

Gordon, Eric A. "A Morning with Ernesto de la Loza." *SPARC Plug* 1, no. 3 (May/June 1991): 3–5.

Grambau, Hugh. "Mural: *La Revolución Mexicana* by Victor Ochoa." *Community Murals* (Fall 1981): 20.

Graves, James Bau. *Cultural Democracy: The Arts and the Public Purpose.* Urbana and Chicago: University of Illinois Press, 2005.

Griswold del Castillo, Richard. *The Treaty of Guadalupe Hidalgo: A Legacy of Conflict.* Norman and London: University of Oklahoma Press, 1990.

Griswold del Castillo, Richard, Teresa McKenna, and Yvonne Yarbro-Bejarano, eds. *CARA. Chicano Art: Resistance and Affirmation.* Los Angeles: Wight Art Gallery, University of California, 1991.

Gutiérrez, Ramón. *When Jesus Came, the Corn Mothers Went Away: Marriage, Sexuality, and Power in New Mexico, 1500–1846.* Stanford, Calif.: Stanford University Press, 1991.

Hall, Stuart. "Cultural Identity and Diaspora." In *Identity: Community, Culture and Difference,* ed. Jonathan Rutherford, 222–237. London: Lawrence and Wishart, 1990.

————. "Ethnicity: Identity and Difference." *Radical America* 23, no. 4 (October–December 1989): 8–20.

————. "New Ethnicities." In *Stuart Hall: Critical Dialogues in Cultural Studies,* ed. David Morley and Kuan-Hsing Chen, 441–449. London and New York: Routledge, 1996.

Haraway, Donna. "A Cyborg Manifesto: Science, Technology and Socialist-Feminism in the Late Twentieth Century." In *The Cybercultures Reader,* ed. David Bell and Barbara M. Kennedy, 291–324. London: Routledge, 2000.

Harris, Jonathan. *Federal Art and National Culture: The Politics of Identity in New Deal America.* Cambridge, U.K., and New York, N.Y.: Cambridge University Press, 1995.

Healey, Heather. "Kahlo Redux." *L.A. Weekly* (May 1–7, 1987): 93.

Healy, Wayne Alaniz. "Letter to Chismearte." *Chismearte* 1, no. 2 (Winter/Spring 1977): 53.

Hernández, Daniel. "Mural or Graffiti? City Draws Line; L.A. Is Cracking Down on Wall Art, Ordering Businesses to Redo or Remove Works." *Los Angeles Times,* August 25, 2005, A1.

Herring, Adam. *Art and Writing in the Maya Cities, A.D. 600–800.* New York: Cambridge University Press, 2005.

Hicks, Emily. "Textual Migration: Issues of Chicano American Culture." In *Postmodernism and New Cultural Tendencies in Latin America: 500th Anniversary of the Encounter of Two Worlds,* ed. Emily Hicks, Beatriz Jaguaribe, Mari Carmen Ramírez, and Marc Zimmerman, 1–24. San Francisco: San Francisco State University, 1993.

Hicks, Emily, Beatriz Jaguaribe, Mari Carmen Ramírez, and Marc Zimmerman, eds. *Postmodernism and New Cultural Tendencies in Latin America: 500th Anniversary of the Encounter of Two Worlds.* San Francisco: San Francisco State University, 1993.

Hoefer, Jacqueline. *A More Abundant Life: New Deal Artists and Public Art in New Mexico.* Santa Fe, N.M.: Sunstone Press, 2003.

Holscher, Louis M. "Tiene Arte Valor Fuera del Barrio: The Murals of East Los Angeles and Boyle Heights." *The Journal of Ethnic Studies* 4, no. 3 (Fall 1976): 42–51.

Hurlburt, Laurance P. *The Mexican Muralists in the United States.* Albuquerque: University of New Mexico Press, 1989.

Hutcheon, Linda. "'Scare Quotes': Irony versus Nostalgia." In *Quotation: Re-presenting History.* Winnipeg, Canada: Winnipeg Art Gallery, 1994.

Jacob, Mary Jane. "Ashé in the Art of Ana Mendieta." In *Santería Aesthetics in Contemporary Latin American Art,* ed. Arturo Lindsay, 189–200. Washington, D.C.: Smithsonian Institution Press, 1996.

Johnson, Kaytie. "Charles 'Chaz' Bojórquez." In *Contemporary Chicana and Chicano Art: Artists, Works, Culture, and Education,* Vol. 1, ed. Gary D. Keller et al., 74–75. Tempe, Ariz.: Bilingual Press/Editorial Bilingüe, 2002.

Johnson, Troy R. *The Occupation of Alcatraz Island: Indian Self-Determination and the Rise of Indian Activism.* Urbana: University of Illinois Press, 1996.

Juárez, Miguel. *Colors on Desert Walls: The Murals of El Paso.* El Paso: Texas Western Press, 1997.

Juárez, Nicandro F. "José Vasconcelos and 'La Raza Cósmica.'" *Aztlán: Chicano Journal of Social Science and the Arts* 3, no. 1 (1973): 51–82.

Justice, Daniel Heath. "Seeing (and Reading) Red: Indian Outlaws in the Ivory Tower." In *Indigenizing the Academy: Transforming Scholarship and Empowering Communities,* ed. Devon Abbott Mihesuah and Angela Carvender Wilson, 100–123. Lincoln and London: University of Nebraska Press, 2004.

Kanjo, Kathryn, ed. *La Frontera = The Border: Art about the Mexico/United States Border Experience.* San Diego: Centro Cultural de la Raza, 1993.

Kaplan, Caren, Norma Alarcón, and Minoo Moallem, eds. *Between Woman and Nation: Nationalisms, Transnational Feminisms, and the State.* Durham: Duke University Press, 1999.

Karlstrom, Paul, ed. *On the Edge of America: California Modernist Art, 1900–1950.* Berkeley: University of California Press, 1996.

———. "Rivera, Mexico and Modernism in California Art." In *Diego Rivera: Art and Revolution,* ed. Consejo Nacional para la Cultura y las Artes, 219–234. Mexico City: Landucci Editores, 1999.

Keller, Gary D. "Esteban Villa." In *Contemporary Chicana and Chicano Art: Artists, Works, Culture, and Education,* Vol. 2, ed. Gary D. Keller et al., 294–295. Tempe, Ariz.: Bilingual Press/Editorial Bilingüe, 2002.

Keller, Gary D., et al. *Chicano Art for Our Millennium: Collected Works from the Arizona State University Community.* Tempe, Ariz.: Bilingual Press/Editorial Bilingüe, 2004.

Keller, Gary D., et al. *Contemporary Chicana and Chicano Art: Artists, Works, Culture, and Education.* Vol. 1. Tempe, Ariz.: Bilingual Press/Editorial Bilingüe, 2002.

Keller, Gary D., and Amy Phillips. *Triumph of Our Communities: Four Decades of Mexican American Art.* Tempe, Ariz.: Bilingual Press/Editorial Bilingüe, 2005.

Kim, Howard. "Judithe Hernández and a Glimpse at the Chicana Artist." *Somos* 2, no. 7 (October–November 1979): 8–12.

Kim, Sojin. *Chicano Graffiti and Murals: The Neighborhood of Peter Quezada.* Jackson: University Press of Mississippi, 1995.

Klahr, Flora Lara. *Jefes, héroes y caudillos.* Mexico City: Fondo de Cultura Económica, 1986.

Klor de Alva, J. Jorge. "Aztlán, Borinquen, and Hispanic Nationalism in the United States."

In *The Latino Studies Reader: Culture, Economy, and Society*, ed. Antonia Darder and Rodolfo D. Torres, 63–82. Malden, Mass.: Blackwell Publishers, 1998.

Kwon, Miwon. "One Place after Another: Notes on Site Specificity." In *Space, Site, Intervention: Situating Installation Art*, ed. Erika Suderburg, 38–63. Minneapolis and London: University of Minnesota Press, 2000.

Lachmann, Richard. "Graffiti as Career and Ideology." *American Journal of Sociology* 94, no. 2 (September 1988): 229–250.

Latorre, Guisela. "Latina Feminism and Visual Discourse: Yreina Cervántez's *La Ofrenda*." *Discourse: Journal for Theoretical Studies in Media and Culture* 21, no. 3 (Fall 1999): 95–110.

Lawal, Babatunde. "From Africa to the Americas: Art in Yoruba Religion." In *Santería Aesthetics in Contemporary Latin America*, ed. Arturo Lindsay, 3–37. Washington, D.C.: Smithsonian Institution Press, 1996.

Leal, Luis. "In Search of Aztlán." In *Aztlán: Essays on the Chicano Homeland*, ed. Rudolfo A. Anaya and Francisco A. Lomelí, 6–13. Albuquerque: University of New Mexico Press, 1991.

Lee, Cynthia. "The Writing on the Wall." UCLA *Magazine* (Fall 2000): 2–5.

Lefebvre, Henri. *The Production of Space*. Oxford: Blackwell, 1991. (Orig. pub. 1974.)

Leuthold, Steven. *Indigenous Aesthetics: Native Art Media and Identity*. Austin: University of Texas Press, 1998.

Limón, José. "La Llorona, the Third Legend of Greater Mexico: Cultural Symbols, Women, and the Political Unconscious." In *Between Borders: Essays on Mexicana/Chicana History*, ed. Adelaida R. Del Castillo, 399–432. Encino, Calif.: Floricanto Press, 1990.

Lindsay, Arturo, ed. *Santería Aesthetics in Contemporary Latin American Art*. Washington, D.C., and London: Smithsonian Institution Press, 1996.

Lipsitz, George. *Dangerous Crossroads: Popular Music, Postmodernism and the Poetics of Place*. London: Verso, 1994.

Lopez, Gerard. "Estrada Murals." *La Luz* 4 (June 1975): 21.

Loucky, James, and Marilyn M. Moors, eds. *The Maya Diaspora: Guatemalan Roots, New American Lives*. Philadelphia: Temple University Press, 2000.

Lowe, Seana S. "Creating Community: Art for Community Development." *Journal of Contemporary Ethnography* 29, no. 3 (June 2000): 357–386.

Lozano, Luis-Martín. "María Izquierdo: Sobre la pintura moderna mexicana." In *María Izquierdo 1902–1955*, ed. Mexican Fine Arts Museum, 19–62. Chicago: 1996.

Lugo Saavedra, Denise. "Arte de 'East Los' y el movimiento muralista público de los setenta." In *Los Chicanos: Origen, presencia, destino*, ed. Segundo Foro Internacional, 121–126. Colima, Mexico: Universidad de Colima, 1987.

Lutz, Christopher, and W. George Lovell. "Survivors on the Move: Maya Migration in Time and Space." In *The Maya Diaspora: Guatemalan Roots, New American Lives*, ed. James Loucky and Marilyn M. Moors, 11–34. Philadelphia: Temple University Press, 2000.

Lyon, David. "The Information Society." In *Globalization: The Reader*, ed. John Beynon and David Dunkerley, 205–206. New York: Routledge, 2000.

Maciel, David R., Isidro D. Ortiz, and María Herrera-Sobek. *Chicano Renaissance: Contemporary Cultural Trend*. Tucson: University of Arizona Press, 2000.

Madill, Shirley J.-R. Introduction to *Quotation: Re-presenting History*. Winnipeg, Canada: Winnipeg Art Gallery, 1994.

Martínez, Rubén. "Going Up in L.A." *Centro de Estudios Puertorriqueños* 5, no. 2 (Spring 1992–1993): 8–17.

Mesa-Bains, Amalia. "Quest for Identity: Profile of Two Chicana Muralists." In *Signs from the Heart: California Chicano Murals,* ed. Eva Sperling Cockcroft and Holly Barnet-Sánchez, 68–83. Albuquerque: University of New Mexico Press, 1993.

Mexican Fine Arts Center Museum, ed. *María Izquierdo 1902–1955.* Chicago: Mexican Fine Arts Center Museum, 1996.

Michael, Mike. *Reconnecting Culture, Technology and Nature: From Society to Heterogeneity.* London and New York: Routledge, 2000.

Mihesuah, Devon Abbott, and Angela Cavender Wilson, eds. *Indigenizing the Academy: Transforming Scholarship and Empowering Communities.* Lincoln and London: University of Nebraska Press, 2004.

Miller, Ivor L. *Aerosol Kingdom: Subway Painters of New York City.* Jackson: University Press of Mississippi, 2002.

Miller, Mary Ellen. *The Art of Mesoamerica: From Olmec to Aztec.* London: Thames and Hudson, 1986.

———. "The Image of People and Nature in Classic Maya Art." In *The Ancient Americas: Art from Sacred Landscapes,* ed. Richard F. Townsend, 159–170. Chicago: Art Institute of Chicago, 1992.

Mirandé, Alfredo, and Evangelina Enríquez. *La Chicana: The Mexican American Woman.* Chicago: University of Chicago Press, 1979.

Moraga, Cherríe. *The Last Generation: Prose and Poetry.* Boston, Mass.: South End Press, 1993.

———. "Queer Aztlán: The Re-formation of Chicano Tribe." In *The Last Generation: Prose and Poetry,* 145–174. Boston, Mass.: South End Press, 1993.

Morley, David, and Chen Kuan-Hsing, eds. *Stuart Hall: Critical Dialogues in Cultural Studies.* London and New York: Routledge, 1996.

Moure, Nancy Dustin Wall. *California Art: 450 Years of Painting and Other Media.* Los Angeles: Dustin Publications, 1998.

Mujeres Muralistas. "Manifesto." *Imagine: International Chicano Poetry Journal* 3, nos. 1–2 (Summer–Winter 1986): 148.

Mullan Burnham, Patricia, and Lucretia H. Giese, eds. *Redefining American History Painting.* Cambridge: Cambridge University Press, 1995.

Muñoz, José Esteban. "Memory Performance: Luis Alfaro's 'Cuerpo Politizado.'" In *Corpus Delecti: Performance Art of the Americas,* ed. Coco Fusco, 97–113. London and New York: Routledge, 2000.

Muñoz, Lorenza. "Distinctive L.A. Art Legacy Under Siege." *Los Angeles Times,* July 23, 1999, A1–A9.

Murphy, Michael. "Understanding Indigenous Nationalism." In *The Fate of the Nation-State,* ed. Michel Seymour, 271–294. Montreal and Kingston, Canada: McGill-Queen's University Press, 2004.

Museo Soumaya, Mexico City, and Mexican Fine Arts Center Museum, Chicago, eds. *La Patria Portátil: 100 Years of Mexican Chromo Art Calendars.* Mexico City: Asociación Caso A. C., 1999.

Museum of Fine Arts, Houston, ed. *Hispanic Art in the United States.* New York: Abbeville Press, 1987.

Nelson, Alondra, Thuy Linh N. Tu, and Alicia Headlam Hines, eds. *Technicolor: Race, Technology, and Everyday Life.* New York and London: New York University Press, 2001.

Nuckolls, Charles W. *The Cultural Dialectics of Knowledge and Desire.* Madison: University of Wisconsin Press, 1996.

Ochoa, María. "Creative Collectives: A Study of Chicana Artistic Expressiveness." Ph.D. diss., History of Consciousness, University of California, Santa Cruz, 1995.

Oguibe, Olu. "Appropriation as Nationalism in Modern African Art." *Third Text* 16, no. 3 (September 2002): 243–259.

Padilla, Genaro M. "Myth and Comparative Cultural Nationalism: The Ideological Uses of Aztlán." In *Aztlán: Essays on the Chicano Homeland,* ed. Rudolfo Anaya and Francisco A. Lomelí, 111–134. Albuquerque: University of New Mexico Press, 1991.

Pasztory, Esther. *Aztec Art*. Norman: University of Oklahoma Press, 1983.

Paz, Octavio. "Art and Identity: Hispanics in the United States." In *Hispanic Art in the United States,* ed. Museum of Fine Arts, Houston, 13–42. New York: Abbeville Press, 1987.

Peabody, Melissa. "San Francisco's Chicano Mural Movement." *Lector* 5, no. 2 (1988): 16–17, 32.

Penn-Hilden, Patricia. "How the Border Lies: Some Historical Reflections." In *Decolonial Voices: Chicana and Chicano Cultural Studies in the 21st Century,* ed. Arturo J. Aldama and Naomi H. Quiñones, 152–176. Bloomington and Indianapolis: Indiana University Press, 2002.

Pérez, Emma. *The Decolonial Imaginary: Writing Chicanas into History*. Bloomington and Indianapolis: Indiana University Press, 1999.

Pérez, Laura. "Spirit Glyphs: Reimagining Art and Artist in the Work of Chicana Tlamatinime." *Modern Fiction Studies* 44, no. 1 (1998): 36–76.

Pérez-Torres, Rafael. *Movements in Chicano Poetry*. Cambridge: Cambridge University Press, 1995.

Phillips, Susan A. *Wallbangin': Graffiti and Gangs in L.A*. Chicago: University of Chicago Press, 1999.

Pina, Michael. "The Archaic, Historical and Mythicized Dimensions of Aztlán." In *Aztlán: Essays on the Chicano Homeland,* ed. Rudolfo A. Anaya and Francisco A. Lomelí, 14–48. Albuquerque: University of New Mexico Press, 1991.

Prigoff, James, and Robin J. Dunitz. *Walls of Heritage/Walls of Pride: African American Murals*. San Francisco: Pomegranate, 2000.

Quintero, Victoria. "A Mural Is a Painting on a Wall Done by Human Hands." *El Tecolote* 5, no. 1 (September 13, 1974): 1–4.

Quotation: Re-presenting History. Winnipeg, Canada: Winnipeg Art Gallery, 1994.

Radin, Rick. "Tag! S.F. Property Owners Are It. New Ordinance Makes Residents Responsible for Removing Graffiti on Their Homes, but the City Still Helps Out a Little." *San Francisco Chronicle,* Home and Garden, June 8, 2005, F2.

Ramos, Miguel "Willie." "Afro-Cuban Orisha Worship." In *Santería Aesthetics in Contemporary Latin American Art,* ed. Arturo Lindsay, 51–76. Washington, D.C.: Smithsonian Institution Press, 1996.

Rangel, Jeffrey J. "Art and Activism in the Chicano Movement: Judith F. Baca, and the Politics of Cultural Work." In *Generations of Youth,* ed. Michael Nevin Willard and Joe Austin, 223–239. New York: New York University Press, 1998.

Reents-Budet, Dorie. *Painting the Maya Universe: Royal Ceramics of the Classic Period*. Durham and London: Duke University Press and Duke University Museum, 1994.

Rodríguez, Antonio. *David Alfaro Siqueiros: Mural Painting*. Mexico City: Fondo Editorial de Plástica Mexicana, 1992.

Romero, Rolando, and Amanda Harris Nolacea, eds. *Feminism, Nation and Myth: La Malinche*. Houston: Arte Público Press, 2005.

Romero Galván, José Rubén. "La ciudad de México: Los paradigmas de dos fundaciones." *Estudios de Historia Novohispana* 20, no. 9 (1999): 13–32.

Romo, Tere. "The Chicanization of Mexican Calendar Art." A presentation delivered during the Interpretation and Representation of Latino Cultures: Research and Museums, a national conference at the Smithsonian Museum, Washington, D.C., November 20–23, 2002.

Romotsky, Jerry, and Sally R. Romotsky. "L.A. Human Scale: Street Art of Los Angeles." *Journal of Popular Culture* 10, no. 3 (Winter 1976): 655–661.

———. *Los Angeles Barrio Calligraphy*. Los Angeles: Dawson's Book Shop, 1976.

———. "Placas and Murals." *Arts in Society* 2, no. 2 (Summer–Fall 1974): 286–299.

Romotsky, Sally R., and Jerry Romotsky. "Plaqueaso on the Wall." *Human Behavior* 4, no. 5 (May 1975): 64–69.

Rosales, F. Arturo. *Chicano! The History of the Mexican American Civil Rights Movement*. Houston: Arte Público Press, 1996.

Rutherford, Jonathan, ed. *Identity: Community, Culture and Difference*. London: Lawrence and Wishart, 1990.

Salas, Elizabeth. "The Soldadera in the Mexican Revolution: *War and Men's Illusions*." In *Women in the Mexican Countryside, 1850–1990*, ed. Heather Fowler-Salamini and Mary Kay Vaughan, 93–105. Tucson and London: University of Arizona Press, 1994.

Salomon, Larry. "Taking Alcatraz." *Third Force* 5, no. 3 (August 31, 1997): 32.

Sánchez, George J. *Becoming Mexican American: Ethnicity, Culture and Identity in Chicano Los Angeles, 1900–1945*. New York: Oxford University Press, 1993.

Sánchez-Tranquilino, Marcos. "The Chicano Codices: Feathered Reflections of an Aztlanic Archaeology." In *The Chicano Codices: Encountering Art of the Americas*, ed. Patricia Draher, 4–19. San Francisco: The Mexican Museum, 1992.

———. "Mi Casa No Es Su Casa: Chicano Murals and Barrio Calligraphy as Systems of Signification at Estrada Courts 1972–1978." Master's thesis, University of California, Los Angeles, 1991.

———. "Murales del Movimiento: Chicano Murals and the Discourses of Art and Americanization." In *Signs of the Heart: California Chicano Murals*, ed. Eva Sperling Cockcroft and Holly Barnet-Sánchez, 84–101. Albuquerque: University of New Mexico Press, 1993.

———. "Space, Power, and Youth Culture: Mexican American Graffiti and Chicano Murals in East Los Angeles." In *Looking High and Low: Art and Cultural Identity*, ed. Brenda Jo Bright and Liza Blackwell, 55–88. Tucson: University of Arizona Press, 1995.

Sánchez-Tranquilino, Marcos, and John Tagg. "The Pachuco's Flayed Hide: The Museum, Identity, and Buenas Garras." In *Chicano Art: Resistance and Affirmation, 1965–1985*, ed. Richard Griswold del Castillo, Teresa McKenna, and Yvonne Yarbro-Bejarano, 97–108. Los Angeles: Wight Art Gallery, 1990.

Sandoval, Chela. *Methodology of the Oppressed*. Minneapolis and London: University of Minnesota Press, 2000.

———. "New Sciences: Cyborg Feminism and the Methodology of the Oppressed." In *The Cybercultures Reader*, ed. David Bell and Barbara M. Kennedy, 374–390. London: Routledge, 2000.

Sartiliot, Claudette. *Citation and Modernity: Derrida, Joyce and Brecht*. Norman and London: University of Oklahoma Press, 1993.

Scarborough, Vernon L., and David R. Wilcox, eds. *The Mesoamerican Ballgame*. Tucson: University of Arizona Press, 1991.

Scheben, Helmut. "Indigenismo y modernismo." *Revista de Crítica Literaria Latinoamericana* 5, no. 10 (2nd Semester 1979): 115–128.

Schele, Linda, and Mary Ellen Miller. *Blood of Kings: Dynasty and Ritual in Maya Art.* Fort Worth, Tex.: Kimbell Art Museum, 1986.

Scheuler, Steven. "Revising the Paths of Discovery in the Spanish Borderlands and Re-examining the 'Black Legend.'" *Journal of Borderlands Study* 14, no. 2 (Fall 1999): 116–122.

Scott, Diana. "Unfurling a Maestrapeace: Mythic and Mortal Female Ancestors Grace This San Francisco Landmark." *On the Issues: The Progressive Woman's Quarterly* 4, no. 1 (January 31, 1995): 43–46.

Segundo Foro Internacional, ed. *Los Chicanos: Origen, presencia, destino.* Colima, Mexico: Universidad de Colima, 1987.

Seymour, Michel, ed. *The Fate of the Nation-State.* Montreal and Kingston: McGill-Queen's University Press, 2004.

Shohat, Ella, ed. *Talking Visions: Multicultural Feminism in a Transnational Age.* Cambridge: MIT Press, 1998.

Social and Public Art Resource Center (SPARC). *World Wall: A Vision of the Future without Fear.* Venice, Calif.: SPARC Publication, 1991.

Sommer, Robert. "Some Psychological Aspects of Community Murals." *Community Murals* (Fall 1982): 50–51.

Sorell, Victor. "The Photograph as a Source for Visual Artists: Images from the Archivo Casasola in the Works of Mexican and Chicano Artists." In *The World of Agustín Victor Casasola, Mexico: 1900–1938,* ed. Fondo Casasola, 35–47. Washington, D.C.: Fondo del Sol Visual Arts and Media Center, 1984.

Storey, John, ed. *An Introduction to Cultural Theory and Popular Culture.* Athens: University of Georgia Press, 1998.

Suderburg, Erika, ed. *Space, Site, Intervention: Situating Installation Art.* Minneapolis and London: University of Minnesota Press, 2000.

Taube, Karl. *Aztec and Maya Myths.* Austin: University of Texas Press, 1993.

Thompson, Robert Farris. *Flash of the Spirit: African and Afro-American Art and Philosophy.* New York: Random House, 1983.

Townsend, Richard F. *The Ancient Americas: Art from Sacred Landscapes.* Chicago: Art Institute of Chicago, 1992.

Tréguer, Annick. *Chicanos: Murs peints des Etats-Unis.* Paris: Presses de la Sorbonne Nouvelle, 2000.

Umberger, Emily. "Aztec Sculptures, Hieroglyphs, and History." Ph.D. diss., Columbia University, New York, 1981.

University Art Museum, Berkeley, ed. *The Fifth Sun: Contemporary/Traditional Chicano/Latino Art.* Berkeley: Chicano Studies, University of California, 1977.

Vargas, George. "A Historical Overview/Update on the State of Chicano Art." In *Chicano Renaissance: Contemporary Cultural Trends,* ed. David R. Maciel, Isidro D. Ortiz, and María Herrera-Sobek, 191–232. Tucson: University of Arizona Press, 2000.

Vasconcelos, José. *The Cosmic Race/La raza cósmica.* Los Angeles: Centro de Publicaciones, Chicano Studies, California State University, 1979. [Orig. pub. 1925.]

———. *La raza cósmica: Misión de la raza iberoamericana.* Barcelona: Agencia Mundial de Librería, 1924.

Vélez-Ibáñez, Carlos. *Border Visions: Mexican Cultures of the Southwest United States.* Tucson: University of Arizona Press, 1996.

Villa, Raúl Homero. *Barrio-Logos: Space and Place in Urban Chicano Literature and Culture.* Austin: University of Texas Press, 2000.

Villagrá, Gaspar Pérez de. *Historia de la Nueva México, 1610.* Albuquerque: University of New Mexico Press, 1992.

Villarino, José, and Arturo Ramírez. *Chicano Border: Culture and Folklore.* San Diego: Marion Publications, 1992.

Von Blum, Paul. *Other Visions, Other Voices: Women Political Artists in Greater Los Angeles.* Lanham, Md.: University Press of America, 1994.

White, Michelle-Lee. "Afrotech and Outer Spaces." *Art Journal* 60, no. 3 (Fall 2001): 90–91.

Widdifield, Stacie G. *Embodiment of the National in Late Nineteenth-Century Mexican Painting.* Tucson: University of Arizona Press, 1996.

Wilkerson, S. Jeffrey K. "And Then They Were Sacrificed: The Ritual Ballgame in North-eastern Mesoamerica through Time and Space." In *The Mesoamerican Ballgame,* ed. Vernon L. Scarborough and David R. Wilcox, 45–72. Tucson: University of Arizona Press, 1991.

Wilson, Angela Cavender. "Reclaiming Our Humanity: Decolonization and the Recovery of Indigenous Knowledge." In *Indigenizing the Academy: Transforming Scholarship and Empowering Communities,* ed. Devon Abbott Mihesuah and Angela Cavender Wilson, 69–87. Lincoln and London: University of Nebraska Press, 2004.

Winnipeg Art Gallery. *Quotation: Re-presenting History.* Winnipeg, Canada: Winnipeg Art Gallery, 1994.

Ybarra-Frausto, Tomás. "Arte Chicano: Images of a Community." In *Signs of the Heart: California Chicano Murals,* ed. Eva Sperling Cockcroft and Holly Barnet-Sánchez, 54–67. Albuquerque: University of New Mexico Press, 1993.

———. "Rasquachismo: A Chicano Sensibility." In *CARA Chicano Art: Resistance and Affirmation 1965–1985,* ed. Richard Griswold del Castillo, Teresa MacKenna, and Yvonne Yarbro-Bejarano, 155–162. Los Angeles: Wight Art Gallery, University of California, 1993.

Young, Stanley. *The Big Picture: Murals of Los Angeles.* Boston: Little, Brown, 1988.

Ziff, Bruce, and Pratima V. Rao, eds. *Borrowed Power: Essays on Cultural Appropriation.* New Brunswick, N.J.: Rutgers University Press, 1997.

Ziff, Trish, ed. *Distant Relations: Chicano Irish Mexican Art and Critical Writing.* New York: Smart Press, 1996.

Primary Source Material

Baca, Judy. Interview by Amalia Mesa-Bains, August 5 and 6, 1986. Archives of American Art, Smithsonian Institution.

Botello, David. Interview, August 10, 1983. Transcribed in *Califas, Chicano Art and Culture in California,* Conference Proceedings Vol. 4 (April 15–18, 1986). Santa Cruz: University of California.

Cervántez, Yreina. "*La Ofrenda* Artist Statement," 1989. Manuscript in artist's collection.

"Emigdio Vasquez, June 15, 1984." Oral History. Emigdio Vasquez Papers, California Ethnic and Multicultural Archives, University of California, Santa Barbara.

Gronk, Interview by Jeffrey Rangel, January 20 and 23, 1997. Archives of American Art, Smithsonian Institution.

Leaños, John Jota. "Imperial Silences." Presentation delivered at the University of California, Santa Barbara, May 17, 2006.

The MEChA *Mural: Twentieth Anniversary 1974–1994*. Brochure published by Rancho Santiago College, available in Nealley Library, Santa Ana College, 1994.

Ortiz, Gloria. "Interview with Emigdio Vasquez," March 29, 1995. Emigdio Vasquez Papers, California Ethnic and Multicultural Archives, University of California, Santa Barbara.

Vasquez, Emigdio. Undated artist's statement. Emigdio Vasquez Papers, California Ethnic and Multicultural Archives, University of California, Santa Barbara.

Discography

Mulford, Marilyn, director; Mario Barrera and Marilyn Mulford, producers. *Chicano Park*. Video. San Diego: Redbird Films, 1988.

Pilots of Aztlán: The Flights of the RCAF. KVIE-TV Sacramento, Calif., VHS, 59 min., 1995.

Siqueiros, David Alfaro. *Integración plástica*. Sound recording, n.d. Salvador Roberto Torres Papers, California Ethnic and Multicultural Archives, University of California, Santa Barbara.

———. *El nuevo realismo mexicano, 1966*. Sound recording, n.d. Salvador Roberto Torres Papers, California Ethnic and Multicultural Archives, University of California, Santa Barbara.

Treviño, Jesús Salvador, producer. *América Tropical*. Los Angeles: KCET film, 1971.

Index

www.ingramcontent.com/pod-product-compliance
Lightning Source LLC
Chambersburg PA
CBHW020729180526
45163CB00001B/169